A HISTORY OF IRELAND

A History of
IRELAND

EDMUND CURTIS
M.A., LITT.D.

*Late Lecky Professor of Modern History
in the University of Dublin*

METHUEN & CO LTD
11 NEW FETTER LANE · LONDON EC4

First published 1936 by Methuen & Co Ltd
Sixth edition 1950
Reprinted six times
Reprinted 1968
SBN 416 33960 3

First published as a University Paperback 1961
Reprinted five times
Reprinted 1973
SBN 416 67730 4

Printed in Great Britain by
Butler & Tanner Ltd, Frome and London

Distributed in the USA by
HARPER & ROW, PUBLISHERS, INC.
BARNES & NOBLE IMPORT DIVISION

PREFACE

NATURE has placed the two islands of Britain and Ireland in such close neighbourhood that it was inevitable that their destinies should be interwoven in various ways, and the Irish themselves have long spoken of 'The Three Kingdoms' which they formed and which for some centuries have been in one royal line. Ireland, lying to the west of the greater island, has by geography and history been made to feel the impact of it from early times. She contains some twenty million statute acres and 32,000 square miles of territory, while England, apart from Wales, has thirty-two million statute acres, and Scotland nineteen. Ireland is, however, far more fertile than Scotland, and compares well with rich England in this regard, for the limestone plain, which makes up nearly half her soil, forms the best grazing land in Europe, and everywhere, indeed, good land and poor land lie side by side. In Tudor and Stuart times the officials who made plans for confiscation and colonization reckoned that out of the twenty millions of acres some twelve millions were 'profitable land', to be set apart for settlers, English or Scotch. But a great deal of the island is lake, bogland, and mountain; up to three centuries ago our country was very untraversable and greatly severed by natural features. Its abundance of all that the natural man desires has tempted many invaders, but no country has resisted invasion more successfully, for it is a difficult country to hold though easy to overrun, as the Normans found. The soft air and abundant rain, the extent and fertility of good soil, the food-producing richness of Ireland all conspire to make life easy and enable the native race to recover quickly after the most devastating wars. Hence the high 'survival value' of the Irish people, who have beaten invader after invader, not so much by arms as by the constant revival of 'man-power'. It is worth recalling that as late as 1800 out of every three men in the British Isles one was an Irishman, and in view of their military disposition and hostility to the Saxon (much of it well deserved) it is not to be wondered at that militarists in the greater island for long regarded Ireland as a danger This explains much of our history and the measures frequently taken for the 'reduction of Ireland', when wise kings and statesmen should have taken other courses to win her people over. It is only one of the difficulties in writing Irish history that a close political connexion has bound Ireland and Britain together for long centuries, and the story has to include at once the native race, Anglo-Ireland, and English government in Ireland.

To make a country's history intelligible, the historian naturally seeks for some point of unity, and this has been long deferred in Ireland's history. Of ancient Erin under its High kings we can only say that, as with England itself at the time, political union was slow, whatever we may say of a remarkable cultural unity and the 'nation-making' that we owe to native heroes such as Brian Boru. And even the old Gaelic State was destroyed by the Norman-French invasion, though its laws, language, and order of life lived on locally among the Gaelic septs of Ireland till the Tudor conquest. Since this latter event, the political State has seldom (save for a brief spell under the Stuarts) been representative of the majority who believed themselves to be the true and historic Irish nation. For the establishment of a central government representing the nation and able to rule justly over all its elements, Ireland has had to wait till the present generation.

The Treaty of 1922 and the attainment of true self-government, with the willing assent of Great Britain, gives meaning and justification to the long-continued struggle which fills so many of these pages, and permits us to treat dispassionately a story around which great and enduring passion has been woven. But though Ireland is now free to write her future history in brighter pages, the difficulties of writing her past remain and are admitted by all who have honestly attempted it. For centuries almost any point of unity seems lacking, and though Henry VIII set up the Kingdom of Ireland and Elizabeth's reign saw the whole island welded into an apparent whole, the religious and political despotism of the titular Monarchy unfortunately made the general acceptance of it impossible. Yet even as it was, the Kingdom of Ireland, though its monarchs for nearly three centuries never visited their second realm, has had historic greatness and national appeal, and to restore it as it was in the days of Grattan has been the aim of most of our leaders since the Union of 1800.

Politics and religion take up a disproportionate space in our history, but these questions, the unfortunate heritage of the past, have left a deeper mark here than elsewhere in Europe, and though they have been dissolved in the light of modern reasonableness their importance in our history and on the shaping of the national character cannot be minimized. When we add to them the Land question and the agrarian fight, we have a union of passionate forces on which Irish nationality has been reared.

On the matter of our religious differences, one treads on sacred and dangerous ground, and the historian can only treat conscientious religious belief with the respect it deserves and view the Churches of the past in the light of their own day. The three-fold distinction of 'Catholic, Protestant, and Presbyterian' has for Irishmen a clear and historic significance, and can be used without apology or offence. Minorities, social, religious, and political, have played a great part among us, and the former 'Protestant Ascendancy' and all that it has meant in the field of civilization, literature, and political freedom, as well as its faults, are immortalized in the pages of Froude and Lecky. The Protestant Dissenters of the North have an honoured place in patriotic history for their democratic record and their part in the agrarian fight which has left Ireland, in spite of all the confiscations and plantations of the past, a land owned by 600,000 peasant proprietors. The historian can only register and regret the fact that the counties where the Presbyterians are most dominant are now severed politically from the rest of Ireland.

The main task, after all, must be to trace the story of the majority who have finally achieved nationhood, and who in the struggle have always found among the Protestant minority leaders and heroes, and a constant body of sympathy and aid. The natural ties between Irishmen are indeed stronger than their political and religious divisions; strong enough indeed, if encouraged by our leaders, to effect that true union of all Ireland which, in spite of many great victories, remains unachieved. We have traced the course of a remarkable race-consciousness from far back in Irish history into the nation-consciousness of to-day, and it is the story of a constant absorption of all later elements into the Irish nation which emerges from 1603 onwards.

To carry through a history which begins with the Gaelic Celts and reaches almost to the present time is no light task of compression and selection. The writer has sought to give cultural, social, and economic factors their due weight with the rest, and throughout has selected what seemed to him the moving forces, the deciding facts, and the men that mattered, and to present them in a story that has movement and meaning. Some thirty years' study and twenty years' teaching of Irish history have clarified it for him, and will, he trusts. do so for his readers.

E. C.

TRINITY COLLEGE
DUBLIN

CONTENTS

MAPS

CHAPTER I

FROM THE ORIGINS TO A.D. 800

THE traditions of the Irish people are the oldest of any race in Europe north and west of the Alps, and they themselves are the longest settled on their own soil. When they learned to write they recorded the tradition that they originally came from northern Spain. The ancient *Leabar Gabála* (the *Book of Invasions*) tells how the three sons of Mileadh of Spain, namely, Heremon, Heber, and Ir, came to Erin about the time of Alexander the Great and conquered the land from the Tuatha Dé Danann. Of the races that were in possession before them, the Tuatha Dé Danann were a superior race, semi-divine in their arts of magic and wizardry, the Firbolg were a race dark, short, and plebeian, the Fomorians were gloomy giants of the sea. From the three sons of Mileadh descended all the royal clans of later Ireland. To this day, wherever Irish is spoken, the story of 'Meela Spaunya' is remembered, and to be of the old Milesian race is an honourable distinction.

Modern scholars agree that Ireland was first peopled by neolithic men, users of flint, and then by dark, small people from the Mediterranean, users of bronze, who are perhaps the Firbolg of our traditions. Later, Scotland and Northern Ireland were peopled by a race called the Picts, in Irish 'the Cruithne'. Then about 350 B.C. came Celts from the centre of Europe, a tall race, red-blond of hair, speaking a language close to Latin. The Gaelic Celts, coming direct by sea from south France and perhaps northern Spain, conquered Ireland; the British Celts, their cousins, coming from France and the mouth of the Rhine, invaded and conquered Britain. A great Celtic empire had once covered central Europe, but now between the Germans on the east and Rome on the south was at last narrowed down to Gaul and northern Spain. Britain and Erin were the last conquests of the Celts, and Ireland is to-day the only Celtic nation State left in the world.

The victory of the Gaelic invaders came from their weapons of tempered iron, their greater stature, their superiority in battle to the bronze-using aborigines, and their warlike, aristocratic, and masterful temper. They were destined to become the political masters of Ireland, and by the year A.D. 800, though they were an upper-class minority, they had completely imposed their empire, language, and law upon our whole island. To the Romans they were known as the Scots, to themselves they were the Gaels, and they called their country Ériu, a name familiar to us as Erin, and to the Latin world as Hibernia.

Ireland was already a land of ancient cultures. From the Tuatha Dé Danann and Firbolg the Gaels added to their gods such deities as Angus Oge, the Dagda, and Dána, the Mother of the gods. Ireland was full of sacred places of the dead, groves of deities, and great hill-fortresses, such as Tara, Emain Macha, and Aileach. The traditional memories, the music and the art of the older races blended with the arts of the Gaels. Politically they also took over many things. Monarchy became a feature of their government, though on the continent the Celts were republican. Ireland was already divided into the five 'Fifths' or kingdoms, and this division has lasted until to-day, though Meath no longer is a province. Ulster, Connacht, Munster, north and south Leinster formed this pentarchy, and the province-kingdoms were divided again into petty states called *Tuatha*, of which by A.D. 1000 there were about one hundred.

The religion of the Irish was Druidism; this was of Celtic origin, but blended with much earlier paganism. Celtic, too, was the earliest form of writing, the Ogam, based on the Latin alphabet, but serving for little more than funeral inscriptions on upright stones or short writings on wooden staves. A remarkable institution of the Irish Celts was their learned class the 'Filí' (poets or seers),[1] who were greatly venerated and feared. It was they who preserved the traditions, epics, laws, pedigrees, and history of the race. When Christianity came this powerful caste took on a veneer of the new faith,

[1] Singular 'File', pronounced 'Filla'; plural 'Filidh', or in modern spelling 'Filí', pronounced 'Fill-ee'.

but until the fall of the Gaelic order in 1603 they were
the hereditary keepers of the ancient lore and learning of
Ireland as expressed in the Irish language. When writing
came in with Christianity, Gaelic became a cultivated language
and the sages wrote down in it the epics and records which they
formerly kept orally.

In our earlier history tradition and fact are blended together,
and it is not till St. Patrick's arrival in 432 that we may regard
ourselves on historical ground. The oldest of our national
epics, the *Táin Bó Cualgne*, takes us back to the time of Christ.
It tells how Maeve, queen of Connacht, made war on Concobar,
king of Ulster, and his famous Red Branch heroes, whose seat
was the hill-fortress of Emain Macha near Armagh, and their
most famous name that of Cú Chulainn. In this we read of
five kingdoms, but there is no supreme king, and Ulster is the
greatest of the five, stretching south to the Boyne and across
to the middle Shannon. Later, Leinster received its name from
the 'Broad spears' of two thousand Gauls, with whom its
exiled king Labraid recovered his kingdom. The early records
of Munster also show Gaulish immigration, and this did much
to make a distinction between the south and the Gaelic-
Pictish north.

THE RACE OF CONN

The Gaels were a military and oppressive aristocracy, and
about the year A.D. 100 there was a great revolt of the pre-
Celtic subjects under Cairbre Cinn Cait, 'the Cat-head'. This
was crushed by a Gaelic prince called Tuathal, and there
followed a great historic event, the formation of a united
kingdom of Meath and Connacht, which provided Ireland for
centuries with a central High kingship. The Firbolgs never
revolted again, and the pride of their Gaelic masters remained
unbroken. Henceforth anybody 'who was anything' boasted
a pedigree derived from Heremon, Ir, and Heber.

Tuathal's first capital was Maeve's fortress of Rath Croghan
in Roscommon. East of the Shannon he built a second capital
on the hill of Uisneach near Mullingar. A hundred years after
him, about A.D. 200, his descendant Conn Céd-cathach ('of
the hundred fights') formed a central monarchy, of which the

eastern part was called Midhe or 'the Middle kingdom'. He had a rival in the south in Eoghan Mór, also called 'Mogh Nuadat' (devotee of the god Nuada), who created the kingdom of Munster, but the two at last came to terms, and divided their spheres of influence north and south of a line from Dublin to Galway along a ridge of sandhills called Escir Riada. Henceforth 'Mogh's Half and Conn's Half' were recognized divisions of our island.

In Conn, from whom Connacht gets its name, we have the first of the line of the High kings of Ireland, the Dál Cuinn or 'Race of Conn', who lasted till 1022 and gave Ireland a centre of national unity. The expansion of this victorious race was a defeat for both Ulster and Leinster. Ulster lost the Boyne valley, and built 'The Great Wall of Ulster', reaching from Newry to Lough Erne. Leinster fell back from Tara to the Liffey, and the Connacht-Meath kingdom reached the eastern sea. Meanwhile the race of Eoghan Mór, called later the Eoghanacht, by the year 400 built up a powerful kingdom, including the present Munster and Clare, and made their capital on the hill of Cashel.

Of the Dál Cuinn, Cormac, son of Art son of Conn, is the next great name (A.D. 275–300). In Gaelic tradition he is the first founder, legislator, and nation-maker, who made Tara's ancient and sacred hill the capital of Ireland. On its broad green summit were the great banqueting place and the timber halls of kings, princesses, and nobles, and here every third year as High king (*Ard Rí*) he presided over the Feis of Tara, a great national assembly for law, homaging, music, games, and literary contests. In such gatherings, which were also held at Tailten, was the national unity in language, culture, and government testified and affirmed, right up to the Norman conquest.

Tradition attributes to Cormac MacArt the five great roads of Ireland, which ran from Tara north, south, and west, and the formation of a standing warrior force, the Fianna, whose chief was Finn MacCumhaill, which finally grew too strong for the Árd Rí and was crushed in a battle at Gavra by Cormac's grandson, Cairbre. Round the Fianna grew up a body of dramatic legend which is remembered to this day among all Gaelic speakers, and the wise Finn, his son the poet Oisin, his grandson the valiant Oscar, Diarmaid 'of the love-spot', and all their company have been the first and most lasting darlings of the folk-lore of the Gael.

THE HIGH KINGSHIP, A.D. 380–1022

In Niall of the Nine Hostages, who ruled at Tara from 380 to 405, appears the greatest ruler of the race of Conn. Ulster and Leinster had steadily shrunk before the Connacht expansion. Leinster could not forgive her defeats and remained an enemy of the High kings, but Ulster had to surrender her pride of place. Seeking new lordships of their own, in 332 the 'Three Collas', princes of the race of Conn, marched against the 'Great Wall of Ulster' and slew in battle Fergus, the last king of Concobar's race. The defeated Ultonians had to retreat east of the Bann and Lough Neagh, and there, behind a third defensive wall, now called the 'Danes' Cast', they retained their independence in the petty kingdom called Ulidia, which covered Antrim and Down. The three Collas then set up a new kingdom called Oriel (Oirgialla: 'Eastern vassals'), which covered the present Monaghan, Louth, and Armagh. It was regarded as an offshoot of Connacht, and is part of the expansion of the Dál Cuinn. But Emain Macha became a grass-grown solitude, as all the great pagan forts, even Tara, were destined to be after the coming of the Faith.

The time of Niall is a remarkable one for Irish unity, the ruin and reshaping of Roman Britain, and the first coming of the Christian faith to Erin.

Niall was a splendid hero of the Gaelic blood, tall, fair-haired, and blue-eyed, a great and noble-minded warrior, 'kind in hall and fierce in fray'. Of his many sons, Laeghaire succeeded him as Árd Rí, from others descended the High kings of Ireland, who were known till 1022 as the Ui Néill, or 'de-scendants of Niall'. Two of his sons, Eoghan and Conall, about A.D. 400 marched northwards, conquered north-west Ulster, and founded a new state variously called the kingdom of Aileach, the Northern Kingdom, or Ulster. Its capital was Aileach, a great stone-built cashel on a hill north-west of Derry.

Eoghan, the senior, took for his share Inishowen (Inis Eoghain) and Tír Eoghain (the land of Eoghan), and his descendants the O'Neills were lords in central Ulster till 1603, while
Conall, the younger, took as his domain Tír Conaill (Conall's
land), and from him descended the O'Donnells. In time this
new kingdom subjected both Oriel and Ulidia and by 1000 had
built up a new kingdom of Ulster. About the same time
bands of Gaels began to cross the thirty-mile strait between
Antrim and Argyle and make settlements among the Picts of
'Alba' (the Irish name for Caledonia).

The Roman empire in Britain, only sixty miles by sea, could
not fail to cast its influence upon Ireland. Wales was a Roman
province, and all the western coast from Galloway to Cornwall contained petty towns and rural villas, where dwelt a
romanized population of Britons, who spoke a kind of Latin,
were already Christian, and prided themselves on their imperial speech and citizenship. Not a single Roman legionary
ever set foot on the soil of Ireland but much Roman influence
was bound to radiate upon her. The full light of civilization
and the Faith were, however, not to fall upon Ireland till the
Empire itself was destroyed. As it decayed from A.D. 350,
the Scots of Ireland and the Picts of Caledonia began
to assail Britain from the north and west, the Roman
legions were finally withdrawn in 407, and then the
savage and pagan Angles and Saxons assailed her from
the east.

In the fifth century was founded a new Britain. The Anglo-
saxons finally Teutonized most of what is now England and
the south-east corner of Scotland, while the Celtic Britons
held out in Cornwall, Wales, and Strathclyde and colonized
Brittany. In Ireland the Picts succumbed to Milesian rule,
in Scotland they went under before the Angles and Scots. In
Britain the Roman speech of men like Patrick vanished and the
Latin tradition and language survived only in the Church.
The Irish now seemed about to become masters of both Wales
and Scotland. The High kings of Tara, such as Niall, directed
constant attacks upon Roman Britain and a large part of its
western coast was for a time Gaelicized. A later Irish book
records that in the fifth and sixth centuries 'great was the

power of the Gaels over the Britons, and they divided the isle of Britain between them, and not more numerous were the Gaels at home than those who dwelt in Britain'.

The Gaelic conquest of Wales, however, was not to be permanent, for in the sixth century a British prince, Cunedda, marched from North Britain and mastered all Wales, which received its name of Cambria from his followers the Cymry ('Companions'). Thus the western front of Britain remained with the British Celts, who preserved for centuries an intimate alliance with Ireland in art, law, education, and Christianity, though their Celtic dialects were too far apart to serve as a common link. But in northern Britain the Gaels made a lasting conquest and gave Scotland (Alba) a stamp she has never lost. Up to this time it had been (north of the Roman wall) a Pictish kingdom, divided in two by Drum Alban. The Scots of Ireland were destined to become masters of the northern and western parts and to give Scotland their name. In 470 Fergus Mac Erc, prince of Dalriada in north Antrim, and his three brothers crossed over and founded the kingdom of Argyle ('the eastern Gael'), or Scottish Dalriada, and so began the long history of Gaelic Scotland.

ST. PATRICK, 390–461

In the spiritual history of Ireland the first great name is that of Patrick, 'the Apostle of Ireland'. He gave to this pagan island the priceless gift of the Christian faith and the moral order of the Christian Church. He opened it up to Latin civilization and the culture of Rome, which, though the Empire died, survived in the Church. He turned a land that had no written literature into a land where scholars and poets cultivated both the Latin, or learned speech, and the Gaelic, the dearly loved native speech. He turned the Irish from a race of cruel conquerors, whose galleys were dreaded on all the coasts of Britain and Gaul, into a race whose enthusiasm was for missionary labour, Latin learning, and the contemplative life. To the fifth century no name sounded more barbarous and brutal than that of the plundering Scots, but to later centuries no names were sweeter or nobler than that of

Columba, Aidan, and Adamnan, or more famous in learning or religion than John Scotus or Columbanus.

The Ireland to which Patrick was to give a new direction, though barbarous and isolated, had a remarkable culture and unity of her own. The High king of Tara was only a sort of president over the several kings of Erin, but his was a high name to evoke, and his safeguard was essential to any stranger landing at an Irish port. He could call out the national host to repulse or invade foreign enemies, and it was his prerogative to settle the disputes of under-kings and preside over the great periodic Aonach or all-Ireland gatherings at Tara or Tailten. If he lacked the prestige of medieval Christian kings he was on the other hand surrounded with pagan taboos and privileges, for the High king of Tara was by ancient tradition a priest-king. As such, a king like Niall was the head and centre of a powerful and greatly feared pagan religion and culture.

The Druidic priests were numerous, highly respected, and greatly feared among the Irish Celts. Socially they were the equals of the kings and warriors; they were the augurs and interpreters of the calendar, and magical gifts for spells of enchantment against enemies or for surrounding a battle-field with a 'Druid mist', and so on, were attributed to them. The 'brehons' or jurists of later times inherited their law-giving office. Of the best as well as the worst side of the Druid religion unfortunately we know little, but much of the pagan lore has survived, and the 'Shee' or fairy people of peasant lore to-day are the dwindled-down survivors of the gods of two thousand years ago.

The 'Fili' or learned class were the hereditary custodians of the national memory and of the oral literature, in which they spent long years of training. It was believed of the 'File' that he had supernatural gifts and could by his satires inflict blemish or evil upon the subject of his dispraise. His knowledge of pedigree and history enabled him in return for handsome gifts to feed the pride of the Gaelic aristocracy or by poetic exhortation to bring victory to a patron. With the coming of Christianity the priestly caste died out, but the learned class survived, and until 1603 were the main support and champions of the old Gaelic order.

The life of our national apostle may be said to cover the
years 390–461. Patrick was born a Roman citizen, speaking
a kind of Latin, in a small town called Bannavem Taberniae,
the site of which is disputed but at least was at some point
of western Britain where the land was fertile and a considerable
Romano-British population dwelt. The raids of Niall of the
Nine Hostages were constant up the Severn and the Solway,
and it seems as if fate brought together in the high light of history the great warrior-king and the humble Christian boy who
was destined to end the pagan monarchy. In one of these raids,
about A.D. 405, among the horde of slaves that were brought
back to Ireland was Patrick or 'Patricius', son of Calpurnius,
then a youth in his sixteenth year. The Roman empire had
not yet fallen in Britain, and the Catholic church had long
flourished there. The two proud boasts of Patrick in his
writings were Roman civilization and the Christian church,
and he urged the Irish to be at once Christians and Romans.
As a slave under a pagan master, tending sheep on Slemish
in Antrim, the serious boy meditated on his fate and pitied the
pagan people to whom the Light had not come. Six years
afterwards he escaped, got away to Britain, and thence to
Gaul, where he spent long years at Auxerre, learning the Bible
and the grounds of the faith, and later received priestly orders.
Everything now worked for his return to the land of his captivity, from which, in a vivid dream, he heard the 'voices of
the Irish' calling on him to come and walk once more among
them. The Church of Gaul was the greatest organized branch
of the western Church and had a special care to keep Christian
'the Roman island (Britain) and the pagan island (Ireland)'.
At its request, Pope Celestine sent one Palladius to convert
Ireland in 431, but a sudden death removed him, and Patrick
seemed the appointed man. The Church of Gaul consecrated
him bishop and sent him in 432 on the mission which was to
fill the rest of his life.

Patrick's mission finally centred itself in north-east Ulster,
where after twelve years a local prince presented him with
the site of a church at Armagh, which was destined to be the
metropolis of Irish Christianity. Helpers came to him from

Gaul or Britain, such as Auxilius, Iserninus, Secundinus and Benignus. He appointed the first of these bishop in northern Leinster, the second in southern Leinster, the third in Meath; while Benignus succeeded him in Armagh. When Patrick died in old age about 461 he had laid the foundations of the Church in Ireland, but the house itself was long to build. Wherever we find the word 'domnach', now 'donagh' (from 'dominicum'), in place-names we see the hand of Patrick.

We may be sure that the democratic Christian faith was gladly accepted by the under-races and oppressed peoples, but that it was resisted by the High king and the Gaelic aristocracy, as well as by the Druids and the Fili, is equally certain. Patrick's famous meeting with the High King Laeghaire may be a legend; this son of Niall indeed died a pagan, but at least offered no active opposition to the new faith. It is not till 490 that the first Christian king of Cashel, Oengus, appears. But the opposition was not a fierce one and the Church did not need to be founded in the blood of martyrs.

Under 440 the annals say, 'Leo was ordained bishop of Rome and Patrick was approved in the Catholic Faith'. Further proof of a papal commission we have not; it is enough that Patrick was a bishop ordained by the Church of Gaul and obeyed the call of Christ 'to go forth and teach all nations in my name'. From his *Confession* and what we know of the Church of his time, we cannot doubt that Patrick was a typical western Christian of his age, holding by the Latin Eucharist, the invocation of saints, the sacraments and the doctrine of the Catholic faith as held generally in his time. Above all he must have regarded the Bishop of Rome as in spiritual matters the final authority.

Patrick intended to found in Ireland a branch of the Church in which, as in Gaul or Britain, bishops with large dioceses would rule the Church, and parish clergy and regular monks would exist side by side. Ireland, however, was a country of many tribal states, without great roads, towns, proper communication, or a strong central authority. Instead of the episcopal church he had planned, there developed from the work of others a monastic church with a strong national spirit, well suited to the conditions of the country, and this remained the dominant character of the Church till the twelfth century. As a result not only the work but the memory of St. Patrick was for long obscured, and other names than his were claimed as founders of our Church. The pagan structure of Ireland itself made his mission for a century difficult. In the poets or 'Fili' Ireland had a rampart of native culture which was hard to dislodge. The race of Conn, whose kingdom was rooted in the Gaelic past, did not yield easily. Laeghaire died like a pagan fighting against Leinster in 463, and by his own orders was buried upright in his armour facing the hereditary foe. It was not till the High king Diarmait died in 565 that the old pagan order as enthroned in Tara ended and the ancient hill became the abandoned fortress that we see now. Kings, however, were for centuries to count less than monks in Ireland.

THE IRISH CHURCH, 500–900

In the sixth century the Church began to take a characteristic form which we call Celtic, a word applied also to the sister churches of Scotland, Wales, and Brittany. The Anglosaxon conquest of Britain and the Frankish conquest of Gaul cut them off for a century or more from the Continental Church and its head, the Pope. This intercepted the communications, with the result that later the Celtic churches were found to have tenets and rites older than those of the existing Roman Church. In isolation also they developed that monastic character and body of native customs to which the term 'Celtic particularism' is applied. But all these, though they caused great controversy later, never amounted to independence of the papal authority or the rejection of Catholic unity.

The division of Ireland into province-kingdoms and petty 'tuatha' led to the bishops being numerous and each of them ruling a 'tuath' or two with spiritual functions only. On the other hand, numerous monasteries were founded by gifts of land from some local chief to some prominent saint. The abbot became more important than the bishop, and the bishop generally resided modestly in some monastery. In the endowment of an abbey the first abbot's kin were generally given the succession in the office, and his successors or 'Coarbs' were for centuries members of his family. So much did the monastic system triumph that soon after 500 Patrick's own see became a monastic community and soon there was both an abbot and a bishop at Armagh. It was to the great abbots that in later times the Pope had to address himself as the heads of the national church.

The Latin tongue and the study of the Bible and Catholic theology now entered the country. First among those to whom we owe this stands St. Finnian, abbot-bishop of Clonard in Meath. Under the influence of British monasticism at St. David's, Finnian about 540 organized Clonard as a centre of Latin studies and education. From thence Latin letters spread and the 'Filí' began to use the Latin alphabet to write their own Gaelic.

By 600 Clonard was followed by other great foundations such as Clonmacnois, Clonfert, Lismore, Derry, Kildare, and others, the work of Ciaran, Brendan, Carthach, Columba, and Brigid. These made a new world in Ireland. In the abbeys and their many daughter houses not only was the peaceful life possible but religion, learning, and education flourished, and the Irish monasteries were at once the schools, the libraries, and the universities of the land. Because of their sanctity and security they became also the capitals, the markets, the art and craft centres of Ireland, and such monastic 'cities' as Glendalough were till the Norse period the nearest thing to towns that Ireland had.

In the midst of this renaissance a youth came to manhood, whose name was destined to excel the founders of Irish Christianity, including even Patrick himself, in the hearts of the Gaelic race. In 521 was born at Gartan in Tyrconnell a boy of the race of Niall of the Nine Hostages, whose devotion to the Church soon won him the name of Columba or Colum Cille, 'the Dove of the Church'. Ordained priest at Cloonfad, he did the round of the schools of his time, and studied for a time in Leinster with a Christian 'file' called Gemman. From him the saint was strengthened in his natural attachment to the poetry and lore of the past, which he combined with a passion for the new faith. About 546 he founded a church at Derry on

Lough Foyle; he was its first abbot, and thence founded other houses, such as Durrow in Meath. For them he drew up the Columban rule, just as Ciaran, Brendan, and others drew up rules for their foundations. Not for five centuries did any continental religious Order enter Ireland.

An event in which Columba saw the hand of God sent him upon the true mission of his life. While staying with Finnen, abbot of Moville, he secretly copied out a portion of a Bible which modern scholars think was perhaps the earliest copy in Ireland of St. Jerome's Latin Vulgate. Appealed to by the angry host who wished to keep the precious book to himself, the High king Diarmait gave the famous decision, 'To every cow her calf, to every book its copy'. Columba in anger rejected the decision, and others both of Church and State joined in the dispute, which led to a great battle in 561 at Culdremna in Sligo between the High king and Columba's royal kinsmen in the North. For this the saints of Ireland united to condemn Columba. His own noble nature soon repined at the slaughter of thousands in a quarrel due to himself, and he decided to redeem his soul by winning in a foreign land as many souls for Christ as perished at Culdremna.

Fergus Mac Erc had already founded the petty kingdom of Argyle, but among his people and among the Picts lay a land of pagan barbarism. Thither in 563 Columba sailed with a few monks and received the island of Iona from the king as the seat of his mission. For nearly three centuries this little island was to be the most famous seat of learning and piety in all the Celtic lands, 'a soil,' says Dr. Johnson, 'made sacred by wisdom, valour, and virtue'. Before his death in 597 Columba, 'abbot-bishop of the isles', had evangelized Alba, and is the apostle of Scotland as Patrick is of Ireland.

His name indeed became the greatest in the Irish Church, and Ireland in 575 needed his wisdom and authority on several great matters. At the convention of Drumceat (in county Derry) the High king Aed presided over a national council of kings and abbots, and Columba spoke both as a prince and a churchman. The relations of Scottish Dalriada and Ireland were in dispute, and on his advice it was settled that this little kingdom, whose capital was still northern Antrim, should give its military service to the High king and its naval service to the king of Argyle. Ireland and Scotland were still one empire and remained so till the Norse raids cut them politically asunder. A cultural dispute had also to be settled. The poets ('Filí') had accepted the faith with their lips but in their hearts retained the pagan lore and the pride of their caste. Numerous and great were the rewards they demanded for their compositions and encomiums, so that their exactions became a national nuisance and a proposal was made to exile or outlaw them. But Columba, who had been trained under a Christian 'file' in youth, was their saviour; a prince of the ancient race, his ardent Gaelic soul was on their side. His casting vote saved the Filí and turned them from a race of wandering visitants into a privileged caste of letters and learning. He advised that every province king and every lord of a 'tuath' should have a supreme poet or 'ollamh', and in the course of the centuries the Filí became the ancestors of the professional, endowed, and hereditary poets, bards, and chroniclers whose order survived till 1603.

To their deliverer the poets paid the greatest tribute they could render, and there were attributed to him in later times many lyrics personal in note and tender with the love of Nature and of Ireland. Colum Cille was a poet in Latin and left one or two hymns of lofty quality, but whether he was a poet in his own tongue we know not; at least it is eloquent of his well-known love of Ireland and the native tradition that wandering bards and unknown monks fathered on his name their most inspired verse.

Columba died in Iona in 597, and in the same year the Roman missionary Augustine, sent by Pope Gregory to convert the pagan English, landed in Kent. Columba had founded a spiritual empire in the North, and from Iona not only Scotland but much of England was christianized, while Wales and Cornwall looked towards Ireland as their culture centre. In 633 Edwin, king of Northumbria, fell in battle, and two brothers of the rival dynasty, Oswald and Oswy, returned from the exile into which he had driven them. Both had been taught among the monks of Iona, had learned Irish, and favoured the generous and simple faith of Columba's monks.

Oswald in 633 brought into his kingdom the monk Aidan with a band of monks from Iona and the rocky isle of Lindisfarne became their home. So began what Bede called the 'thirty years' episcopate of the Scots'. In 625 the Roman Paulinus had been sent to Northumbria, but his mission failed in the north with the rise of the heathen Penda of Mercia and receded to Kent. In its place the Iona mission reached as far as the Thames, and Irish bishops and monks were all over Mercia and East Anglia and as far west as Glastonbury. Northumbria was their great conquest and its kings for a hundred years spoke Irish.

In 642 Penda slew the saintly Oswald at the battle of Maserfield, but after dreadful ravages in central England Oswy in 655 at last slew the heathen monarch in battle at Winwaed. The triumph of the Irish mission, however, was checked by the Northumbrian Wilfrid, abbot of Ripon, a man of vigour and genius, who was determined to link the English Church on to that of the Continent rather than remain with the Church of Armagh and Iona, and finally the differences between the Irish and Roman forms came to a head at the Synod of Whitby held under King Oswy in 664.

These differences had already evoked correspondence between the Roman headquarters and Ireland. The Irish monks wore a tonsure of their own, in which the front of the head was shaved, leaving long locks behind. Other small differences existed, but what was serious was the Easter question. Under papal authority the Paschal date had been fixed for the Church by Victorius in 457, but the Celtic churches adhered to the Paschal term as fixed by Anatolius in the third century. As a practical result the Irish were found keeping Easter from the fourteenth to the twentieth of the lunar month and the Continental church between the sixteenth and the twenty-second. On this matter of controversy many letters had passed between the Irish leaders and Rome. Popes Honorius and John IV had urged the Irish to conform and had been answered by Cummian and by Columbanus. The latter, writing to Gregory the Great, boldly maintained the Irish position over Easter, but conceded to the Holy See a primacy of honour and a measure of supreme authority, adding, 'it is known to all that our Saviour gave Saint Peter the keys of the kingdom of Heaven, and that Rome is the principal seat of the orthodox faith'.

By the middle of the seventh century southern Ireland had accepted the Victorian Easter and only northern Ireland and Iona, strong in the name and memory of Columba, stood out. At the Synod of Whitby, Colman, Bishop of Lindisfarne, spoke for the Irish side, but was no match for the arrogant Wilfrid, who said of the Scots, Picts, and Britons who opposed the rest of the world, 'though your Fathers were holy, do you think that their small number in a corner of the remotest island is to be preferred before the universal Church of Christ? Would you put your Columba before the Prince of the Apostles to whom was said "Thou art Peter, and on this rock I will build my Church"?' This was final. Colman might plead that his side held the same Easter as Saint John, and that Columba was their master, but no Catholic at that time could stand against the argument that Christ had made Peter the head of the Church and that the Pope (now against them on the Easter question) was his successor. Colman did not deny this, and when Oswy, as president of the synod, decided that he preferred to be with Saint Peter and the Church of Rome the conference decided against the Irish monks. We may note that they made no claim for their Church to be independent of papal authority and they did not even mention Patrick, a proof of how nationalistic their Church had become and how the great name of Columba had overshadowed the name of the first apostle.

Thus defeated, the Irish withdrew to Iona and left England to the orthodox side, but on the Easter question even Iona conformed in 716 and soon after so did northern Ireland. Wilfrid as bishop of Ripon brought Northumbria over, and five years after Whitby Archbishop Theodore of Canterbury began the career in which he organized the Anglo-Saxon church solidly in bishoprics and parishes. Such an established Church threw into prominence the monastic character and isolated customs which the Celts still retained, though con-verted on the Easter and tonsure questions, and in spite of the piety, learning, and enthusiasm of the Irish, the more organized

Churches of England and the continent continued to accuse them of unorthodoxy in practices, though not in faith.

Checked in England, the missionary genius of the Scots found a greater field in Europe, where the wide empire of the Franks enabled them to penetrate far. Whether as organizers of local churches, teachers in Palace schools, wandering scholars and scribes or solitary preachers, they won for ever the unspoiled glory of pioneers and restorers of the Church and the tradition of Latin culture in the seventh to the ninth centuries, the Golden Age of the Irish Church. Many of those whose aim was solitude sailed away to lonely islands of the western sea, and got as far as Iceland and the Faroes. Others have left their names in the loneliest mountain glens of Switzerland. Others, educated in Latin at home, wandered from abbey to abbey in Europe and earned their bread as scribes and won fame for their beautiful handwriting. The books *Scottice scripti* were highly prized. To such scribes is due the preservation of much classical literature which otherwise would have perished in the Dark Ages. Some of the superior members of this class wrote poetry or prose in Latin worthy of the best standards of the time, some such as John the Scot and Sedulius were appointed chief professors in the Palace schools of Charlemagne and his successors, and won fame in philosophy and the science of the time.

Columbanus is the first great name among our missionaries abroad. An alumnus of Bangor, in 590 he left Ireland with a few companions and arrived in Burgundy. Before his death in 615 he converted or restored to the faith large parts of Lombardy and Burgundy and founded two monasteries, Luxeuil and Bobbio, while his disciple Gall carried on his work in Switzerland. The map of Europe before the year 900 shows the footprints of many such men; among the great names are Cataldus of Taranto, Killian of Franconia, Colman of Lower Austria. In the Low countries and north-east France Irish monks and scholars were particularly in evidence, and at Peronne on the Marne about 670 they founded a monastery which was their first on the continent and which was followed in later centuries by other houses in Cologne, Ratisbon, Vienna, and other places which formed a chain of 'Monasteria

Scotorum', keeping alive the name and fame of Ireland on the Continent and strengthening the Church at home. Unfortunately after the Norman conquest of Ireland these houses fell into the hands of others.

In general the Irish monks and teachers were in doctrine orthodox, though unorthodox in many of their practices, in their preaching evangelical, and in their organization weak. But in John Scotus 'Eriugena' Ireland produced a man of independent and unorthodox genius. After learning all that the Irish schools could teach, John came about 845 to France and became chief professor at the Palace school of the Emperor Charles the Bald at Laon, where he remained for twenty-five years. John has been called 'the greatest intellect given by Ireland to Europe in that age', and one of the most brilliant of all those scholars whom the Renaissance of Charlemagne's time produced. A skilful writer in Latin, he stood alone in his knowledge of Greek; a daring speculator and a Neo-Platonist he won universal attention by his teachings on Free will and Original sin, on which men were free to speculate but in which the orthodox regarded him as near to heresy.

By the year 800 the Irish Church at home attained an ordered form which she kept little changed till the year 1100. The Easter and the tonsure questions had been settled, and no controversy of importance brought Armagh into conflict with Rome. The unity age succeeded to the missionary age. The name and true importance of Patrick were revived again at Armagh, where about 800 the scribe Ferdomnach in the *Book of Armagh* wrote down various traditional lives of Patrick. From henceforth the supremacy of Armagh over the whole of Church of Ireland was affirmed. This was a return to that Roman unity which Patrick had desired and it was natural that an admission of Papal authority should go with it. An ancient canon in the *Book of Armagh* says that 'whensoever any cause that is very difficult and unknown to all the judges of the Scottic nation shall arise, it should rightly be referred to the See of the archbishop of the Irish, to wit Patrick, and the examination of the prelate thereof. But if by him and his wise men such a cause cannot be determined, we have decreed that it shall be sent to the Apostolic see, that is, to

the Chair of the Apostle Peter which has the authoritv of
tne city of Rome.'

THE 'GOLDEN AGE' OF IRELAND

By A.D. 800 Ireland had become a unity of civilization and
law, and no languages save the Gaelic of the ruling classes and
the Latin of the Church were spoken.   The Gaels had subjected
or absorbed the former peoples and created a race-consciousness which has never been lost.   For all that there was little
centralized authority.   The High king Laeghaire, son of Niall,
was slain in 463 while at war with Leinster.   He was succeeded
by Ailill, king of united Connacht and Meath, son of Dathi the
son of Niall's brother Fiachra.   In 483 Ailill's two cousins,
Murchertach 'Mac Erca', grandson of Eoghan, son of Niall and
head of the northern 'Dál Cuinn', and Luguid (Lewy), son of
Laeghaire, son of Niall, united and in the battle of Ocha
defeated and slew Ailill.   He was then succeeded as High king
by Luguid, and he again, according to their compact, by
Murchertach in 509.   The royal succession was thus recovered
for Niall's line, and Diarmait, great-grandson of Niall, is the
first High king who can be called a christian (544–565).   But
meanwhile Connacht had found a king of its own in the line of
Brion, another brother of Niall.   In short, the connexion of the
Connacht-Meath kingdom was severed finally by the battle of
Ocha.   It was established that the High kingship henceforth
went alternately between the Ui Néill of the North and of the
South, or Meath.   From Murchertach Mac Erca descended
the local kings of the Ui Néill of the North.   The High king
Diarmait, head of the southern Ui Néill, had two sons, Colman
and Aed Sláine.   From the first of these came the later kings
of Meath, who had rivals for centuries in the descendants of
Aed.   The succession in the High kingship was uncertain up
to the year 734, then up to 1022 it ran alternately between
the Ui Néill of the north and the Ui Néill, that is, the Clan
Colman, of the south.

Such a succession-rule alone was sufficient to prevent con-
tinuity and therefore strength in the High monarchy.   The
south also paid little obedience, and the Árd Rí remained

merely the president of a union of Irish states, which was now
a heptarchy of Connacht, Meath, Leinster, Munster, Aileach,
Oriel, and Ulidia. The real genius and interest of Ireland lay
in her art and culture. The world-famous books of Kells and
Durrow are of this age and attest the Irish genius for illumina-
tion and Latin calligraphy. The great monasteries had their
libraries and schools, which trained the scholars who won the
respect of Europe. Side by side with the enthusiasm for Latin
and theology went a passion for the native language, which
was now a written speech. The higher clergy with their Latin
tradition despised the old language, charged as it was with
pagan tradition, and the abbot Adamnan of Iona, writing the
life of Columba in Latin, though himself an Irishman, speaks
scornfully of the *lingua Scottica vilis*. But the Filí remained
a powerful body attached to their ancient law and language.
With them and many nameless wandering monks began the
writing of Irish poetry in metres based on the Latin hymns.
Others compiled the old laws of the 'Féni' or free Gaels, now
called the Brehon laws, and the writing of Irish history begins
about 600. The marginal jottings and glosses of Irish missionaries, familiar with Latin and Gaelic, on the continent, upon
copies of the Gospels, have enabled scholars to reconstruct the
Scottic language in what is called the early Irish stage, which
ends about 900, and is then replaced by Middle Irish, which
goes on till 1500. Apart from the more accurate records, the
abundant fancy and imagination of Irish writers and poets
expressed itself in charming lyrics, prose romances, historical
tales, and the reconstruction of the great pagan epics such as
the *Táin Bó Cualnge*.

The Irish mind was now fresh and vivid and seemed likely
to achieve great things in poetry, prose, and drama. Along
with that, it must be added, went a strong pedantic and antiquarian strain. It is tragic that not only did the Scandinavian
and then the Norman invasions dislocate and partly destroy
Irish learning, but they also did much to cripple the natural
inspiration of the Irish mind. Of the Golden Age the greater
part of the manuscripts have perished and can only be partly
deduced from the reconstructions made after the Norse
period. The pedantic spirit of the professional literary man

unfortunately got the better of the inspired but anonymous poet. It is, however, a real glory for Ireland that she was the first nation north of the Alps to produce a whole body of literature in her own speech, to be followed in this by Anglo-Saxons, Norsemen, and Welshmen.

The structural unity of Ireland had now remained intact for four centuries in language, law, religion, and culture. Scholars and poets could freely pass, be understood, and entertain all listeners throughout the whole island. The national unity was visible in the High king, in occasional 'Rig-Dáil' or national gatherings, and in the general assemblies held by the High king at Tailten and such centres. Unfortunately the political weakness of Ireland was to be now put to a cruel test by the Scandinavian onslaught.

CHAPTER II

THE NORSE TYRANNY, 800–1014

ABOUT the year 800 the Scandinavians, moved by an uncontrollable impulse, took to the sea. Led by their 'jarls' and free warriors, in galleys superior to anything yet invented, which could at once face the Atlantic seas and sail far up any navigable river, they soon became the constant terror of civilized lands. Ireland is rich in navigable streams and great inland lakes, and is nowhere more than fifty miles from the sea. She was thus from the Norse point of view an ideal land to attack, with her broad pastures, abundant cattle, unorganized people, and rich and numerous monasteries.

Of the two Scandinavian races which took to the Atlantic, the Norwegians sailed boldly out westward to Iceland, where they founded a republic in 870, and south-west to the Scottish isles. Here they colonized first Orkney and Shetland, then the Hebrides ('Sudreyas' or 'southern isles') and Man, then various points in Galloway, the Solway Firth, and as far south as Pembroke. This took a century or more, and the Hebrides soon witnessed a blending of the Gaelic inhabitants and the Norsemen, which, speaking Gaelic but keeping many Norse traces, remains to this day in the Scottish isles. The kings of Norway from the time of Harold Fairhair (*circa* 900) did not easily abandon these roving subjects of theirs, and for centuries claimed the Norse colonies as their 'Tribute-lands'.

The Danes, on the other hand, kept nearer in and attacked England and Normandy. The differences between these two races were slight, but the Irish, who had a strong sense of colour, called the Norseman a 'Finn-gall' or 'fair foreigner' and the Dane a 'Dubh-gall' or 'dark foreigner'. The land of the vikings they called 'Lochlann', and they hated and dreaded them as ruthless and pagan invaders.[1]

---

[1] The traditional name in Ireland for our Scandinavian invaders is 'the Danes', but it is accepted that the greater part of them were Norwegian, hence I use the word 'Norse' as most convenient.

The first raids of the sea-kings fell upon Orkney, Shetland, and the Hebrides, where they set up petty earldoms. In 830 the pressure was so severe that the abbot of Iona and his monks fled to Downpatrick with the relics of Columba. Thus was Iona, that 'light of learning and piety' which had shone so long in the north-west, extinguished. Armagh took its place definitely as the head-quarters of Irish Christianity. As the hordes of viking ships grew, the kingdoms of Ireland and Scotland were cut off, Scottish Dalriada was united with the kingdom of the Picts, and about 840 Kenneth Mac Alpin became the first 'king of Picts and Scots'.

Turgesius (in Norse 'Thorgest') was the first viking to attempt a kingdom in Ireland. His ships sailed up the Shannon and the Bann into Lough Ree and Lough Neagh, whence he commanded the kingdoms of Ulster, Connacht, and Meath. With a grim humour he made himself abbot of Armagh, while his wife Ota sat as a priestess at the high altar of Clonmacnois and delivered heathen oracles. But after lording it in this fashion from 831 to 845 Turgesius was treacherously taken by Malachy ('Maelsechlainn'), king of Meath, and drowned in Lough Owel.

After many defeats the Irish began to recover, and in 848 this Malachy, now High king, crushed a Norse army at Sciath Nechtain. He felt that the cause of Ireland was part of the general Christian cause of Europe and reported his victory to the Emperor Charles the Bald along with gifts and a request for safe conduct for Irish pilgrims to visit Rome. But, soon after, two vikings, Olaf the White and Ivar 'Beinlaus', landed in Dublin Bay in 852 and fortified the hill above the Liffey where Dublin Castle now stands.

The straightforward character of 'the war of the Gael and the Gall'[1] soon vanished. A mixed race grew up in Ireland and Scotland and in the islands, to whom the Irish gave the name of 'Gall-Gaels'. Irish kings began to intermarry with

[1] The name of an historical tract in Irish commemorating the life and victories of Brian Boru. 'Gall' in Irish meant originally a Gaul; it now came to mean a 'Norseman'; next it was applied to Normans, and till about 1540 was the general name for the Normans who became practically Irish. It still means 'the English' in the native language, along with 'Sasanach'.

the Norse and to adopt such names as Magnus, Lochlann, Sitric, etc. Cervall, king of Ossory, who died in 888, was accepted as king of Dublin; daughters of his married Norse chiefs and from them descended many famous vikings of later times. The weight of the Scandinavian attacks on Ireland was also diverted to England in the time of Alfred the Great. From the death of Ivar in 873 'there was rest for forty years to the Men of Erin', and during this lull another Cervall, king of Leinster, occupied Dublin.

Meanwhile Cashel was ruled for a century by a race of Eoghanacht priest-kings, which at last produced a remarkable man in Cormac Mac Cullenan, a scholar-king and a man of sincere and noble character. For or by him was compiled one of the famous lost books of Ireland, the *Psalter of Cashel*. Of the portions that survive, one is called *Cormac's Glossary*, an attempt to compare Irish words with contemporary languages. Another is the *Book of Rights*, drawn up in Irish and in verse by the orders of Cormac and agreed upon by the chief poets and kings of Ireland. As revised later under Brian Boru it describes the prerogatives of the High king and the rights and duties of the province-kings and their vassal-states.

Cormac, who was bishop-king of Cashel, was prematurely slain in 908 in war against the Leinster men at Ballaghmoon, when, against his own wish and impelled by wicked advisers, he attempted to subject Leinster to Cashel. With him ended the priest-kings, and another branch of the Eoghanacht soon after took the throne of Cashel in the person of one Cellachan.

The century 914–1014 is a date easily remembered for the whole story of the Norse attempt to subdue Ireland and its failure. It begins and ends dramatically in Dublin. In 914 two grandsons of Ivar, Ragnall and Sitric, arrived in Waterford Harbour and built a fortress there. Next, in 916, Sitric sailed up the Liffey and recovered Dublin, which, after the death of Cervall, king of Leinster, in 909, had been left undefended. The occupation of Dublin was a challenge to all Ireland which the High king Niall 'Glúndubh' (Black-knee), head of the Northern Ui Néill, nobly took up in 919. Collecting the levies of Ulster, Meath, and Connacht, he marched upon

Dublin. Sitric's forces met him at Kilmohavoc ('Cell-mo-shamoc'), a ford on the Liffey west of Dublin, and there the hero-king was slain and the Irish defeated. After this 'battle of Dublin' the capital remained in the hands of the race of Ivar, and it was clear that all the valour of the Irish was of little avail against the trained courage of the armoured Norsemen.

Next the race of Ivar occupied Limerick in 920, and so was finally spread a whole chain of viking colonies and fortresses round the coast from the Liffey to the Shannon, of which the strongest points were Dublin, Wexford, Waterford, Cork, and Limerick.

Now came the zenith of Scandinavian power in Ireland. A line of kings of the race of Ivar followed in Dublin, which became a kingdom covering the two counties of Dublin and Wicklow, stretching down to Arklow and reaching inland to Leixlip. Among these kings, Olaf 'Cuaran' ('of the Sandals') ruled Dublin victoriously from 944 onwards, and reached the height of his victories when in 977 his army defeated the forces of the High king Domnall, whereupon all Meath from the Shannon to the sea was placed under a Norse oppression so severe that the Gaels called it a 'Babylonish captivity'. It is significant of the disruption of things that the Fair or Aenach of Tailten, which it was the prerogative of the High king to hold, was intermitted for some eighty years till Brian revived it again in 1007. At the same time a yoke almost as heavy was placed upon Munster, whose rivers the Norsemen could easily penetrate, and where they had the centres of Waterford, Cork, and Limerick to operate from. The race of Ivar seized on the capital, Cashel, itself, and though bravely resisted by the Eoghanacht king, Cellachan, could not be overthrown. Cellachan died in 954, and with his son the direct Eoghanacht dynasty ended, leaving the way open to a greater line.

At last the Norse yoke was broken by two remarkable men, Malachy (Maelsechlainn), king of Meath, and Brian Boru 'of the Tributes'.

The oppression of Munster under the race of Ivar is graphically described in the opening pages of the *War of the Gael and the Gall.* Thomond (North Munster) was the kingdom of Cennedig, head of the Dál Cais, one of the royal free tribes of Munster, which sprang a long way back from the royal stock of Ailill Olum, father of Eoghan Mór and Cormac Cas. Cennedig had two sons, Mahon and Brian, and Mahon succeeded him. Brian, the younger, was born about 940 and grew up during the worst days of the Norse tyranny when the Dalcassians had been driven into the present county Clare, and Ivar of Limerick planned a great rampart between Limerick and the Fergus to hem them in. Mahon was ready to accept terms but Brian urged resistance, and in a number of petty battles trained a Dalcassian army to face the Norsemen. The two brothers triumphed so far that on the death of Donnchad son of Cellachan in 963 Mahon claimed the throne of Cashel. But first Ivar, who had Eoghanacht allies, had to be overthrown. In 968 at Sulcoit in Tipperary the two brothers completely overthrew Ivar's forces and marched upon Limerick, and took it, while Ivar fled with the two Eoghanacht princes, Donovan and Maelmuad. The Norse tyranny in Munster thus collapsed and Mahon ruled peaceably for eight years as king of Cashel until Ivar returned from oversea, conspired again with Donovan and Maelmuad, and slew him by treachery. This cleared the way for the really great man in Munster. Brian honourably enough, by open battle or fair challenge, slew Ivar and disposed of his two allies, whose death removed for the time any Eoghanacht claimants to Cashel.

From 976 to 1014 Brian reigned as king of Munster, which in the eyes of orthodox annalists was his first usurpation. He justified it by a work of reconstruction which puts him on a footing with Alfred, Edgar, and Otto the Great as restorers of Europe after the Scandinavian fury.

Meanwhile Malachy had arisen like another star in the North. He was born in 948, became king of Meath, and in 980 High king. This he signalized at the battle of Tara in 980, where he overthrew a Norse army, marched upon Dublin and forced Olaf to surrender, and so ended at one blow 'the Babylonish captivity in Meath, which was like the captivity of Hell'. Olaf went oversea and died next year a Christian in

Iona, for already the settled Norsemen of the southern lands were giving up the pagan gods.

Malachy thus became master of Dublin, but had no wish to destroy so rich a city and so useful a vassal-state, and therefore finally installed there in 994 a son of Olaf, Sitric called 'Silk-beard'. Sitric, who was the son of Olaf Cuaran by Gormflath, sister of Maelmora, later king of Leinster, was to survive all the drama of the age and die in 1042. Irish on his mother's side, and at least a nominal Christian, he shows how mistaken it would be to regard the Brian saga as a war of Irish against Norse and Christians against pagans. Malachy had married Gormflath some time after the death of Olaf, and both he and Brian were to show a fatal leniency to her son.

Gormflath was one of the fateful women of Irish history. Her career was long and disastrous for Ireland, however much she justified it as a Leinster patriot and for the sake of husband and brother. She is described in a Norse saga (for the Norse knew her well as 'Kormlada'), as 'fairest and best-gifted in everything that was not in her own power, but it was the talk of men that she did all things ill over which she had any power'. This beautiful, dangerous woman was the wife in turn of Olaf, Malachy, and Brian, and in the end for the sake of revenge was ready to give her hand to the invader Sigurd.

Brian was already king of Munster and his next step was to subject Ossory and Leinster and so rule the Southern half. Leinster was in a state of weakness and the royal succession was disputed, so Brian was able to subject it, and by 984 was supreme over southern Ireland. A clash between himself and Malachy was inevitable, but in the contest Brian was the greater man and could send the viking ships of Limerick up the Shannon to dominate both Connacht and Meath. At last in 998 the two leaders, who were able to fight or parley like gentlemen, divided Ireland between them, and Brian became supreme king of the Southern half, with the vassalage of Dublin and the Norse towns. According to his opponents, this was his second usurpation.

Leinster and Dublin were, however, soon leagued against Irish unity and a woman's heart was thrown into the scale. Malachy was now tired of Gormflath and finally repudiated her. Turning to her brother Maelmora, she urged him to take the kingdom of Leinster, to which he had a royal claim, to unite with Sitric, and then between them break the double yoke of Malachy and Brian. Brian, however, marched up from Kincora, and in 999 at Glenmama, on the mountain slope of Saggard, west of Dublin, routed the Norse and Leinster allies under Maelmora and Sitric and marched victor into Dublin.

Brian was now an elderly man and had already two sons, Murchad and Taig, but he too fell under the spell of Gormflath, who became his wife and bore him a son Donnchad. For her sake he restored Sitric in Dublin and installed Maelmora in the kingdom of Leinster.

The joint sway of Brian and Malachy could not last. In 1002 Brian met his rival at Tara and gave him time to decide on open battle with the aid of the northern Ui Néill, or peacefully to surrender the High kingship. Malachy called in vain on the princes of the North and so gave in. Brian became High king of Ireland. It was his third usurpation, and a final breach of the Ui Néill succession, which had lasted for six centuries.

Both Church and State, however, admitted the fact. In 1004 Brian carried out the Circuit of the High king with a pomp never equalled before or after his time, and marched from his capital at Kincora up through Connacht over the Erne, through Ulster to Armagh, down into Meath and to Dublin and back by Leinster and Ossory to Cashel again. In the great church of Armagh after mass he laid twenty ounces of gold as a gift upon the altar and bade his scribe Maelsuthain enter in the *Book of Armagh* words which can be still read there in Latin:

'The holy Patrick, when going to Heaven, ordained that the whole fruit of his labour as well of baptism as of church matters and alms should be paid to the apostolic city which in Irish is called Ardmacha. So have I found it among the books of the Scots and have written it in the sight of Brian, emperor of the Scots, and what I have written he has confirmed for all the kings of Cashel.'

This was the greatest moment in the history of native Ireland. Brian by this title was claiming the monarchy of the whole Gaelic race. To sanctify his rule he accepted the supremacy of Armagh over the whole Church of Ireland. Brian, whose nobility and depth of character shines through the ages, was a sincere Christian and saw the necessity of religious and political bonds for the salvation of society.

Ten years remained to him to lift Ireland out of the ruin of the Norse age. He had already made Munster a strong kingdom and its monasteries the seats of a revived culture, and now he did this work for all Ireland, and the loyal Malachy supported him. He rebuilt ruined churches or founded others, sent overseas to replace the lost books, and in other ways healed the ruin of the past two centuries. In 1007 he presided over the Fair of Tailten, which had been suspended for eighty years, and so all Ireland celebrated the ending of the Norse terror.

But gradually the disruptive forces stirred again. Malachy had enough to do in keeping order in the Northern half. The baleful genius of Gormflath still burned against the two great men who had repudiated her, and again she stirred up Maelmora and Sitric with taunts on their vassalage. Summoned by Malachy to his aid, Brian had to march up from Kincora and besiege Dublin from September to Christmas 1013, and to retire for lack of provisions. He was now an aged man, but with brain and energy as active as ever. Sitric was meanwhile seeking viking aid for the Leinster-Dublin alliance. Sigurd the Stout, earl of Orkney, offered himself and two thousand Norsemen in mail and was promised in return the hand of Gormflath, and with it the kingdom of Erin. The rendezvous was to be on the high ground between Dublin and the Tolka. There on Good Friday, April 23, 1014, Brian, marching up from Kincora, faced the allies on the slope of Crinan's Hill north of the river. His army, levied from all Munster, was swelled with his vassals from south Connacht, of whom Taig O'Kelly was the most ardent spirit. He only required of Malachy to keep his forces stationed behind the line of battle. On the other side Sigurd commanded two thousand men, the pick of the Norse world of Scotland and Man, and was supported by the levies of

Leinster and of Dublin. Maelmora led his men, but Sitric watched the battle from the ramparts. Brian himself, too aged for battle, stayed in his tent behind the lines. In the fierce fighting Murchad broke the opposing Norsemen and Sigurd fell, so did Maelmora, and the allies were swept away in rout, the Leinster and Dublin men making for the bridge back to the city, and the vikings for the weir of the Tolka to get to their ships at Clontarf. It was, however, flooded by a high tide, and most of them perished there, and among the pursuers the young Turloch, son of Murchad, was drowned. The hero Murchad himself fell in the battle, and Brian, unhappily left unguarded in his tent, was slain by one of the flying Norsemen, Brodir, seizing such an opportunity. Such was the battle of Clontarf and what the Norse sagas commemorated as 'Brian's Battle'. Of Gormflath we hear no more. The body of Brian was borne with the utmost honour by the clergy to Armagh, and buried near the high altar there. His army, badly shattered in the fighting, could not take Dublin, and retreated back to Kincora, under the command of his son Taig.

CHAPTER III

THE END OF GAELIC INDEPENDENCE, 1014–1166

WITH the fall of Brian at Clontarf ended an heroic age. There was for a time a restoration of the old order. Malachy resumed the High kingship but died in 1022 at an advanced age, and with him ended the Ui Néill succession, which had lasted for six centuries. There followed 'kings with opposition', and the struggle of province dynasts for the supreme power lasted till the Norman invasion. Brian had set the bad example of usurpation; others imitated him but could not, like him, justify it. The Heptarchy kingdoms recovered their independence. Taig remained with difficulty king of Cashel till his death in 1023, when his brother Donnchad replaced him, and Leinster regained her freedom. When Maelmora's son Broen died in 1018 the way was left for another branch of the royal race.

Nevertheless Brian's reign is of unique importance, both as ending and beginning a period. He brought the viking terror to an end, gave Munster a predominance which might have led to a real monarchy for Ireland, restored the Church, and gave Ireland a new impetus of art, literature, and culture not unworthy of her former Golden Age. By such great men was the national consciousness created. He settled the political structure of Ireland as it lasted till the Normans came. To him is attributed the general adoption of the patronymics of O and Mac (grandson and son), which gave us the famous surnames of O'Brien, O'Connor, MacCarthy, and so on. These surnames had in fact already begun, but it may well be that Brian hastened their general acceptance. Henceforth the succession of kings was limited to the heirs male of these founders, though descent from father to son had to fight long against the 'Derb-fine' law, by which all the male descendants of a king to the fourth generation were eligible.

The recovery of the native Church followed on Brian's victories, and before a century was passed a reform began

IRELAND
IN 1014

Scale of Miles

0   20   40   60

TIREE
Iona
MULL
ARGYLL o
ISLAY
DA

Rathlin
INISHOWEN
IRISH
Aileach
Derry
DALRIADA
TIR EOGHAIN
KINGDOM
TIRCONAILL
OF
Donegal
KINGDOM OF THE
NORTH
Lough
Neagh
ULIDIA
L.Derg
Lough
Erne
R.Erne
R.Blackwater
L.Melvin
Armagh
SUBKINGDOM
KINGDOM OF
Carlingford
Lough
L.Allen
OF
ORIEL
L.Gara
BREFNI
KINGDOM
Monasterboice
OF
L.Sheelin
Slane
Rathcroghan
Kells
KINGDOM OF
R.Boyne
L.Mask
CONNACHT
L.Ree
Uisneach
MEATH
Tara
Cong
L.Corrib
Tuam
R.Suck
Durrow
Clonard
Howt
Clonmacnois
Dublin
Clonfert
Kildare
Glendalough
KINGDOM
R.Liffey
L.Derg
Kincora
THOMOND
SLIEVE-
Wicklo
Limerick
R.Nore
MARGY
NORSE CITY
Kilkenny
LEINSTER
Arklow
OF LIMERICK
OSSORY
R.Barrow
R.Slaney
Ferns
R.Shannon
KINGDOM
Cashel
Mount
OF
R.Suir
Wexford
Brandon
MUNSTER
Lismore
Waterford
NORSE CIT
Killarney
R.Blackwater
OF WEXFOR
Dungarvan
NORSE STATE
R.Lee
OF WATERFORD
Cork
Youghal
DESMOND
NORSE CITY
OF CORK

which merged in the general Reform of the Church under the lead of Rome. Many of the old abbeys never revived, but others such as Clonmacnois did, and new ones arose, and Ireland still remained the culture centre of the Celtic lands.

In the revival of civilization Brian's patronage and inspiration was strongly marked. The collection of what could be saved from the past began, and abbots and kings prided themselves on the possession of great books such as the *Book of Leinster*, into which careful scribes gathered the epics, poetry, history and science of the past. The metal-work in gold and bronze, in which Ireland excelled in the former age, revived and gave us such gems as the processional Cross of Cong. So too the great stone High crosses mark the artistic revival of this age, such as we have still at Tuam and Monasterboice. In architecture the Irish evolved a Hiberno-Romanesque style, of which the great examples are Cormac's Chapel at Cashel and the doorway at Clonfert. In this period of 1014 to 1166 Ireland had one more chance of a native civilization and political unity, but unfortunately her political weakness was to prove fatal.

The political structure of Ireland was now as follows. The Scandinavian menace had been ended for good, and the population of the Norse towns turned Christian and finally in speech and habit almost Irish. The name Ostmen ('Eastmen') is applied to this new race, now cut off from the great viking world. They chose their own bishops and built their own cathedrals, Sitric of Dublin setting the example by founding Christchurch in 1040 and installing Donatus as bishop.

The Ostman states were of considerable size. Dublin-shire, as the Norse called it, stretched from Skerries down to Arklow, and the country north of the Liffey was a thickly populated country, still called Fingall (Fine Gall, 'the land of the Norsemen'). Waterford, Limerick, Cork, and even Wexford, though much smaller, had each before the Normans came a considerable territory round their walls called 'the cantred of the Ostmen'. In Dublin by 1100 the old race of Ivar died out and their place was taken by a family of Norse earls called Mac Torcaill. Waterford also, and apparently Limerick and Cork, had their petty independent rulers. The Norse attempt to

conquer Ireland had failed, but Irish generosity and the loose
structure of the Irish State now allowed these petty republics
to enjoy citizen rights under the High monarchy. Nevertheless their hearts were not entirely with Ireland or their
nationality absorbed. Their sea-towns were now to serve the
Irish province kings as they deserted their inland raths, and
within a century Dublin, Cork, and Limerick had become
respectively a second capital for MacMurrough, MacCarthy,
and O'Brien.

The political balance of Ireland, as it now stood, is summed
up in the *Book of Rights,* which Brian for his own purposes
caused to be re-edited. In this new form the book provided
for the claim of Munster, Leinster, Ulster, and Meath to enjoy
the High kingship, but not Connacht, which by ancient tradition was part of the old Meath-Connacht kingdom. Again,
Brian's edition increased the King of Cashel's power in his own
province: he was to have the military service of the Gaels of
Dublin and Ireland and, if he were not King of Erin, to be
King of Mogh's half. The result of this design for a central
monarchy proved very different in the outcome. The struggle
of 'kings with opposition' began, and though three of these
kingdoms in turn produced able men nothing so promising as
Brian's monarchy emerged again.

In Munster, after the death of Donnchad, a weak man,
Turloch, son of Taig, and then his son Murcertach ruled till
1119. These were able and enlightened men, but their brave
efforts to revive their ancestors' greatness ended with them.
They were threatened too by a revival of the Eoghanacht line,
whom the Dalcassians had thrust aside, and in 1050 we read of
Carthach, king of Desmond, whose race was destined to
challenge the O'Brien kingship. In Leinster the line of north
Leinster kings ended with Maelmora, and in 1040 their place
was taken by Diarmait or Dermot, whose family demesne was
Hy Kinsella in Carlow and north Wexford. Dermot was a
man of ambition and force and ended up as king both of
Leinster and of the Galls of Dublin in 1071. From his son
Murchad came the royal name of MacMurrough.

In Meath, though the descendants of Malachy (the O'Melaghlins) were of the old Uí Néill of the South, their line produced
no great men, and their small but fertile kingdom became the

prey to the neighbouring kingdoms. In the North the surname
of MacLochlann became pre-eminent out of the race of Niall
Glúndubh, and these vigorous kings of Cenel Eoghain seemed
about to create a single kingdom in Ulster. In Connacht arose
the O'Connors, whose demesne in county Roscommon was
called Síl Muiredaig (by the Normans 'Shilmorthy').

The *Book of Rights* gives us an almost complete picture of
the High king and his prerogatives, the duties *inter se* of the
High king and the province kings, and their rights again over
their vassals. In all there are some hundred sub-states in
Ireland called *Tuatha*, each with its petty *Rí* or king, several
of them sometimes uniting again into a *Mór-Tuath*, such as
the seven tribes of Leix. It was a patriarchal society in which
the king must be the senior and best fitted to rule of an
ancestral line. Once accepted by his chief vassals and inaugurated with ancient rites on some sacred hill in the open air,
he then became a considerable despot. But his rights came to
him by popular acceptance, and no 'stranger in the sovereignty'
could for long hope to govern an Irish state. The strength and
the weakness of the Irish political structure were to be sorely
tested again before long, and it was shown that though weak
in central command it was strong in local resistance. The
survival-value of the Gaelic order was a high one.

We now briefly follow the political events that led up
to the Norman invasion. In 1086 Turloch O'Brien died at
Kincora at the great age of seventy-seven, 'King of Ireland'
according to the annals of Loch Cé. He was succeeded by his
son Murcertach, a man of intellectual ability, a friend and
patron of Church reform and a statesman of ability. But the
task of welding Ireland together could only be achieved by
the continued supremacy of one kingdom, and this the others
generally combined to prevent. In Connacht there arose a
determined rival, Rory O'Connor; in Ulster another, Donal
MacLochlann. Had Ireland but realized it, the situation from
abroad should have taught the necessity of union. In 1066
Anglo-Saxon England fell before the Conqueror and his
Normans, and this aggressive race was bent upon further
expansion. In 1072, say the Irish annals, the 'Franks'

invaded Scotland, and in 1090 the Norman adventurers in Wales slew Rhys, king of south Wales, in battle. Thus, says the Welsh chronicler sadly, 'fell the kingdom of the Britons'. From another side Lanfranc, the new archbishop of Canterbury, was claiming a supremacy for his see over all the British islands, and Ireland it was clear would have to set her ancient Church in order.

Murcertach strove valiantly to meet the new order of things. After long warfare with his northern rivals, he secured homage enough in 1101 to make the 'Circuit of the High king'. He pleased the Church in that same year by presenting his former capital of Cashel as the site of a proposed archbishopric for Munster, and before his death he presided as High king in 1110 at the first Reforming synod at Fiadh-mic-Oengusa.

The islands and coasts of Scotland and Ulster were still the home and haunts of Norsemen and vikings. Among the names of the mixed Gall-Gael race who ruled earldoms from their galleys we may notice Somerled, in 1164 'king of the Gall-Gael' or 'Lord of Argyll', ancestor of the MacDonnells of the Isles, and an earlier 'Suibhne', ancestor of MacSweeny. In 1102 there appeared in these waters Magnus 'Barefoot', one of the last sea-kings of Norway, a gallant and heroic figure, claiming tribute from the Hebrides and Man. Murcertach made friends with him and entertained him at Kincora. He then prepared to sail home for Norway, but, landing in Ulster to forage, he and many gallant vikings were slain by a local levy, in 1103. Murcertach had marched north, and like his great ancestor placed a gift of gold on the high altar of Armagh, but was suddenly attacked and routed by his rival MacLochlann at Moy Cova on August 5th 1103. The O'Brien glory never recovered, and on his death in 1119 Munster fell out of the race for supremacy. Turloch O'Connor, who became king of Connacht in 1106, took his place and became Ireland's last great king.

Meanwhile forces other than political were moving. The reformation of the Church had begun in Europe a century ago. For Ireland the necessity, too, was pointed out by Rome and Canterbury and realized by a band of native reformers. The eleventh and twelfth centuries were for Europe an age of recovery in the intellectual and spiritual life, and this impulse Ireland was destined to feel also. Her monastic centres had long played a noble part, but they had become rich and stagnant, devoted to their local interests, and yet subjected to the tyranny of temporal lords. Only the churches of the Ostmen had the Order of Benedict or Augustine; the native abbeys obeyed the Rule of Columba, Ciaran, Brendan, and other ancient founders. The Irish Church was still monastic, and a proper Episcopate with due authority and endowment was lacking. The practice of simony, the intrusion of men with minor orders into high Church offices for selfish reasons, and hereditary succession in the great abbeys, were abuses similar to those that the Cluniac reform on the Continent had already assailed. From 957 the abbacy of Armagh was for a century and a half continuously in the hands of a single family, the Clann Sinach, who as laymen or in minor orders attained the Coarb-ship and then appointed an insignificant bishop or added this office to their own.

The Hildebrandine reform added still further emphasis, and Ireland was included in the programme of 'Unity and Purity' which Gregory VII pronounced. The Norman archbishops of Canterbury from Lanfranc on, in virtue of their claim derived from Augustine to be supreme over all the British isles, pointed out in various letters to the Irish leaders the need of a general purification. Ireland was asked to accept all the essentials of the Western Church, the supreme authority of Rome, conformity to one ritual, canonical marriage, a proper episcopate under Roman authority, celibacy and tithes for the clergy, and the freedom of the Church from lay domination.

Once again, as in the seventh century, the Irish Church came into conflict with the papal head-quarters. Catholic unity and doctrine it had no wish to reject, but attachment to old custom was tenacious and opposed to the centralizing and unifying programme now set forth. But the forward wave was against Irish conservatism. Of the Churches which had clung to 'Celtic particularism', Scotland was brought into

Roman conformity under Queen Margaret, and when Wales succumbed to the Norman advance the independence of St. David's vanished also.

The interference of Canterbury began with the Ostmen, who turned from the Celts and looked towards England for their church government. Of the bishops of Dublin before the Norman invasion almost all sought Canterbury's approval. After Donatus (1035–1074), Patrick was sent to Canterbury by the citizens, was consecrated by Lanfranc, and swore obedience to him. Lanfranc took the opportunity to address a letter to Turloch O'Brien as King of Ireland, pointing out the abuses of the Irish church, which was the beginning of a long correspondence between England, Ireland, and Rome on the church question. The next two bishops of Dublin, Donatus and Samuel O'Haingli, again were confirmed by Canterbury, and Anselm also claimed the Primacy of all the Britains. Not till 1152 did Dublin give in to the Irish church. So it was with Waterford. Its first bishop, Malchus, a monk from Winchester, was consecrated by Anselm and two English bishops. The letters recommending him to Anselm from the Ostmen townsmen were attested by 'Murchertach, our king', and four Irish bishops. In 1105 the Norse city of Limerick also got its first bishop, Gillebert, who, however, was Irish.

A band of native reformers now appeared alongside of this Ostman movement. A number of Irish bishops aspired to have in Ireland the status of their Continental brethren and were ready to accept Roman reform. In Gillebert of Limerick, who had been a monk at Rouen with Anselm, they found an inspiring writer who provided them with a tract on the 'status of the Church', outlining a proper episcopal and parochial organization for Ireland and advocating a uniform liturgy.

Reform was now fully launched in the South, and the High king Murcertach gave it his blessing by presenting at a council of Cashel in 1101 the famous Rock to the Church, as the seat of an archbishop. Next the North of Ireland joined in and Armagh took its rightful place as head of the Church. In 1105 Celsus (Cellach) was elected Coarb; he also was of the Clann Sinach and a layman, only twenty-five years old, and

married, who took holy orders only after his election. The
next year he took episcopal orders when the bishop of Armagh
died, and united in himself the double office of abbot-bishop.
He was thus an example of all the abuses of the time, but
justified himself by joining the Reform party and throwing
his great name and influence into it. Welcomed by the
southerners, in 1106 at Cashel he was accepted by all as
Archbishop and Primate of the Irish Church. It was a title
up to then unknown. In return Celsus erected Cashel into
an archbishopric for Malchus of Waterford. Rome showed
its approval by appointing Gillebert papal legate in 1107,
but deferred its sanction to the new archdiocese. The next
advance was made at the national synod of Rathbreasail or
Fiadh-mic-Oengusa in 1110, presided over by the High king
and Celsus, which divided Ireland into twenty-four proper
sees. But this programme needed a long working out. Again
in 1122 the Dublin Ostmen got a bishop, Gregory, consecrated
at Canterbury, rejecting an act of the synod which subjected
their bishopric to that of Glendalough. To be ruled from a
Celtic monastery somewhere in the mountains was not to the
taste of the Norse burgesses, who preferred to have a bishop
of their own within their walls.

While unity was evolving in the Church, Turloch More
O'Connor was attempting the unity of the Irish State. He
was Ireland's greatest king since Brian, and, like him, strove
to make one province supreme in order that the others should
be subject to it, but again success to be permanent needed a
line of successors equal to himself in ability. All that could
be done to make the fluctuating monarchy real he did; as
king of Connacht, and then as High king, girdling Connacht
with forts at all the vital points, spanning the Shannon with
a bridge, dismembering the other kingdoms and striving to
appoint their rulers. On the death of Murcertach in 1119 he
secured the High kingship and held it till his death in 1156.
He accepted the High king's position as patron of Church
reform and of national culture. From his own kingdom,
which he made into a bastion dominating the rest of Ireland,
he enforced his personal will upon the other princes. It is

tragic that such a man was not in charge of the national destiny when the Normans arrived. Instead, he was succeeded in Connacht by a son who was a weakling and the old game of 'Kings with opposition' began again.

Divide et impera was a maxim well understood by Turloch. He expelled from Meath its king, Murchad O'Melaghlin, in 1126 and set up in his place his own son Connor, but the young prince was soon slain in a local revolt because he was 'a stranger in sovereignty'. The same policy was attempted with Leinster. Its real triumph was the permanent division of Munster, a kingdom formerly so pre-eminent. In 1127 he invaded it in great force and at Cork divided it between Conor, nephew of Murcertach O'Brien, and Cormac MacCarthy. The former took for his kingdom Thomond or North Munster (the present counties of Clare, Tipperary, Limerick, and north Kerry) and the latter Desmond or South Munster (south Kerry and county Cork as far east as Lismore). Cormac was an amiable prince, a friend to Reform and the builder of a beautiful church at Cashel. But the division of Munster was disastrous. Turloch O'Connor was reviving for selfish reasons the Eoghanacht claim which Brian had extinguished a century ago, and it would appear that Carthach, the founder of this name in 1050, had no particular claim to the kingdom of Cashel. But again in 1151 Turloch More invaded Munster in full force, overthrew Turloch O'Brien at Móin Mór near Cork, and once more divided the province.

This policy caused an alignment of rival forces which ended in the Norman invasion. Murcertach MacLochlann, king of the Cenel Eoghain ('the Race of Eoghan'), subjected Ulidia and Oriel and united Ulster. He was Turloch O'Connor's chief rival, and Leinster joined him from the south. Here Dermot (Diarmait) MacMurrough, great-grandson of the first Dermot, came into the kingdom of Leinster about 1126. In that year, in a vacancy, the High king Turloch imposed his son Conor upon Leinster, but Dermot asserted his claim and expelled the Connacht prince. Henceforth he was enemy to O'Connor and friend to MacLochlann. This bad man was to be the ultimate cause of the loss of Ireland's independence.

Among other princes of the time we may note Donnchad

O'Cervall, king of Oriel, a patron of Church reform, who gave
the land for Mellifont; Murchad O'Melaghlin, last king of
undivided Meath; and Tiernan O'Ruairc, lord of Brefni.
Tiernan was a man of Dermot's stamp, full of fierce energy,
and an out-and-out partisan, who, though on the native side,
proved no less disastrous to the native cause. Brefni, now
the modern counties of Cavan and Leitrim, was a vassal-state
of Connacht and defended it on the north-east against Ulster.
O'Ruairc made it one of the chief minor states and aimed at
annexing to it western Meath.

Irish kings could seldom rise above a temporary greatness,
but Dermot at least showed how strong a province-king could
be. The chiefs of northern Leinster had little affection for
his southern branch of the royal race. The border state of
Ossory under Mac Gillapatraic resisted Leinster's claim to
suzerainty. The Ostman states of Dublin, Waterford, and
Wexford owed homage and service to the king of Leinster,
according to the *Book of Rights*, though their supreme allegiance was due to the High king. To be at once 'king of the
Leinstermen and of the foreigners' was a proud title which the
Leinster kings had not enjoyed since the first Dermot, but
Dermot II meant to be all this. In the struggle of province-
kingdoms Leinster too should play its old part, and according
to the *Book of Rights* there was nothing to bar its claim to
the High kingship.

Dermot was not a complete barbarian; indeed he was a
patron of culture and religion. His palace at Ferns had in its
library one of the glories of Irish literature, the *Book of Leinster*,
written about 1150; here he founded an abbey, and similarly
he endowed All Saints in Dublin as well as Jerpoint and
Baltinglas. But all his political activities betrayed ferocity
and violence. Early in his career he sacked the abbey of
Kildare and shamefully treated the abbess. The indignation
of the Church at such deeds of the Irish princes had much
to do with the surrender of the bishops later to the English
king, who they thought alone could guarantee order. Against
Dublin, Dermot had a special animus, because it had expelled
his race, and the townsmen returned his hatred. He only
finally became king of Leinster by hard battling, in which he

had to subdue Ossory, besiege Waterford, and similarly to force Dublin under its earl Asgall Mac Torcaill into reluctant submission. In 1141 he had to suppress a revolt of the north Leinster chiefs and blinded or slew seventeen of them. In no case did he win affection or loyal submission, save in his native domain of Hy Kinsella.

But for a time the strong hand was effective, and by 1150 Dermot was the admitted king of Dublin and Leinster and could play a great part in the general war of Ireland. In 1151 the High king Turloch invaded Munster to enforce the submission of O'Brien, and in the general strife MacMurrough carried off Dervorgilla, the beautiful wife of Tiernan O'Ruairc. It was by her own invitation it seems, for Dermot was a tall, handsome, and imposing man, but his offence was made no better when he soon sent her home again. The High king made an award between him and the prince of Brefni, but O'Ruairc never forgave his enemy and a deadly private feud was added to their public rivalry.

But until the death of the High king Turloch there were some years of peace, and in 1152 he presided over the Synod of Kells, where the cause of native reform reached its summit.

The North had now in Maelmaedoc O'Morgair, who is known to history as St. Malachy, produced the greatest of the reformers. Born in Armagh in 1095 and made a priest in 1119, as vicar to Celsus he enforced the new ideas upon this stubborn and backward province. His first see was Connor, where he made Bangor his head-quarters, but when Celsus died in 1129 he named Malachy his successor in Armagh. The old Clann Sinach was strong enough to resist, but finally Malachy was put in possession of the arch-see by the reforming party and the princes who supported them. In 1137, however, he resigned it to his successor Gelasius, and retired to Bangor again, where he devoted himself to enforcing Roman reforms in the North-east. So far, papal confirmation of these changes was lacking, and in 1139 Gelasius and the other bishops sent Malachy to Rome to secure for Armagh and Cashel the archbishop's pallium.[1] On the way he was received by

---

[1] A collar of lamb's wool which an archbishop must receive at the hands of the Pope or his legate before Rome accepts him.

St. Bernard, abbot of Clairvaux and head of the Cistercian
order, who later wrote a life of the Irish saint. To the great
churchman Malachy recited all the evils of Ireland's Church
and State and Bernard marvelled that so saintly a man should
come out of a race so barbarous as he described.

We may suppose that Malachy and the bishops who later
sent similar reports to Rome were so impressed with the need
of reform in the spiritual life of Ireland that they could not
realize the effect they had upon Rome.

When Malachy reached the Holy city, Innocent II would
only grant the pallia at the request of a national synod, but
he made Malachy papal legate in place of Gillebert in order
to convoke it. Malachy returned to Ireland with a band of
Cistercian monks provided by St. Bernard, for whom a site
was provided on the banks of the Boyne by the king of Oriel.
Gillacrist (or Christian), bishop of Lismore, a zealous reformer,
was their first abbot, and a beautiful church which they
built at Mellifont was the first Gothic building in our
country.

In 1148 a synod of bishops, assembled at Inispatric, again
sent Malachy for the pallia, but he died on the way at Clairvaux in November, and the pallia remained ungranted until
a full national synod was summoned to Kells in 1152, 'in
order to set forth the Catholic Faith, to purify and correct the
morals of the people, to consecrate four archbishops and give
them the pallia'. At this assembly the High king Turloch
and the princes of Ireland gave secular approval to the
decrees issued by Cardinal John Paparo, legate from Rome,
Christian of Lismore, Gelasius, and the bishops of the Irish
Church. The island was divided into thirty-six sees, and
instead of two archbishoprics four were now admitted and
given the pallia by Paparo, namely, Armagh, Cashel, Tuam,
and Dublin. Armagh was to be supreme over all the rest.
The arch-see of Leinster was located in Dublin instead of
Glendalough, in order to detach the Ostmen from Canterbury.
The present bishop, Gregory, accepted the new title and
Ostman separatism came to an end. Many at the time thought
it sufficient to have only two archbishops, Armagh and Cashel,
for Ireland, but it seems that Tuam and Leinster were added

to gratify provincial pride. Unfortunate Meath, whose kings were weak, had no metropolitan granted to it.

On paper the lines of a national self-governing and episcopal church had been laid down with the approval of Rome, but to be a success it needed a reformed and powerful State, and of this there was little hope. Everywhere in Europe the revived Church, in order to carry out its great mission, allied itself with growing Monarchy. Many of the Irish reformers came to regard without dismay foreign intervention. By the donation of Adrian, granted three years after the Synod of Kells, the Pope is said to have commissioned Henry II to reform Ireland. Whether this donation is genuine or not, is one of the great questions of history. But we cannot doubt that political confusion caused good and zealous men to despair of the State and disposed them towards what followed.

In 1156 the death of Turloch O'Connor removed Ireland's last great king. The High monarchy collapsed once more. His son Rory succeeded him in Connacht, but in his claim to the High kingship was thrust aside by Murcertach MacLochlann. It was an office easily won, easily lost. Once more the under-kings did homage to a successful candidate, and finally, in 1162, Murcertach was acknowledged High king in Dublin by Earl Asgall and the Ostmen, who also admitted Dermot to be their immediate lord; after which the two kings installed as archbishop of Dublin Laurence O'Toole, now Ireland's greatest churchman and brother-in-law of Dermot, in succession to Gregory. Thus the king of Ulster became, as the annals say, 'High king of Erin without opposition,' and four years more of national independence were left to Ireland.

In 1155, it is said, Pope Adrian IV had, by the so-called Bull 'Laudabiliter', commissioned Henry II of England to invade Ireland and reform its Church and people, and at a royal council at Winchester talk had been made of carrying this out, but Henry's mother, the Empress Matilda, had protested against it.[1] In Ireland nothing seems to have been

[1] For the Bull 'Laudabiliter' *see* later, pp. 56-57.

known of the matter, and no provision was made against English aggression.

It was an unexpected event in Irish politics that ended native independence. The High king Murcertach was at war with his vassal Eochy Mac Dunlevy, king of Ulidia, and, taking him prisoner, had him blinded, though Eochy had submitted on terms and on the guarantee of Donnchad O'Cervall, king of Oriel, and other princes (1166). Shocked by this atrocity, his vassals revolted against him under O'Cervall and slew him in a petty battle at Leitir Luin. The High kingship again became vacant, and Rory O'Connor secured it and made 'the Circuit of the Ard Rí'. At the same time Tiernan O'Ruairc seized the opportunity to avenge his private feud against Dermot MacMurrough. Dublin and Waterford, Ossory and the chiefs of north Leinster also revolted against their brutal overlord, and when Tiernan invaded Leinster, Dermot was left without supporters save in Hy Kinsella. But Dermot was a man of action and took a rapid decision to appeal for English aid. On August 1st 1166 he sailed for Bristol with his daughter Eva, whose rank and beauty made her a matrimonial prize, leaving behind him to guard his domain his favourite, though, it would seem, illegitimate son, Donal Kavanagh.

No such momentous event had happened since Ireland became a monarchy. MacMurrough's expulsion was not the work of the High king or the decision of a national council, but of his enemy O'Ruairc acting in concert with his Leinster rebels. The High king Rory, however, confirmed the event, and proceeded to confirm Ireland to the princes, dividing Munster between Dermot MacCarthy and Donal Mór O'Brien, Meath between O'Ruairc and Dermot O'Melaghlin, Leinster between Donal MacGillapatric of Ossory and Dermot's brother Murchad, and the kingdom of the North between Murcertach's son Niall and Aedh O'Neill. He then celebrated the Tailten games, and the political structure of Ireland seemed to be restored. But the banished king of Leinster had already found in Wales allies who were to reverse it for ever.

CHAPTER IV

THE NORMAN INVASION, 1166–1172

IRELAND had already for a century been threatened by the powerful monarchy of Norman England, and still more immediately by the aggressive Norman baronial race. The fall of Celtic Wales heralded the fall of Celtic Ireland. The earldoms of Chester, Shrewsbury, and Gloucester, and the Honour of Glamorgan had by 1100 brought most of Wales under the feudal yoke. When in 1090 Rhys ap Tewdwr, king of Dyved, was killed by the Normans the independence of southern Wales perished. Pembroke became a Norman lordship under Arnulf of Montgomery, who in 1097 made castellan of his castle at Pembroke Gerald of Windsor, ancestor of the Geraldines of Ireland. Arnulf was banished by Henry I in 1103 along with his brother Robert, Earl of Shrewsbury, but the Norman advance was not checked, and in 1109 Henry I granted to Gilbert de Clare 'all the land of Cardigan, if he could win it from the Welsh'. This was the sort of 'speculative grant' which was to be common in Ireland.

Within a few years all Pembroke, Glamorgan, and the peninsula of Gower were full of Norman forts and had a medley of Welsh, Norman, Saxon, and Flemish population. The first Henry planted in Gower and south Pembroke a colony of Flemish men-at-arms, no longer needed in English wars, and they and the Welsh bowmen were to be the rank and file of the Norman bands. A Welsh revolt of 1136 showed how stubborn the Britons were, when in open battle Richard, son of Gilbert de Clare, Earl of Hereford, and many other knights perished. King Stephen, however, in 1138 created Richard's younger son Gilbert Earl of Pembroke, and he again reduced the Welsh. His son, Richard FitzGilbert ('Strongbow' of our Irish tradition), welded Pembroke into a feudal State.

It was in southern Wales that the Norman conquerors of Ireland grew up. The younger son and the gentleman-soldier who has made so much English history was abundant there.

The first feudal band to invade Ireland, Maurice FitzGerald and the rest, were a family party, putting their stock into a common enterprise and ready for the great jump-over into Ireland. The Earl of Pembroke was their overlord and the King of England their still remoter lord, but loyalty to both sat light upon them. Had events brought the Geraldines and their race to Ireland in times better suited to their genius for conquest we cannot doubt that they would have founded an independent Norman monarchy in Ireland.

A Welsh princess, Nesta, daughter of the Rhys who was slain in 1090, was the queen-bee of the Norman-Welsh swarm. By her love-affairs with Henry I and Stephen, constable of Cardigan, and her genuine marriage with Gerald of Windsor, she was the mother or grandmother of the Fitzgeralds, Barrys, Carews, and other sharers in the conquest of Ireland. Almost every one of them had Welsh blood in him, and was thereby qualified to master and to understand the Irish Celts.

The dominant genius of the 'Franks' was feudal, military, and romantic. They belonged to the older feudalism, which found its best expression on the borders, but which in England was bridled by the masterful genius of Henry II. In Wales they could conquer as widely as their swords, carry on private war, invade the Welsh mountaineers and divide the spoil among the barons. This was to be their spirit in Ireland. But it was something the Gaels could understand, and such men before long were to become almost as Irish as the Irish. The feudal class lived also in the tradition of the minstrels and the great *chansons de geste* of Charlemagne, Arthur, and Godfrey; it was no great step for them to delight in the music, language, and ancient epics of Ireland. Nationalism was scarcely known to these men, who had come over a century ago as Frenchmen and had not yet become English. Adaptability was their genius, and proud as they were of their own blood, speech, and traditions, they were ready to treat as equals any race that they could respect and freely to inter-marry with it. In Wales they had absorbed Welsh blood and doubtless knew something of the Celtic speech. In Ireland the first generation of them were only too ready to make 'happy marriages' with Irish princesses.

The feudal and military organization of the Normans was to give them a surprising victory in Ireland. In the knightly land-holding class, son succeeded father, and there was thus no disputed title. If the heir was under age, his overlord protected his interests and safeguarded his succession. Compared with this, the uncertain 'derb-fine' rule of succession among the Irish kings put the latter at a disadvantage. On the other hand, the Normans were to find that when there were a dozen or more 'royal heirs' eligible for the kingship of an Irish state the ruling stock was 'unkillable' and could rarely expire like the feudal family. When it came to the art of war and fortification the superiority of the Normans had been displayed already in England, south Italy and Palestine. The *'miles'* or mounted soldier of gentle blood wore a mail shirt covering his body, thighs, and arms, and a conical iron helmet, with a guard for the nose and a chain covering for the neck and throat. Their horses were light coursers which had no armoured protection. A much more elaborate plate armour for man and horse was to become fashionable by 1200, but the equipment of the Geraldines and their companions proved the right thing for Irish war and lingered for many generations. The art of castellation was yet in a primitive stage, and the castle of the Norman when he first appeared in Ireland was a tower of wood rapidly erected on some eminence which a few archers could hold and with an outer stockade or 'bretesche' as a defence against attack. Again it was not till about 1200 that these numerous mote-fortresses could be abandoned and in central places arose stone castles with donjon and bailey almost impregnable to the Irish enemy. But it was still more in their mentality that the Normans were a race made to conquer. The Irish Gael, though given to war and with plenty of natural courage, for the most part fought in linen tunics with light axes, swords, and spears. To the Irish kings a battle was intended to achieve an immediate object; that achieved, their armies retired. To the Norman-French, war was a business proposition and their enterprise a joint-stock company out of which profits were expected. A battle once gained, the next step was to throw up an impregnable castle, the next was to organize the conquered country into a manor or barony and seek if necessary a charter for it from Earl or King.

Such was the race to whom King Dermot turned for allies. At Bristol he was received by one Robert FitzHarding, who sent him on to his sovereign, and in Aquitaine Henry gave him letters patent to enlist among his subjects. Returning to Wales, Dermot won over Richard, Earl of Pembroke, with the promise of his daughter's hand in marriage and the succession to Leinster with rich fiefs for his lieutenants. Strongbow was in bad odour with the King, who disliked Stephen's baronage, and welcomed the prospect of adding a rich kingdom in Ireland to a poor earldom in Wales. The bargain took four years to carry out, but Dermot returned to Leinster in August 1167 bringing a small Norman force under Richard FitzGodebert. The High king offered to restore to him the ten cantreds of Hy Kinsella on paying an 'honour price' to O'Ruairc and giving two sons as hostages. Dermot accepted the offer, but when he brought in further Normans Rory put the two hostages to death, leaving him only one son, Donal Kavanagh.

On May 1st 1169 there arrived in Bannow bay in south Wexford a number of ships carrying Robert FitzStephen, Maurice Prendergast, thirty knights, sixty men-at-arms with breast-plates, and three hundred archers. There on the grassy headland of Baginbun they built the first Norman earthwork in Ireland, whose ramparts can still be traced. A traditional Anglo-Irish rhyme records that:

> At the creek of Baginbun,
> Ireland was lost and won.

The Irish annals say: 'The fleet of the Flemings came to Erin, they were ninety heroes dressed in mail, and *the Gaels set no store by them.*' Backed by this small but professional force, Dermot held his ground until in the next year Maurice FitzGerald and Raymond le Gros of Carew arrived. Finally on August 23rd 1170 Earl Richard landed near Waterford with his bride Eva and one thousand men-at-arms. He was joined by Dermot and Donal Kavanagh, and without delay they attacked and took Waterford, which resisted its rightful king. Its earl, Sitric, was beheaded and Strongbow married Eva in the city cathedral.

Dublin was the supreme objective. The High king brought a national levy to defend it on the west side, but Dermot led the allied army inland by the Wicklow mountains and early in September reached the city where it was undefended on the south. The Ostmen under their earl Asgall offered to parley, but while this was hanging fire Raymond le Gros and Milo de Cogan, who, like true Normans, preferred a *fait accompli*, suddenly attacked and took the fortress. Asgall fled over-sea and Dublin became the capital of English power in Ireland. To all appearance Dermot had by the swords of his Norman allies now recovered the whole kingdom of Leinster.

The Gaels could no longer afford to 'set no store' by these new-comers. Dermot now talked of winning the High king-ship, and the High king collected a great national army to recover Dublin. But suddenly the king of Leinster died at Ferns on May 1st 1171, destined to be remembered with execration as 'Diarmaid na nGall' ('of the Foreigners').

Strongbow thus became king of Leinster, but he was threatened at once by an overwhelming combination. A Norse fleet sailed up the Liffey, having on board a thousand vikings whom Earl Asgall had hired in the Hebrides and Man, who were led by a famous berserk, John 'the Wode' or 'Mad'. Giraldus Cambrensis says admiringly of them: 'They were men with iron arms and iron hearts.' The High king was bringing up an Irish army to besiege Dublin from the west, and had the two forces united, Strongbow would have been in a desperate situation, cooped up in Dublin with most of his forces. Unluckily for themselves, the Norsemen attacked first, and were outside the eastern gate attacked and cut to pieces by a Norman force under Milo de Cogan. John the Wode died like a berserk, while Asgall was taken and beheaded in his own hall.

For all that, Strongbow was in danger from an all-Ireland rally which blockaded Dublin for two months. Rory O'Connor offered Strongbow the kingdom of Leinster under the High

monarchy if he would send his soldiers back, but the Earl
refused, and at last a desperate sally was decided upon.
Maurice FitzGerald pointed out that England had rejected
them and Ireland was against them; let them therefore sally
forth in arms, so that 'by their valour they should reduce
the five kingdoms of Ireland into one'. Strongbow's lieutenants were ready to renounce England and found a new
Norman monarchy in Ireland, but the Earl was a weak and
hesitating man who preferred to be a great baron in Ireland
rather than a small king. Faced with an Irish rally, he was
ready to submit himself to his sovereign, King Henry. But
the sally advocated by FitzGerald was necessary. A vanguard
of six hundred horsemen, followed by Donal Kavanagh and
his Leinster men, marched out in the early morning and,
making a detour by Finglas, took the High king's army,
encamped in the present Phoenix Park, by surprise, scattered
it, and broke up the siege. It was mid-September, and the
victors captured enormous stores of provisions.

Such a double victory for Norman *élan* gave point to
FitzGerald's boast that he and his companions could unaided
have conquered Ireland. But already the Earl had sent in
his submission to Henry II, who was marching to Pembroke
to cross over into Ireland. To the Angevin, Ireland was for
the moment a welcome refuge from the storm raised by the
murder of Archbishop Becket on December 29th 1170, for
which he was threatened with a papal interdict.

HENRY II IN IRELAND

King Henry landed at Waterford on October 17th 1171
with an army of four thousand men. But he did not intend
a military conquest; he came first to ensure that the gains of
the adventurers should depend on the Crown of England,
and secondly to secure a voluntary submission of the Irish
Church and princes. If he had with him the donation of
Adrian IV (the Bull 'Laudabiliter') he did not proclaim it,
but then he was out with the Papacy. For all that, it appears
evident that its purport was already known or was now revealed to the Irish leaders. Short though his stay of less

than six months in Ireland was, it was sufficient to establish
the basis of English sovereignty.

His first measure was to confirm to Strongbow 'the land of
Leinster' as an appanage of the earldom of Pembroke, and to
FitzGerald and the others the baronies granted to them by
Dermot, to be held of the Earl. Henry seems to have scolded
the adventurers before accepting their homage. They, on the
other hand, accepted with a poor grace these gifts from the
royal hand. They had hoped to be kings in Ireland and had
to remain mere barons.

The Waterford citizens submitted to so great a king, and he
rewarded them by confirming 'the liberties of the Ostmen'.
He then marched inland from Waterford to Cashel, then back
to Waterford and so to Dublin. At Lismore 'he held a council
where the laws of England were received and confirmed';
whether this applied only to the English in Ireland or included
the Irish we cannot tell. There also he arranged for the
holding of a national synod under Bishop Christian, who was
papal legate. On the strength of such fair assurances, the
leaders of Church and State prepared to accept him.

At Waterford began the submission of the native chiefs.
Dermot MacCarthy, king of Desmond, came in and for a yearly
tribute got back his kingdom under royal suzerainty, saving
to the Crown the city of Cork and the 'cantred of the Ostmen'
round it. Next came in Donal More O'Brien, king of Thomond,
the king of Ossory, and other local chiefs. Arriving in Dublin
on November 11th, Henry wintered there and received the
homage of further kings, including even Tiernan O'Ruairc,
until only the High king and the princes of the North held out.
Their surrender entailed a general though ill-informed acceptance of a great European king, based on his show of peace,
his rights under a papal concession, and a naïve belief that he
would be content to be an absent Ard Rí, receiving their
homage and tributes but otherwise leaving them undisturbed
in their province kingdoms. But that they failed to grasp
what the Angevin monarchy was was soon shown.   The
submission of the clerical leaders of Ireland, men of intelli-
gence and education, is more surprising. We must suppose

c

that they accepted as genuine Adrian's donation and,
despair of achieving the regeneration of the Irish Church
without the protection of a powerful monarch, decided to
accept this great foreigner.

The Synod of Cashel met towards the end of 1171. Laurence
of Dublin and the archbishops of Tuam and Cashel presided
along with Christian of Lismore and a representative of
Henry, the archdeacon of Llandaff. Gelasius of Armagh was
too old to attend but came later to Dublin and accepted
Henry. The synod put the coping-stone on the long work of
Reform but accompanied it with submission to the English
king. Decrees were passed ordaining tithes for the clergy,
Peter's pence for Rome, regulations on marriage and baptism,
and the freeing of churches from secular exactions. Nothing
was said as to the claims of Canterbury over the Irish Church,
and the supremacy of Armagh over the whole island with
final obedience to none but Rome was accepted. An episcopal
and parochial church was thus finally provided. As regards
the native liturgies, their day was ended. 'The divine offices,'
ran one of the decrees, 'shall be celebrated according to the
usage of the Church of England.'

So when the bishops and the chiefs who had done homage
went home, Henry could indeed feel that he had added a new
crown to his many realms.

Meanwhile he gave to Dublin its first charter of municipal
liberties. He wished to favour and control this old Teutonic
race of Ostmen who commanded the towns of Ireland and were
her merchants and mariners; and finally their towns, and the
cantreds around them, of Wexford, Waterford, Cork, and
Limerick were brought directly under the Crown. Dublin
itself was thrown open to the traders of Henry's wide empire
and soon became a populous merchant town.

Henry's final care was to provide for the royal government.
He appointed Hugh de Lacy 'Justiciar' or viceroy, and placed
constables and garrisons in Dublin, Wexford, and Waterford.
As Crown demesne he annexed the greater part of county
Dublin, the cities of Dublin, Waterford, and Wexford with
their cantreds (territories), and the coast from Waterford to

Dungarvan. The new barons of Ireland would naturally form the council under the King's deputy, and in later times the Anglo-Irish believed that a 'statute of Henry FitzEmpress' gave this council the right to choose a justiciar in case of a vacancy until the king should decide.

The new Lord of Ireland now showed the Irish chiefs what he meant by his full sovereign powers. They had submitted of their own free will, and only one province had been 'conquered' by the barons. But the forceful Angevin proved that, whatever the Gaelic chiefs might expect, he meant to be in Ireland the complete Anglo-Norman king. In England all land-titles depended on the king, who could grant or recover them as 'Dominus Terrae' or supreme landlord. This was a conception unknown in Irish law and foreign to the Irish mind, but essential in feudal law. Henry now exercised it in the case of Meath, a whole kingdom of which the O'Melaghlins were hereditary princes, which he granted to Hugh de Lacy in as ample a manner as its last undisputed king, Murchad O'Melaghlin, had held it. Meath, a whole province which covered the present counties of Meath and Westmeath with Cavan and Longford, now became a feudal earldom, held of the Crown by service of fifty knights. There can be no question that Henry acted with bad faith towards the submitting chiefs, both in this and in later cases.

Henry left Ireland on Easter Monday, April 17th 1172, recalled by the threat of a papal interdict owing to Becket's murder. From the point of view of a strong government which would have protected the Irish from the Norman aggressors, it is regrettable that his stay was so brief. Nor did he ever again visit Ireland, which was destined for his youngest son, John, born in December 1166. The royal power was for thirty years little more than nominal and the feudalists had it their own way.

On the conclusion of the Synod of Cashel, Henry sent envoys to Pope Alexander III, asking for a papal privilege for Ireland. He was in May 1172 reconciled with the Papacy, and in September Alexander not only absolved him but from Tusculum published three letters on the Irish question. One was

addressed to Christian of Lismore as legate and the bishops of
Ireland. It reproved the evil customs of the Irish as made
known to Rome by the bishops themselves, and enjoined on
them to assist Henry in keeping possession of Ireland. A
second, to Henry, urged him to continue his good work of
reforming the evil customs of the Irish people. A third com-
mended the lay princes of Ireland for receiving him as king of
their own free will. Finally the Pope sent a privilege which
was published by papal envoys soon after at the Synod of
Waterford; it conferred on Henry the dominion over the Irish
people. Whatever, then, we may think of the so-called 'Bull'
of Adrian, there can be no doubt that the letters and privilege
of a later Pope conferred the lordship of Ireland upon Henry II.

Over the authenticity of the so-called Bull 'Laudabiliter',
the text of which we have only in Giraldus Cambrensis'
Conquest of Ireland, great controversy has raged; some writers
holding it to be a pure forgery, others regarding it as a
touched-up version of a genuine document, others believing
in its authenticity. It is certainly hard to explain the general
and voluntary submission of the Irish bishops at Cashel and
the Irish kings at Waterford and Dublin unless some such
document was in the air at least. True, it was not published
by Henry when in Ireland, but that can be explained by his
being alienated from Rome over the murder of Becket. There
is still better evidence for a grant of Ireland in 1155. In that
year the famous writer and churchman, John of Salisbury,
went from Henry II to the Papal Curia and obtained from
the English Pope, Adrian IV, a grant of Ireland for the
Angevin king. 'At my prayer,' he says in his book *Metalogicus*,
'he granted Ireland to Henry as an inheritance, as his letter to
this day testifies, and also sent by me a golden ring adorned
with an emerald for the purpose of investiture, and this is
still kept in the State archives.'

This was written about 1159. Giraldus did not write his
History of the Conquest of Ireland till about 1188, and his
dating is not accurate, but we can hardly doubt that he had
some such genuine document before him.[1] In the 'Bull' of

---

[1] There is no original or copy of 'Laudabiliter' in the papal archives.

Adrian, as given by him, the Pope addresses Henry 'as a Catholic prince labouring to extend the borders of the Church and teach the truth of the Christian faith to a rude and unlettered people. It is beyond all doubt that Ireland and all other islands which have received the Christian faith belong to St. Peter and the holy Roman Church.' Henry has signified his proposal 'to enter Ireland in order to subdue the people and make them obedient to laws, and that he is willing to pay from every house there one penny to St. Peter and to keep and preserve the rights of the churches in that land whole and inviolate'. The Pope therefore gives him permission to enter and take possession of the island on these terms, and charges the Irish people to accept and duly obey him as their liege lord, saving only the rights of the churches.

The grant of Ireland by the Papacy to Henry II constituted a 'moral mission' under which Adrian and Alexander III constituted Henry king or lord of Ireland for certain purposes. Too much stress can hardly be laid on the moral and legal terms which accompanied the grant, especially the preservation of the rights of the Irish Church. When Alexander praises the lay princes for receiving Henry willingly, he assumes a bargain which had to be kept. Later generations of Irishmen right up to the seventeenth century fully accepted the papal donation as a fact—witness the Remonstrance of the Irish chiefs to the Pope in 1317—but both then and later they accused the Crown of England of having violated the rights of the Irish Church and the Irish people.

CHAPTER V

THE ORGANIZATION OF THE CONQUEST, 1172–1216

SELDOM has so great a country been thrown open to a race of gentleman buccaneers as Ireland was now, and as it was again in the sixteenth century. Raymond le Gros, Strongbow's marshal, not content with the grant of county Carlow, attacked Cork in defiance of the rights of the Ostmen and Dermot MacCarthy. Limerick was also threatened, but Donal More O'Brien, king of Thomond, gave the Normans their first overthrow at Thurles, where Strongbow had his force of Dublin Ostmen cut to pieces. Then began a war of resistance, in the course of which several chiefs were removed by very dubious methods; thus in 1172 Tiernan O'Ruairc was slain while engaged in a parley with Hugh de Lacy.

Finally, by the mediation of Laurence O'Toole, in October 1175 Henry made the treaty of Windsor with the High king by which Rory was left as king of Connacht under Henry and over-king of the unconquered area on payment of an annual tribute of hides. We have no record that the tribute was ever paid, and though Rory remained Árd Rí over half of Ireland till his death in 1198 he was but a shadow-king. Yet until the death of his brother and successor Cathal in 1224 Connacht remained a Gaelic kingdom. Henry himself soon violated the spirit of this treaty by granting out Munster and Ulster. It was a shameless business, especially for a king who in England was a great constructive statesman, but comment would be vain. There was as yet no central government worth speaking of. The feudal horde was bent upon the conquest and division of Ireland, and the Crown gave way to their demands. The Irish, too, were a warlike race, and on recovering from their first complaisance made it clear that only a general conquest by fighting barons, little troubled by law or conscience, could make English rule a success. For a century or more 'speculative grants' were the order of the day. The rights of the friendly Irish and of those who had aided

Strongbow or de Lacy had to be regarded, and up to the Statutes of Kilkenny in 1366 the legal equality of the 'Five Bloods' or provincial dynasties were admitted in Anglo-Irish courts. But in general the native owners were regarded as rightless, and even when they received royal grants these were generally interpreted to cover but the life of the grantee. So different did the Conquest become from that 'moral mission' with which the Pope had commissioned Henry and from the legal acknowledgment which the Irish chiefs, when they submitted, believed they had secured. In the fighting itself the Norman superiority was everywhere displayed, and in the general break-up of Gaelic Ireland well might the Irish poet say:

> 'Conn of the hundred fights,
> Rest in thy grass-grown sepulchre
> And reproach not our defeats with thy victories.'

Few of the adventurers lived beyond middle age. On June 1st 1176 the death of Strongbow removed the chief figure of the Conquest. His only child by Eva MacMurrough, Isabella de Clare, was an infant, and Leinster passed into the hands of the Crown. He had, however, given it a feudal structure which his son-in-law, William the Marshal, was later to complete.

The 'Land of Leinster' covered the five modern counties of Wexford, Carlow, Leix, Kilkenny, and Kildare. For its defence Strongbow fixed the site of castles at New Ross, Kilkenny, Dunamase, and other points, and planted his vassals out to rule and garrison the land. Among the chief of these, Maurice FitzGerald became lord of Naas and Robert de Bermingham of Carbery or Tethmoy in Kildare; in Carlow, Raymond de Carew received the baronies of Idrone and Forth; in Wexford rich fiefs went to the Prendergasts and others; and so were founded in Leinster many names famous in later history. In the treatment of the native race the line was drawn between those who had aided and been loyal to King Dermot and his heir Strongbow, and those who had resisted. Among the latter the Ui Faelain and Ui Dunchada septs, who ruled the rich plain of Kildare, were ousted and removed themselves into the Wicklow mountains. The latter, whose patronymic became O'Toole, henceforth ruled as lords of Imaal and Fercullen in north and western Wicklow, while the O'Byrnes or Ui Faelain commanded the rest of the county southwards to Arklow. Among the faithful, or those who received terms, MacGillacolmoc, lord of south county Dublin, retained under the name of FitzDermot for two centuries the barony of Rathdown. For his great services to his brother-in-law, Donal Kavanagh was left in possession of most of Hy Kinsella, while a nephew of Dermot, the ancestor of O'Morchoe, was left in possession of lands about Gorey. The conquerors contented themselves with the rich lands and the key points for planting towns, manors, castles, and abbeys, but great tracts of mountain and forest country were left to the native chiefs. The new manors of the Norman lords were stocked with labourers of the native race called 'betaghs' (*biatach*, a 'food-provider'); among the superior tenants were English freemen, townsmen, and military vassals.

Hugh de Lacy left an equally enduring mark upon medieval Ireland. His earldom of Meath was a palatinate containing half a million acres of the rich midland plain. Having removed the native chiefs by battle or treachery, he proved a great organizer and in many ways a tolerant lord. His castles at Trim, Kells, and elsewhere, built in stone after the later fashion, were such as no native attack could overthrow. As in Leinster, the land was organized in manors, of which the rude labour was done by the native 'betaghs', town-life began, and abbeys, founded or brought under a Continental rule, formed a strong Anglo-French element. His enfeoffment of the eighteen baronies of Meath created an English nobility which lasted almost to the battle of the Boyne. Thus began the famous names of Tyrel of Fertullagh and Castleknock, Fleming, baron of Slane, and Petit of Mullingar, Nangle, baron of Navan, Nugent, baron of Delvin, and others. A cousin of the earl, Robert de Lacy, founded the barons of Rathwire and Ferbill. Thus the English land was pushed almost to the Shannon, but of necessity or policy some of the old chiefs were left undisturbed; thus an O'Melaghlin was left in the barony of Clonlonan, O'Farrell in Longford, and in other western parts of this great earldom O'Carroll, lord of Ely,

O'Connor, lord of Offaly, and elsewhere Mageoghegans and O'Molloys. In them, as in the Leinster mountains, were the makings of a Gaelic resurgence in the future, as yet unsuspected. The Norman seed, indeed, though thrown widely, was too thin; a sufficient influx from England to reinforce the first settlers did not happen, and the feudal advance into central Ireland was more like a spear-head than a broad shield.

The Norman success inspired a fresh attempt upon Munster and Ulster, provinces which were rich in the river, wood, meadow, cornland, hunting, and fishing which tempted the conqueror. Henry sanctioned it and also provided the Irish barons with a permanent over-lord. At a Council in Oxford in 1177 he created his son John 'Dominus Hiberniae', and thus began that lordship of Ireland in the English Crown which lasted till 1540. The Papacy had designed a royal title for John, but Henry preferred a lesser one in order to keep Ireland subordinate. 'Dominus' was a title implying mere feudal suzerainty, but John later showed that to him it implied full royal rights. At the same council Robert Fitz-Stephen and Milo de Cogan were granted the kingdom of Cork, or Desmond, jointly between them, while to Philip de Braose, lord of Brecknock in Wales, was granted the kingdom of Limerick, or Thomond. In each case the Crown reserved the cities of Cork and Limerick with their 'cantred of the Ostmen'.

The Norman adventurers were always ready to make good with their swords that which was granted them on parchment. De Braose failed to occupy Limerick, which Donal More O'Brien retained until his death in 1194, but FitzStephen and de Cogan took Cork, induced Dermot MacCarthy to surrender, left him twenty-four cantreds in Desmond under tribute to them, and divided between themselves the seven cantreds east and west of Cork. Dermot, the first Irish king to submit to Henry II, was undoubtedly a much-wronged man, and when he died in 1185 the former native kingdom of Desmond expired with him. FitzStephen and De Cogan left no direct heirs, but up to 1330 Carews, representing Fitz-Stephen, and De Cogans, representing Milo, remained answerable to the Crown for the 'kingdom of Cork'.

The conquest of Ulster makes the finest story in the Conquest

after that of Leinster.   John de Courcy was the younger son
of a Somerset knight and had come to Ireland as a good field
for the adventurous.   Collecting a band of his fellows, he decided, without waiting for royal leave, to invade and conquer
Ulster.   It was the most warlike and impenetrable of the Irish
kingdoms, but his onslaught was worthy of the Norman race at
its best.   The petty kingdom of Ulidia was his first objective.
Its capital, Downpatrick, fell into his hands on February 1st
1177, and when its king, Rory MacDonlevy, appeared to
recover it De Courcy proved the victor.   MacDonlevy had done
homage to Henry II and resisted this aggression.   He appealed
to his suzerain, MacLochlann, king of Cenel Eoghain, but in a
desperate encounter on June 24th of that year the united
Irish were again routed.   The Northern men were hard to
beat, but in several more battles De Courcy's force of knights,
archers, and mail-clad foot showed the superiority of the
professional over the amateur soldier.   At last he was able to
organize his conquest.   He had no definite title from the King
nor did he try to obtain one, and he survives in history in the
titles accorded by contemporary writers of 'Princeps Ulidiae'
and 'Conquestor Ultoniae'.   His whole career of some thirty
years in Ulster shows him ruling like an independent prince.
Beyond the sea, Somerled was lord of Argyle under the King
of Scots, and also, under the Crown of Norway, 'King of the
Isles of the Norsemen' (the Hebrides), while Godred, Norse
ruler of Man, retained the southern half of the Isles.   In order
to win allies among such men De Courcy married Affreca,
Godred's daughter.

   In Ulidia, De Courcy was a noble founder of abbeys, castles,
and petty towns.   His stone castles arose at Carrickfergus,
Dundrum, and other places; into Down, Inch, Greyabbey, and
Coleraine he introduced Benedictine and other monks; and
along the coast of Antrim and Down and inland to Lough Neagh
he enfeoffed his companions, the Hackets, Russels, Savages,
Whites, and Logans of later times.   The old kingdom of Ulidia
disappeared and in its place arose a Norman-French state and
colony, but it was rather a veneer than a true English plantation.

   By 1180 the native Monarchy of Ireland had gone to pieces,

and the death of the noble Laurence O'Toole marks the end
of the native Church. The new Anglo-Norman government
could not conceive of anything but a State Church of prince-
bishops, ruling their wide dioceses with ample revenues and
powers of justice, and serving the State as loyal officials.
The place of Laurence when he died at Eu in Normandy in
November 1180, on his return from a visit to Henry, was
taken by John Comyn, first of the feudalized bishops of Ireland.
This practical prelate, who was elected in England by English
bishops in 1181, in a long episcopate of thirty years served the
government well, built St. Patrick's as a second cathedral for
Dublin, and organized the rich lands of his see as taken over
or increased by Crown grants until they stretched from Dalkey
on Dublin bay south to Glendalough and west to Dunlavin,
and in north Dublin included Swords and other manors. The
Gaelic mind took long to grasp the conception of the new kind
of bishop, endowed with feudal lands and privileges, serving
the interests of the State, peers in Parliament, having courts of
their own for spiritual and other cases and elected with papal
and royal confirmation, foreigners unable to speak their
language or understand their law. This new episcopate in
time controlled all the colonized land, but did not succeed
in the West and North.

The wave of Norman aggression now slackened. By 1190
Strongbow, FitzStephen, De Cogan, Maurice FitzGerald, and
Raymond le Gros were all successively dead. Henry could now
devolve the care of Ireland on his favourite son John as Lord
of Ireland. This Benjamin of the royal flock was now seventeen and was a graceless and insolent youth, but his appearance
in Ireland might give reality to things. Hugh de Lacy had
recently taken as his second wife a daughter of the High king;
this aroused suspicions that he meant to make himself King
of Ireland, and he was dismissed as justiciar. John himself
landed at Waterford on April 25th 1185 with a considerable
army. Among his close companions were three young men
destined to found great families in Ireland, namely, Theobald
Walter, John's butler, Bertram de Verdun, his steward, and
William de Burgo. The court marched by Lismore and

Kildare to Dublin, where John received the homage of several kings and chiefs of the South, but with detestable manners he and his minions mocked the long beards and speech of these men who knew nothing of French or court ways. John's real achievement, in addition to building a few castles, was to make numerous parchment grants of Irish land and still further increase the royal demesne. He annexed to himself the barony of Louth and gave the rest of the former kingdom of Oriel to Bertram de Verdun as lord of Dundalk and to Roger Pipard as lord of Ardee. Munster was also sub-infeudated, but, as Donal O'Brien still ruled, only the nearer parts of Thomond could be appropriated, and Philip de Worcester got five cantreds in south Tipperary, Theobald Walter five and a half cantreds in north Tipperary, and William de Burgo also large fiefs in the north part of the country along the Shannon and facing Clare. To Theobald, John also gave the manor of Arklow, and later his descendants enjoyed the profits of the office of Butler of Ireland. John again confirmed to William and Gerald, sons of Maurice FitzGerald, the manors of May-nooth and Naas, and to the Barrys and Roches in eastern Cork the lands FitzStephen had granted them. Finally he departed from Ireland on December 17th 1185.

Among those first invaders whom John especially feared and hated the greatest was now Hugh de Lacy. The Earl of Meath had built up in the centre of Ireland a powerful feudal State, and after the death of his Norman wife, by whom he had two sons, Walter and Hugh, he married Rose, daughter of the High king Rory O'Connor, and had by her a son called William 'Gorm'. A suspicion arose that he was preparing the way for an independent Norman kingdom of Ireland. But suddenly De Lacy was struck down by an unexpected hand. Like most of the Normans, he had little fear or veneration for the Church when it stood in his way, and the stones of ancient Irish abbeys were excellent material for the new castles with which he bridled the Gael. In nothing could he have more offended the native race. And so when on a day in July 1186 Hugh was aiding at the building of a castle at Durrow from the stones of the ancient monastery there, a young man called O'Miadaigh,

taking it on himself to avenge his people, struck off his head as
he stooped to the work, and fled away. The earldom of Meath
was taken into royal hands, for the heir, Walter, was a minor
till 1194, and so the two great fiefs of Meath and Leinster
lacked adult lords at a time when they were so important to
the Norman cause.

Among the new arrivals William de Burgo was a man both
in thought and action. No advance could be made in Munster
while Donal More O'Brien lived, and indeed De Burgo protected
him and married a daughter of his in 1193. We note how De
Courcy, Strongbow, Hugh de Lacy and the first De Burgo all
married Irish or half-Irish princesses; it was part of their
programme for taking root in Ireland, but it alarmed the
Crown. And again we may note how through the De Burgo
marriage with an O'Brien the blood of the great Brian Boru
has flowed down through the Mortimers and the House of
York to the present royal House of England.

On the death of Donal More in 1194 the advance was resumed.
The De Braose grant was put into effect, all Limerick was
occupied, and De Burgo shared in the spoils. His great stronghold of Castleconnell dominated the Shannon. Among those
who were now enfeoffed in county Limerick was Thomas
FitzGerald, younger son of the first Maurice, who got lands
about Shanid. He is the ancestor of the earls of Desmond
whose war-cry was 'Shanid Abu', and from this centre his race
acquired most of county Limerick. The city itself ceased to be
the O'Brien capital, and in 1197 Prince John granted to
Limerick the liberties of Dublin and confirmed the rights of
the Ostmen there. De Burgo advocated a further advance,
and showed that to round off the Conquest the occupation of
Connacht was essential.

The High king Rory had played little part in the events of
these later years and in 1198 died in obscurity in the abbey
of Cong on the banks of Loch Corrib. As a modern poet has
said:

> There he died and there they left him,
>   Last of Gaelic monarchs of the Gael,
> Slumbering by the vast eternal
>   Voices of the western vale.

The O'Connor candidate was now the valiant and subtle Cathal 'Crovderg' ('Red-hand'), a younger brother of Rory. It would appear that a grant of Connacht was made to De Burgo, but he died in the winter of 1205 without making it good, for John had already changed his mind as to permitting the already great barons of Ireland to aggrandize themselves further.

In 1199 John succeeded to the English throne, and the Lordship of Ireland was merged for good in the Crown of England. John had learned that the Monarchy, as reconstructed by his father, and the Baronage were natural enemies. Whatever his fortunes in the struggle were in England, in Ireland at least he succeeded in depressing the feudal interest and exalting the royal authority, by the policy of raising up against the old a new and more limited baronage and favouring the Irish chiefs as a counter-balance to the Norman conquistadors.

Among the new men stands boldly out William the Marshal, Earl of Pembroke, who in 1189, already an elderly man, had married Strongbow's heiress, Isabella. Among the other magnates were Walter de Lacy, heir to Meath, and Richard and Walter, the sons of William de Burgo and his Irish wife, who succeeded at their father's death to his lands in 1205.

We may now at this date consider the effects of thirty years of Norman aggression and English rule on Ireland. There existed a titular 'Lord of Ireland', but of central authority there was almost nothing. The feudal class had no wish for it save that they valued 'the laws of England' which protected them in the enjoyment of their conquests. No attempt had been made to bring the Irish under one law with the English, and after the first submission it was clear to the Irish kings that they had no legal protection. Overborne by the first rush of the Normans, the kings of Ireland still sought a secure position for their kingdoms under the Crown. But a Dublin government scarcely existed, there was a fortress in Dublin under a constable, there was a royal deputy and royal demesnes, but no coinage, courts, or administration of State.

In so far as a Council of State existed, it was the body of baronial tenants-in-chief themselves. The real strength of the colony lay in the feudal element whose 'conquered' lands covered half the island.

The native losses were overwhelming. The kingdoms of Leinster, Ulidia, Oriel, Meath, Thomond, and Desmond had disappeared. De Courcy had carried the Norman flag to the Giant's Causeway, and, in brief, everything south and east of a line drawn from Limerick to Lough Neagh and Coleraine was 'English land'.

Leinster was now a great feudal State. Strongbow had laid down the lines and his son-in-law, the Earl Marshal, continued his work and planted in new feudal families. Meath and Ulster too were great feudal principalities, one of which De Courcy ruled more like a king than a baron. Oriel too had been sub-infeudated under Prince John, the Clintons, Gernons, and other families were planted there, and thus Meath was linked up with Ulster.

In the south most of Munster had been granted away, though Kerry was as yet untouched. The Norman confidence that it could hold down these great countries was superb, but in fact the organization was not deep enough nor was a sufficient Anglo-saxon population introduced, and in time a Gaelic recovery was inevitable. Had the invaders proceeded by one kingdom at a time the event would have been more of a success. But rapid and extensive conquest and immediate exploitation was more to the feudal mind. And from the first they waged feuds over the border lands which they claimed from one another and thus prevented common action.

Of the unconquered kingdoms, that of Aileach or Cenel Eoghain was the most dangerous and warlike. De Courcy had subdued Ulidia but had little success west of Lough Neagh. He may have claimed that his 'Ultonia' included the whole North, but in fact his grants are never outside of Antrim and Down. Not a single Englishman had yet put permanent foot in the greater part of Ulster, and save for a few attempts in the next generation this remained so till the end of the sixteenth century.

In war and fortification the Normans still for a century were to retain their pre-eminence. The wooden tower or 'bretesche' built on a high mound or 'motte' gave way to elaborate stone castles such as those of Trim or Kilkenny. Armour was developing and the plain '*miles*' of the earlier time was becoming the elaborately armed and mounted knight of medieval chivalry. But in Ireland the invaders found the conical helm, the mail shirt, the light unprotected horse and easy saddle, the bow, spear, and sword the best fitted for Irish warfare in the wooded and trackless country against the active and ill-armed Irish foot. Save for a few encounters such as that of Thurles or Downpatrick battles between Norman and Gael had been soon decided, and the Celts had yet to learn the use of armour and professional soldiery.

As Lord of Ireland, King John pursued an anti-feudal policy at least in reducing the powers of the 'First Families' and introducing new ones. He renewed in 1200 the Honour of Limerick to William, nephew of Philip de Braose, though at a huge price of five thousand marks, and granted to his kinsman Meiler FitzHenry all central Kerry as far south as the lakes of Killarney. In the 'kingdom of Cork' he made fresh grants to Barrys, Roches, Barrets, Condons, Prendergasts, and Fitzgeralds, the latter of whom entrenched themselves at Imokilly in south-east Cork, while the Roches became lords of Fermoy and the Barrys of Buttevant.

But in 1205, when he deprived De Courcy of Ulster and made it an earldom for the younger Hugh de Lacy, he brought an almost independent State to an end, and in 1207 in granting new charters for Meath and Leinster he reduced their liberties. He showed also signs of wishing to balance the Irish baronage by favour to the Irish when he granted Connacht in 1205 and 1210 to Cathal O'Connor and Thomond to Donough O'Brien, and confirmed in their estates several petty chiefs.

In government John brought to an end the almost purely feudal régime that had prevailed in the Colony for thirty years. He set up a royal administration and created a State Church, dealing as best he could with the outlying feudal and Gaelic lords. His agent in this was Meiler FitzHenry, his justiciar from 1200 to 1208, under whom the building of Dublin Castle was begun, and the colony was secured in 'the laws of England' as defined under Henry II. The King's court in Dublin was to be the supreme court of the realm, while the Justiciar in the council of the tenants-in-chief was the final authority. A coinage for Ireland was struck and those assizes in which Henry had applied the jury system to criminal and land cases were extended to Ireland. No freeholder need henceforth answer in any court for his freehold except before the King, his justiciar or justices, and by jury of his equals. During the reign nine Anglo-Norman bishops were introduced into the Church of Ireland and, to show that bishops must be loyal men, in the last year of his reign he decreed that no native Irishman should hold office in a cathedral church. Armagh, Tuam, and Cashel, however, remained under Gaelic bishops. John's later visit of 1210 put the coping-stone to the royal policy, and in so far as his short reign and his difficulties allowed we may say that John 'implemented' the Lordship of Ireland on government lines, whereas his father had only 'acquired' the kingdom of Ireland by consent of the native kings and bishops.

The greatest of the Anglo-Irish magnates in nobility of character was William the Marshal, Earl of Pembroke and Lord of Leinster in virtue of his wife, Strongbow's daughter. Whereas few of the great barons felt anything but contempt and hatred for John, the Marshal had played a leading part in getting the English magnates to accept John instead of his nephew Arthur. But he found it hard to maintain his loyalty in face of John's double-dealing. The murder of the young Arthur in April 1203 inspired feelings too deep for words in honourable men, but for the time they were silent.

The fall of De Courcy followed next. He was the sole survivor of the early conquistadors, the ruler of an almost independent State for which he had no royal patent, and he is said to have spoken indignantly of the murder of Arthur. Unfortunately for himself he was also a childless man. In August 1204 he was summoned by the justiciar FitzHenry to submit himself, he refused, and in May 1205 the young Hugh de Lacy was created Earl of Ulster. De Courcy made a stand in his

castle of Rath or Dundrum on the Down coast against Fitz-
Henry and De Lacy, but was taken prisoner, then released, and
finally died in France in 1219. So 'the Conqueror of Ulster'
vanished from Irish history.

The creation of the Ulster earldom was a decisive event for
the Gaelic chiefs of the North. West of Ulidia they had not
yet submitted to the King of England, but when an Earl of
Ulster was created there was interposed between the Lord of
Ireland and them a feudal suzerain. Till the fifteenth century
the O'Neills on several occasions did homage to an Earl of
Ulster, but the O'Donnells never.

John, in pursuance of his anti-baronial aims, soon repented
handing over two vast provinces to the De Lacy family. The
Irish baronage was full of rebellious spirit. William the
Marshal spent three years in Leinster, from 1207 to 1210,
organizing it on the lines laid down by Strongbow and founding
towns at New Ross, Kilkenny, and other places. He did his best
to stand loyal to the King, but the two De Lacys and William
de Braose went into open rebellion. The latter was by John's
grant lord of the great Honour of Limerick. He got into
trouble with John over his rents, but the De Lacys stood by
him and William the Marshal sheltered him. John's difficulties,
such as the loss of Normandy in 1204, the quarrel with Rome
in 1206, and a papal interdict in 1208, did not, however, lessen
the Angevin energy. He resolved to pursue the Irish rebels
home to prevent their leaguing with King Philip against him,
and finally landed in Ireland near Waterford on June 20th
1210 with a large army. He spent only three months in Ireland, but it was a marvellous example of daemonic energy.

Marching up to the Nore at Kilkenny he proceeded by
Dublin, Trim, and Carlingford, driving the De Lacys and De
Braose before him till they made a stand at Carrickfergus.
On his way he was joined by two of the leading Irish kings,
namely, Cathal O'Connor whom he had recognized as king of
Connacht in 1201, and Donough O'Brien, son of Donal More.
It is recorded as illustrative of Irish warfare that when John
presented the king of Connacht with a richly caparisoned steed,
Cathal thanked him and mounted the horse, but first removed

the saddle, and so rode all day beside the King, much to the surprise of the Normans, who thought the heavy saddle indispensable.

After a short siege Carrickfergus yielded and the two De Lacys and William de Braose fled oversea, whereupon John took into his hands the two earldoms of Meath and Ulster and the Honour of Limerick. This latter fief was never renewed.

Ireland now lay at John's feet. He sent Cathal O'Connor and Donough O'Brien back to be kings of their own countries, and returned to Dublin to put his hand to the royal government. There he held a council of his Irish barons, where 'by common consent the laws and customs of England' were extended to Ireland. Twenty Irish chiefs, whose names we have not, are said to have done homage to him there. During his short but active stay he set working not only the machinery of central government but that of the local areas also, which were organized into counties under sheriffs, and with county courts.

On the departure of John in August 1210 episcopal justiciars continued his royal policy, and the frontiers of the colony were pushed forward to Athlone, Clonmacnois, Roscrea, Clones, and Cael-uisce on the Erne, where royal castles were built. The two latter were intended to bridle the Ulster kings, who stood sternly aloof. In Aedh O'Neill the Cenel Eoghain of Tyrone found a great man who ruled the kingdom from 1196 to 1230. He represented one branch of the royal stock descended from the Niall Glúndubh of 919, but the MacLochlann branch had long been dominant and the O'Neill ascendancy had yet to be secured. Aedh found a natural ally in an O'Donnell, who similarly had to establish his family among kindred stocks. In 1201 Egnechan O'Donnell united with O'Neill to crush a MacLochlann candidate in battle near Portrush, and thus the O'Neills and O'Donnells, side by side, established kingships which lasted unbroken till 1603.

John's reign continued in triumph for five years until the baronial revolt that led to Magna Carta shook his throne.

IRELAND
IN 1216
AFTER 40 YEARS OF
NORMAN INVASION

Scale of Miles

0   20   40   60

Iona

MULL

ISLAY

Rathlin

INISHOWEN

Coleraine

Derry

EARLDOM

Larne

Carrickfergus

TIR

CONAILL

TIR

EOGHAIN

Condor

Antrim

OF

Donegal

L. Derg

Lough Neagh

Belfast

Lough Erne

FERMANAGH

Enniskillen

ULSTER

Armagh

Dundrum

Sligo

TIRAWLEY

TIRERAGH

Monaghan

Newry

L. Allen

ORIEL

Boyle

BREFNI

Cavan

Dundalk

Carlingford

KINGDOM

ANNALY

Ardee

Kells

Mellifont

Drogheda

OF

Cong

Tuam

SHILMORTHY

Lough Corrib

Athlone

Mullingar

DE LACY

Navan

Trim

Tara

Slane

FINGALL

EARLDOM OF

Rathwire

Clonard

Maynooth

Galway

Athenry

Clonmacnois

Durrow

Clonfert

MEATH

Dublin

CONNACHT

STRONGBOWS

COUNTY

OF

DUBLIN

Bray

Kildare

Naas

Lough Derg

Dunamase

Norragh

GLEN IMAAL

Delgany

Ennis

Killaloe

Nenagh

LAND OF

Glendalough

Wicklow

KINGDOM OF

Thurles

Holycross

Carlow

Gorey

Arklow

Limerick

Gur

LIMERICK

ORMOND

Kilkenny

LEINSTER

Ferns

River Shannon

Shanid

Cashel

OSSORY Gowran

Enniscorthy

Mount Brandon

Tralee

OR THOMOND

Clonmel

Jerpoint

New Ross

Wexford

Fermoy

Waterford

BARGY

FORTH

Killorglin

Killarney

R. Blackwater

Lismore

DECIES

Dungarvan

KINGDOM OF CORK

Kenmare

Cork

Youghal

OR DESMOND

Bantry

Head of Kinsale

The Irish baronage, inspired by William the Marshal, was for him. In 1213, when Philip Augustus collected an army to invade England, John summoned the national hosts of earls, barons, knights, and freemen to be at Dover at the close of Easter week for the defence of England. The main body took up their position at Barham Down near Canterbury, and the Marshal brought over the whole body of Irish barons, five hundred in number. But the King was reconciled with the Pope by the legate Pandolf, and on March 15th 1213, in a charter attested by himself, the justiciars of England and Ireland, the archbishop of Dublin, and six earls, John of his own free will and by the common advice of his barons, granted to God and His Church and to the Pope and his successors the whole realm of England and Ireland at tribute of a thousand marks per annum, saving his royal rights. The charter ended with an oath of homage. It was not till 1360 that the English parliament repudiated this papal suzerainty, but in Ireland it was not forgotten on the native side as a fresh affirmation of the papal grant of 1155 and 1172.

After the further surrender of Magna Carta in 1215, it was a small thing for John to make concessions in Ireland. There he restored Walter de Lacy to the earldom of Meath, though his brother Hugh was not restored in Ulster. The faithful Cathal O'Connor was formally granted the kingdom of Connacht, to hold in fee of the Crown by rent of three hundred marks per annum, to pay five thousand marks for the charter and not be dispossessed without judgment of the King's court in Dublin. Whether this was an hereditary grant the next reign was to show.

CHAPTER VI

THE EXPANSION OF THE COLONY, 1216–1272

THE death of John in 1216 left the Crown of England on the head of a child of nine years, Henry III, who till 1232 was ruled by the regents, William the Marshal, who died in 1219, and then Hubert de Burgo, justiciar. The Irish government was in this reign organized, and the Anglo-Irish were secured in the rights and laws of England. Dublin castle had its Exchequer, Chancellor, Treasurer, and Justices of assize, who put the Common law and jury system into effect. The Viceroy or justiciar was supreme judge, political officer and commander of the feudal levy, and named the lesser officials while the King reserved to himself the appointment of the chief ministers. Appeals against his judgments could be carried to England, and the Crown regarded Ireland as a land controlled from Westminster and for which it could legislate by edict. Justiciar or chief justice remained the title of the viceroy until the appointment of Mortimer as King's lieutenant in 1316 marked the beginning of a higher title with greater powers. The shire-organization spread with sheriffs, coroners, and later 'keepers of the peace' and county courts, and by 1260 there were seven counties, Cork, Limerick, Waterford, Kerry, Tipperary, Connacht, and Uriel (Louth). The parliament of the colony till Edward the First's time was the council of bishops, abbots, and lay peers, summoned from time to time by the justiciar; while the tenants by knight service, who numbered some five hundred, formed the feudal host of the Crown. Outside the counties, the great Liberties of Meath, Ulster, etc., were areas which the justiciar did not directly control.

The Anglo-Irish were now secured in the rights and liberties of Englishmen, which, as 'the laws and customs of Ireland', became the proud heritage of the colonists. In 1217 Magna Carta was sent over and published in Ireland. Henceforth the Anglo-Irish could appeal to this document as securing to them, as to born Englishmen, their rights, liberties, and lands, and that they should not be dispossessed or suffer in life, limb, or liberty except by due trial before royal judges and by the jury of their equals.   By several enactments of the reign the Crown directed that Common law was to be used in Ireland and all writs of Common law were to be current there.   In 1228 John's charter requiring English law and customs to be observed in that land was ordered to be proclaimed in every county.

So much for the Norman-English invaders of Ireland, who since 1170 had become a numerous population.   But what of the native race and their legal position?   Here we have to distinguish between the kings and chiefs of the unconquered land, and the lords and people of districts in or adjoining the conquered areas.   The kings of Connacht and Thomond were now *reguli* or local sovereigns by royal grant and under royal suzerainty.   Cathal O'Connor till his death in 1224 and Donough O'Brien till his death in 1240 were practically Gaelic kings of the old order, though O'Brien had little more left than county Clare.   Only in the North, west of the Bann, were there Gaelic kings who had not even admitted the English over-lord. John had also admitted as tenants of the Crown several chiefs of the Decies in Waterford and elsewhere, but, as with Cathal O'Connor, were the grants for life or hereditary?   Under his son advantage was taken of these surviving chiefs to treat their tenures as merely temporary and to oust them in favour of Englishmen.   Had the Crown now, when it was so strong in Ireland, made an honest attempt to turn the Irish kings into tenants-in-chief on honourable and hereditary terms it is possible that the work of Henry VIII would have been antici- pated when he made peers of the realm out of various Gaelic chiefs.   The great opportunity was lost, but it would appear, as a result of John's council at Dublin in 1210 or even the earlier decrees of Henry II, that the chief Irish dynasties, called the 'Five Bloods', were at least regarded and treated as freemen in the courts of the colony.

A further question rises on the treatment of the free population of the native race.   Ever since the invasion the

Normans had been reducing the free tenants on the manors they founded to serfdom and villeinage. There was a large existing class of Irish villeins called 'betaghs', whom the Normans naturally retained to work the soil. In addition they sought to reduce ordinary free tenants to forms of bondage familiar to them in England and Wales, for they had brought few English peasants with them. Their ancestors had done this with Anglo-Saxon 'ceorls', and it was now done even more shamefully in Ireland, until the word 'hibernicus' became a general equation for 'villein'. Many of the free and even of the noble were thus reduced in status, or had to fly from their patrimony. To deny the Irish the right of freemen was to make them ignoble of blood and 'to reduce to slavery the blood that has flowed in freedom from of old'.[1] A race so proud as the Gaelic aristocracy and which put the 'free clans' so high in estimation was well aware of what such legal injustice meant.

The State had to have some policy on this question, for a wise government would try to bring both races under a common law. But how were the new occupiers and lords to be protected from the Irish demand for redress if the native race were given the full benefit of the 'laws and customs of Ireland'? How were the Irish to be treated justly if also claims rising from the Conquest were to be legalized and protected, or how were sufficient labour and service to be found for the exploitation of the land?

In 1214 the writ 'of villeins and fugitives' was extended to Ireland; its action was to go back as far as 1170, so to cover the Conquest period and to enable landlords to claim and recover their serfs. When the land-assizes of Henry II were extended to Ireland under John it was provided that that of Novel Disseisin, protecting freeholders from unjust dispossession, should not operate from before 1199 and the others not from before 1172. When the Assize of Clarendon was sent over in 1204 it was directed that no one should be impleaded for the goods or life of an Irishman until after Michaelmas 1205. Thus the injustices of the past thirty years were protected and the gains and oppressions of the Anglo-Irish covered.

Still it was obviously implied that after 1205 the Irish might

---

[1] See the *Remonstrance of the Irish* in 1317, p. 97, here.

plead, answer, and receive redress in Anglo-Irish courts. This seems to have been John's intention. Unhappily, as the century proceeded events showed that this implication was dead in law, and finally the Statutes of Kilkenny in 1366 debarred the native race definitely from the law and even deprived the Five Bloods of their admitted privilege.

This demand for English law on the part of the Irish did not necessarily mean that they liked it. While the law was strong and they were under feudal lords or the county administration they naturally sought its protection, but some of its penalties were dreadful to the native race, whose law rarely applied death or mutilation as punishments. Royal permission to a feudal lord 'to erect a gallows and to have assizes with judgment of thieves and all other liberties and free customs belonging thereto, and also free warren in all his demesne lands', would strike the resident native population with horror. The English law with its good and bad features might have been forced upon them, and indeed many asked for it, especially for the protection of their lands and personal freedom; but when, after a century, they were able to shake it off, the majority reverted gladly to their own ancient code.

The Anglo-Irish had stood by John in his latter end and expected the favour of his son. While the Earl Marshal lived and when, on his death in 1219, Hubert de Burgo ruled till 1232, the feudal class was favoured, for Hubert was an uncle of Richard de Burgo. Walter de Lacy was restored at once to Meath, though his brother Hugh did not get Ulster back till 1227, and so the baronage were able at every point to resume their plan of a final conquest.

Meiler FitzHenry had been granted all central Kerry from Tralee to the lakes of Killarney. He died childless in 1220 and the Munster Geraldines became his heirs. Thomas of Shanid left two sons, John and Maurice. From the former descended the earls of Desmond and the knights of Kerry; from the second the FitzMaurices, barons of Kerry and lords of Clanmaurice and Lixnaw. The Geraldine brothers now led a Norman advance in which the whole coast from Bantry to Castlemaine was bridled with a ring of fortresses, such as Killorglin. 'The foreigners overran all Desmond even to the sea and built castles for themselves against the Gael', say the *Annals of Innisfallen*. John got the FitzHenry lands, Kerry became a Geraldine inheritance, and by 1228 the south-west was all feudalized. The Irish of Desmond were thus cooped up in their last stronghold. Partly by Norman aggression and partly by the attacks of Donal O'Brien, who seized the occasion to oust the Eoghanacht rivals, the MacCarthys had now been driven out of the rich plains of Cashel along with their vassals the O'Sullivans of Knockgraffon into the country west of Cork. There they subjected the older races and built up a new lordship. Dermot MacCarthy of the Conquest time was succeeded by his son Donal More, and he again by his son, Dermot 'of Dundrinan', who died in 1230; both were addressed as 'king of the Irish of Desmond' in royal letters.

Meanwhile the two Lacys attempted the conquest of the Erne and upper Shannon. The First Families rooted themselves in and benefited by the extinction or return to England of original grantees. William, son of the first William de Braose, had been restored to his Irish lands but not to the Honour or kingdom of Limerick, and he now made large grants in Tipperary to Theobald Butler (for such became the family surname), which the latter thus held in chief of the Crown. Butler also got the De Worcester cantreds in south Tipperary, he owned the great manor of Gowran in Kilkenny, and so the fortunes of the house were made.

The second William Marshal, Earl of Pembroke, had his father's nobility of character, but found it hard to be loyal to Henry III's government or to endure the unjust treatment of loyal Irish chiefs. As justiciar from 1224 to 1226 he attempted to befriend the O'Connors against the Lacys and their sort. On the death of Cathal O'Connor in 1224 his son Aedh succeeded to the kingship and the Marshal supported his cause in the disorder due to the De Lacy ambitions. O'Connor, however, was summoned to the King's court at Dublin 'to surrender the land of Connacht which he ought no longer to hold on account of his own and his father's forfeiture, for by King John's charter, granted to Cathal, he only held the land as long as he faithfully served the King'. This was a most unjust reading of the terms of the treaty of 1215, for Cathal had believed that the grant of Connacht was made to him and his heirs. But the baronial faction led by Richard de Burgo had the ear of the justiciar Hubert, and De Burgo claimed Connacht under the grant made to his father. Aedh O'Connor himself was murdered in a petty affair in Dublin, and in May 1227 the 'Land of Connacht' was adjudged to his enemy, Richard de Burgo, with a reservation to the Crown of five cantreds about Athlone, henceforth called 'the King's cantreds'.[1] In 1228 Richard was himself made justiciar and so united both public and private powers. He devoted himself to the conquest of Connacht but could not achieve it at once, and for some years Felim, brother of Aedh, ruled the kingdom of Connacht.

Norman Ireland now became a second field in which to fight out the battle of Crown *versus* Baronage. William, second Earl Marshal, had been succeeded by his brother Richard, and Richard became the leader of Henry's barons. After a protest against the King's foreign favourites, he withdrew to his lands in Wales and finally to Ireland, in which he arrived as a proclaimed traitor. An Anglo-Irish party was worked up against him by the government, and finally at a conference with these secret enemies at the Curragh of Kildare he was treacherously wounded to death (April 1st 1234). The Earl had declared his cause to be that of 'justice, the laws of England, and the expulsion of foreign favourites', but the English government might well fear that the grandson of Strongbow and Eva Mac-Murrough would proclaim himself King of Ireland.

In these baronial clashes of the thirteenth century the knights were in the full panoply of medieval armour, the pot helmet, surcoat of linen or silk, 'gambeson' or padded garment under the coat of mail, mail hose, sleeves extending to the mail glove, a heavy charger (or 'destrier'), an expensive animal, which itself was protected with housings of mail and quilted cloth. In their 'gentlemanly encounters' men and horses did little fighting and suffered little loss. But such a baronage was not destined to rule Ireland; the Normans in this land had to

---

[1] Really the O'Connor royal demesne, Sil Muiredaig or Shilmorthy.

fight with lighter armour and more active steeds, and the Irish
themselves soon showed what serious things battles could be.

The kingdom of Cenel Eoghain, under O'Neill, stood boldly
aloof from these confusions. Egnechan O'Donnell ruled the
Cenel Conaill till 1208 and was then succeeded by his son Donal
More. He too entered into alliance with Aedh O'Neill, and
before he died in 1240 reduced Brefni and its chiefs O'Ruairc
and O'Reilly to submission, and made himself over-lord of
Fermanagh. On the death of Aedh O'Neill in 1230, 'a king who
never gave pledge or hostage to Gael or Gall', a Donal Mac-
Lochlann for some years revived the claim of his race, but at
last Brian, son of Aedh, with O'Donnell aid, recovered the
kingship of Tír Eoghain for his race at the battle of Cameirge
in 1241, in which the MacLochlann name was practically
extinguished and Donal and ten of his 'derbfine' fell in the
battle.

The great event of these years was the Conquest of Connacht,
of which we may say that had Ulster suffered the same fate
the Normans would have ruled Ireland from sea to sea.
Hubert de Burgh fell from office in 1232, but the feudal caste
was still in the saddle, and in 1235 Richard de Burgo called on
the whole feudal host of Ireland to install him in his land
of Connacht. The justiciar himself, Maurice FitzGerald, lord of
Offaly, sanctioned and joined in one of the finest buccaneering
exploits in all feudal history. Almost all the great names of
feudal Ireland followed De Burgo in the army that invaded
Connacht and easily drove Felim O'Connor out of his kingdom.
There then followed the enfeoffment of a whole province.
De Burgo took for himself in chief all the rich land of county
Galway between the Corrib and the Shannon, later called
from him Clanrickard, and a large but less fertile area in
county Mayo, with Loughrea as his chief manor. Maurice Fitz-
Gerald received from him most of Sligo county with other
baronies in Mayo and Galway, and Hugh de Lacy further
conveyed to him his claims as Earl of Ulster over Tyrconnel
and Fermanagh. There were now founded by De Burgo's
lieutenants other great Norman names in Connacht, such as

the Berminghams, lords of Athenry, and the Prendergasts, Stauntons, D'Exeters, and De Angulos of Galway and Mayo. The rank and file also received their shares, and in east Mayo was planted a whole group of Welsh tenants, the Barrets, Lynnets, Merricks, and Walshes, called in later times 'the Welshmen of Tirawley', while in the mountain barrier between Mayo and Galway was planted the race of the Joyces.

The conquerors founded towns, such as Galway, the work of De Burgo, Sligo, the work of FitzGerald, and Athenry, a Bermingham town. For the most part, however, it was a feudal conquest which created a mere Norman noblesse which for some time retained a veneer of French blood and speech, but whose tenantry were almost wholly native and Gaelic-speaking, and who took over the whole existing Gaelic structure of the province. It is doubtful if outside their castles and the walls of these petty towns the Saxon speech was ever heard in medieval Connacht. Within a century even this veneer wore through and the Normans of Connacht were the first of their class to turn Irish.

Of the present five counties of Connacht only Roscommon and Leitrim, the least fertile, were not infeudated and were left to the Gael. Felim O'Connor returned to bow the knee and was granted the five 'King's cantreds' at money rent of the Crown. Henceforth the lordship of his race was confined to county Roscommon. They continued for over a century to call themselves kings of Connacht, but in fact the O'Connor kingship now vanished and De Burgo became 'Dominus Connaciae'. Norman arms had thus reached the Atlantic, making Connacht for a time part of the great French-speaking world of Europe.

Richard de Burgo died in 1243 and Maurice FitzGerald, lord of Naas and Offaly, took the lead of the conquerors. We note now the disappearance of many great names of the Conquest whose dead grants came into the hands of the Geraldines, Butlers, and De Burgos. The two greatest of all, De Lacy and Marshal, suddenly disappear from history. In 1241 Walter de Lacy, earl of Meath, died leaving only two daughters, and two years later his brother Hugh, earl of Ulster, died without heirs at all. In 1243 died Anselm, last of the five sons of the elder William, earl of Pembroke, and only heiresses, daughters of the first Marshal, survived. The De Lacy lordship in Meath was divided between Matilda, the eldest daughter, who was married to Geoffrey de Genville, and Margery, the second daughter, wife of John de Verdun. The former portion was called the Liberty of Trim, the second, a smaller area, the lordship of Lochsewdy or Westmeath. In the case of Leinster there was a five-fold partition among the daughters of the first Earl Marshal and their husbands or heirs. Thus Roger Bigod, Earl of Norfolk, came to be lord of Carlow, Aymer de Valence, lord of Wexford as well as Earl of Pembroke, Roger Mortimer, lord of Leix, the De Clare earls of Gloucester, lords of Kilkenny, and William de Vescy, lord of Kildare. All were Englishmen and absentees. Strongbow's original fief of Leinster, as a single unit, had been a great 'English land'; now, split into five portions, it could not resist the future Irish resurgence.

As for Ulster, in 1264 Walter de Burgo, already lord of Connacht, was created earl there, and so began a line which lasted till 1333.

Maurice FitzGerald of Offaly was a great lord in both Leinster and Connacht, and from this latter vantage-point set himself to make good the claims conveyed to him by Hugh de Lacy. From Sligo he invaded Tyrconnell, and for a time dominated this land of mountain and glen; but he died in 1257 and the heroic Goffraidh O'Donnell turned the Norman tide, invaded Sligo, and defeated an English force at Credran. But now Brian O'Neill appeared in the field; after his victory at Cameirge he styled himself 'king of Ulster', and so claimed the homage and tribute of the whole province. He was defeated on the Swilly river by Goffraidh, but Tyrconnell's hero died of his wounds, and his country was only saved by the arrival in 1258 of Donal Oge O'Donnell from Scotland, where he had been fostered and had married Catriona MacSweeney, a descendant of the Suibhne of 1034. Donal brought with him a band of Scottish galloglass, led by his brother-in-law, and this was the first appearance in Ireland of these first-rate fighting men. Backed by them, he shook off the O'Neill claim, and by his death in 1283 had become over-lord of Tyrconnell, Sligo, and Fermanagh. The Norman advance was checked for good in the north-west, and not till 1540 did an O'Donnell do homage to a king of England.

The galloglasses were to remain till the sixteenth century the most formidable element in Irish warfare, and English accounts of the sixteenth century describe them as tall, fierce footmen, with battle-axes as tall as themselves, clad in helmet and coat of mail, refusing to fly and bearing the brunt of the battle till the last.

The origin of the galloglasses must be sought in the Hebrides, which in Irish were called the 'Innse Gall' or 'Isles of the Norsemen'.[1] The name (*gallóglach*) itself means 'Norse' or 'Foreign soldiery'. In these islands there had grown up a mixed Gaelic and Norse race, having the tall stature and war-like spirit of both races, lovers of the sea, speaking a Gaelic full of Norse words and following the wandering and fighting traditions of the vikings and using their weapons. Within the next two centuries the galloglass mercenaries penetrated every part of Gaelic and Norman Ireland, and to have a band of Scots was the thing for every chief or lord who valued his reputation. The MacSweeneys were the first to come, as marshals to O'Donnell, and in time there were three branches of them in Tyrconnell, of Doe, Fanad, and Banagh. The MacDonnells or 'Race of Sumerled', lords of the Isles, provided marshals for O'Neill's forces, and later MacCabes, MacDugalls, and Sheehys took service with the chiefs of Ulster, Connacht, and Munster.

In the military and political history of Ireland the galloglass proved a turning-point. Up to this the Irish, though brave enough, in their light dress were no match for the heavily armed Normans, but now they found in these Scottish mercenaries trained and traditional soldiers who could endure the Norman arrows and repulse their foot, and who before long turned the tide of battle against them. To them we may attribute much of the resurgence of Gaelic Ireland in the next three centuries.

---

[1] 'Gall' at first meant a Gaul, next a Norseman, then was applied to the Normans or early English settlers in Ireland.

Brian O'Neill now sought to revive the old High kingship, and secured the support of O'Connor and O'Brien, but when it came to battle only O'Connor supported him. In May 1260 he advanced upon Downpatrick with a levy of the Ulster chiefs, but at Drumderg near that town was defeated and killed with many of his vassals. The battle showed that in the old style of war the Irish could never prevail, for there were no galloglasses with them, and they fought in linen tunics with sword, spear, and light axe. A poem of the time which is a lament for the hero Brian and his vassals, the O'Cahans, testifies to this.

> Unequal they came to the battle,
> The Foreigners and the race of Tara;
> Fine linen shirts on the race of Conn,
> The Foreigners one mass of iron.

The glory of the O'Neills for the time departed. In 1264 Walter de Burgo became earl of Ulster and as such set up in place of Brian a 'tame O'Neill', Aedh Buidhe (the yellow-haired), from whom descended the O'Neills of Clandeboy, the Clann Aedha Buidhe.

The tide of Norman expansion fluctuated also in the west and south-west. Until 1242 Donough O'Brien remained king of Thomond, but after him the O'Briens were more and more menaced by royal grants to Normans. In Desmond, John FitzThomas had climbed to pre-eminence, inheriting various claims, and was the greatest man in the counties of Cork, Limerick, and Kerry. To crown his greatness, in 1259 he got a royal grant of Desmond and Decies (west Waterford) in fee. After Dermot, king of Desmond, who died in 1230, the Mac-Carthy royal succession was disputed between the race of Cormac Finn and Donal Got, his two brothers, and Finghin ('Fineen'), son of the latter, became the family hero and levelled the Norman castles built round the coast from 1215 to 1228. When the grant of 1259 was made, Fineen MacCarthy rallied his people, and in July 1261 at the battle of Callann near Kenmare the Irish won a complete victory over the army of FitzThomas and the justiciar, and the Geraldine himself, his son Maurice, and many gallant knights and barons fell there. Only an infant grandson, Thomas, son of Maurice,

D

survived to represent FitzThomas. The battle ot Callann was as decisive in Desmond history as the career of Donal Oge was in the history of Tyrconnell. The MacCarthys, though they no longer held the plain of Cashel or the city of Cork, henceforth built up a great lordship, covering finally all south-west Munster from the lakes of Killarney south to Bantry Bay and east to Macroom. The senior line, descended from Cormac Finn, retained the sovereignty as MacCarthy More and till 1394 called themselves 'kings of Desmond', while the junior branch of Donal Got, called MacCarthy Reagh, were lords of Carbery between Bantry and Inishannon. The grant of Desmond and Decies to FitzThomas did not indeed lapse and was renewed later to his grandson, but in the interval the MacCarthy power became too strong to be uprooted again.

The persistent hope of the Irish race that they might find another native or foreign Ard Rí instead of the new English over-lord now turned towards a king of Norway. In 1263 there appeared off the coast of Scotland Haakon, last of the sea-kings of Norway, demanding tribute and homage of the Outer isles. The Irish sent envoys to him, asking him to come to their aid, but he was concerned only with his Scottish claims, and on landing there was defeated at Largs in an indecisive battle by Alexander III, king of Scots. Thereupon he sailed home and the Norwegian suzerainty of the Scottish Isles lapsed. In its place the MacDonnells became to all intents independent Lords of the Isles, and so lasted till James IV extinguished their lordship in 1499.

Thrown on their own resources and unable by their mutual jealousies to unite, still the native princes by local victories defeated the great Conquest design. At the end of Henry III's reign the justiciar D'Ufford built a royal castle at Roscommon and in 1270 advanced with Walter de Burgo against Aedh O'Connor, son of Felim. Backed by a force of galloglass, O'Connor defeated them at Athankip on the Shannon. Henceforth the O'Connors retained the Five cantreds and from Roscommon were accepted by the local chiefs as 'kings of the Gael of Connacht'. The war of the two races thus ended in a drawn fight, the Irish unable to make a central union but strong in local resistance, the Normans divided from one another by their feuds and ambitions, and already through residence and intermarriage knowing the Irish speech and allying themselves with Irish princes. The plan of a final Norman conquest had failed, but the failure was only admitted openly a century later by the Statutes of Kilkenny.

CHAPTER VII

ENGLISH LORDSHIP AT ITS HEIGHT, 1272–1327

THE Conquest of Ireland was destined now to go no farther than the points it had reached, namely, Ulster east of Lough Neagh, Meath, Leinster, most of Connacht and Munster. The English Lordship was legally admitted, but in fact Ireland was already divided into the three areas of the Gaelic territories, still unconquered, the feudal Liberties, and the 'English land' divided into counties and ruled by sheriffs, which, and which only, the Dublin government could effectively control. The strength and success of this 'English land' depended on efficient government and effective support from England.

Under Edward I the Crown made an attempt to create in Ireland a replica of the English monarchy. The persistent flaw in English rule in Ireland was the absence of the monarch himself. 'The Lion himself came not to the hunt,' wrote Davies under James I, 'and left the prey to the inferior beasts.' Edward, a man of English and rigid mind, did not admit the rights of the native race, and in two instances, that of Desmond and that of Thomond, he granted to feudal lords two Irish kingdoms. He was not likely to sympathize with Brehon laws any more than he sympathized with Welsh laws. But he might be expected to sympathize with the native demand to be made equal in English law with the colonists. In 1276 the Irish through the justiciar D'Ufford offered him the sum of eight thousand marks for the benefits of English law. After three years' delay Edward referred the question to a parliament of Irish barons, but they seemed to have shelved the question, and the selfish spirit of this class, who did not wish their serfs set free or their exploitation of the native race checked, was too strong for the Crown. Edward is much to be blamed, for the royal power was then very strong, and indeed he did later by royal fiat secure legal equality to such individual Irishmen as sought for it, but to have general effect this

88

needed enactment in Parliament and fearless execution by royal judges.[1]

The baronial class had now a fresh generation of leaders. In 1280 Richard de Burgo, son of Earl Walter, succeeded in the lordship of Connacht and the earldom of Ulster, which he ruled till his death in 1326 and raised to their greatest power and extent. Known as the 'Red Earl', he was the admitted leader of the Anglo-Irish and popular with the Gaels by his descent from the O'Briens. The Munster Geraldines had their chief in Thomas FitzMaurice, grandson of the Thomas slain at Callann. When he received in 1292 a re-grant of all Desmond and Decies there was on this occasion no native revolt, for MacCarthy More was friendly to the Geraldines, and Fitz-Maurice admitted the lordship of their race in south-west Desmond. The great name among the Leinster Geraldines was John FitzThomas, fifth baron of Offaly, who by bequest or the extinction of other branches of the family finally concentrated in his hands vast possessions in Leinster, Limerick, and Connacht. In eastern Munster the Butlers, in virtue of their own grants and succession to the extinct De Braoses, Worcesters, and others, ruled most of Ormond. After five short-lived Theobalds followed one another, in 1299 Edmund succeeded and was the founder of a race of Earls. When we add to such men Geoffrey de Genville, lord of Trim, and others, we have a handful of men who controlled the greater part of Ireland, and whose feudal interests formed a thick-set hedge which the Crown was not likely to break down.

During the reign the balance of power was shifted among them. After a long dispute between Richard de Burgo and FitzThomas, in 1299 the Crown compelled FitzThomas to surrender Sligo and his baronies in Mayo and Galway to the Earl. Richard, however, refrained from using Sligo as the base of a renewed attack upon the O'Donnells. It was from the eastern side that he extended the earldom of Ulster, which finally took in the great peninsula of Inishowen and reached to the eastern shore of Lough Swilly. The leading

[1] In or about 1292 Edward commanded a Great Council held in London that a grant of English law should be made to all Irishmen who demanded it, 'for his council had shown him that it would be greatly to his advantage'.

Ulster chiefs were subjected to the Earl and eleven of them
from O'Neill downwards consented to hold their lands and
regalities from the Earl of Ulster by military sevice, providing
355 men in all or payment of one pound per man.   This military
service was called by the Irish 'Bonnacht'; it was claimed by
the Earls of Ulster till the middle of the fifteenth century.

In two directions King Edward favoured pure feudal expansion.   One was his grant of Desmond and Decies to FitzMaurice,
the other was when in 1276 he granted 'the whole land of
Thomond' (county Clare) to Thomas de Clare, a kinsman of
the Earl of Gloucester, as a feudal liberty.   De Clare was a
brave soldier; he invaded Thomond at once, built a strong
castle at Bunratty, and colonized the land around it with
Englishmen.   Following the usual Norman ruse, he supported
Brian Ruadh O'Brien against his nephew Turloch, son of the
former reigning chief, Conor.   But the young Turloch was a
gallant fellow; he took up arms against the Norman claim and
there followed a long and sporadic war which did not end till
1318.   In this De Clare and the race of Brian Ruadh fought
endless battles against Turloch which are the subject of a
glowing historical tract in Irish, called the *Wars of Turloch*,
written by Seán Magrath some fifty years afterwards.

On the non-feudal side, Edward aimed at making the
Lordship of Ireland the second jewel in his crown.   A number
of viceroys, generally English, were instructed to make the
government both efficient and lucrative and strengthen it
against the feudal lords.   The ordinary revenue of the colony
was seldom more than five thousand pounds per annum, but
State taxation might be made to grow.   In 1275 a council of
Irish magnates granted to Edward I the 'Great Custom' on
the export of wool, hides, and leather, and Ireland began to
provide a State revenue for the Crown.   Since the Anglo-Irish
were to be treated as Englishmen, many of the great public
statutes of Edward I were now, by royal writ, extended to
Ireland, such as that of Gloucester in 1285.   But Ireland
remained lacking in many of the great acts passed in England
from 1272 onwards, such as the Statute of Treason of 1352;
hence it was that Poynings' parliament of 1494–5 applied

here all the great 'acts made formerly for the public weal' in England.

The Statute of Gloucester contained the 'Quo Warranto' writ by which the Crown could inquire into feudal and episcopal privileges. This was a powerful weapon in England, but how was a mere viceroy without a strong government behind him to question the liberties of the Irish magnates? Several of the justiciars attempted it, but it was not till John de Wogan, a knight of Pembroke, arrived as justiciar in 1295 to rule with intervals till 1312 that the great attempt to extend the shire-land was made. De Wogan was sent to reconcile the feuds of the nobles and to make the colony not only self-supporting but a treasury to draw upon for Edward's Scottish and French wars. The feuds of the Irish magnates were many, a proof how selfish and local-minded a nobility can be without the restraining hand of a national monarch.

It was Wogan who settled the feud of FitzThomas and De Vescy in 1297 and that of De Burgo and FitzThomas in 1299. His great achievement in Irish history is the foundation of the Irish Parliament in 1297. Edward wanted an army from Ireland for his Scottish war and ordered that the widest possible approval of the Irish colony should be obtained. The usual council of the prelates and lay peers was summoned to meet the justiciar and his ministers, and in addition for the first time two knights were summoned from each of nine counties and each of five liberties with the sheriff or seneschal in each case. The counties summoned were, in Leinster, Dublin, and Louth (Uriel); in Munster, Waterford, Tipperary, Cork, Limerick, and Kerry; in Connacht, Roscommon; while the liberties were Meath, Wexford, Carlow, Kilkenny, and Ulster. By acts of this parliament Kildare and Meath were made shires, and the eleven counties and five liberties represented may be taken as what was then regarded as the 'English land'.

Other acts passed attest how Irish the outlying colonists were becoming and how hostile both to them and the native Irish the Dublin parliament was to be. Such of the English as wore their hair in the flowing locks or 'coolun' which were the Irish fashion were to be taken for Irish and treated as such, and the name of 'degenerate English' was for the first time applied to them. Another act forbade the maintaining of kern, that is Irish footmen, and by another every holder of twenty ploughlands was to keep horse and armour and be ready to serve the State.

The first step was thus taken towards a representative parliament for the Anglo-Irish colony.

As Edward's representative, Wogan showed firm will and ready action in inquiring into the privileges of lords, prelates, and abbots. He got Meath and Kildare made into shires, and the forfeiture of De Vescy in Kildare and death of Roger Bigod, earl of Norfolk, without male heir in 1306 enabled Edward to resume two great feudal liberties. But the King let his servant down and before long renewed the Liberty of Carlow to his second son Thomas of Brotherton, whom he created Earl of Norfolk. So, after all the efforts of Edward's viceroys, the feudal magnates of Ireland continued to guide the fortunes of the colony.

The accession of the worthless Edward II made little difference to Ireland as long as Wogan ruled. In 1310 he summoned to Kilkenny a still more representative parliament, for, in addition to the prelates and eighty-eight magnates each summoned by writ, he called for two knights from each shire and two members from each of a number of towns. Parliament so formed was an Anglo-Irish assembly and no Irishman sat among the deputies, or even among the magnates unless it were some bishop or abbot of Gaelic blood. In this body, which seldom rose above one hundred and twenty, the council remained the important nucleus; it spoke for the 'English land', for it could not speak for Gaelic Ireland; its language was French or English, and yet it claimed to be the final law-maker and court for all Ireland, which it bound with its decisions as far as they could be enforced.[1] It was not, however, till 1372 that the medieval Irish parliament received the final shape which it kept until 1537.

[1] Thus the Statutes of Kilkenny, passed by a small Anglo-Irish parliament in 1366, bound the whole island with disastrous results till 1613.

The parliament of 1310 passed an act that 'no mere Irish-man shall be received into a religious order among the English in the land of peace'. This is the first use of the famous phrase 'mere Irish' (*merus hibernicus*), and it implied that Gaels living by Irish law and under their own chiefs were not possessed of civil rights among the English race. The phrase 'land of peace' is also significant of the feeling that only the shires were the true English land, while the lands of the great feudal lords were 'march lands', and those of the Irish were a 'land of war', beyond English control. It is to the credit of Walter Jorz (or Joyce), the English archbishop of Armagh, that he got the act at once revoked by appeal to the King.

Wogan ruled till 1312. During his period the Lordship of Ireland became profitable to the Crown and the colonists contributed great supplies of men and provisions for the Scottish wars. Of the Irish levies the Earl of Ulster was the leader, and he fought several campaigns in Scotland, but as he was the father-in-law of Robert the Bruce we may assume that he was not whole-hearted in the business of suppressing Scottish independence.

There arrived in Ireland in 1308 a young Englishman who was the legal heir to vast estates. This was Roger Mortimer, lord of Wigmore in Herefordshire, by descent from the Marshals and Lacys lord of Trim and claimant to Leix. He was soon to find how the return of an absentee of English birth could arouse the hostility and opposition both of Irish and Norman. In Leix, Mortimer had to force O'More, who in Irish eyes was king there, into submission and to bridle the country with his great castle on the rock of Dunamase. In Meath the aged Geoffrey de Genville had retired into a monastery and the old Lacy earldom had to be divided again between Mortimer, as husband of the heiress Joan de Genville, and Theobald de Verdun, already lord of Westmeath. But the junior Lacys and Verduns, who were rooted in the Irish soil, resented the feudal law by which fiefs passed through females and like the Irish believed in male succession as long as there were men of the name who could defend and maintain their country, accord-ing to the maxim '*tír mharbh tír gan tighearna*' ('a land without a lord is a dead land'). In a land of border wars the patriarchal and kin spirit became imperative and captured the invaders also. Naturally it was more felt among the junior De Burgos, Verduns, Lacys, etc., than their seniors, who were great tenants of the Crown and men of State. Before a century the annalist Clyn speaks of the 'clans and surnames' (*naciones et cognomina*) of the Geraldines, Roches, Poers, and others.

When therefore Meath was redivided in 1308 the junior Lacys of Rathwire resisted, and even the younger Verduns had no love for the chief of their name. Wogan's last public action was to lead an army against the Verduns and receive a defeat at their hands. But such rebels against the State did not therefore join the Irish chiefs, and for a long time yet war upon the Irish was the sport of the Englishry. Among those most praised in this field was Piers de Bermingham, baron of Tethmoy, the ruins of whose strong castle in the 'Carrick' or Rock of Carbery near Edenderry may still be seen. The O'Connors, lords of Offaly, were his neighbours, and in open war could not be subdued. He therefore, on Christmas Day 1295, invited their chief men to a banquet at the Carrick, and after they had feasted well had Calvach O'Connor, the chief, his two brothers, and twenty-nine of his leading men massacred. It was a determined attempt to wipe out a whole royal 'derb-fine', but actually several O'Connor 'royal heirs' survived and it was shown once again how unkillable was an Irish dynasty. But not only did the Dublin government reward Sir Piers with a hundred pounds for this callous deed, but a stirring con-temporary ballad in English, as spoken in Ireland, praises him enthusiastically as 'a hunter out of the Irish'. In the eyes of the law and its supporters Irish chiefs were 'felons' and out-laws, or rebellious vassals of a Norman grantee.

THE BRUCE INVASION AND ITS AFTERMATH, 1315–1327

On June 24th 1314 at Bannockburn was established the freedom of Scotland. The English government had to abandon Scotland, but the King of Scots was not so easily got rid of. Robert Bruce had a very capable brother Edward, earl of Carrick in Galloway, whose energies and ambitions needed an outlet. He had also thousands of veterans unemployed and as the war was unfinished he boldly carried it into the enemy's quarters. In Ireland he saw the makings of a great anti-English combination, the Irish chiefs ready to welcome a deliverer, the Irish Church wronged by the English lordship, numbers of the feudal Anglo-Irish discontented, and his father-in-law the Earl of Ulster neutral or even friendly. Scotland was a country of mixed languages and races, Norman, Gaelic, and English. In Ireland the same situation existed, and Bruce, who was on his father's side a feudal Norman and on his mother's side descended from the ancient Gaelic kings of Alba, felt himself able to manage the Irish situation.

On May 25th 1315 Edward Bruce arrived in Larne harbour (then called Olderfleet) with the greatest foreign force ever yet landed in Ireland, an army of six thousand veterans clad in mail. He was joined by Robert Byset, lord of the Glens of Antrim, a man of Scottish descent, and by Donal O'Neill, son of Brian 'of the battle of Down'. With such a union of veteran soldiers and light Irish troops Bruce proved invincible in every battle till his last.

The first serious encounter was at Connor in Antrim, where he defeated the Red Earl. He then invaded Meath, was joined by the Lacys of Rathwire and the Verduns, and crumpled up the large but untrained levies of the colony in a series of battles.

The Scottish victories caused a general Irish resurgence and many local triumphs of the native race. Numbers of their clergy and many of the Irish members of the Franciscans openly welcomed the Scots, and according to the Anglo-Irish annalist Clyn, 'there adhered to them almost all the Irish of the land and few kept their faith and loyalty'. Donal O'Neill failed to unite the kings in common action, but almost nowhere was the English cause safe and many of the Norman race joined the Scots or stood neutral. At Kells in Meath Edward Bruce defeated Mortimer and at Ardscull Edmund Butler. All the north was in his hands save Carrickfergus, and finally on May Day 1316 he was crowned on the hill of Knocknemelan near Dundalk; 'the Gaels of Erin' say the annals of Loch Cé 'proclaimed him King of Erin'.

Edward, King of England, was slow to move till Ireland

was almost lost; then, to win over the Anglo-Irish magnates, he created Edmund Butler earl of Carrick and John Fitz-Thomas earl of Kildare and appointed Roger Mortimer his Lieutenant.

It was to Connacht that Bruce looked for a striking victory. There had been since 1274 among the royal race of O'Connor a long and deadly succession war. The race of Cathal Crovderg had ruled till the death of Aedh, the victor of Athankip. Then for forty years the kingship was contested by the respective heirs of Cathal and of his younger brothers, Murcertach and Brian of Leyny, among whose numerous descendants some ten names of 'kings' appear, till in 1310 Felim, the true heir of the senior line of Cathal, was elected. But he had a strong rival in Rory, head of the Clan Murcertach.

Felim had marched with the Red Earl to Connor but accepted the offers of Bruce and returned home. There he slew his rival in battle and assumed the whole sovereignty of Connacht. His nominal over-lord, the Earl of Ulster, was now a defeated man and 'a wanderer throughout Erin without sway or power' but William 'Liath' ('the Grey') de Burgo, cousin of the earl, and Richard de Bermingham, lord of Athenry, raised a Norman force and met Felim in battle at Athenry on August 10th 1316. The young king commanded a great levy of chiefs from Connacht, Meath, Thomond, and Brefni, and the fight was worthy of the great occasion, but in the end the Norman horse and archers triumphed, over a thousand Irish fell, and Felim was slain beneath his own leopard standard. It was the most determined fight made by the Irish since the Conquest and evidently they now wore mail, for it is recorded that the victors walled Athenry out of the profits of the arms and armour taken from the Irish dead. So fell the O'Connor kingdom of Connacht.

Edward Bruce was at least master of the North, he took Carrickfergus after a long siege in September, and his brother Robert arrived to join him. They were irresistible in the open field, and when they invaded the Midlands again they found almost no foe to face them, for the magnates could not unite and the government was paralysed, but their ravages created such a famine and general ruin as to lose them many hearts.

Early in 1317 they marched upon Dublin, in which the Red Earl had sought refuge, thinking he might deliver the city to them, but the mayor and citizens boldly manned the walls, and as they had no siege train to take so strong a town the Scots retreated from Castleknock in February and marched to the west and then back to Ulster.

Thence Robert returned to Scotland. On April 7th 1317 Mortimer arrived at Youghal as Lord lieutenant with an army and a commission to admit the Irish to the full use of English law. He drove the Lacys out of Meath and at Athlone made a treaty with Cathal O'Connor, 'prince of the Irish of Connacht', and confirmed to him the Five cantreds. So weakened were now the O'Connors that this Cathal, head of the Clan Brian, could show no king among his ancestors for six generations back to Turloch More himself, and thus was not even a 'royal heir'. This interloper, however, did not last long, and Turloch, brother of Felim, in 1324 recovered the kingship for good for the race of Cathal Crovderg. But the full glory of the O'Connors never returned.

It is now (1317) that a combination of the Irish chiefs under Donal O'Neill sent to the Avignon pope, John XXII, their Remonstrance against English oppression.

In this great indictment both of the Lordship of Ireland and the Anglo-Irish, they charge the kings of England with violating the spirit of Adrian's grant, especially as regards the native Church. They have sought redress from the present king but he has made no answer, they therefore appeal to his suzerain the Pope. They charge the 'men of the middle nation', that is, the colonists, with constant cruelties against the native people, robbing them of their land and reducing them to slavery, 'so bringing into servitude the blood that has flowed in freedom from of old'. They quote the case of the O'Connors murdered by Sir Piers de Bermingham, and the remark of an Anglo-Irish cleric who had said in Edward Bruce's court at Carrick that to kill an Irishman was no more than to kill a dog. The charges are in one important case untrue, but the relations of the races since 1170 justified the general charge and the passion does not invalidate the truth.

They have asked the King of England to divide the island between them and the English, but no reply has been received, and despairing of justice from him they have decided to repudiate his authority; therefore Donal O'Neill, 'by hereditary right King of Ireland', surrenders his rule to Edward Bruce 'Earl of Carrick, sprung from the most illustrious of our ancestors'.

The days of great popes were over and the only response to Ireland's appeal was a letter from John XXII to Edward II early in 1318, urging him to do justice to the Irish according to the Donation of Adrian, and a Bull of excommunication against Edward Bruce and his adherents.

It was already late in the day, for Bruce's chance of an Irish monarchy was by now on the wane. But before it expired a great local victory was recorded for the native side. In Thomond the war of De Clare and the O'Briens had gone on for nearly forty years, Richard de Clare taking the place of his father Thomas and Murcertach O'Brien replacing his father Turloch. At last on May 10th 1318 the issue was fought out at Disert O'Dea near Ennis. In the picturesque account given in the *Wars of Turloch* the comparison between the well-armed Englishry and the light and active Gaels is well drawn and the picture is shown of De Clare and his Normans forming themselves at last into a 'battle hedge' and being slain to a man. 'So dour the hand-to-hand work was that neither noble nor commander of them left the ground, but most of them fell where they stood, both knight and battle-baron, lord and heir.' On the news of the battle De Clare's wife abandoned Bunratty castle and went off with what remained of the garrison in their fast galleys to Limerick. 'From which time to this never one of their breed has come back to have a look at it,' concludes the triumphant chronicler.

So the O'Briens, unlike the O'Connors, recovered their former kingship, which they only exchanged for an earldom in 1540.

Bruce had retired to Ulster and might have held the North for long had he but waited for men and supplies from his brother Robert, but when a colonial army led by John de

Bermingham, lord of Tethmoy, marched against him, he rashly faced it with an inferior force of Scots, Irish, and Meath rebels at Faughart near Dundalk, on October 14th 1318. In the battle he himself was slain after a gallant stand, his allies suffered severely, and the remnant of the Scots got back to their native country as best they could. So ended the Bruce enterprise of Ireland. Edward had attempted to be that foreign Árd Rí which the Irish had sought for in Haakon of Norway and had received great support, but though he was a gallant soldier we cannot feel that he had the gifts of a nation-maker.

Thus was the English lordship of Ireland restored. The Red Earl recovered Ulster and Connacht and banished Donal O'Neill into the wilds of Tyrone, while John de Bermingham was created earl of Louth. There was little thought of vengeance, and even the De Lacys and Verduns were restored to most of their estates. The lesson was not without its effects. In 1320, at a Dublin parliament, Mortimer, in the name of the King, granted Magna Carta once more to the clergy and people of Ireland. Further, in accordance with his instructions, he issued charters of English liberty to some Irish chiefs, and by edict in 1321 admitted all Irishmen, 'both within and without the liberties, who have been, or shall be, admitted to English law, the English law of life and limb', saving to the King and the lords the chattels of their serfs called 'betaghs'.[1]

Henceforth the emancipation of the Irish was more a matter of individual grant by letters patent of the Crown, purchased for money in accordance with this declaration, rather than a general enfranchisement by statute. This would have encountered the selfish interest of the lords and their villeins; indeed, as it was, the Statutes of Kilkenny fifty years later settled the question in a manner fatal to the Irish.

For the moment there was an apparent revival of Anglo-Ireland, and it seemed that the ship of State might resume a better course. When the Red Earl, greatest of the magnates, died in 1326 his grandson William 'Donn' ('the Brown Earl')

---

[1] Under the feudal system, the villeins and their property belonged to the manor lord.

succeeded to the earldom at its height. But in fact the ravages and victories of the Scots had been fatal to those Anglo-Irish towns and manors which had been widely founded all over the midlands. The crops could soon be replaced after the famine but men and buildings could not. From this time the strength of the colony had to lie in the coast towns and the settled nearer districts.

The Irish chiefs had failed to secure a general triumph but won many local victories. Many of them recovered lost lordships, as did the O'Briens, while Aedh O'Donnell levelled De Burgo's castle of Sligo and enforced the permanent supremacy of Tyrconnell over that O'Connor branch, sprung from Brian of Leyny, which was later called O'Connor Sligo.

The feelings of the Irish with regard to Bruce varied, and some of the comments no doubt were made after his failure. Whether a Scottish feudal monarchy in Ireland instead of an English one would have bettered things Fate was not to attest. Some of the chiefs preferred the advantage they could get from terms with the English. Among the expressions of feeling we have that of the O'Maddens, a strong sept in county Galway. After the Bruce war the Red Earl got Mortimer to grant English law to Eoghan O'Madden of Hy Many, his brothers, and his heirs, and the Earl divided this country between him and O'Kelly. 'One-third of the province of Connacht to be under O'Madadhain, no English steward to preside over his Gaels, and he and his free clans to be equally noble in blood with his lord De Burgo, contrary to the former decisions of these English lords that the Gael was a bondsman while the Saxon was a noble.' No wonder that in a Gaelic tract of the time written for this O'Madden there is a long eulogy of the Anglo-Norman lords and reproof of the Connacht chiefs for wanting to call in 'Scottish foreigners less noble than our own foreigners, in imitation of the O'Neills', which goes on to praise 'those princely English lords who gave up their foreignness for a pure mind, their harshness for good manners, their stubbornness for mildness and their perverseness for hospitality'. Also the pitiless ravages of the Scots impressed many, and the native annals call Edward Bruce 'the destroyer of Ireland in general, both of the English and the Gael', and say that 'there was not done from the beginning of the world a better deed for the men of Erin than that deed, for theft, famine, and destruction of men occurred throughout Erin for the space of three years and a half, and people used actually to eat one another throughout the island'.

CHAPTER VIII

THE DECLINE OF THE COLONY AND THE STATUTES OF KILKENNY, 1327–1366

AFTER the overthrow and murder of the unfortunate Edward II, Roger Mortimer ruled England for three years along with the Queen-mother Isabella. He was himself an Irish magnate, and in the parliament of Shrewsbury in 1329, when he got himself created earl of March, favoured his Anglo-Irish supporters by getting Maurice FitzThomas created earl of Desmond and James, son of Edmund Butler, earl of Ormond. By later grants of Edward III James was granted a palatine Liberty in Tipperary and confirmed in the prise of wines throughout Ireland as Butler; while Desmond equally received palatine rights in Kerry.

In the year 1330 Mortimer was overthrown and executed by his enemies, and Edward III began his reign, that of a warrior rather than a statesman. He had to take Ireland into account with the decay of the government there, the decline of revenues, the revival of the Irish, the question of their admission to the law, the absenteeism of titular landowners, and the overgrown powers of the magnates. The Fitzgeralds and Butlers were by way of owning the whole south, and the fewer the great nobles were the greater they became. In 1316 on the death of Theobald de Verdun the Liberty of Westmeath expired, and on the death of Aymer de Valence in 1324 the Honour of Wexford was left vacant. When it was renewed to his grandnephew Laurence Hastings, in 1399, it was only another case of an English absentee getting what rents he could from his distant Irish estates.

In 1331 Edward sent over as his deputy Sir Anthony Lucy with these instructions. The Irish were to be brought under English law 'but the betaghs to remain subject to their lords', Mortimer's grants as being made in the King's minority were to be resumed, and twenty-four great absentees must return or garrison their lands. On the first point, the legal equality

IRELAND
IN 1330
ANGLO-NORMAN LORDSHIP
AT ITS HEIGHT

Miles
0   20   40

FANAD
INISHOWEN
DOE
EARLDOM
GLENS
OF
ANTRIM
TIR
Derry
THE
ROUTE
OF
CONAILL
Lifford
TIR
Carrickfergus
RANAGH
Donegal
EOGHAIN
Lough
Neagh
ARDS
Ballyshannon
Omagh
ULSTER
Inch
Dungannon
Downpatrick
Enniskillen
Armagh
Dundrum
Sligo
FERMANAGH
IRISH
LECALE
Newry
TIRAWLEY
TIRERAGH
ORIEL
L.Allen
ENGLISH
DE BURGO
BREFNI
ORIEL
Carlingford
(O'CONNOR)
L Gara
Carrick
on Shannon
Ardee
LOUTH
LORDSHIP OF
THE KING'S
Slane
Drogheda
CANTREDS
Kells
Navan
Roscommon
MEATH
Tuam
HYMANY
LIBERTY OF TRIM
COUNTY
CONNACHT
(O'KELLY)
Rathwire
Trim
Dublin
Athenry
Ballinasloe
Athlone
OF
Galway
DELVIN
CARBERY
Bray
Loughrea
OFFALY
EARLDOM
Naas
FERCULLEN
OF
DUBLIN
O'BRIEN
ELY
Dunamase
Kildare
Newcastle
O'CARROLL
KILDARE
GLEN
Glendalough
LORDSHIP OF
LIBERTY
IMAAL
Wicklow
Ennis
Killaloe
OF LEIX
Glenmalure
THOMOND
Bunratty
Nenagh
Carlow
LIBERTY
PALATINE
LIBERTY
OF
Arklow
Limerick
Kilkenny
OF
CARLOW
Gorey
Glin
Shanid
EARLDOM
Cashel
Ferns
Croom
OF ORMOND
OF
LIBERTY OF
Kilmallock
Clonmel
KILKENNY
Enniscorthy
PALATINE
Tralee
EARLDOM
Carrick
on Suir
WEXFORD
New Ross
COUNTY OF KERRY
Buttevant
COUNTY
Wexford
Dingle
Fermoy
Lismore
OF WATERFORD
Killorglin
Killarney
OF DESMOND
(LE POER)
valentia
Kenmare
THE MacCARTHY
PECIES
Dungarvan
Cork
Cloyne
COUNTRY
Bandon
Bantry
Kinsale

J.T.RANKIN

of the Irish was not confirmed by any Irish parliament but was pleaded many times in Irish courts. The absentees failed to obey the order. The second point was taken as an attack upon the Earls of Desmond and Ormond and others who owed their titles or grants to Mortimer. Even the mere sending over of an ordinary knight as viceroy was resented by the proud magnates of Ireland, who had hoped that, if not the King himself, at least some great English nobleman would be sent to rule them. 'For this race, both English and Irish did ever love to be ruled by great persons';[1] a saying very true of all Irish history and fatally ignored by Ireland's rulers throughout the centuries.

To the 'English in Ireland' this royal programme was more serious even than the revival of the Gaelic race. Magna Carta, with its protection of men in their estates, life, and liberty, had been re-extended to Ireland as late as 1320, Edward III had re-issued it at his accession in England but not in Ireland, and Lucy's edict of Resumption seemed a direct violation of Anglo-Irish rights. The result was the first beginnings of a 'Patriot party' among them, who disliked the officials, 'the English by birth', and made the claim for their own native and aristocratic caste to control Ireland. Up to the end of the eighteenth century the Anglo-Irish of every kind maintained this spirit of colonial independence. Beyond this, or to achieve an Irish nationality like that which the Bruces won for Scotland, they never seriously contemplated to go.

Maurice, earl of Desmond, took the lead of this opposition and Lucy had to be recalled, but for thirty years the struggle went on. And before the King could proceed further, a disastrous event in the North struck the colony an even deadlier blow than the Bruce war.

On June 6th 1333 William, the young Earl of Ulster, was murdered at the 'Ford of Carrickfergus' by some of the Mandevilles and other tenants of his as the result of a family feud. This was the second assassination of the kind within four years, for John de Bermingham, the victor of Faughart, had been murdered in the same way by his own tenants at Balibragan

---

[1] Sir John Davies in his *Discovery of the True Causes why Ireland has never been subdued to the English Crown* (1612).

in 1329. Rebellion and disloyalty now marked the lesser Normans, who resented great earls over them and wanted to be supreme 'captains of their nations'.

The murder of the Brown Earl had irreparable effects. His wife fled to England with her only child, Elizabeth, and the male line of the De Burgo earls came to an end. They had been the great rampart of the colony on the North and had their lordship endured through the Middle ages Irish history would be written differently. Now the greatest feudal State in Ireland became a nominal lordship for another English absentee, this time a royal one, namely, Lionel, Duke of Clarence, Edward's second son, to whom later the infant Elizabeth was married. Seizing their opportunity, the Ulster chiefs, former vassals of De Burgo, recovered their ground and reduced the vast earldom to the limits of the coast of Antrim and Down.

The De Burgos thus vanished from Ulster. But in Connacht there was a junior branch of the De Burgos of whom a different story was to be told. William 'Liath' had left two sons, Ulick and Edmund 'Albanach' ('the Scotsman') so called because he had spent twenty years of his youth in Scotland. By feudal law all the De Burgo lands should go to the young heiress, but the two brothers stood by the Gaelic law of male succession in despite of royal wardship. Ulick seized upon all the family lands in county Galway, where he founded the Clan-rickard Burkes, and Edmund equally upon the Mayo lands, where he founded the Mayo Burkes. Thus arose two great families who lorded it over most of Connacht for two centuries without a legal title. On the borders of Limerick and Tipperary a third branch, called the lords of Castleconnell or Clanwilliam, were at this time founded by another Edmund, a younger son of the Red Earl.

The victory of these Norman-Irish was a triumph also for the Gaelic tradition and showed how little they cared for feudal titles compared with building up a kingship on the hearts of the native race. 'Twenty years did Edmund remain in Scotland,' says a Gaelic history of the family, 'when by the death of the Brown Earl tribe-extinction came upon the Burkes, and Edmund returned and landed in Umhall of

O'Maille ("the Owles of Mayo"), and his chief poet and ambassador to the Connachtmen was Donn O'Breslin, and Edmund took to wife the daughter of O'Maille.' The families which the two brothers founded became Irish chieftains; the Clanrickard branch were known as the 'Upper MacWilliam', the Mayo one as the 'Lower MacWilliam'. The O'Kellys of Hy Many, the O'Connors and other chiefs profited by the turn of events, and Connacht to all intents was lost to the English law and language. Thus in 1340 MacDermot, already lord of Moy Lurg and Airthech in north-west Roscommon, 'extended his sway over Sliabh Lugha (De Angulo's county) by the strong hand', and in 1317 O'Dowd 'recovered Tireragh from the English and divided it among his sept'. The feudal veneer alone remained. The Norman families which in 1235 had French names and spoke French were by the sixteenth century Irish speakers and known by such patronymics as MacCostello, MacJordan and so on. The feudal influence, however, was never lost, these families remained proud of their English blood, and up to recent times the population and the gentry of Connacht were a blend of Norman and Celt in which the blood of De Burgo's companions preponderated.

This revolution had its influence on the Ulster border, where the difficulties of mountain, lake, and river reinforced the warlike spirit of the native race and made Ulster in the sixteenth century the last province to succumb. The county and town of Sligo ceased to be a De Burgo lordship and O'Connor Sligo, a race descended from Brian of Leyny, became lords there with O'Donnell as suzerain. In Fermanagh also arose the ruling race of Maguire, the first of whom was Donn, installed by O'Donnell in about 1300. In Leitrim the O'Rourkes, and in Cavan the O'Reillys became rulers, and save for the eastern coast of Ulster English influence disappeared in the northern province.

Within a hundred years all over Ireland the Gaelic chiefs recovered large parts of their former lordships in hundreds of petty battles of which we have few details, in which Scottish galloglass and Irish kern defeated the horse and foot of the Norman stock. The general pressure due to the greater numbers and fertility of the native race also steadily pushed the invading stock back to the areas nearer to the towns and the coast. Many a castle built by the Normans fell to the Gaelic chiefs and became the strongholds of native lordships. In the use of armour, heraldry, banners, and fortifications the Irish chiefs became the imitators and then the equals of their feudal neighbours, with whom they began to intermarry and ally.

In east and central Ulster within seventy years there emerged several new native states: in Monaghan the lordship of MacMahon, in north Derry ('Cianacht') that of O'Cahan, in Inishowen O'Doherty, all founded on the ruin of the earldom. Only on the sea-coast did De Courcy's settlers survive, such as Byset, lord of the Glens, Savage, lord of the Ards, and Mande-ville of the Route in north Antrim. Even these feudal families soon lost their French character and adopted Gaelic law and surnames; thus did Mandeville become MacQuillan ('son of Ugolin').

The Irish chiefs had never willingly abandoned their ances-tral rights, and the disappearance of legal over-lords and absentees enabled them to rise again. A striking instance is recorded in Lysagh O'More, who about 1340 made himself again lord of Leix, where the Mortimers were titular possessors. 'He stirred up to war all the Irish of Munster and Leinster by persuasion, promises, and gifts, and expelled nearly all the English from their lands by force, for in one evening he burned eight castles of the Englishry, and destroyed the noble castle of Dunamase belonging to Roger Mortimer, and usurped to himself the lordship of the country. From a slave he became a lord, from a subject a prince.'

About the same time Taig O'Carroll 'slew or expelled from Ely (the country about Slieve Bloom) the nations of the Brets, Milbornes, and other English and occupied their lands and castles'. A similar triumph of O'Kennedy, the native heir to Ormond, lost to the Earl of Ormond his great lordship or manor of Nenagh in Tipperary and drove his dominion back to the south of that county and to county Kilkenny. It was also shown how fatal to the 'Land of Leinster' as an English colony was the wide mountain land which lay so near to the capital. The O'Byrnes and O'Tooles occupied by the strong hand the great tracts which by law belonged to the Crown and the archbishop, and O'Byrne finally ruled from Delgany down to the Butler manor of Arklow.

The race of Donal Kavanagh, descended from Donal, son of King Dermot, and called from him MacMurrough Kavanagh, as long as the Bigods remained lords of Carlow accepted their position as tenants under Strongbow's heirs and were favoured as 'Irishmen and kinsmen of Roger le Bygod, Earl Marshal'. But on the extinction of this family the rich county of Carlow lay open to them and they began to assert their former claims over Idrone and Hy Kinsella. By ancient right they were monarchs of Leinster, and in 1327 'the Irish of Leinster elected to themselves a king, Donal MacMurrough'. From this time on the MacMurroughs called themselves kings of Leinster and their domain finally stretched from Idrone to Ferns, where they recovered the old palace of King Dermot, which had been long in Norman hands.

Since the conquest of 1172 the native race, though they had made some valiant efforts to revive the High kingship, either in a Gael or a foreigner, had failed in their central objective. They did, however, in local combinations recover most of their old lordships and became in every part of the island what the English called 'captains of their nations' and 'lords of countries'.

THE CROWN AND THE ANGLO-IRISH

In later days Poynings' parliament attributed the decay of English rule to the beginning of Edward III's reign, from which the long decline of one hundred and sixty years set in. Edward indeed made a long attempt to bring the colony under imperial control, but, instead of coming himself with a large army, he could do nothing more than to issue ordinances and edicts from London and to send over English viceroys and officials to control and administer the government. This was resisted by the Anglo-Irish, led by several of the great magnates, who insisted that the affairs of Ireland should be settled in an Irish parliament and in Irish law courts subject to the royal supremacy and who favoured the appointment of native lords. We may call it, to anticipate modern terms, the clash of Unionism and Home Rule.

In 1341 the King sent over Sir John Morris with an edict that none but English-born should hold high legal office in Ireland. This was resisted by a patriot party, and when the viceroy called a parliament to Dublin the Earls of Desmond and Kildare instead summoned an assembly of their party to Kilkenny in November of that year which sent a long address to the King. Ireland, they said, is a third part lost to the Irish, the justiciars know nothing of Ireland, they override the rights of the subjects and enrich themselves at the expense of the country, the ministers are corrupt and negligent, cases are cited to England which could be settled in Ireland, and finally the act of Resumption of 1331 'is contrary to Magna Carta by which no man can be deprived of his freehold without due process of law'. Theirs, however, was a constitutional protest, and they ended by saying that while Scots, Gascons, and Welsh have often risen against the Crown 'your loyal English of Ireland have ever been loyal and please God will ever be so'.

The King withdrew the statute excluding the Anglo-Irish from office, but later, in 1344, Sir Ralf D'Ufford was sent over as viceroy for the reformation of Ireland, accompanied by his wife, widow of the murdered earl of Ulster. This strong governor made an expedition into Ulster in the attempt to recover the earldom and proclaimed a general pardon for the Anglo-Irish, but did not please them all the same. According to the Anglo-Irish annals 'This justiciar was an invader of the rights of the clerics and of the lay, rich and poor, a robber of goods under the colour of good, the defrauder of many, never observing the law of the Church nor that of the State, inflicting many evils on the native-born, the poor only excepted, in which things he was led by the council of his wife'. This statement reflects that Anglo-Irish sentiment which has so often thwarted English viceroys when bent upon crushing the great, whether Irish or Old English.

In the next year Desmond again called a rival parliament to Callan, but D'Ufford outlawed him, marched into Munster, and subdued the earldom. On taking the Earl's castle of Castle-island he had the Earl's seneschal and two others put to death for treason in 'exercising, maintaining, and inventing many foreign, oppressive and intolerable laws'. These apparently were that combination of Irish and feudal exactions, generally called coyne and livery and 'March law', which were so odious to the government and the loyal colonists.   After D'Ufford's death in 1346 the royal policy was again suspended; a general pardon proclaimed; and the Anglo-Irish had Magna Carta again confirmed to them.

Finally the Earl of Desmond was pardoned and restored. In Earl Maurice we see the first case of a Norman-Irish magnate openly opposing English government in Ireland.   While he led the Anglo-Irish the Gaels also regarded him as the greatest of those settlers who by now showed an affection for Irish speech and Irish poets, and the Geraldines, who had never been English in England, were soon to become Irish in Ireland.

In the midst of this struggle, the Black Death fell upon Ireland and proved a scourge to the colony not less than Bruce's invasion.   The native Irish, being a rural and scattered race, escaped better than the Anglo-Irish population who were clustered in towns and manors.   The plague was to reduce still further their limited numbers.   The Friar Clyn, whose Latin annals are the best we have for this time, ends his chronicles with this pestilence of which he himself died at Kilkenny. 'This pestilence raged so', he says, under 1349, 'at Kilkenny that on the 6th day of March eight Friars preachers died in one day, and in the city seldom did one only die in a house, but commonly the man and the wife with their children and servants together took the one road of death.'

Among the later English viceroys the most meritorious was Sir Thomas Rokeby, who ruled from 1350 to 1355, and with the usual small but well-equipped force of the time, paid for from England, of light horse (hoblers), archers, and men-at-arms, at least preserved the borders of 'the English land'. Under him we note an attempt to secure obedience and responsibility among the Irish septs whom no longer either the government or the colonists could dispossess.   In 1350 Rokeby made terms with three chiefs of the Dublin border, namely John O'Byrne, captain elect of his nation, Walter Harold, and Matthew Archbold, who had been elected chiefs by the leading men of their name.   The government confirmed these men as captains of their nations and as responsible for keeping their people in order.   Of the three we note that two are old Ostmen names, of families which had become lords along the slopes of the Dublin mountains and turned themselves into Irish septs. Henceforth the recognition of such Irish captains was a frequent practice of the government, to the end of the sixteenth century.

After the death of Maurice, earl of Desmond, in 1356 Anglo-Irish magnates ruled Ireland as justiciars till the coming of Lionel of Clarence.   Royal ordinances to appease the wounded feelings of the 'English by blood' declared that 'the affairs of the land of Ireland shall be referred to our Council *here* but shall be determined in our parliament *there*'.   'All Englishmen born in Ireland shall be taken to be true Englishmen like those born in England, bound by the same laws, rights, and customs.' An edict of 1361 declared that 'no pure-blooded Irishman of Irish nation shall be made mayor, bailiff, or officer in any place subject to the king or hold a canonry or living among the English; yet at the request of Irish clerics living among the English we ordain that such Irishmen, of whose loyalty our judges are assured, shall not be molested'.   In this decree the Crown drew the distinction between the independent Irish living under Brehon law and those individuals who dwelt peaceably among the English.

LIONEL, DUKE OF CLARENCE, IN IRELAND, 1361–1367

The Anglo-Irish had often asked for the King or a prince of the blood to come over, and now in Lionel of Clarence, Edward's second son, a tall, handsome, young Plantagenet, they had all they had looked for.   Lionel, who was appointed lieutenant in July 1361 with almost sovereign powers, was already in virtue of his wife earl of Ulster and lord of Connacht.   To recover these lost lordships was his personal object, to extend 'the land of peace' and organize the colony was his public object. The evil of absenteeism was now shown when no less than sixty-four titular lords of land in Ireland were specially ordered to accompany him, who included the inheritors of Leix, Carlow, Wexford, and Kilkenny.   With several of these he landed at Dublin in September 1361 with an army of fifteen hundred men, all that the King could spare from the French war.

When Lionel called on the Anglo-Irish to reinforce him he found that they were far from zealous in a war against their Irish neighbours, and the Earl of Kildare and others stood aloof when he marched against the Irish at Wicklow. For all that he waged some vigorous campaigns against the septs of Leinster, captured Art More MacMurrough, king of Leinster, and in Cork restored to their wasted lands some of the old English. For a time he checked the loss of Ulster, but a resident lord was needed there and Lionel like all young Englishmen of his time chafed at the Irish service and longed to be in France, where chivalric glory and rich booty were to be made at every battle. It was partly due to this weariness that he finally summoned as a solution of the Irish problem the ever-famous Parliament of Kilkenny in February 1366. His one lasting contribution to Irish history was to be the division and estrangement of the two races in Ireland for nearly three centuries.

In this assembly thirty-five acts in all were passed in the Norman-French which was the legal language of the time. The preamble runs thus: 'Whereas at the conquest of the land of Ireland and for a long time after, the English of the said land used the English language, mode of riding and apparel, and were governed and ruled, and their subjects called Betaghs, by the English law, in which time God and Holy Church, and their franchises according to their conditions, were maintained, and they themselves lived, in subjection; now many English of the said land, forsaking the English language, fashion, mode of riding, laws and usages, live and govern themselves according to the manners, fashion, and language of the Irish enemies, and have also made divers marriages and alliances between themselves and the Irish enemies aforesaid; whereby the said land and the liege people thereof, the English language, the allegiance due to our lord the King, and the English laws there, are put in subjection and decayed.'

To prevent these evils stringent laws are enacted. The English are forbidden by severe penalties to make fosterage, marriage or gossipred with the Irish or in law cases to use

Brehon law or the 'law of the Marches', or to entertain Irish minstrels, poets or story-tellers.[1] They must not sell to the Irish in time of peace or war horses or armour, or in time of war any victuals. They and the Irish among them must use English surnames of colour, trade, place, etc., must speak English and follow English customs. For the purpose of war they must practise with the bow and ride with the saddle after the English fashion. If they use the Irish speech they shall forfeit their lands to their lords until they undertake to use English. The Irish are excluded from cathedrals, abbeys, and benefices among the English. Every 'chieftain of English lineage' shall arrest evildoers of his own lineage or following until they are delivered by the law. Only on the Marches shall kerns and hired soldiers be maintained. In every county of the land of peace there shall be four keepers of the peace to assess and review the English for military service. This 'land of peace' is reckoned as the counties and liberties of Louth, Meath, Trim, Dublin, Kildare, Kilkenny, Wexford, Waterford, and Tipperary.

The statutes of Kilkenny remained in force for over two centuries. After enacting them, in November 1366 Lionel left Ireland for good, and in October 1368 died in Italy. He left by his wife, Elizabeth de Burgo, only one child, Philippa, who later marrying Edmund Mortimer, earl of March, passed the earldom of Ulster to the Mortimers and in the end to the crown of England.

The Statutes of Kilkenny marked the failure of the Conquest of Ireland as it was meant to be, viz. a complete reduction of the whole island to English law and Norman lordship. Their object on the English side was 'to cut the losses' and in abandoning a large part of Ireland to enforce in the still 'English land' the use of English law, custom, and speech. It was only in the so-called 'obedient shires', covering about a third of Ireland, that the government hoped to count on a continued English population, the enforcement of royal orders, and the

[1] A parliament of 1351 had already spoken of this 'March law' thus: 'Whereas in disputes among English and English they have been wont to be governed by the law of the March and the Brehon law, *which is not law and ought not to be called law and is not the law of the land,*' etc.

use of the Common law. The 'degenerate' English on the Marches were by origin Frenchmen, in the course of two centuries they were becoming Irish, and they lived in a feudal world of their own, in which Irish and feudal law were strangely mingled, and in which they ceased to pay their homages, dues, and services to the Crown. In order to keep them for the English connexion, they were now allowed to maintain Irish troops, and were made responsible for not only their families but their followers and retainers as if they were 'captains of their nations'. It was hoped that penalties or concessions would prevent their becoming still further Irish. The loyal English, for their part, were to return to the use of the bow and the heavy Norman saddle, for it was by such that their first victories had been won. In the obedient shires the militia duty was to be enforced and wardens of the peace were to supervise it. Thus between the common folk of the counties and the feudal bulwark in the Marches the English land might be kept intact.

The phrase 'chieftains of the English lineage' is significant. These were the Butlers, Burkes, Roches, Geraldines, and such who now lorded it over a third of the island. A further phrase, 'captains of their nations', is henceforth a legal phrase and fact applied till the end of the sixteenth century to the chiefs and lords, both Gaelic and Norman. But, whatever government might enact, in fact the Gaelic speech and culture with all its attraction of music, poetry, and epic was destined to capture the chiefs of lineage and their English vassals. That which might have prevented it was not attempted, such as a fresh influx of the more modern English race or a university which might have made an English culture-centre of Dublin.[1]

The phrase 'Irish enemy' is equally significant. Since John's reign the admission of the native Irish to English law and liberty had been a burning question, it had often been asked for and on the royal side granted and by the selfish colonial feeling thwarted. Now the question was solved in a way fatal

---

[1] A university had been attempted in Dublin in 1310–1320 by Bikenor, archbishop of Dublin, but came to nothing, and Ireland had no State university till Trinity College was founded in 1592.

to the union and fusion of both races.   It is not too much to
speak of the *Outlawry of the Irish race* as enacted by these
statutes.   Admission to English law was henceforth limited to
the Irish 'living among the English' and accepting the English
tradition, or to grants made for fee or favour to some head of
an Irish sept and his kinsmen.   The charters of emancipation
frequently granted, of which many survive or are recorded,
attest by the provisions of the rights to which the recipient
is now admitted the disabilities that the Irish suffered when
'rightless' in the eyes of the law.[1]

The Irish themselves, it must be admitted, contributed to
this final division.   Clinging proudly to the Irish language and
their own law, what did they know or care for sheriffs, assizes,
juries, the procedure and the dreadful penalties of the Common
law, expressed in French and English.   The time had now
come, they thought, to reverse the Conquest and recover large
parts of Ireland, in which they could enjoy as before the old
Gaelic ideal of life.

From the English point of view no area was properly English
and no population truly under the Crown unless it was organized shire-land, and hence till the reign of James I large areas
in the west and north were not subject either to the benefits
or duties of law.   Nevertheless the legal titles of the first
conquerors and the rights of the Crown, even if for two centuries they were abandoned, did not become dead in law, and
it remained for many a chief in the sixteenth century to be
told that legally he and his people were mere encroachers and
intruders upon some Englishman's land or an inheritance of
the Crown.   For such an injustice the statutes of Kilkenny
remained the first legal quotation.

The mass of the Irish had never been in full possession of
English liberty, but by tacit acceptance the chief dynasts, the
so-called Five Bloods, had been law-worthy.   Now even this
was taken away from the proudest of the Irish kings, who

[1] These charters, granted to an individual 'of Irish nation', which
went on till the end of Elizabeth's reign, allow the recipient and his
issue to buy, inherit, bequeath, and transfer land and property, to
trade freely and follow professions, to have justice done to himself and
to answer for himself in the King's courts, to enjoy Church livings and
offices (if a cleric) and to have and use all other such rights as the
King's liege subjects use and enjoy.

henceforth were regarded as rightless and of 'Irish conditio and servitude'. They were no longer subjects and could not inherit or hold land, or have office or living among the Englishry or have justice done in their courts. Thus did the old native race, in so far as it lived its own life, become in legal parlance *'the King's Irish enemies'*, a very significant phrase. But the English, however 'degenerate' and rebel they might become, remained always 'English lieges', who might be recovered to loyalty and their duty.

To enforce these discriminating acts was to prove a task almost impossible. What was to prevent the feudal English from intermarriage and fosterage with so attractive and proud a race as the Gaels? Many instances prove that they could not be prevented, though for long the great earls did not take to themselves Irish wives. Royal licence could be obtained or purchased to break these laws, and later on acts of parliament could be passed to that effect; nevertheless they hung over the heads of offenders, and in the next century an earl of Desmond was executed on the charge of violating them.

English law once enacted, even by a petty parliament of the Pale, was a sharp-edged sword, even though it was generally suspended. Two outstanding instances of when it fell are those of Art Oge MacMurrough Kavanagh, king of Leinster, who, when he married Elizabeth le Veel, heiress of the barony of Norragh in Kildare, was not allowed as an 'Irish enemy' to enter upon a feudal estate; the other is that of Conn O'Neill, son of the reigning O'Neill, who married a daughter of the Earl of Kildare, yet this marriage was not valid in law for him or her until an act of Parliament in 1480 enfranchised him and his issue by her.

The statutes of Kilkenny were given the most solemn force possible by the signature of the royal duke and the full consent of the council and parliament, and at the request of the archbishops of Dublin, Cashel, and Tuam, and the bishops of Waterford–Lismore, Killaloe, Ossory, Leighlin, and Cloyne, who, 'all being present at the said parliament did fulminate sentence of excommunication against those contravening the aforesaid statutes'.

There was no protest on the part of the native Church and lay leaders. For over two hundred years the chiefs cared for little but the recovery of their local lordships, nor did they realize the future danger for them in the acts of a parliament which, though it only represented the colonists, could legislate for all Ireland and had now legalized the outlawry of the native race. Yet up to 1625 the law had little difficulty in proving the Irish mere squatters on 'Englishmen's or Crown lands' and so dispossessing them or reducing them to mere leaseholders or tenants-at-will. According to the English, after 1366 all the 'mere Irish' living under Brehon law were *of Irish and servile condition*. Even a man of Irish surname, living in a town or manor, might have his right to his property or trade questioned. The Irish knew well the difference between 'free races' ('saor-chlanna') and 'unfree races' ('daor-chlanna') in their own law, but ignored or did not understand the hidden machinery of royal or feudal law which could be used to destroy them. The Anglo-Irish, on the other hand, though many of them became 'degenerate', never lost the protection of Common law and Magna Carta, and thus between the 'King's Irish rebels' and the 'King's Irish enemies' there remained always a world of difference.

Few could have seen how the Kilkenny statutes would work. After 1366 the English language ordained in them dwindled away and until the seventeenth century had no great history in Ireland. The French of the feudal class became rusty and died out among them, save in the nearer parts, but it was Irish and not the English of Chaucer that they acquired instead.

The statutes of Kilkenny became to the colonists almost as sacred as Magna Carta and were many times reissued. The penalties were always there and served to keep all privileges in the hands of the Englishry. But when in Poynings' parliament in 1495 they were once more enacted, there had to be passed over those two acts which forbade the speaking of Irish and riding after the Irish fashion. So common by that time among the English and even in the Pale had the language and horsemanship of the 'Irish enemy' become.

E

CHAPTER IX

LAST EFFORTS OF THE ENGLISH LORDSHIP,
1366–1399

ROYAL visits, such as those of Lionel, covering a number of years, would doubtless have preserved a large part of Ireland to the English Crown. But not for many years again was a royal prince to be seen in Ireland, and after the departure of Clarence the native chiefs continued their re-conquests. The Englishry were pushed back in many a point along the border, and among the states founded by the warrior chiefs we may note two in Ulster and one in Desmond. In the latter there were already the two MacCarthy chiefs, MacCarthy More and MacCarthy Reagh of Carbery; now there arose a Dermot MacCarthy whom Lionel had for a time checked, but who by his death in 1368 had created by the strong hand a third lordship for this race, that of Muskerry in west Cork. In Ulster the earldom was assailed by chiefs bent upon carving out new lordships, and among these Cumhaidhe O'Cathain, called in English tradition 'Cooey na Gall' ('of the Foreigners', because he spent his youth among the English and learned their use of armour and tactics), founded a lordship in the present county of Derry, called Iraght O'Cahan.

A still greater state was that of the O'Neills of Clandeboy, a race descended from the Aedh Buidhe who was king of Tír Eoghain in 1280. Because the Earl of Ulster had favoured him, his children were allowed to expand at the expense of older native chiefs on the east side of the Bann, while Donal O'Neill, son of Brian, continued the line of 'The Great O'Neill of Tyrone'. In the course of a century from about 1350 the O'Neills of Clandeboy founded a Gaelic state which stretched from the Glens of Antrim to Belfast and the north part of Down. They conquered not only the colonial land but also wiped out the MacDunlevys and O'Flynns, who had formerly ruled in Ulidia.

Meanwhile the Dublin government could command little

more than Leinster and the towns. On the borders it left the feudal lords and 'the chieftains of lineage' to cope with the Irish as best they could, and in order to do so these earls and barons hired kerns and 'bonnaughts' (Irish mercenaries). Already in 1314 Edmund Butler had 'put Dermot son of Turloch O'Brien and his kerns at coign on the English farmers of his country'. 'Coign' was the billeting of troops on one's tenants according to old Irish law, but it was hateful to the feudal class and caused the exodus of many of the lesser Englishry from Ireland.

The three Earls of Kildare, Desmond, and Ormond were now the leaders of the 'English by blood'. Of the three, Gerald, third earl of Desmond (1359–1398), ruled four counties in the south, while James Butler, second earl of Ormond 1350–1382), by royal grants had the Palatine lordship of Tipperary and the prisage of wines throughout Ireland. The Desmond Geraldines were before long to turn Irish, but the Butlers remained loyal to the English connexion, and this was due to a royal marriage. The first Earl of Ormond, James, married Eleanor Bohun, a granddaughter of Edward I; their son, called the 'noble earl' as a kinsman of the King, inherited rich lands in England.

It was the 'land of peace' which continued to occupy the main attention of the English Crown. In 1368 at a council in Guildford the King stated that he had heard from the faithful subjects of Ireland 'how that the Irish ride in hostile array through every part of the said land so that it is at point to be lost if remedy be not immediately supplied'. He therefore had summoned a parliament to Dublin in May 1367, which advised that the only salvation was in the continuous residence of the Earls and others who have inheritance in Ireland. The King therefore now by the advice of his English peers and council ordained that those in England who have lands in Ireland should return to reside or supply men for the defence of the same before next Easter, or in default be deprived of those lands. This was the first Absentee act; there was to be a still more severe one in 1380.

The French war was now proving a failure and England had little money or men to spare for Ireland, but among the transient viceroys a strong man was found in Sìr William de Windsor (1369–1376), who came in June 1369 with the title of Lieutenant. In the first year of his office a great triumph for the Irish took place in Munster. Brian O'Brien, king of Thomond, crossed the Shannon and at Monasteraneany defeated his enemy, the Earl of Desmond, and took him prisoner on July 10th 1370. He then occupied and looted Limerick and the Earl was only ransomed after a tedious captivity by the lieutenant. O'Brien and the Irish of Munster, Connacht, and Leinster were now, it was said, 'confederated to make a universal conquest of Ireland'. To cope with such a rising, Windsor attempted to wring money out of the colony, and in 1371, besides getting local grants, he forced one parliament at Kilkenny into granting three thousand pounds and another at Baldoyle two thousand pounds. This was more than the Anglo-Irish could pay in one year and on their protest the aged King recalled him but soon sent him back to raise the needed supplies. In 1375 Edward directed the Irish parliament to send sixty representatives to appear before the English Council with their complaints in February 1376, namely, two from each county to represent the nobles and commons, two from each town, and two clerics from each diocese. Although they sent these delegates, the united Parliament declared that 'according to the rights and liberties enjoyed from the time of the Conquest and before, they were not bound to send such representatives, and though they now elected them they reserved the right of assenting to any subsidies made in their name; moreover, their present compliance was not hereafter to be taken in prejudice of the rights, laws and customs which they had enjoyed from the time of the Conquest and before'.

Nothing came of the visit of the Irish deputies to England, save that the council superseded Windsor and made Ormond justiciar in July 1376. They attempted to impeach Windsor and their complaints were heard in the Good Parliament of April–July 1376. In this famous parliament the process of Impeachment originated, and possibly the Irish complaints aided it; in fact, however, as long as it lasted the Irish parliament was never able to impeach ministers of state, who were responsible only to the Crown in England. But from this time the Irish parliament took a final shape, which lasted till 1537. It was now established that for taxation purposes the assent of parliament was necessary and local taxation by agreement with towns, estates, and counties ceased. In the parliament or council of 1372 two clerical proctors from each diocese were added to the commons. The obligation of lay magnates to attend parliament became a matter of tenure-in-chief of the Crown and the writs of individual summons were restricted to the earls, barons, and prelates.

After the departure of Windsor the Irish in their various combinations attacked the colony on every side. Of all the losses since that of Ulster the worst was that of the once English 'Land of Leinster'. It might almost be said that had geography made this province a land as level as Meath England's first conquest of Ireland would never have been a failure. Though Norman towns and manors encircled Leinster, the whole wild inland country, which was the nominal demesne of the King and Archbishop, in reality remained in the hands of the O'Byrnes and O'Tooles. By 1400 the whole lovely eastern coast from Bray to Arklow was a solitary stretch where scarcely an English ship appeared, where there was scarcely a colonist and where only the royal castles of Wicklow and Newcastle kept a precarious hold. The O'Byrnes became lords not only of the mountains but of the coast from Bray to Arklow and so inland to Shillelagh. And Glenmalure, the wildest and most impenetrable defile in Wicklow, was their final stronghold.

The natural leader of the Leinster Irish was MacMurrough Kavanagh, the descendant of Donal Kavanagh. For over a century his race, left in possession of part of Hy Kinsella, and favoured by the Bigod descendants of Strongbow, remained fairly peaceable, but on the extinction of the Bigods in 1306 they reasserted their old kingdom of Leinster. Carlow was renewed as a fief to Thomas of Brotherton, younger son of Edward I, but on the passing of this feudal state to an absentee English prince the MacMurroughs seized the opportunity to assert their ancient kingship, and in 1327 the Irish of Leinster had met and chosen as king over them Donal son of Art MacMurrough.

From this time until the days of Henry VIII MacMurrough Kavanagh styled himself 'Rex Lagenie'.

Absenteeism and the extinction of Anglo-Norman families favoured the Irish recovery. The two baronies of Idrone and Forth O'Nolan, formerly the heritage of Raymond le Gros in Carlow, fell into MacMurrough hands when the Carews, barons of Idrone, expired about 1370. So did the Kavanaghs build up the old Hy Kinsella again, rich and level country backed by the inaccessible range of Mount Leinster and by great woods from which no Norman force could hope to dislodge them. The Dublin government realized so pressing a danger, and Duke Lionel made war on the Leinster Irish and captured Art More, son of the Donal of 1327, who ended his days in Dublin Castle. But his elder son Donal took his place and in 1372 had to be bought off with a fee of eighty marks from the Exchequer, which became an annuity regularly paid to the MacMurroughs up to the year 1536.

ART OGE MACMURROUGH, KING OF LEINSTER, 1376–1417

In Art Oge appeared the greatest of Donal's descendants and of the medieval chiefs of Ireland the one who most ruined the English colony. Inaugurated king of Leinster in 1376, Art took the field with colours flying, and, summoning all the hereditary vassals of the old kings of Leinster, the O'Mores, O'Connors, O'Byrnes, O'Dempseys, and the rest, ravaged the colonial lands until the terrified officials of the Exchequer renewed to him the grant made to his uncle.

And now the Anglo-Irish at last got a Prince of the Blood as viceroy. Edmund Mortimer, third earl of March, was husband of Philippa, daughter of Lionel of Clarence. In May 1380 he landed as the King's lieutenant with a considerable army, bent upon the recovery of his Irish estates, but after a long and gallant march as far northwards as Coleraine and then back to Dunamase in Leix, where he made O'More swear vassalage again, and then down to Cork, he died suddenly in December 1381. Himself a young man, he left by Philippa an infant heir, Roger, a boy of eight, who in 1385 was declared heir to the throne after Richard.

Richard II succeeded to the throne of England in 1377, a boy of eleven, who as he grew to manhood proved himself of a sensitive and artistic temperament marred by weakness and indecision and ill-fitted to cope with the violent nobles who surrounded the throne. For Ireland Richard seems to have had a real solicitude and a desire to set things right. His lordship there was full of lapsed fiefs, and Ulster, Connacht, Westmeath, and a large part of Leinster might be reckoned as gone. Close to Dublin the Irish septs held the great mountain plateau and menaced Wexford, Carlow, and Kildare. The absentee evil was a very great one, for by it English lands passed to the neighbouring Irish and Normans. An exodus had set in of the more English tenantry, while the further Englishry were becoming Irish in language, law, dress, and warlike pursuits. The more the colony dwindled in size and English order, the greater became the heads of the original families. The two Burkes dominated most of Connacht, the Kildare earldom spread from Kildare to meet in Carlow the power of the Butlers, with whom the lands of the Desmond earls marched at Clonmel and Kilfeakle. The Earls of Ormond had lost to the O'Kennedys upper Ormond, but in south Tipperary and in Kilkenny they formed a compact power which reached its height when in 1391 the Despenser heir of the Liberty of Kilkenny conveyed to James, third earl of Ormond, his manor and castle at Kilkenny with numerous rich lands and manors attached. This great territory with its centre in the noble castle that overlooks the Nore became under its Palatine lords an almost sovereign state and an 'English land' in speech and culture second only to the Pale itself.

The Irish chiefs were now all bent on building up their local lordships, and the dream of restoring the High kingship was abandoned. They did, however, admit the judicial, political, and military supremacy of the old province kings, and even as MacMurrough was admitted to be king by his 'urraghts' so were O'Neill and O'Connor. The Irish mind could well conceive of a De Burgo as 'Lord of the English of Connacht' and an O'Connor as 'king of the Gael of Connacht', existing side by side. For this later title there were now two claimants.

Turloch Donn and Turloch Ruadh O'Connor; their feud was fatal to the old kingship, and though in 1385 they came to an understanding, the kingship was never united again.[1]

Imitating the Normans in war, castles, and heraldry, the Irish chiefs strove also to attain that primogeniture which gave the feudal class much of its stability. The 'derb-fine' rule for the succession to chieftainships lasted indeed till 1603 with the claims of the 'Rig-domnas', or royal heirs, but *Tanistry* was now general, by which in the lifetime of a chief a 'Tanist' or successor was appointed who would rule till the chief's son came of age. This narrowed down the succession, and it would seem that the Tanist's son rarely claimed to succeed his father after the interim. In one or two families such as MacCarthy and O'Neill of Tyrone a long-sustained and successful effort took place to secure the succession from father to son, but the claims of 'royal heirs' according to law were often asserted and led to long and destructive succession-wars.

The way for Richard's visit was prepared by a number of viceroys, of whom the most gallant figure is James, third Earl of Ormond, a brave knight who spoke the native language fluently and was trusted by the Irish. The King's Irish advisers, such as John Colton, archbishop of Armagh, sent long and eloquent reports on the Irish situation. In these reports the name of Art MacMurrough often occurred and inspired Richard with the determination that in him was the chief 'Irish enemy'. Art with an army of his vassals had occupied most of county Carlow and further in 1390 had married Elizabeth Calfe, heiress of the barony of Norragh in county Kildare. In her name he claimed this estate, but the law did not admit that a 'mere Irishman' could hold English land, and so he was denied possession. In his anger he committed dreadful ravages, with a great host burned the town of Naas, and wrought ruin among the Englishry of counties Kildare, Wexford, and Carlow.

King Richard landed at Waterford on October 2nd 1394 with

[1] From this Turloch 'Donn' ('the Brown') we get the still surviving title of O'Connor Don.

a large army, and all the royal power was for once exercised in Ireland by the monarch. The English parliament had granted large sums for the recovery of Ireland and Richard called upon the great absentees to accompany him.[1] Before his departure he restored the Honour of Carlow to Thomas Mowbray, earl of Nottingham and Earl Marshal, who came with the King, as did also Roger Mortimer, heir to the throne, and earl of March and Ulster.

From Waterford Richard marched up the Barrow, admiring on his way the luxuriant beauty of Leinster, and sending his lieutenants inland to wage war on Art MacMurrough, who burned New Ross but fell back before the English on to his woodland fastness of Garbh-choill at the foot of Mount Leinster.

Marching by Kilkenny, Richard reached Dublin in November and spent the Christmas there in the castle. There the great plan for Ireland was evolved. In a letter to his uncle, Edmund of York, Regent of England, Richard divided Ireland into 'the wild Irish, our enemies; English rebels; and obedient English'. Of the English 'rebels' he wrote 'they have become disobedient through injustice practised upon them by our officers and if they are not won over they will join the Irish enemies'. As for the Irish, he had already written from England to O'Neill, as the greatest of the Irish, promising 'to do justice to every man'.

According to the plan which the Earl of Ormond, the archbishops of Armagh and Tuam and others suggested to the King, the Irish were to be induced into an honourable submission and recognized as vassals of the Crown, with the exception of Art MacMurrough. On the Irish side, it seems that O'Connor and other chiefs urged Niall More O'Neill to lead a general resistance to Richard, but Archbishop Colton induced the king of Tír Eoghain to submit, Ormond and

---

[1] A statute of Absentees for Ireland was passed in the English Parliament of 1380 by which all subjects who have lands, rents, benefices, offices, and other possessions in Ireland shall return to reside there and hold such lands, etc., or send men to defend them; otherwise two-thirds of the profits shall be forfeited to the use of the justiciar and government for the use and defence of the State. This important act was often put into force in the next two centuries.

Desmond induced MacCarthy, O'Brien, and the southern chiefs to do the same, and the result was the greatest homaging of native Ireland to an English king that took place between 1172 and 1540.

The royal policy had four distinct objects:

(a) The Irish chiefs except MacMurrough and his Leinster vassals were to surrender the lands they had 'usurped' from the English and promised a double obedience in future to the King as liege-lord and to the Norman earls to whom they owed simple homage as their suzerains. In return they were to be confirmed in their 'Irish lands', namely, those territories which they had always held from the time of the Conquest.

(b) The 'rebel English' were to be pardoned and restored to their due allegiance. Of these, however, only eight, from Munster and Connacht, appeared to claim their pardon.

(c) A definitely 'English land' was to be created in eastern Ireland, east of a line drawn from Dundalk to the Boyne and down the Barrow to Waterford. In this English 'Pale' a new colony was to be planted and grants were to be made to new Englishmen.

(d) In order to carry out the latter, the warlike Art Mac-Murrough and his vassals must be compelled to quit the lands of Leinster.

On January 20th 1395, at Drogheda, Niall More made his submission to Richard, and his example was followed by all the chiefs of the Gaelic race save O'Donnell, his vassals in Fermanagh and Sligo, and the barbarous chieftains of the Connacht seaboard. Between January and May 1395 the King, the Earl Marshal, Ormond and other magnates received at Dublin or other centres the homage and submission of eighty paramount chiefs, who sometimes appeared with their tanists. At Drogheda on March 16th Niall Oge O'Neill sub-mitted to the King in the name of his father, 'prince of the Irish of Ulster', and also did simple homage to the Earl of Ulster. He promised to surrender all lands, lordships, and liberties unlawfully possessed by him or others under him, surrendering to the Earl the 'Bonnacht' or military service of the Irish of Ulster, and to come to parliaments and councils when summoned by the King, his heirs, or his deputies. He was followed by a whole body of his vassals, such as Magennis and MacMahon, who took the same terms; while John or Shane MacDonnell, who called himself 'constable of the Irish of Ulster', submitted separately.[1] From south Ulster and Meath came in O'Reilly of Brefni and other 'captains of their nations' and so further south the chiefs of northern Munster, O'Kennedy and others, who accepted Ormond as their over-lord. On March 1st, at Dublin, Brian O'Brien, 'prince of the Irish of Thomond', did homage and was followed by a group of vassals in Clare. In like fashion did Turloch Donn O'Connor, 'prince of the Irish of Connacht', submit at Waterford for himself and a group of vassals covering a large part of that province; while at Kilkenny Taig MacCarthy More ('Major'), 'prince of the Irish of Desmond', submitted and accepted Desmond as his over-lord; along with him MacCarthy, lord of Muskerry, bowed the knee.[2]

The title 'Prince of the Irish of Ulster', etc., in the case of O'Neill, O'Connor, O'Brien, and MacCarthy attests the survival to this time of the old provincial kingships, at least in the mind of the native race. In one or two areas, such as Meath and north Munster, they had ceased to exist. But it is significant that after this solemn and general submission to their English lord the greater Irish chiefs dropped the title of 'king', and henceforth MacCarthy is MacCarthy More, instead of 'king of Desmond'. But MacMurrough Kavanagh continued on his seal and elsewhere to use 'Rex Lagenie' up to Henry VIII's reign, and the annals, which are very conservative, continue to use the name 'Rí' for the great princes.

For the Leinster rebels against whom Richard had sent his troops with fire and sword the terms were to be different. The Earl Marshal as Lord of Carlow dealt with Art Mac-Murrough, who by this time found himself abandoned in his

[1] This John was a brother of Donal MacDonnell of Harlaw, Lord of the Isles; expelled by Donal, he had taken to the galloglass profession under O'Neill. In 1399 he married Margery Byset, heiress of the Glens of Antrim, and founded a MacDonnell lordship there.

[2] The chief vassals of the province kings, such as MacMahon, vassal of O'Neill, are called by the Anglo-Irish 'urraghs' or 'urraghts', a corruption either of 'oirrigh', under-king, or 'oireacht', the assembly of a king's chief vassals and electors.

resistance, and on January 7th 1395, at Tullow in Carlow, the king of Leinster pledged himself with all his vassals and fighting-men by the first Sunday of Lent to quit Leinster and go at the King's pay to conquer lands elsewhere occupied by rebels and enemies, which lands they should hold for ever of the King and his successors. Further, Art was granted the barony of Norragh and the annual fee of eighty marks for life. To these terms his 'urraghs', O'Byrne, O'Toole, O'Connor, and others, also bound themselves, and at Ballygory on February 16th Art and his under-chiefs did homage to the Earl Marshal.

In the midst of all this homaging, on March 25th Richard knighted four Irish kings in Dublin, and of this ceremony and their behaviour Froissart gives a picturesque account. Charmed with so easy a surrender, Richard made several fine grants of lands in Leinster to his admiral, John de Beaumont, and others. By the end of April, however, Richard began to think of his return to England, to which the Lollard and other problems recalled him. Probably the King's facile imagination, which had been kindled with the idea of setting Ireland right, had now subsided. Though he had intended a parliament in Dublin, none such met to ratify the Irish submission or possibly to reverse the Statutes of Kilkenny. On May 1st, on board his ship at Waterford, Richard knighted William de Burgo of Clanrickard, Walter de Bermingham of Athenry, two 'English rebels' and Turloch O'Connor Don, and so on May 15th he departed with all his chivalry for England, thus repeating the mistake of Henry II and John in leaving Ireland before their work was completed. It was, however, regarded as a spectacular triumph in England.

The Irish chiefs had done their homage and taken their oaths in one language only, Irish, while the Norman 'rebels' took theirs in French or English. From what we read in Froissart of their taciturn pride and democratic sense and from their letters to the King, we can gather the difficulty of making these patriarchal kings into liege vassals of the Crown and members of the English-speaking parliament of Dublin.

It is doubtful if the 'English land' was increased by a single acre as a result of these imposing submissions of 1395. They had been a triumph for the Gaelic chiefs, who were now admitted to be legal possessors of the land they had inherited, even if they must surrender lands 'usurped'. In return they had admitted the King as their sovereign, and in the case of Mac-Carthy, O'Kennedy, and O'Neill, admitted the Earls of Desmond, Ormond, and Ulster as their immediate lords, so that no doubt could now exist that they had received a status in English law for their lands and chieftainships. Successfully completed on both sides, these treaties might have solved the great problem of the relation of the Irish princes to the English Crown. But in fact the bargains were not carried out, and O'Neill and the rest made no attempt to hand over the 'English lands' which they were said to have usurped, while Mac-Murrough and the Leinster chiefs made not the slightest attempt to quit the land of Leinster. Nor was the great submission ever legalized by enactment of the Dublin parliament.

On the English side the refusal of the chiefs, especially MacMurrough, to fulfil the terms was denounced as a breach of faith and led to Richard II's second expedition. Nevertheless their submission was regarded as binding the future, and one of the arguments put forward by Henry VIII in taking the Crown of Ireland in 1540 was the general acceptance of Richard II as over-lord in 1395.

Roger Mortimer was now left as Lieutenant to enforce the terms and to recover his lordships of Leix and Ulster. In doing so he was slain in a battle of Kellistown in Carlow on July 20th 1398 against an army of the Leinster Irish, in which he was said rashly to have worn only the linen dress of an Irish chief. Himself but twenty-five years of age, Mortimer left only an infant son, Edmund, and a daughter Anne.

The news of this disaster filled King Richard with fury and despair, for Roger was heir to the childless king and his chief lieutenant in his struggle with the baronial party. He revoked MacMurrough's grant of Norragh, and on June 1st 1399 landed at Waterford with a large army, vowing to burn MacMurrough out of his woods. Again he marched by Kilkenny and sent the Earl of Gloucester to bring MacMurrough to submission.

A meeting of the feudal host in its full panoply of armed knights in serried ranks and the light levies of the Irish under the king of Leinster in some unnamed glen of these wild mountains is the subject of one of the few illuminated pictures we have of Irish medieval history. Art MacMurrough is represented as riding a splendid black horse, without saddle or housings, which had cost four hundred cows. He wears a high, conical cap covering the nape of the neck, a parti-coloured cloak. long coat and under-coat, all of gay yellow, crimson, and blue.[1] He is described as a fine, large, handsome man, of stern, indomitable bearing, who refused to submit and boldly declared, 'I am rightful king of Ireland and it is unjust to deprive me of what is my land by conquest.'

From Dublin Richard himself marched back to Waterford, for events in England compelled the return of him and his grand army. There the news of Derby's landing at Ravenspur reached him, and the last of the Plantagenets sailed from Ireland on August 13th 1399 to meet his tragic doom of deposition and death.

---

[1] *See* 'King Richard', a contemporary French poem by Jean Creton, printed in *Archæologia* (1824); illuminations reproduced in Green's *Short History*, illustrated ed. 1898, p. 905.

CHAPTER X

THE GAELIC RECOVERY AND ARISTOCRATIC HOME RULE, 1399-1477

HENRY IV began his reign with conciliation to Ireland and restored to MacMurrough the barony of Norragh, which, however, Art kept for only a few years, and neither he nor his heirs ever claimed again.

A new period now began between England and Ireland. With justice we may say that 1394 to 1399 is 'the last effort of the English lordship' till Tudor times. The Lancastrian dynasty was too weak to attend to Ireland, and before long all England's ambition was diverted to the French wars and later all her energies to the Wars of the Roses. Only in an odd breathing-space up to 1485 did the English Crown turn its serious attention to the lordship of Ireland. The 'first conquest' begun by Henry II was now an obvious failure. As a result of a government which had no money or men to spare for Ireland, the native race recovered two-thirds of Ireland and spread once more the language and culture which during the Conquest had receded to remote parts. The national spirit reasserted itself and proved victorious over the alien one; unfortunately political unity was not restored with the racial unity, and the ideal of the fifty or sixty Gaelic 'captains of their nations' was simply to recover the old aristocratic tradition and the pedantic culture of the bards, Brehons, and chroniclers who surrounded them. The traditional world of Gaelic Ireland became as strong again as in the eleventh century, and a great body of manuscript literature in Irish comes down from these times.

Not only did the colony dwindle but its language died away, for no University existed in Dublin, and the French-speaking feudal class took to Irish rather than English. There was an exodus of the common English and of the clerics, who preferred to stay in England in spite of the severe Absentee act of 1380, numbers of the tenantry abandoned the country unable to endure the Irish advance or to tolerate the exactions of the March lords, and so there was a steady diminution of the Anglo-Irish race. In this Irish world the part which the government played became less and less. But the Pale of Leinster and Meath was still large, though destined to dwindle during the century. It becomes necessary to treat as almost separate entities the history of the Gaelic chiefs, the great earls and the feudal class, and the 'land of peace', as ruled by the Dublin government under the final control of the Crown. But the relations between the three were never entirely suspended, much as each moved on its own orbit.

The high title of King's Lieutenant, now generally superseded the lesser title of Justiciar, his salary was increased, but such was the decline in the revenue that the expenses of Ireland had often to be met from the English exchequer. The pride of the Anglo-Irish was gratified by the appointment of great nobles or even princes of the Blood; while the Home Rule sentiment was occasionally met when the sword of State was committed to men like the Earl of Ormond, who was lieutenant several times during this period.

On the accession of Henry V in 1413 a memorable viceroy appeared in John Talbot, Lord Furnival, afterwards earl of Shrewsbury, and one of England's most famous captains in France. He arrived in November 1414 and remained till 1419, grappling with the threefold problem of how to maintain the 'English land', repulse the Irish enemy, and give force to the central government. By this time there was a sturdy and narrow Anglo-Saxon patriotism in England, equally hostile to Irish, Scots, Welsh, and Frenchmen, and Talbot felt this both for the Irish and the English of Ireland. In Dublin, where he ruled as viceroy for several periods till 1447, he tried to build up a pro-English officialdom which would ensure a strong and impartial government. His brother Richard, archbishop of Dublin and Chancellor, was his right-hand man against the Home Rule and aristocratic party led by James of Ormond, who is called the 'White Earl'. By this time the colonial feeling was expressing itself in parliamentary form and did not rest till it secured the legislative autonomy of Ireland.

Talbot was succeeded by the Earl of Ormond, and he again in 1423 by a prince of the Blood who it was felt could command the general respect and allegiance of Ireland. Edmund Mortimer, earl of March and Ulster, son of the Roger slain in 1398, was now a man, but a man of unambitious character. By blood, if succession through women was allowed, he had the better right to the throne than the young Henry VI, but neither Henry IV nor Henry V had felt any reason to mistrust him. When Mortimer arrived in 1423 both Irish and English greeted him as the greatest of all the native magnates, and when he held his court at Trim five Ulster chiefs with Eoghan O'Neill at their head did homage to him, both as the King's deputy and as earl of Ulster. But Mortimer died suddenly of the plague early in 1425, leaving only a sister Anne, the wife of Richard, duke of Cambridge, and mother of the still more famous Richard, duke of York. Thus was extinguished the almost royal name of Mortimer.

Talbot was at once appointed justiciar by the Council, and before the chiefs could depart compelled them into a further submission, and in all some nine of the greater chiefs made terms with the government, among others Eoghan O'Neill admitted the rights of the young Richard of York as earl of Ulster and his over-lord. After his uncle's death, Richard united in himself the lordships of Ulster, Trim, Leix, and Connacht in Ireland, of the Marches in Wales, and in England the duchy of York. He also had a double claim to the throne, that of Clarence and that of York, but for the present he was a loyal man, attached to the court and the cause of Humfrey, duke of Gloucester, the King's youngest uncle.

After the death of Mortimer it was some twenty years before Ireland became important again in English eyes. Archbishop Richard Talbot strove to maintain an English faction in the government, but in fact the Home Rule party was now in the saddle and England, immersed in a losing war in France, had to cut Ireland out. Not till the appointment of Richard, duke of York, as Lord Lieutenant in 1447, did Ireland count again in English politics.

On their part, the Gaelic chiefs continued their local triumphs and built up lordships based on the old domains of their race or at the expense of the English colonists. Among these we may note the O'Connors, former kings of Connacht. Cathal Crovderg's line maintained itself till 1385, ousting the rival stocks, and then split into the two races of O'Connor Don and O'Connor Roe. In Ulster Eoghan O'Neill succeeded in 1432 when he was made king of Ulster 'on the flagstone of the kings at Tullahoge by the will of God and men, bishops and sages'; he ruled till 1455 and built up a great O'Neill supremacy. In the north-west the great name was that of the O'Donnells, who dominated Tyrconnell and Fermanagh and in Sligo were over-lords of O'Connor Sligo.

In the south-east, the great name was that of MacMurrough Kavanagh. In his later years Art Oge MacMurrough had shown himself more peaceful, for he had revived the vast family lordship in Hy Kinsella. In a deed of July 1417 he sought a safeguard for his son Gerald to travel freely through Ireland and the King's dominions, and in doing so he admitted himself liege-man and subject of Henry V. Early in 1418 Art died in his own fortress, having earned the title of 'the most fierce rebel, against whose power all Leinster could not stand'. Art was succeeded by his son Donough, who again was succeeded by his nephew Donal Reagh ('Riabhach'); he ruled till 1476 and under him the domain of the MacMurroughs stretched from the Dullough in north Carlow to Enniscorthy in Wexford. Donal's seal is extant which bears the title 'Rex Lagenie', and this title his race retained till 1522.[1]

The great earldoms and the feudal English dominated a large part of Ireland and were an element on which the English connexion might still reckon. These were the 'Middle nation' who stood half-way between the English and the Irish division in their sympathies and, reared as they were among a dominant Irish population, were familiar with Irish speech, culture, and law. A typical example is Gerald, third earl of Desmond, who died in 1398. In Irish tradition Gerald was

---

[1] Nevertheless the law never recognized such Irish lordships as MacMurrough's to be legal, see later p. 191.

the 'Gearóid Iarla' who was a poet and a lover of the Gaelic spirit. He composed verses both in Gaelic and French, and in the annals of Clonmacnois is described as 'a nobleman of wonderful bounty, cheerfulness in conversation, easie of access, charitable in his deeds, a witty and ingenious composer of Irish poetry, a learned and profound chronicler, and in fine one of the English nobility that had Irish learning and the professors thereof in greatest reverence of all the English of Ireland'. Gerald got leave from the Crown to have his son James fostered among the O'Briens of Thomond, but his heir was his grandson Thomas, who succeeded in 1399. What followed is a signal example of how the Anglo-Norman race of Ireland was turning Irish. The young Thomas was about 1416 ousted by his uncle James, who was backed by the O'Briens, on the grounds that he had married a low-born Irishwoman, Catherine MacCormac, and so violated not only the Statutes of Kilkenny, but the pride of the Geraldine race. Earl Thomas died in France in 1420, and his uncle James took his place, for the English government was powerless to prevent him. It was practically an assertion of Irish chieftainship and Tanistry among this great and once-feudal Norman race. James, the new earl, entered into alliance with the White Earl of Ormond, who procured many grants from the Crown for him, and as a result before his death in 1462 he lorded it over the four counties of Cork, Limerick, Kerry, and Waterford, and commanded the ports of Dingle, Tralee, Limerick, Youghal, and Cork.

The three great earls of the South were destined to build up a supremacy over Ireland which passed successively from Ormond to Desmond and from Desmond to Kildare. Their junior branches began freely to intermarry with the Irish, and even in the loyal Butlers we find Richard, brother of the White Earl, marrying a Catherine O'Reilly. From this Richard 'of Polestown' in Kilkenny descended a Butler line which after a century succeeded to the earldom. His son Edmund, generally called 'MacRichard', married Catherine O'Carroll, and these junior Butlers became full of Gaelic blood. But the great Earls themselves maintained the purity of their stock and for some generations never married Irish. This did not prevent a gallant knight such as James, fourth or White Ear of Ormond, from having Gaelic sympathies and speaking Irish, or, on the other hand, making war upon the neighbouring septs. His aunt Joan had married Taig O'Carroll, lord of Ely, and yet in September 1407 the Deputy and Ormond won a great victory at Callan, in which Taig was defeated and slain, a native hero and 'a man of great account and fame with the professors of poetry and music of Ireland and Scotland'.

That great and widespread class in Munster, Meath, and the borders whom the law called 'chieftains of lineage' and 'degenerate English', now aspired to great local lordships like the Irish themselves, and, against the whole spirit of English monarchy, built up whole 'countries' twenty or thirty miles square, in which they ruled partly like feudal seigneurs and partly like Gaelic kings.

The Gaelic and the Norman lords, indeed, in their use of the Irish language, their patronage of Brehons and bards, their standing forces and love of local independence, were becoming almost indistinguishable, and the prohibition of intermarriage and fosterage went by the board. Ireland became a chequer-board for an aristocracy derived from both races, in many ways acting together, though for long the 'Old English' boasted that they were of the blood of the Conquest and thought themselves a superior race.

The course of events had made them the masters of Ireland, save for the Pale, which remained England's one foothold and bridge-head here.

In England after the death of the Duke of Bedford in 1435 everything made for the Wars of the Roses. The growing loss of France and heavy taxation led to the formation of two parties at Court, the one led by Humfrey, duke of Gloucester, Henry V's only surviving brother, which was for continuing the war, and the other led by the Dukes of Somerset and Suffolk, which wanted to make terms with France while possible. Henry VI was 'a good, innocent, and simple man', ruled by his masterful wife, Margaret of Anjou. As they were childless, Gloucester was next in succession, so when he was removed or died mysteriously in February 1447 the Court party seemed to triumph. But this only threw into more prominence Richard of York, whom many regarded as a more legitimate heir to the throne than Henry himself. Along with this went universal 'lack of governance', the passion for getting local lordship, often by ousting other men, and the evils called 'livery and maintenance', namely, the enlisting of retainers and maintaining by force the lord's law-suits and quarrels.

In Ireland the same passion for lordship was displayed, and man-power was what the local magnates desired. The Anglo-Irish lords more and more quartered upon their tenants their armed retainers, kern, galloglasses and bonnaughts, and hence arose what the English government regarded as the evils of 'coigny, livery, kernety, bonnaught, cuddies', etc., which in the sixteenth century Tudor officials denounced as 'abominable Irish exactions' and 'Irish cuttings and spendings'. They were derived from Gaelic custom and hence to the numerous Irish tenants of these earls and 'chieftains of lineage' seemed endurable, but to the English tenants they were intolerable and to the government odious. But even the viceroys from time to time maintained the State army by quartering it on the Pale by the rule of 'coigny'.[1]

The feuds of the great men in England in the shires and at court were finally to end in the wars of the Roses. The Somerset party in England thought to get rid of their greatest opponent by appointing Richard of York as Lieutenant of Ireland in December 1447 for ten years. By this they hoped to get him out of the way, but Richard was a skilful politician and determined to use this office in such a way as to enlist Ireland for his cause in the inevitable struggle.

In Ireland parliament and government were falling into the hands of the Patriot party, and when in 1447 the Earl of Shrewsbury retired from office the Anglo-Irish came into full power. Already, however, the great family of Ormond had taken their side in the war that was to break out in England, for James, son and heir of the White Earl, married Eleanor, sister of the Duke of Somerset, and was created earl of Wiltshire.

[1] 'Billeting', from the Irish 'coinmhedh', maintenance.'

On July 6th 1449 Richard landed at Howth accompanied by his beautiful wife Cecily Nevill, 'The Rose of Raby', with a considerable army, and supreme powers as lieutenant. Richard was a tall and handsome man of princely and affable bearing; to the Anglo-Irish he stood for the great names of De Burgo, Lacy, and Mortimer, his ancestors; to the Irish he was 'the lord of the English of Ireland', in whose veins was the blood of Brian Boru. Richard cared less for setting the government of Ireland right than for enlisting the country on his side. The result of his thirteen years of power was to put the aristocratic Home Rule party into power for nearly a century and to win the hearts of nearly all Ireland for the romantic cause of the White Rose until every hope of it was extinguished.

Such was the charm that Richard displayed that, according to a later English chronicler, 'he got him such love and favour of that country and its inhabitants that their sincere and lovely affection could never be separated from him and his lineage'. At Trim and Carlingford, where he displayed the 'Black dragon' banner of the earldom, he received the homage of Magennis, MacMahon, O'Reilly, and MacQuillan (formerly Mandeville), whose forces in all amounted to over three thousand men, proof of what a 'land of war' Ireland had become. He then turned south and marched into Wicklow where Brian O'Byrne submitted to him, and altogether over twenty-four of the leading Irish chiefs of Ulster and the midlands and the Old English of Munster came in and did homage and provided for his table. O'Neill of Tyrone in particular admitted the suzerainty of his over-lord, the Earl of Ulster, and in August of this year at Drogheda Henry O'Neill, eldest son of Eoghan, acting for his father, made a solemn treaty. By this he bound himself and his sept to be the men of the Duke, to restore all lands and castles formerly possessed by the Duke's ancestors as earls of Ulster, as well as the ancient 'bonnacht' or military service due from the Irish chiefs of Ulster, and to support the Duke if necessary with a thousand men. In such terms the Duke saw the makings of an Irish army which would maintain his cause in Ireland or even provide recruits for him in England. Actually, the treaty had little effect, for an Irish chief was not likely to surrender his conquests, but an *entente* was established between the House of York and the O'Neills which lasted for several generations and aided the race of Niall More in establishing an hereditary succession which lasted to the end of the next century.

In October 1449 was born in Dublin Richard's third son, George, future duke of Clarence. This was a highly popular event; the Irish henceforth regarded Clarence as 'one of ourselves', and it was in the belief that Lambert Simnel was his son that he was crowned in Dublin.

In May 1450 the King's chief minister, William de la Pole, duke of Suffolk, was murdered by the mob in escaping to France, and on hearing of the removal of his enemy York returned to England, where the Court had to take him into favour and confirm him as lieutenant. In October 1453 the birth of a royal prince, Edward, knocked him out of the succession, but on the King's becoming imbecile he was made Protector. On May 22nd 1455 the first clash in the Wars of the Roses took place at St. Albans, and there the Duke of Somerset was slain. On Lady Day 1458 a 'love-day' was staged in London in which the Duke of York and the Queen walked in procession hand in hand, but the lords who were there 'never came together again after that time to parliament or council unless it were in field with spear and shield'.

Next at 'the Rout of Ludlow' in October 1459, the Yorkist forces were scattered, and York made for Ireland and his son Edward of March and his nephew Richard of Warwick for Calais. An English parliament attainted York and all his adherents, so that his office of Lord Lieutenant legally ceased. But this meant nothing to the Anglo-Irish, for they now had a 'king of their own' and meant to make use of him. On Richard's return he was welcomed with enthusiasm and when he summoned a parliament to Drogheda in February 1460 it gave almost sovereign powers to the superseded viceroy and proceeded to assert its legislative independence in those words: 'The land of Ireland is, and at all times hath been, corporate of itself by the ancient laws and customs used in the same, freed of the burden of any special law of the realm of England, save only such laws as by the lords spiritual and temporal and

the commons of the said land had been in great council or
Parliament there held admitted, accepted, affirmed, and
proclaimed.'

Thus did Ireland, or rather the English colony, assert its
separateness from England except for the personal link of the
Crown. Richard accepted the declaration with some mis-
givings, no doubt, for he was a true Englishman and a possible
king, but for the present his purpose was to enlist on his side
the magnates and people of Ireland.

The invasion of England from the two points of Dublin and
Calais was the next Yorkist step, and when Warwick took the
King prisoner at the battle of Northampton in July 1460,
York returned at once with many devoted followers from
Ireland, and made an almost royal entry into London, while
Parliament under pressure admitted his claim to succeed to
the Crown on the death of Henry. But Richard did not live
long to enjoy his triumph, for on December 31st 1460 he was
killed outside his own castle at Wakefield, in an encounter
with a large Lancastrian army. His son the Earl of March,
however, marched upon London, was crowned there as
Edward IV, and secured his kingdom at Towton in March 1461.
After this decisive battle, among others who paid for their
defeat, James, fifth earl of Ormond and earl of Wiltshire, was
taken and finally beheaded. In the new king Ireland welcomed
with enthusiasm the triumph of hereditary succession and of
a gallant and handsome youth who through his Irish descent
was regarded as one of the English of Ireland. In Edward
the vast, though at present unprofitable, estates of Ulster,
Connacht, Trim, and Leix were merged in the English Crown.

The popularity which Duke Richard had won for the House
of York was to be deep and to last long. 'This race has ever
desired to be ruled by great persons' and no better example
of such a ruler has appeared either before or since, but that
he had Ireland's interests at heart we can hardly suppose, and
he did not scruple to drain the colony of men to such an extent
that, as the chronicler says, 'the English domination was utterly
dissolved and spoiled'. Another writer not long afterwards

says: 'He so gained the hearts of the Irish nobility, that divers
of them, especially those of Ulster, Clandeboy, the Glinnes,
and the Ardes, which at that time was better inhabited with
English nobility than any part of Munster or Connacht, came
over with him against Henry VI to divers famous battles,
lastly to Wakefield, where they not only lost their lives with
him, but also left their country so naked of defence that the
Irish, in the meantime, finding the enterprise so easy, cast up
their old captain O'Neill, relyed with their ancient neighbours
the Scots, and repossessed themselves of the whole country,
which was the utter decay of Ulster.' His most lasting achievement, indeed, was to give the parliament of the Anglo-Irish
the opportunity under his great name to declare their right
to determine their own laws at home. Of this sentiment the
high peak was touched in 1460; it was one of the first objects
of the Tudors to repeal it and so to end fifty years of Home
Rule, but in some form or other the claim has never been
abandoned.

The Yorkist cause was not immediately won in Ireland.
John, brother of James who had fallen at Towton, and who
was attainted along with other chief Lancastrians, returned
to Ireland and summoned Edmund MacRichard and the local
Butlers and the towns of Kilkenny and Clonmel to arms. But
at Pilltown near Carrick-on-Suir in 1462, their forces were
overthrown by Thomas, the new Earl of Desmond, and the
Lancastrian attempt failed. The results were to be decisive in
the history of this great and pro-English line of earls. Attainted
by both parliaments (till the attainder was removed in 1476),
Earl John and his brother Thomas remained absentees in
England, leaving the Polestown branch their deputies in Ireland, and on the death of Thomas in 1515 the senior line
of the Butlers expired.
The accession of Edward IV in England was a party
triumph, not the work of the whole nation, and the wars of
the Roses were far from ended. During their unsteady twenty-
four years of rule, Edward and his brother Richard after him
had practically to abandon Ireland to the great lords there
who had supported their father. Their brother George, duke

of Clarence, was nominal lieutenant most of the time until his execution in February 1478, but Irish earls ruled as his deputies. The system of governing Ireland by English-born viceroys had to give way to one in which 'over-mighty subjects' ruled the Pale, divided government offices among their supporters, used the revenues and forces of State for their own purposes, and at the same time ruled their vast earldoms like petty kings.

The supremacy among the three great Earls passed successively from Ormond to Desmond and then to Kildare, whose line kept it for some sixty years. The Butlers passed off the Irish stage when Earl John became an absentee. The Polestown Butlers, their Irish deputies, had a hard struggle to maintain themselves between the two Geraldines of Desmond and Kildare, but loyally maintained the Lancastrian tradition. Irish marriages were becoming common, and these junior Butlers were already half Gaelic. Edmund MacRichard married Catherine O'Carroll, and his son James about 1463 married Saiv Kavanagh, daughter of Donal Reagh, king of Leinster, and had by her a famous son, Sir Piers 'the Red', in later times earl of Ossory and Ormond.

The power of the Desmond earl was now princely. James, who ruled from 1416 to 1462, had made it supreme in the four south-west counties, and the main Desmond line was supported by four junior branches, the Knight of Kerry at Dingle, the Baron of Clanmaurice at Lixnaw, the Knight of Glin in Limerick, and the White Knight or Fitzgibbon at Kilmallock. He himself founded the important family of the Fitzgeralds of Decies in West Waterford which district he gave to his younger son Gerald. Among his English tenants James was a great palatine lord, to a widespread Gaelic population he was like an Irish 'Rí' to whom as a great prince of an accepted stock they gave generous obedience. In defiance of the Statutes of Kilkenny he granted portions of the earldom to Irish chiefs, thus he planted an O'Brien in the great castle and lordship of Carrigogunnell on the Shannon. The ruling race of Thomond were his allies, for he had been fostered among the O'Briens, and in the south-west MacCarthy More was true to the vassalage which the head of the race had admitted in 1395, even if MacCarthy Reagh was hostile.

The fame of the Earl reached even to Florence where the Secretary of State to the Republic in 1440 wrote him a flattering letter, congratulating him of being of Florentine stock, of the ancient family of the Gherardini, 'so that the Florentines themselves could rejoice that through him they bore sway even in Ireland, the most remote island in the world'. When the Desmond power fell with a crash in 1583, it was written: 'the Earl of Desmond grew into the greatest estate, power, and riches of any subject perhaps in the world, which is manifest by this that at his attainder he forfeited near 500,000 acres of land and had not less than 20 great houses and castles big enough for the residence of a prince.'

This vast power, however, was built upon the subjection of his tenants, both English and Irish, to those impositions which were especially detested by later Tudor officials, and in the sixteenth-century history of Holinshed we read: 'James, Earl of Desmond, being suffered and not controlled, during the government of Richard, Duke of York, his godsip and of Thomas Earl of Kildare his kinsman, did put upon the King's subjects within the counties of Cork, Kerry, Limerick and Waterford the Irish impositions of quinio (coign) and livery, cartings, carriages, lodgings, cosherings, bonnaght and such like, which customs are the very breeders, maintainers and upholders of all Irish enormities.'

For the law-cases of his Irish tenants Earl James introduced Gaelic brehons into Munster, and, since every great man must now have his family bard, he made an O'Daly his court poet. To maintain his troops, for every great man must now have an army, he brought in a Scottish galloglass family, the MacSheehys, from the North and quartered on his tenants numbers of kern, bonnachts, and other hired troops.

Thomas succeeded his father James as earl and became deputy for the Duke of Clarence from 1463 to 1467. He held a parliament at Trim and Drogheda in 1465, some of whose acts are memorable. The attainder of Edmund MacRichard was reversed and the revolt of 1462 was thus pardoned. The

Irish living in the counties of Meath, Louth, Dublin, and Kildare were ordered 'to take English surnames, to go as English, and be sworn as lieges within a year'. This provision is notable, because it is the first recognition of *the Pale* of four counties as the only portion left of the true 'English land', into which, however, the native race and language were fast intruding.

Son of a father who had been fostered among the O'Briens and of a Burke mother, the Earl of Desmond had strong Irish sympathies. When he summoned parliament to Dublin in 1464, MacWilliam of Clanrickard, Red Hugh O'Donnell, and other chiefs, both English and Irish, attended him, and the sight was seen of Irish chiefs and their galloglasses walking the Dublin streets, a token that the Norman and Celtic aristocracy were blending and become joint lords of Ireland. Yet Earl Thomas was a noble-minded man who spoke English, tried to reconcile the Butlers, and founded at Youghal a splendid collegiate church of the Blessed Virgin Mary, well endowed by him, which had a long history. Yet he was suspect of the English monarchy, both for his father's and his own favour to the Irish, and for his continuance in 'Irish impositions'. There was, further, a suspicion that so great and splendid a lord might assume the Crown of Ireland, and whether Desmond ever entertained it we know not, but it is certain that for over seventy years there was a constant fear in England that some Irish lord would take upon him the sovereignty of Ireland.

Suddenly, by one of the most dramatic surprises in Irish history, the greatest man among the English of Ireland was overthrown. King Edward was persuaded into an attempt to crush the Home Rule aristocracy, and in 1467 sent over as lieutenant Sir John Tibetot, earl of Worcester, a devoted partisan of the Yorkist House and a classical scholar and child of the Renaissance. Tibetot as Constable of England had ruthlessly sent to execution many enemies of the House of York and had earned the name of 'the Butcher'. He came over to assert the English control of Ireland and summoned a parliament to Drogheda at the end of 1467, wherein the sovereignty of Edward as Lord of Ireland was re-asserted and the bishops were ordered to preach general obedience to him. James Butler, son and heir of Edmund MacRichard, had his marriage with Saiv Kavanagh legitimized by act of Parliament. But the real thunder-bolt was fired when suddenly the two Earls of Desmond and Kildare were attainted 'for horrible treasons and felonies as well as in alliance, fosterage, and alterage with the Irish enemies of the King as in giving to them horses, harnesses, and arms'. Desmond was taken and beheaded at Drogheda on February 14th 1468, but Kildare was lucky enough to procure a pardon.

The judicial murder of Earl Thomas struck both the Irish and English of Ireland with universal horror. It was a deadly and determined blow at the Home Rule aristocracy, and, above all, a clear warning from the English government that even the greatest of the Anglo-Irish was not to be permitted to favour the Irish race or to forsake the strict lines of English loyalty as laid down by the statutes of Kilkenny. The fatal result was to drive the great house of Desmond over to the Irish side and to ensure its almost permanent disloyalty till its tragic fall in 1583. James, son of the executed earl, at once rose in arms and swore that he and his would never attend parliament or council again or enter any walled town of the King except at their own pleasure. This James, sixth earl, went even more Irish than his father and by marrying Margaret O'Brien started the tradition among the Desmond Geraldines of marrying Irish wives.

The blow, however, was premature and King Edward himself in 1470 had to fly to Holland before an uprising of the Lancastrian party, in which Tibetot himself was taken and executed after his own fashion, and on Edward's restoration in 1471, nothing remained for him but to leave in power in Ireland the Home Rule aristocracy. Thus did Thomas, earl of Kildare, become Deputy under the Duke of Clarence from 1470 till his own death in March 1477. The houses of Ormond and Desmond now passed out of the running, and from this time to 1534 the Earls of Kildare became the real rulers of the country.

All this time the independence of the Irish parliament was

growing, and an act of 1468 asserted that English statutes to be valid in Ireland must be ratified by the Irish parliament. In 1470 Thomas of Kildare was elected justiciar by the Irish council in the vacancy caused by the attainder of Tibetot, and according to the 'statute of FitzEmpress'. George of Clarence, attainted and executed in February 1478, was followed by a line of nominal lieutenants, royal princes, whether Yorkist or Tudor, but the real power was with native deputies.

And so we come to the all-but-kingship of the Earls of Kildare, the great fact in Irish history for some sixty years, which became complete under Gerald, son of Thomas, eighth earl of Kildare, called by the Irish 'Garret More', the real king of Ireland from 1477 till his death in 1513. Already the Irish parliament, a body which represented only the counties of Leinster and a few towns, had accepted the Kildare supremacy and was ready to clothe its doings with legality. By a grant of 1474 it gave Earl Thomas a retinue of a hundred and sixty-three spearmen, and by the creation of the Guild of St. George for the defence of the Pale it placed under the command of the deputy a force of two hundred fully equipped men, chosen out of the four counties of the Pale, so that some four hundred of the best equipped soldiers in Ireland for twenty years were at the disposal of Kildare.

CHAPTER XI

THE KILDARE SUPREMACY AND THE REFORMATION,
1477–1540

THIS period marks the culmination of the Home Rule demand of the English in Ireland, asserted definitely in 1460. Though interrupted by Poynings' law in 1495, it continued in effect till the fall of the House of Kildare.

In Garret More we get a remarkable character, perhaps the first example of the blended Anglo-Irish type, the result of influences both English and Irish, to appear in our history in which it has played so large a part. The power of Kildare was already prepared by a number of marriages, both with the Gaels and the Englishry, which it was his policy to continue and which built up for his family a great 'House power'. In 1480 his sister Eleanor married Conn, the eldest son of Henry 'the O'Neill', and an act of parliament made him and his children by her of free estate in the law. By other marriages the house of Kildare secured allies everywhere, but the winning over of the great chiefs of the North was especially a triumph. In the royal race of Tyrone, Henry O'Neill, son of Eoghan, ruled till 1483, continued the lineal succession, and built up a vast lordship in central Ulster. Conn More, as he was called, and his son Conn Bacach, later earl of Tyrone, were kinsmen and loyal supporters of the House of Kildare till it fell and in themselves attested the blending of the two races. In the north-west Red Hugh O'Donnell ruled for the long period of 1461 to 1505, and, though unrelated by blood to Kildare, became his standing ally. It was he who built the noble Franciscan house at Donegal, to which we owe in later times such works as the *Annals of the Four Masters*. The great enemy, on the other hand, of Kildare continued to be the Butlers under James, son of Edmund MacRichard, who was made deputy by the absentee Earl of Ormond for his Irish lands and lordships.

Till 1485 the Anglo-Irish remained in an entire possession

of the Irish government.   In 1477 Gerald was elected justiciar
by the Council of Ireland under the statute of FitzEmpress,
but when the Duke of Clarence was put to death in February
1478 King Edward deprived Kildare of his office and sent
over Henry, Lord Grey, instead. But the Anglo-Irish spirit
now ran high, and in defiance of the royal will Kildare called
a parliament at Naas which confirmed his tenure of office.
The King had to withdraw the appointment of Grey, and a
parliament held at Trim enacted that in future in the case of
a vacancy a justiciar should be elected by the Council and
the consent of parliament till the King's pleasure should be
known. After this defeat of the Crown the Kildare supremacy
was left undisturbed. The smaller grew the Pale the greater
was the Home Rule it enjoyed, and while the real power of
Kildare came from his vast earldom which spread steadily
over Leinster, it was well worth his while to control the revenue
and the offices of State, and, above all, to get the sanction of
legality for all his measures.

The short rule of Richard III made no difference, and an
Irish parliament under Kildare in 1485 enacted that the
Chancellor, Treasurer, and three other chief ministers should
hold for life, and together with the peers should, according to
the statute of FitzEmpress, elect a viceroy in time of vacancy.
On August 21st 1485 King Richard was slain at Bosworth, and
Henry Tudor ascended the throne. With him a totally new
age began for England, and the medieval time passed away.
But in Ireland the medieval age went on and the romance of
the White Rose died hard. The Earl of Kildare, like many in
both England and Ireland, had to face the problem of how
long Henry VII would keep the throne of England and whether
there were not truer princes of the blood alive than he, John
de la Pole, earl of Lincoln, Edward, earl of Warwick, son of
Clarence, and perhaps the younger son of Edward IV. At the
moment of Bosworth, Lincoln was Richard's accepted heir and
legal lieutenant of Ireland. Was Ireland to obey a Yorkist
viceroy or not?

For some twelve years Ireland was the stage of successive
attempts against the new Tudor throne. The first centred

round the name of Lambert Simnel, whom, early in 1487, an Oxford priest brought to Dublin, a handsome boy of ten, who was supposed to be Edward of Warwick, son of George of Clarence. The Earl of Kildare and the Anglo-Irish lords as well as the archbishops of Armagh and Dublin and three other bishops accepted the boy as the real Warwick, son of their Dublin-born Clarence. The Earl of Lincoln appealed to Margaret, duchess of Flanders and sister of Edward IV, and she sent two thousand German mercenaries who landed in Dublin on May 5th 1487. On May 24th of that year the pretender was crowned as Edward VI of England and Ireland in St. Mary's Church at Dublin, with a golden circlet taken from a statue of the Blessed Virgin, and thus did the Home Rule party get a king of their own whom all the country accepted, save for Waterford and the Butler towns.

The next and necessary step was to impose the pretender upon England, and early in June a combined army of Germans and Anglo-Irish, under De la Pole, landed in Lancashire, but at Stoke in Lincolnshire, on June 16th 1487, they were cut to pieces by the Tudor army, and about four thousand of them fell, including the Earl of Lincoln, a brother of the Earl of Kildare, and Martin Swartz, the leader of the German mer- cenaries, while Simnel himself was taken and ended his days as a scullion in the royal kitchens. Henry had procured a papal Bull in support of his right to the Crown, and so he put the Anglo-Irish in the wrong; nevertheless he had to leave Kildare in office as Deputy. In 1488 he sent over Sir Richard Edgecomb to take the oaths of allegiance of the Irish lords, and after some resistance Edgecomb proclaimed a full pardon for Kildare and the chief supporters of the pretender. Again Kildare was left in power, and now we find him interfering everywhere in Irish disputes, traversing the whole country, and in succession-questions putting in the chief that he favoured. Gunpowder had come to Ireland, the Earl's house in Dublin had a guard of musketeers, and he was able to blow down the castles of his enemies with light artillery.

Again in 1491 the Yorkist hope revived and there landed in Cork a handsome boy of seventeen under the care of one

F

John Taylor, who this time was given out to be Richard, the younger of the two sons of Edward IV, while Henry's supporters denounced him as Perkin Warbeck of Tournai. This time a still larger alliance supported this 'French lad', which included most of the Anglo-Irish (though Kildare was now more wary), the Emperor Maximilian, and the kings of France and Scotland. Warbeck soon, however, departed from Ireland, to which he did not return till 1495, and in the interval Henry VII took steps at last to deal with the recurring danger from beyond the Irish sea.

POYNINGS' PARLIAMENT, 1494–1495

At last the new Tudor dynasty took decisive action in Ireland. Kildare was removed from power and on October 13th 1494 there arrived as Deputy to Prince Henry a viceroy such as had not been seen for a hundred and fifty years. Sir Edward Poynings was a typical servant of the new régime; he had but a thousand men, but with these and backed by the new monarchy he was ready to crush the Home Rule party and restore the sovereignty of England. To replace them, he brought with him pure-born Englishmen to be Chancellor, Treasurer, and other officials, in order to purify the Dublin government and discover the King's ancient rights and revenues. The armed resistance to Poynings was but small, and he soon relieved the siege of Waterford which in 1495 was beleaguered vainly by Maurice, earl of Desmond, and Warbeck. His real work was to ensure that the parliament of Ireland should never be used against English interests again.

The famous 'Poynings' parliament' met on December 1st 1494, and lasted into 1495. It was a packed assembly which was easily persuaded to attaint the Earl of Kildare, and on March 5th he was sent to England and lodged in the Tower of London.

Poynings' orders were to reduce the Lordship of Ireland to 'whole and perfect obedience', and to suppress those who practised on 'the innocent and true English subjects, great and divers robberies, murders, burnings, and the universal intolerable and damnable extortions of coign, livery, and pay'.

Henry had held his hand for ten years, he now struck a master-
blow worthy of his cool and inflexible temper. His general
purpose was to proclaim the sovereign rights of the Crown in
Ireland going back to 1327; his more immediate purpose was
to prevent Ireland's remaining a hatching-ground for Yorkist
plots and to end Home Rule as enjoyed by a Yorkist nobility.
The 'Irish enemies' could for the time be disregarded, and
even the 'degenerate English' did not directly menace the
Crown's authority. What was serious was the seizure of the
'State' by an Anglo-Irish party who had made Dublin as it
were the capital of a nation and in whose parliament a Yorkist
claimant might be crowned or a native king be elected or
treaties passed with England's enemies. The real and lasting
result of Poynings' measures was to render harmless the Dublin
parliament as an instrument in Irish hands, and to destroy
it as a Yorkist citadel. It was indeed an act of union, a fore-
runner of the great one of 1800, and intended to link Ireland
once again to the destinies and civilization of England.

Various acts resumed to the Crown the appointing of all
officers of State and constables of royal castles, abolished the
statute of FitzEmpress, brought to an end the Guild of St.
George, declared the army to be the king's only and forbade
any to keep artillery save his deputy, and made it treason to
take the field against the State. The proceedings of the
'pretended parliament' of 1460 were annulled and every royal
writ or command under the Great or Privy Seal declared sacred
as in England.

So ended the Home Rule experiment of fifty years. To
ensure that the Irish parliament should never act freely again
against English policy, was passed the famous 'Poynings' law'
which states that no parliament shall be held in Ireland 'till
the Lieutenant and council of Ireland shall first certify the
King under the Great seal of such causes and acts as them
seemeth should pass; then the King and his Council, after
affirming such causes and acts to be good and expedient for
the said land, shall send his license thereupon, as well in
affirmation of the said causes and acts as to summon the said
parliament under his Great seal of England: that done, a

parliament shall be holden after the form and effect afore rehearsed, any parliament holden hereafter contrary to these forms to be void and of no effect.' This famous law was to have a curious and long history right up to 1783.

The citadel of power being thus recovered, the next step was to defend it against Irish and English enemies. It was provided that a double ditch should be built round the four counties of the Pale to prevent rievers from raiding the cattle there. This ditch was to run from the mouth of the Liffey to Kildare up to Trim and so through Meath to Dundalk. For the defence of this land, every subject must be armed after English fashion and be ready to do military duty as by ancient statutes when called upon.

The great statutes up to this time made 'for the common weal in England' were declared to be of force in Ireland. It was not intended that the English parliament should hence-forth legislate for Ireland, for the Crown was the imperial authority; her parliament was left in control in this matter, but could safely be so left, subject to the veto of the Crown under 'Poynings' law'.

To recover the King's revenues was as important as to assert his prerogative. They had fallen almost to zero, as his financial experts found, and so a great act of Resumption restored to the Crown all royal rights and revenues usurped or lost since 1327. For the most part this was an act on paper; for it was certain that the Crown could not dispossess half the nobility of Ireland, but it could be used on occasion or suspended *in terrorem*.

In order to recall the 'March English' from their degeneracy and warlike habits and to forbid their local tyranny, the great war-cries of the Anglo-Irish, such as 'Butler Aboo' or 'Crom Aboo', were forbidden, and Brehon law was condemned. Coign and livery and all such Irish extortions were severely prohi-bited, so were the black-rents as paid to the Irish enemy. Finally the Statutes of Kilkenny were re-enacted, which had been the first attempt to check the 'degeneracy' of the Englishry, but it is a commentary on their failure that the original acts forbidding the speaking of Irish and riding without a saddle are not repeated. By this time even in the Pale Irish was becoming universal.

Poynings stayed in Ireland till January 1496, having with his small army of a thousand trained soldiers showed how effective such troops with muskets and artillery could be against the numerous but amateur levies of Ireland. The bridling of the Irish parliament for centuries was his real contribution to Irish history. The rest was merely a striking assertion of English sovereignty in Ireland which the Tudor government only resumed after forty years. When he and his Englishmen departed, no increase of the revenue or Crown lands was recorded, Home Rule was restored under Kildare, the degenerate English continued as before, and the tide of Irish language and feeling continued to flow. Once again parsimony and desire to get rid of the Irish problem had asserted itself and meanness of expenditure upon Ireland was to be the continued and fatal note of Tudor rule. A great moment was again lost, and if instead of the Statutes of Kilkenny being re-enacted the Irish had been made equal to the English in law, a union of the divided population might have followed. Henry did indeed admit two MacCarthy chiefs to English law and proclaimed that such of the natives of Ireland as are willing to submit themselves should be admitted to the King's grace, but this general pronouncement had little effect.

It was, however, chiefly to save the Pale that Poynings had come, and, small though the 'English land' had become, henceforth it felt it had a strong monarchy behind it, and the pro-English elements in Ireland showed a confidence and boldness they had not displayed since the days of Talbot.

The end of the Warbeck enterprise was inglorious. His siege of Waterford, the 'urbs intacta', in July 1495, was a failure, and after troubled wanderings, his final fate was to be captured in Cornwall in 1497, and to be executed in November 1499. Five days later the unfortunate Edward of Warwick was beheaded, and so ended the Yorkist hopes, though for thirty years yet two De la Pole brothers survived

Henry VII had already realized in a meeting with Garret More that 'since all Ireland cannot rule this man, this man must rule all Ireland', and so he restored Kildare as Deputy, giving him further in marriage as his second wife his own cousin, Elizabeth St. John, and pardoning the whole body of his supporters. Kildare ruled Ireland for the rest of his life, and the bridling of the Dublin parliament even made him still more master, for as long as the King approved he could manage it and legislate in it as he wished. Save for that, all his former powers were restored and so was Anglo-Irish control in Dublin. All the highest offices in Church and State (saving those of bishops and of Chancellor, Treasurer, and the chief judges) were in the appointment of Kildare; he spent whatever revenues of State there were, commanded its forces, named the constables of the royal castles, and used the royal artillery for his own purposes. In the North he protected the interests of his nephews, sons of Conn More O'Neill, though the second of these, the famous Conn Bacach, did not become O'Neill till 1519. A fine family grew up round him and through his five daughters he allied himself to the great houses of Gael and Gall. One married Ulick Burke of Clanrickard; another Donal MacCarthy Reagh; another Mulrony O'Carroll; another the Lord of Slane; a fifth, Margaret, Sir Piers Butler who, on the death of his father James in 1478, became head of the Polestown Butlers and deputy for the absentee Earl of Ormond

In these years in which he was left in charge of Ireland, Garret More both as deputy and earl, marched over more of Ireland than any viceroy had done for generations, bringing local chiefs into vassalage, securing the succession of the O'Neill or the O'Kelly he favoured, and blowing down with the royal artillery the castles of private opponents. Ireland had found in him an 'uncrowned King', and though she was divided into local combinations, at least they revolved round the great names of Geraldine, Butler, Burke, and O'Brien. The culmination of these armed confederacies was seen in the year 1504. In the west Garret More's great opponent was Ulick Burke, his own son-in-law, who was usurping the royal town of Galway and had ill-treated his wife, Kildare's daughter

It came to a great battle in which the summons of Kildare was answered by O'Donnell, O'Neill, O'Kelly, the Mayo Burke and the English of the Pale, and that of Clanrickard by O'Brien and the chiefs of Ormond and Connacht. In all, Kildare mustered such an army of English and Irish as would have conquered the Pale in twenty-four hours, had he but dared to claim the Crown of Ireland. On August 19th 1504 some ten thousand men faced one another on the low hill of Cnoc Tuagh (Knocktoe) near Galway, armies medievally equipped with bows and bills, spears and swords, light horsemen and heavy axe-men, and so desperate was the fighting that out of Clanrickard's nine battalions of galloglass, eighteen hundred men, only the remnant of one battalion escaped alive.

It was a famous victory, and Kildare entered Galway in glory, but though it was reported to the King as a great triumph for the English cause in Ireland and earned the Garter for the Earl, it was but the final explosion of a long feud and for Kildare the crushing of a great rival. The ability of Garret More cannot be doubted, nor can his popularity with both the races of Ireland, but though he was a secret Yorkist and wished to be a king-maker, he was not one of those Bruces or Vasas who have dared to set themselves at the head of a new and independent nation.

Kildare indeed realized that a new age had come with the failure of the Yorkist hope and the coming of the Tudors, nor could he ignore the news that in 1499 King James of Scotland brought the Lordship of the Isles to an end after two centuries and a half of independence by hanging its lord, John MacDonnell, and three of his sons. The moral was that both in England and Scotland the day of a new and powerful monarchy had come.

In 1505 Hugh Oge O'Donnell succeeded his father as overlord of Tyrconnell, Sligo, Fermanagh, and Leitrim. His race had been allied with Kildare for some forty years against Clanrickard and other enemies, and Kildare and he became the chief leaders of a movement to unite Scotland and Ireland against England with the possible hope of a Yorkist restoration. There were still two nephews of Edward IV alive,

Edmund and Richard de la Pole, and the Yorkist cause simmered on till the death of Richard at the battle of Pavia in
1525. The accession of Henry VIII to England did not dissolve the plan and Henry himself was too full of glowing youth
and European ambition to care for the time about Ireland, in
which he continued Kildare as deputy. O'Donnell was that
new type of Irish chief who could travel and speak other
languages, he visited Rome in 1510, and later on his return
was knighted by the King in London, but did not hesitate to
enter into communication with James IV, King of Scots,
Henry's enemy, who thought of attacking England through
Ireland. But before this design ripened the Great Earl himself
was dead.

It was in a petty skirmish with the O'Mores of Leix that
Garret More's long life ended. He was trying one of the King's
new guns upon them, and in return one of them shot him with
one of their new muskets. On September 3rd 1513 the Earl
was dead, and six days later the King of Scots was slain with
all his chivalry at Flodden Field, while O'Donnell could
only write from Donegal to Henry to clear himself from
suspicion.

Garret More came nearer to being the accepted king of
Ireland than any man since the Conquest, and his popularity
lasted for the forty years of his rule. He is described as 'a
mighty man of stature, full of honour and courage, open and
plain, hardly able to rule himself when he was moved to anger,
easily displeased and soon appeased, of the English well-
beloved, a good justiciar, a suppresser of rebels and a warrior
incomparable'. Under him, though the union of the two races
was not operated, there was a growing sense of a new nationality, and Gaelic chiefs and Old English lords allied and inter-
married openly. The influence of the Renaissance was seen
in Ireland in the founding of Kilkenny school by Piers Butler,
in a splendid college at Maynooth, built by the Great Earl,
and the fine library, both of manuscripts and books, that
the Earl and his son had in their Maynooth castle. It was
a flowering time also for Gaelic culture which both races
honoured, and if Ireland was dominated by a numerous and

IRELAND
DIVIDED INTO GREAT LORDSHIPS
CIRCA 1500
Miles
0   20   40   60

powerful aristocracy without a king, at least civilization under them had a noble and generous character.

The power of the Geraldine had extended itself over the Pale, and over a large part of Leinster and is expressed in the *Red Book of Kildare*, a great family rental drawn up for Garret More. This power rested on affection and loyalty as well as on force, and even after the fall of the Geraldines in 1534 a Dublin official could write to Thomas Cromwell: 'this English Pale, except the towns and a few of the possessioners, be so affectionat to the Geraldines for kindred, marriage, fostering, and adherence, that they covet more to see a Geraldine to reign and triumph than to see God come among them'.

Garret Oge, as the Great Earl's son was called by the Irish, was continued as deputy with similar powers to his father. He was equally able, skilful, and popular, and continued those marriage alliances on which the family power rested. King Henry was content for the present to allow Ireland to be governed by what is called 'the Pale policy', that is, to leave the government and control of the country in the hands of a nobleman whose deputyship had become hereditary. But Garret Oge was threatened both from England and Ireland in a way his father had not known. King Henry was slow to mature, but as he did he began to feel that Tudor sense of the omnipotence of the State and the danger from 'over-mighty subjects' which was the keynote of the new monarchy, and Irish nationalism was likely to receive little consideration from a king to whom English nationalism and English religion were things it was treason to oppose.

In the very year of Garret More's death Wolsey first came into power in England; he soon gained the ear of Henry, and did not cease to mock at the new Earl as 'the King of Kildare', a subject who left the Crown few rights in Ireland. Again, in 1515, Earl Thomas of Ormond died, and his rights went to his grandson, Sir Thomas Boleyn. Sir Piers Butler then claimed the earldom of Ormond, and appeared more and more as a pro-English opponent of the Kildare supremacy. When Anne Boleyn became a royal favourite, the influence of this family too was thrown into the scales. In Dublin itself the loyalist element became more and more emboldened, and from this time frequent reports to the Crown impressed Henry with the belief that a reformation of Ireland must be taken in hand.

In Tudor eyes, Ireland was full of independent and unruly lords whose lands in acreage were greater than many a proud nobleman in England, and these 'mesne' lords stood between the Crown and the common subject, against all the traditions of English monarchy. True, the 'common English subject' was far from common in Ireland, but he was to be found at least in the Pale, in Wexford and other small areas, in the more English part of the Church, and above all in the towns. The seaport towns boasted their old allegiance to English speech and law, while they cherished the many charters which had made them almost into city republics, and a group of southern towns, such as Waterford and Kilkenny, were partisans of the Butler house and of the Tudor dynasty. The towns of the south-west, indeed, were in Desmond hands, but Galway, most remote of all, might well be made a royal fortress in the west. Whenever the 'strong policy' of earlier times should be attempted, it was thought possible to recall the old English colony to its allegiance and stop 'degeneracy' into Irishism.

Medieval isolation also was over, and with the duel that now began of the new centralized monarchies of Europe this island might become a dangerous centre of intrigues against England. This was especially so when the breach with the Church began. The idea of making Ireland first pay for herself and then of making her a second jewel in the English Crown, in view of all her potential wealth, was bound to occur. At present whenever Henry thought of Ireland and his revenues there, it seemed full of 'the King's decayed rents and embezzled lands'.

A series of reports now began in excellent Tudor English, sent from the pro-English element in the Council of Ireland and others who felt it safe to 'appeal to Caesar', directed against the Kildare rule. Gradually a few Englishmen were introduced into the Council, such as John Alen, made archbishop of Dublin and Chancellor in 1528. In league with Sir Piers Butler, who openly became anti-Kildare, this faction made Garret Oge's tenure of office more and more shaky. Sir

Piers himself in 1515 took the title of Earl of Ormond, but Henry did not like it and made Sir Piers content himself in 1529 with that of Earl of Ossory, while the favoured Sir Thomas Boleyn enjoyed till 1539 the title of Ormond, derived from his grandfather, Earl Thomas.

These reports, which begin in 1515 and continue till 1536, tell of an unhappy and dwindling Pale becoming more and more Irish. The common subject is burdened by Black-rents paid to the Irish enemy and by the deputy's army which he quarters on them by 'coign and livery'. English long bows, spears, swords, bucklers, and jacks have been replaced by Irish short bows and darts. The deputy's army is a multitude of galloglasses and kerns, his hostings are for his own advantage, he employs the King's artillery against his particular enemies and, uses the sword the King has committed to him 'to extinguish the fame and honour of any other nobleman within that land' (a Butler touch). The further English practise Irish law, and in Waterford, Cork, Kerry, and Limerick under the Earl of Desmond and in counties Kilkenny and Tipperary use Irish habits and Irish tongue and do not obey the King's laws. Outside the Pale the land is given up to some ninety captains of English blood and Irish chiefs, all independent and maintaining each a small army. The moral is that the King should take the government out of the hands of native lords and send an English Deputy. The complaints are more against 'the old English Irelandized', than against the Irish, who are praised for keeping their own laws justly, 'also there be no more industrious people under the sun than their churls and husbandmen, if their lords do not eat them out'.

At last in 1520 Henry sent over as full lieutenant an English nobleman of royal descent, Thomas, Earl of Surrey, son of that Duke of Norfolk who had died gallantly at Bosworth on the Yorkist side. He came with an army of 1,100, which was as large a force as the Crown generally spared for Ireland, but when he considered the country he informed Henry that if a conquest were to be undertaken to be final it would need 6,000 men. He also told Henry how it was only in the Pale that sheriffs acted and the King's writ ran, and that the common English, in spite of Poynings' acts, still paid those

shameful Black-rents of £740 (some £20,000 of our money)
yearly, a point which particularly stung Henry's pride.

The Tudor monarch, however, rejected the policy both of
Conquest and Plantation. Indeed, in view of the fact that the
armed forces of the Irish chiefs alone were reckoned at some
22,000 at this time, a conquest would have been a hazardous
undertaking. Economy as regards Ireland was to become a
Tudor tradition and cost more in the end than a firm and just
policy would have done.

Several Irish chiefs came in to Surrey, and among these were
Hugh Oge O'Donnell and Conn Bacach, now the O'Neill.
Cormac McCarthy, lord of Carbery, also came in, and in a
letter to Surrey Henry suggested that this chief should surrender his Irish lands and receive them back as an estate-in-
tail from the Crown. 'The Irish lords', he wrote, 'may be told
that though we are above the laws we will take nothing that
belongs to them.' Henry thus renounced the idea of a fresh
conquest, adopting instead the policy of 'Surrender and
Re-grant' which later deputies put into effect, and announced
as the policy of his later reign in Ireland 'sober ways, politic
drifts, and amiable persuasions'.

Surrey was withdrawn in 1522 and Kildare again restored,
but on a less secure basis and with more enemies. Anne Boleyn
became the King's favourite, and for twelve years her family,
allied with the Butlers, were enemies to the Earl. In the south-
west his kinsman, James, tenth Earl of Desmond, and O'Brien
intrigued with Charles V in favour of Richard de la Pole, and
such intrigues were taken seriously in England, for they
seemed to threaten an Irish combination backed by France or
the Empire and Scotland.

In the Reformation Parliament of England, 1529–1536,
Henry made the great breach with Rome, and Thomas Cromwell took the place of chief minister which the fall of Wolsey
left vacant. Till 1540 this resolute and unscrupulous man had
the direction also of Irish affairs and it was now that the fall
of the semi-royal House of Kildare was achieved. In 1532
Garret Oge was wounded in securing the succession of his

nephew Fergananim O'Carroll and was never the same man
again. In 1533 the Council at Dublin, a junta of some twelve
men who were mainly pro-English such as the archbishop and
another John Alen, Master of the Rolls, again sent one of those
long representations which were to be fatal to Kildare, and in
February 1534 the Earl was recalled for the last time and lodged
in the Tower. Before leaving, he appointed as his deputy his
eldest son Thomas, Lord Offaly, a handsome and attractive
youth of twenty-one, known to the Irish as 'Silken Thomas'
(Tomás an tSioda) because of the silken garments of himself
and his bodyguard. The wise Earl realized the danger the
Kildare supremacy was in and adjured his son to be guided by
the advice of the Council. All was ruined, however, by the
rashness of a fiery young man and the coldblooded malice of
the enemies of his house. The pro-English faction and the
Butlers, who did not want Kildare ever to return, spread
a report that the Earl was dead in the Tower, the victim of a
cruel and heretic king, and in a dramatic moment on June 11th
Silken Thomas in the council-chamber surrendered the sword
of State and declared himself not Henry's deputy but his foe.
Although the son of an English mother, Offaly well understood
Irish and was moved to his final gesture by the chanting of his
Irish harper, O'Keenan.

The rising that followed had little military significance.
Archbishop Alen was murdered, when attempting to flee, by
Offaly's followers, and this brought on Thomas the full excommunication of the Church. He failed to take Dublin castle
and retired to his strong castle of Maynooth, from which he
appealed to the Emperor and the Pope against the excommunicate Henry, who had, he declared, forfeited the Lordship
of Ireland for heresy. The rising showed that the majority of
the Irish regarded their country as a papal fief held by the
Crown of England in virtue of Adrian's donation.

The royal lion was now roused to his full fury, and in
October 1534 Sir William Skeffington arrived as deputy with
the largest army seen for some time and occupied Dublin.
Offaly was proclaimed traitor and the 'Curse' of the Church
against him was published in such dreadful terms that when

it was shown to him the unhappy earl of Kildare died of despair in the Tower in December of that year. The crafty earl of Ossory saw in all this the triumph of the Butler house and raised all Ossory and Ormond in arms. The one military event of importance was the capture of Maynooth in March 1535. Skeffington took it after a week's siege, and after two-thirds of its garrison of a hundred were killed the survivors surrendered, but were immediately put to execution 'as an example to others'.

'The pardon of Maynooth' was never to be forgotten in Irish tradition and served as a dreadful precedent for Tudor wars, in which garrisons, however gallant, received little quarter and the priests in particular were given no consideration.

In August 1535 Silken Thomas, who had failed to bring Ireland to his help, surrendered unconditionally and was sent over to London. There, after a miserable sojourn in the Tower, in February 1537 he was executed at Tyburn along with five of his Geraldine uncles, who had been trapped in various ways. Lord Leonard Grey, who had succeeded as Deputy, pleaded for the life of the unfortunate Offaly, but was not listened to, for Henry in his wrath was determined to extinguish in its own blood the whole Geraldine race. In Ireland there was no House of peers as in England for the trial of its own members, and for centuries even the noblest of the Irish, if seized and sent over to England, could first linger untried and miserably in the Tower of London or be finally executed by mere royal order.

Ireland, whether Gaelic or Norman, was shocked to a man at this ending of the great house of Kildare, an example as to what might happen for a century to whoever dared to oppose the Crown. Only one scion of the house was left, Gerald, half-brother of Thomas and a mere boy of ten, who was rescued and in whose interest was formed the Geraldine League of old English and Irish lords by the devotion of his aunt, Lady Eleanor, the widow of MacCarthy of Carbery, who married Manus O'Donnell so as to make a union of north and south.

While this league menaced the Pale, the new policy of Henry for Ireland was put into effect. The fall of the Kildare lordship had given the Crown a foothold such as it had not had for a couple of centuries and brought most of Leinster within the Pale. The pro-English elements were greatly encouraged and a typical member of the ruling junta, Brabazon, Treasurer of War, wrote to Cromwell while Silken Thomas was in prison urging that the whole sept of the Geraldines should be wiped out; 'the poor commonalty, however, be very true people and conformable to all good order, and the destruction of the land is wholly by the extortions of the lords and gentlemen of the country'. If the Government had really cared for the poor and the ordinary people, no doubt Tudor rule in Ireland would have won more hearts than it did.

For the new policy of reforming the Church on English lines and bringing Ireland into English 'civility', Piers Butler, Earl of Ossory, could be well relied on to lead the way. Already in May 1534 he had made a treaty with the King by which he was to have the rule of counties Kilkenny, Tipperary, and Waterford as King's lieutenant, and swore to resist 'the abused and usurped jurisdiction of the Bishop of Rome'. The murder of Archbishop Alen also enabled Henry to provide for Dublin an English prelate, George Browne, who had accepted the King's view and could be trusted to enforce Reform. The religious programme was prepared between Cromwell and the Irish Council and in 1536 the 'Reformation parliament' met under the Deputy, Lord Grey. The non-religious enactments were forced through without much difficulty in a small body which represented some nine counties at most, a small peerage and some dozen towns. The Earl of Kildare and his family were attainted, a subsidy was granted to the Crown, Black-rents were no longer to be paid, intermarriage and fostering with the Irish and the keeping of Irish minstrels, 'rymours' and bards was not to be permitted among the Englishry, the use of Irish dress was forbidden, and English dress and language were to be used. By an act against Absentees the many derelict lordships of the original Conquest were vested in the Crown, such as the lordships of Carlow, Wexford, and other Leinster fiefs. As the King was already by law Earl of Ulster and Lord of Leix and Connacht, this act still further increased that vast area of Ireland to which, when the occasion arose, the King's title could be proved.

The religious programme, however, was not to the liking of the Anglo-Irish, no matter how loyal they might be, and was stubbornly resisted by the bishops and the clerical proctors among the Commons, but finally there were forced through acts dissolving the abbeys of Ireland and putting their properties in the hands of the Crown, and annexing to the King the First-fruits and other perquisites of the Papacy. On the question of Supremacy the opposition was so prolonged that an angry letter from Henry was necessary in February 1537, and the clerical proctors were by act of this assembly excluded from parliament for ever. This enabled the Act of supremacy to be passed, by which the King was declared Supreme Head on earth of the Church of Ireland, and all office-holders in Church and State were to acknowledge him as such. Thus was the papal authority, or as it was styled 'the usurped authority of the Bishop of Rome', rejected for all Ireland by the pressure of the English State and the vigour of a small English faction backed by Piers, Earl of Ossory. It is doubtful whether there was then more than a handful of Protestants in all Ireland among the Irish and Old English.

The justification for these acts was set forth in the words: 'Inasmuch as this land of Ireland is the King's proper dominion of England and united, knit and belonging to the Imperial Crown of the same realm'.

How many of the Irish bishops accepted Henry as Head of the Church cannot be easily established. It was a doctrine unheard-of till then that a lay prince could have the spiritual supremacy over the Church of God in any country. The opposition was headed by Cromer of Armagh, himself an Englishman, and it seems certain that the whole policy of a Reformation enforced from England was opposed by the vast majority of Irishmen. Nevertheless sufficient bishops, perhaps a majority, were found to take the Supremacy oath, and in this matter we must remember that Henry set up a Church 'Catholic without the Pope', and that for the rest of his reign ordinary worshippers continued to receive as before the old sacraments and attend the Latin Mass. The change in any case could only affect Leinster and the nearer areas. Along with it went a policy of anglicization, and bishops and clergy

were expected to use and preach in English.   The wrecking of
the abbeys was especially shocking to the common people, who
saw no fault in the monks, and the civilization of Ireland
suffered a terrible blow by the destruction of these centres of
learning, religion, and hospitality, expecially in a country
lacking in towns, villages, and manor-houses like those of
England.   Relic-burning, as ordered by Cromwell and Browne,
shocked the people in their deepest sense both of piety and
tradition.   Among the most precious objects of veneration
destroyed was the 'Baculum Jesu', the supposed Staff of Christ
which had been St. Patrick's crosier; this was burned publicly
in Dublin by order of Archbishop Browne.

As the years passed and the return of Henry to the fold could
hardly be hoped for, the Pope began to appoint new bishops
for Irish sees, and in 1541 two Jesuits visited Ireland for the
first time.   The idea was already born that Ireland must be
kept true to the old Faith, whatever the cost might be.

CHAPTER XII

THE TUDOR MONARCHY AND THE SECOND CONQUEST OF IRELAND, 1540–1603

WITH the fall of the House of Kildare, the Tudor government which had got to work in England in 1485 could now get to work in Ireland. Aristocratic Home Rule was ended and henceforth the English government ruled Ireland through English viceroys and an officialdom controlled finally from Whitehall and by Star Chamber methods. Never again till the seventeenth century was a great Irish nobleman of any house to be the King's lieutenant. The Pale had been extended to cover most of Leinster and Meath, and in this secure foothold a new policy in Church and State was put into effect, regardless of the alliance of lords and chiefs called the Geraldine league which threatened it all along the borders. The final consummation of the new policy was that Henry was to take the title King of Ireland, to which general approval was to be secured. His agent in this was first Lord Leonard Grey (1536–1540) and then Sir Anthony St. Leger for the rest of the reign. Except for the savage extinction of the Geraldines, Henry preferred the concilation method, one based on the wish not to spend money on Ireland, and expressed in his phrase 'sober ways, politic drifts, and amiable persuasions'. To secure the necessary support was the task of the new English viceroys, and this proceeded slowly. But in Dublin was firmly entrenched a pro-English official class, both English-born and Anglo-Irish, while in the nearer areas in which the religious houses could be safely dissolved grants of rich abbey lands for a mere song won over the local gentry and nobles, as they did in England itself.

To save the person of the only heir of the Geraldines of Kildare was now the passion of Ireland, both English and Gaelic. The Geraldine league included Desmond and the MacCarthys of the south, Brian O'Connor of Offaly, brother-in-law of Silken Thomas, in the centre, and Conn O'Neill in the north. It went so far as that O'Neill was to be crowned King of Ireland at Tara, but Grey and his small but modern army was a match for all enemies, and at Bellahoe in 1539 he routed Conn O'Neill as he invaded the Pale. Nevertheless the main object of the league was achieved when in 1541 the young Gerald was shipped away and sent to the court of Florence, where he grew up. In the Pale, it was reported, the people were 'so affectionat to this house that they would sooner a Geraldine come among them than God', and whatever the military result of the league was it showed at least a common spirit of opposition which the government should have recognized. But with the departure of the young Geraldine quiet fell upon Ireland and the way was prepared for Henry to turn the Lordship into a Kingdom, to secure assent for the breach with Rome, and to win over the aristocracy to support him in his new titles.

The policy of 'Surrender and Re-grant' was designed to win over the Gaelic chiefs and such Old English as could prove no such titles to their lands and lordships as would be valid in law. According to the theory of the English monarchy, all land-titles depended on the Crown, while in Ireland the greater part of the island was owned by Gaelic chiefs whose titles came from Irish law, and even some Normans such as the Burkes could prove no 'legal' claim. Sir Anthony St. Leger, who ruled Ireland from 1540 to 1548, was the chief agent in winning over this nobility to a royal confirmation of their estates.

But first a new title to Ireland had to be found for Henry. In December 1540 St. Leger and the Council of Ireland advised that he should take the title of King, 'for that the Irish have a foolish opinion that the Bishop of Rome is King of Ireland'. A parliament was therefore summoned to Dublin in June 1541, in which Henry was confirmed in the Crown of Ireland. The title was intended to be flattering to Irish pride and as such it was passed, according to the official report, 'to the general joy'. The parliament was a fuller one than had met for a long time, and included four archbishops, nineteen bishops, and twenty peers, of whom four were new.

Thus began the new Kingdom of Ireland, which lasted in

that form till the Union of 1800. Henry, however, laid it down
that he was 'King of this land of Ireland as united, annexed,
and knit for ever to the Imperial crown of the realm of England'. In others words, the Crown of Ireland was *ipso facto*
vested in whoever was king of England, nor was anything
but a mere proclamation in Dublin needed at a royal accession
in England to that effect. In later days this was to have
serious consequences, as when the Parliament of England
deprived James II of his throne while the Irish nation considered that he was still, in law and fact, king of Ireland.
The Tudor monarchs had no intention that parliament in
England should share the control of Ireland, but in later days
when the parliament of England became supreme it claimed
control over the parliament of Ireland. Henry set up in
Ireland all the style and trappings of monarchy, a royal great
seal, courts of law, a Privy Council and so on, but in fact it
was a government controlled from England, in which national
representation found little place, and exercised through
English-born viceroys.

The parliament which declared Henry king represented
only the English part of Ireland, but it was attended by some
nobles who had been absent for generations, such as the Earl
of Desmond, Barry, Roche, and other lords of Munster, while
proxies attended for O'Brien, and four or five Irish chiefs
came in person, of whom one, Brian MacGillapatric (henceforth Fitzpatrick), actually sat as Baron of Upper Ossory, and
all gave their 'liberal consents'. Sir Piers Butler had early in
1539 been created Earl of Ormond in addition to Ossory, his
son James had succeeded him, and it is illustrative of the
prevalence of the Irish language among the nobility that the
Chancellor's speech proclaiming Henry as King of Ireland had
to be translated into the native language by Earl James for
the benefit of the Irish and Norman peers.

It cannot be doubted that there was a considerable enthusiasm for the new Monarchy, and had it been accompanied with
noble conditions it might have had great success. Formerly
the Council of Ireland had included the Lords of the Pale, and
if the native nobility of Ireland as the royal area increased had

kept their place in the Council, which was all-powerful, native feeling could have found expression in a generous loyalty. But in fact Ireland was to be governed by a small council of officials from which the Irish nobility were excluded, though the Lords of the Pale claimed to be that council which under Poynings' law had the initiative of drawing up Bills and sending them over to be accepted or amended in England. Under this famous law also the Irish parliament continued for centuries to be bridled and could not originate or deal with legislation at its pleasure.

Henry's Irish policy after the fall of the House of Kildare was as follows:

(1). He imposed upon Ireland a Reform of the Church on lines similar to that of England, that is Catholic in doctrine but royal in government;

(2). He began a system of government in which the royal will was supreme and in place of native lords English deputies ruled the country;

(3). But, content with the acceptance of his monarchy in Church and State, he then tried to base it on treaties with the nobility, both Irish and Norman, whom he left undisturbed in their lordships and lands if they would accept tenure under the Crown.

(4). His policy included anti-Irish measures in favour of English speech and 'civility', and the Irish language and culture, as expressed in the bards, poets, and others, were again forbidden or even penalized. Ireland was to be made if possible a second England through the complaisant bishops and nobility, and no provision was made for the recognition of Irish and Gaelic tradition.

Under Lord Grey and still more under St. Leger numerous treaties of 'Surrender and Re-grant' were made with the most prominent chiefs and even a few of the 'degenerate English', though in general the Old English of Ireland were taken to be, unlike the Irish, 'natural liege subjects' who needed no new title for their property. Many of these treaties were made with lesser chiefs, such as O'Toole, who had long menaced the Pale, but even the greatest of the old province kings were won over both to accept Henry and to renounce the Pope. Thus in the autumn of 1540 St. Leger got Cahir MacMurrough Kavanagh and his sept to renounce the name MacMurrough and promise that 'in future no one should be elected chief but that they would obey the King's law and hold their lands by knight-service and accept such rules as the King should appoint'. So came to an end the MacMurrough kingship, though as late as 1522 Gerald Kavanagh had styled himself 'king of Leinster and leader of the Leinster-men'. Brian MacGillapatric, through the influence of the Earl of Ormond, submitted and was made Baron of Upper Ossory, for the new policy included the offer of titles to the more prominent chiefs and inducing them thus to come to Parliament.

Among the 'degenerate English' Ulick Burke was made Earl of Clanrickard, and thus the 'usurped' lordship of his race was confirmed to him. To win over the northern chiefs was especially important, for O'Neill was regarded by the Irish as hereditary king of Ireland, and the Ulster Irish were especially warlike and independent. It was therefore a great triumph when in December 1541 Conn Bacach O'Neill submitted to St. Leger on certain terms. He accepted Henry as King and Head of the Church and promised to hold his lands by knight-service of the Crown, and to attend Parliament and answer the summons of the Deputy with a stated number of armed men; in return he was offered and accepted the title of Earl of Tyrone. On October 1st 1542 Conn was at Greenwich created Earl, the title to go after him to his eldest son Matthew as Baron of Dungannon.

The reigning O'Donnell was now Manus, son of Hugh Oge. St. Leger met this chief in Cavan in August 1541, and found him an elegant and handsome gentleman, magnificently attired in crimson velvet. He expressed a warm loyalty and finally signed a treaty on similar terms to those of O'Neill, agreeing to accept whatever title the King should confer upon him.

The head of the great O'Brien race was Murrough, who was, however, the younger brother of Connor, the former chief, had been his Tanist, and succeeded him on his death in 1540. He also was won over and created Earl of Thomond and Baron of Inchiquin. These re-grant treaties had to take into account the expectant rights of tanists, and so Connor's son, Donough, was at the same time created Baron of Ibrackin and later, on Murrough's death, became second Earl of Thomond in which again his son Connor succeeded him.

Thus three feudal earldoms were bestowed on Gaelic kings, with several lesser titles of baron. The history of Tudor Ireland was to be largely the history of the great landlords, for or against the State, and therefore the after-fate of these creations is to be noted. The O'Donnells did not receive the expected title of Earl of Tyrconnell till the accession of James I. Nevertheless the entente now made turned this family for most of the century into a pro-English power in the north-west, used by the Government to balance the still greater O'Neills.

Among the families now won over, the Fitzpatricks, barons of Upper Ossory, henceforth were a strength added to the English connexion. The O'Brien Earls of Thomond by the end of the century had moreover accepted the State church. The Norman-Irish race of Clanrickard, after some vicissitudes, were then also found on the loyal, though not on the Protestant, side. But the greatest of the Gaelic families, the O'Neills of Tyrone, were destined to provide the fiercest opponents of the Tudor policy and to fall with a crash in 1603.

One item in the winning over of the Irish nobility was to induce them 'to come to Court', and thus James Fitzmaurice, later for a short time twelfth Earl of Desmond, was educated at Windsor and was known therefore as 'the Court page'. In the same way the young Barnaby Fitzpatrick, heir to the first Baron of Upper Ossory, and Thomas, son of James, the Earl of Ormond who died in 1546, were brought up along with the young Edward the sixth. One prominent chief, however, was not pardoned or taken into favour. This was Brian O'Connor, lord of Offaly, brother-in-law of Silken Thomas, who had been the bravest and most determined of 'the Geraldine band'. He himself was destined to be banished and his country confiscated.

The future of the 'new earls' was to prove uncertain and troubled, and the comment of the Annals of the Four Masters that by these treaties 'the sovereignty of every Gaelic lord was

lowered' represents the Irish feeling that by accepting tenure and
titles from England they were abandoning the native tradition.

The submission, however, of forty of the greatest chiefs and
lords, the most general submission since Richard II, seemed
for the moment Henry's greatest triumph. He was content to
rule through them and to leave them to enjoy their lordships
undisturbed under this cover of submission to him, and for the
most part to govern their countries by Irish law and custom.
We find O'Donnell still ruling over his 'urraghs' or vassal-
chiefs, Maguire of Fermanagh and O'Connor of Sligo, and so
with the other paramount chiefs. Again, as under Henry II
or Richard II, the Irish chiefs might flatter themselves that
the King of England was merely a great foreign Árd Rí, content
with their homage.

By the end of his reign (1547) Henry's actual sovereignty
had extended over Leinster and was being pushed into nearer
Munster, where the Earls of Ormond and Desmond undertook
to co-operate in suppressing Brehon law and Irish bards and
introducing the principles of English law. The revenue was
but small, some eight thousand pounds at best yearly, and
Henry's policy of moderation was inspired by this fact that
Ireland did not pay for itself.

EDWARD VI, 1547–1553

The success of Henry's policy had been mainly due to St.
Leger, an Englishman of the old aristocratic type, and a fair-
minded man who saw no reason for depriving Irish lords or the
Church of their just liberties. He was continued in office for
another year, till 1548, but was then succeeded by Sir Edward
Bellingham, sent over as Deputy to enforce the reform ideas
of the Protector Somerset. As yet these were of a mild or
Lutheran order, but opposition to the breach with Rome was
stiffening, and while Browne of Dublin spoke for the government, Dowdall of Armagh took the lead of the Catholic party.
The aristocratic cliques that ruled England under an infant
King had little time for strong measures in Ireland, and again
in 1550 St. Leger was restored and the Mass was again sung

in Christ Church. The first prayer book of Edward VI, still a Catholic one, was printed in Dublin, but the second or Genevan one was not sent over. Whatever Protestant population there was was to be found in the towns, and even nobles like the Earl of Ormond, in common with the great men of both countries, waited to see whether Rome would return or what form the State church was to take. Texts and phrases were to play a large part in the decision one way or another. A picturesque story of a Council meeting in March 1551 of the deputy St. Leger and the archbishops of Armagh and Dublin with others, makes St. Leger defend Edward's first prayer book, while Dowdall exclaims against the Mass in English 'then shall every illiterate fellow read mass', and Browne as a loyal servant of whatever was the government, says, 'I submit to the king as Jesus did to Caesar'.

More and more the English government in Ireland was to realize that to get a population loyal both in Church and State an English colony was needed. The greater part of Ireland was not 'shire land' in which sheriffs could rule and the Common law run. To extend the 'English land' was needful, and already under Edward, Leix and Offaly,[1] whose chiefs had been put out of grace, were garrisoned, and in the north-east Sir Nicholas Bagenal, Marshal of the army, was granted the Lordship of Mourne in Down and the rich lands of the abbey of Newry, which became an English foothold in Ulster.

THE CATHOLIC RESTORATION, 1553-1558

A boy-king was now succeeded by an ailing and elderly woman, and though the old Church was restored, it was but for five years. For the moment it all seemed a triumph for Ireland, in which both the nobility and the Catholic bishops could be loyal alike in Church and State. Browne and the married bishops were deprived and Ireland absolved and restored to the faith by the Papacy. Mary, however, retained

[1] The Crown in November 1548 appointed an Englishman, Walter Cowley, as 'Surveyor-General and Escheator-General of Ireland', to receive, value, and re-distribute the forfeited lands. 'Escheator-General' was to prove a dreaded name in subsequent forfeitures and Plantations.

her father's title, and was proclaimed as Queen of Ireland, nor
was it possible to recover from the hands of the grantees, however Catholic, the former abbey lands. The noble-minded St.
Leger was restored with no difficulty about the Mass, and he
ruled till 1556 with his former policy of conciliation. To
reverse acts of injustice and to please those who loved the great
families, three noble youths were allowed to return, Gerald of
Kildare, Thomas Butler, Earl of Ormond, son of Earl James
who died in 1546, and Barnaby Fitzpatrick, Lord of Upper
Ossory. Gerald, the new Earl of Kildare, had been brought
up as a foreigner and never went back to Irish ways. Though
restored to vast estates, he never recovered either the palatine
powers or the political ascendancy of his race. The Geraldines
of Leinster had in effect been tamed, and not till 1798 did they
again produce a patriot name. Thomas, tenth Earl of Ormond,
was to live to a great age, and did not die till 1614. He was
known as 'Black Tom', and because of his good looks and
kinship with her was a favourite of Elizabeth. His grandfather, Piers Roe, had seen and brought about the ruin of the
Fitzgeralds of Kildare; Thomas himself, an able soldier and
politician, continued the loyal policy and before his death saw
the Geraldine house of Desmond completely destroyed. In
so far as a man could be called a Protestant at this stage, the
Earl of Ormond was one, and in any case an unswerving
supporter of the State.

In 1556 a forward policy began with the Earl of Sussex, who
arrived as Lord Lieutenant on May 24th 1556 and superseded
St. Leger. The new viceroy was instructed to restore the whole
Catholic system, to expel the Scots from Antrim, and to plant
Leix and Offaly. A parliament met at Dublin in June 1557,
and a Bull of Paul IV absolved Ireland from heresy and confirmed Mary as Queen.

The Scottish danger had been growing for half a century.
The Lordship of the Isles had been extinguished in 1499, but
the MacDonnells transferred themselves to Islay, Rathlin, and
Antrim, and by 1550 James MacDonnell, who called himself
Lord of the Isles, established himself in the Glens of Antrim,
where an older branch of the race had ruled since 1400. By

this time there were some ten thousand Hebridean Scots, or 'Redshanks' as they were called, in the North, and they spread westward against the MacQuillans, lords of the Route, and south against the O'Neills of Clandeboy. These Scots were gallant fighters, war was their trade, and, like the earlier galloglasses, they began to hire themselves out along with their kinsmen from the Isles in the service of the Ulster chiefs. Sussex made a useless raid against them, and they continued to be a great factor in the North for forty years.

The midland area of Ireland had long been a land of un-conquered septs—the O'Mores of Leix, the O'Connors of Offaly, the O'Dempseys of Clanmalier, and others. From their secure retreat among the great bogs and woods they easily attacked the Pale and year by year exacted their black-rents. Brian O'Connor had been outlawed for his part in the Geraldine league and finally was deprived of his lordship. Under Edward, Leix and Offaly were annexed, and, as was often to be the case later, the Crown's title to these areas, by descent from the Mortimers, etc., was easily found by juries of inquisition. Surveys of the districts were made under Cowley, the Escheator-General, and had the Irish realized it the terrible weapon of confiscation threatened them all. According to the English law, forfeiture followed the crime of Treason and all that was needed then was to get a local jury to declare the lands vested in the Crown and at its full disposal. Under the conditions of the time a jury could be intimidated, bullied, or even fined and imprisoned for not giving a verdict to suit the government, and so obsequious juries, even of native Irish-men, were found for sixty or seventy years ready to attaint their own chiefs. An act of parliament was necessary to complete the attainder by which the convicted man and his heirs were for ever deprived of their lands, but Parliament itself could be subjected to government pressure.

The confiscation of areas so large and the dispossession of a whole body of native lords, still less of all the population, could hardly have taken place in Tudor England, no matter how great the Despotism was, but in Ireland it became common for a century and a half to declare vast countries forfeited and all

the local landowners attainted, the next step being to plant
such areas with English grantees. Thus Confiscation and
Plantation were to go hand in hand, and Leix and Offaly under
a Catholic queen were the first example.

By an elaborate plan the countries of Leix, Offaly, Clanmalier, Slievemargy, etc., were in 1556 thrown open to
planters. The native owners were to retain only a third of
their own country, that lying to the west, while in the nearer
two-thirds land grants were made to a number of settlers on
stated terms. These were to be 'English subjects born either
in England or Ireland'; their estates were to be limited in size
and were to descend to the eldest son by the English law of
succession; the grantees must take only English servants; they
must build stone houses, and serve the Deputy with a stated
number of troops, and to pay a head-rent ('quit-rent') to the
Crown. The Irish chiefs and freeholders were also to receive
grants in the forfeited areas on quit-rent terms, and the confiscated territories were shired as King's and Queen's counties,
with fortresses at Philipstown and Maryborough.

This treatment of the native race was so sweepingly unjust
that the native septs rose in arms, and for some fifty years
their fierce resistance was prolonged by scions of these families.
The terms indeed had to be modified later, in 1561, and more
generous grants made to the chiefs, among whom, for example,
Owny O'Dempsey got a re-grant of his whole country, and his
nephew later became Viscount Clanmalier. But the O'Mores
and O'Connors, who were naturally the main opponents
of a policy which reduced them from Gaelic kings to small
landlords, produced determined and gallant rebels, such as
Rory O'More of Leix, his son Rory Oge and his son again
Owny MacRory, all alike slain in battle against the English.
Not till 1603, at the general reduction of Gaelic Ireland, did
the remnant of these septs lay down the arms which they had
used in every rising that marked Elizabeth's régime. By that
time the O'Connors had disappeared and of the O'Mores one
only, the father of the famous Rory O'More of 1641, was
allowed to retain a small estate.

There was no difficulty in getting the petty parliament of the
Pale to confirm this plantation. But a year after, in November

1558, Queen Mary was dead, and the long reign of Elizabeth was destined to end in a general destruction of Gaelic and feudal Ireland.

Already by 1558 it seemed doubtful if Henry VIII's policy of ruling Ireland through the 'new earls' would succeed. It was hoped on the English side that the great lords and chiefs would gradually introduce and enforce in their own countries the English law, religion, and language. But the Government and even these new earls could hardly foresee what a determined opposition the old Gaelic and Brehon order was capable of, even among the Old English. The poets and bards had long been the chief inspirers of the native tradition and maintained the haughty pride and warlike spirit of their patrons, Gael or Gall, by their encomiums in verse. Similarly, the Brehons and chroniclers kept up the native law and all its records, and while they and the poets were well endowed in the Gaelic system, so also thousands of galloglasses and other mercenary soldiers depended on the native order which they were determined to maintain. The Tudor government had already set itself to proscribe Irish law and language, and hoped that where it could not do so directly it might turn earls and chiefs into agents for doing so. Again, the abolition of Irish captainships and patriarchal titles such as O'Neill had already been urged by officials, and in one or two cases had been included in terms of Surrender and Re-grant. 'Experience showeth that the captainships in Ireland are the undoing of the same', wrote an official in 1544, and this remained the Government idea till the end of the century, when the wise Mountjoy declared, however: 'For believe me with my experience, the titles of our honours do rather weaken than strengthen them (the Irish chiefs) in this country.'

By the terms of Surrender and Re-grant the lord or chief was left in possession of his whole country without provision made for the rights of his tenants or even the introduction of English law and land-tenure. In other words, when Henry made O'Neill, Clanrickard, and others peers of the realm, he actually threatened their Irish vassals with a form of landlordism quite unknown to Irish law. In native law the chief

was not the owner of his whole 'country' (which in O'Neill's
case meant the three modern shires of Tyrone, Armagh, and
Derry)—he was simply the elected head and ruler of a whole
body of vassal septs, some of whom held from him, while
others again held of these vassals, freeholders who bore arms
were numerous, and underneath all there was a large population
of earth-tillers and craftsmen who also had their rights in law,
though they were unwarlike. The chief had but a demesne of
his own, called 'mensal lands', and further to maintain him
in his office he had rights of tributes, food-rents and military
service over his whole 'country'. In the feudal system of
Monarchy, all authority, title, and land-tenure came from above
by the grant of the King or a superior lord. Of Irish law,
however, it would be almost true to say that 'it was the people
who gave the land to the chief, while in the feudal State the
chief gave the land to the people'. The imposition of a great
local tyrant, called an earl or baron, deriving his title and
authority from an English king and intended to serve him,
was resisted by an overwhelming mass of opinion.

ENGLISH AND IRISH LAW

It was no mere romantic sentiment that was involved in
being 'O'Neill', 'MacCarthy More', etc., for whoever had been
duly inaugurated king commanded the allegiance, the military
service, the tributes and above all the sacred awe of his people.
Hence Mountjoy could say fifty years later, 'No subjects have
a more dreadful awe to lay violent hands on their lawful prince
than these people have to touch the persons of their O'Neills.'
It added little as regards the obedience of the people that
some one was Earl of Tyrone or Clancarthy if he were not also
O'Neill or MacCarthy More, for the legal background was one
in which the chief according to ancient custom was supreme
lord. Especially in war, he could bring out the whole armed
forces of his freemen and commandeer food-supplies. To have
such a lord was essential to the unity and strength of an Irish
state, and even if the exactions were numerous, the motto ran
'Spend me and defend me'. Hence the Government itself
continued in many cases to accept chiefs as 'captains of their

nations' because as such it could call them to account; and
hence, to quote one instance, Hugh O'Neill defended his taking
the title of O'Neill (forbidden by law) while he was also Earl
of Tyrone because otherwise some one else would take it and
the people would prefer to obey him rather than an English-
created earl.

This Gaelic resistance, based on chieftainship and Tanistry,
was to last for fifty years, and elective captainships did not
disappear until the law had subdued the whole population.
The old Gaelic world, which had existed for two thousand
years, was now to clash with the modern world as represented
by the Tudor government, strongly entrenched in Dublin.
Its ideal was that of an aristocracy who still lived in the heroic
age, in the atmosphere of battle and foray, and who were
expected by their poets, historians, and followers to be warriors
rather than statesmen. Numbers of them fell in the forefront
of useless battles, while the wise man who let the others do the
fighting and kept himself in power for a long life was rare.
True, the chiefs were now to produce men who perforce
were statesmen and wily politicians rather than mere soldiers,
such as Shane O'Neill; but even his remarkable brain was
stilled by a sudden stab in a drunken quarrel.

The Gaelic resistance against English law and language and
against the State landlords of native blood who 'had gone
over' was not a general one; it could indeed hardly be so, for
each of the many chiefs who ruled the greater part of Ireland
was 'king in his own country', and their feuds and jealousies,
old and present, were too many to sink. Even if a great genius
had risen to unite them theirs was a most unequal struggle
against the machinery of a powerful State, especially as the
Gaelic chief was not even hereditary, and at any moment a
strong or Irish-minded ruler might be displaced by a weak or
loyal kinsman, whom the Government could, as it often did,
make use of as a 'tame' or 'Queen's O'Neill'.   'n spite of our
admiration for some gallant and noble leaders and sympathy
for their attitude to the world, we must admit that they were
hopelessly out of date and destined to lose, since they could
scarcely hope to conquer and seldom knew how to compromise.

Of his Gaelic resistance there were already several striking local instances. Richard, second Earl of Clanrickard (1544–1582), called 'Sasanach' by his people because he had adopted English ways and tried to rule as a Crown earl, was opposed not only by an elected 'MacWilliam' who represented the old order, but even by his own two sons. In Thomond, Donough O'Brien became the second earl, but on his death in 1554 his brother Donal asserted the old captainship and ruled for four years. We have now vehement poems of the bardic poets praising these champions of the old order and pouring contempt upon the 'Queen's Irish'. In Thomond, however, Conor, Donough's son, succeeded as earl, and the O'Briens henceforth combined the powers derived from the old title and the new.

It was in the North that the most striking clash occurred of the new and the patriarchal order and that the latter found its greatest champion. Conn O'Neill, in accepting the title of Earl of Tyrone, had renounced that of O'Neill and his eldest son Matthew, Baron of Dungannon, was to be his heir-at-law. But the next son, Shane (called by the Irish 'the Proud') claimed that Matthew was illegitimate and that he was the rightful heir. Shane was already Tanist to his father, now an old man who died in 1559, but he did not by his birth claim to be next earl. On the contrary, he rejected all English titles and came out as the determined maintainer of Gaelic kingship. In the feud that followed between him and his brother, Matthew was slain, and at the accession of Elizabeth Shane held the field while Matthew's two sons, Brian and Hugh, were mere youths. When Conn Bacach died, Shane had no hesitation in taking on the proud style and the great powers of 'The O'Neill'.

Ireland was now a world of varied elements, in which the most permanent and effective was the State seated in Dublin and able to command most of Meath and Leinster as well as the loyalty of Ormond and a large element among the Anglo-Irish. The proceedings of Council and parliament in the Pale for the present might be disregarded by Gaelic and Norman lords, but they were to be of decisive importance for them and the future of Ireland. Of such a nature were the doings of Elizabeth's first parliament in Dublin.

G

THE REFORMATION PARLIAMENT, 1560

The Earl of Sussex was continued as lieutenant by the new Queen, and like most of the aristocracy of his time was as ready to enforce the English service as he had been a few years before to restore the Mass. He summoned a parliament which lasted from January 12th to February 1st 1560, and in it in less than twenty days was imposed on Ireland by the government and the Irish-born deputies of a third of the island a Reformation of the Church which was certainly unacceptable to the great majority of Irishmen. Parliament now represented ten counties and twenty-eight towns, namely, Leinster, Meath, and two counties of Munster (Tipperary and Waterford), so that Ulster and Connacht were unrepresented save for one town deputy from Ulster and two from Connacht. Twenty-three temporal peers attended, but the only Gaelic ones were Thomond and Fitzpatrick. As to the number of bishops who actually came when summoned authors differ, and possibly only some eleven attended. By the parliamentary constitution the spiritual Estate could not defeat a statute, and so were passed the two acts of Supremacy and Uniformity in wording similar to those already passed by the English parliament.

By the act of Supremacy the monarch became Supreme Governor on earth of the Church of Ireland, and an oath accepting the Queen as such was imposed upon all holders of office in Church and State, all mayors of corporate towns, all taking university degrees, and all tenants-in-chief of the Crown suing out livery of their estates. The Queen was given the appointment by letters patent of bishops. By the act of Uniformity the new Book of Common Prayer was imposed upon all ordained clergy, and attendance at the State Church was made compulsory on pain of a fine of one shilling each Sunday (the 'Recusancy' fine). English was the language of the prayer book, and yet this language was only understood by a minority of the people. It was provided that Latin might be used instead, but no provision was made for the Irish language, which all the Gaelic race spoke and most of the Old English understood. No attempt was made until it was too late to convert the people through the medium of their own language, and it was not till the beginning of James I's reign that the prayer book and New Testament were published in Irish, nor was it till the reign of Charles I that the whole Bible was translated into Irish. So was set up in Ireland that Established Church on Anglican lines which the Irish called the 'Queen's religion' and which was officially called 'that religion which is established by the laws of the land', or 'the Protestant reformed religion established by law'. From this time, however, a Protestant population slowly grew up, at first in the towns and later reinforced by the new colonists.

How was Ireland to accept this Elizabethan establishment, which in theory was the Catholic Church of Ireland merely reformed and cleansed of abuses under the direction of Monarchy and Parliament? How many bishops accepted the royal Supremacy is a disputed point; a Catholic writer declares that out of eleven bishops who attended Parliament seven accepted the Supremacy Oath, while a Protestant divine says that out of all the bishops only two refused the Oath and were deprived. The persecution of those who objected was at the time not good policy, and for some thirty or forty years the Queen in general used the royal Prerogative to dispense with the Oath in the case of officials and protected the ordinary loyal subject from persecution for Religion's sake. But it was clear that the Church had been set up on a basis to which ultimately all must conform, and to be loyal to the Crown both as sovereign and head of the Church was considered the duty of all true subjects. Nor could it be doubted that the old Church of the Papal allegiance to which the majority of the Irish belonged had been dispossessed and disestablished and that the Catholic population had lost the cathedrals and churches and were by law unable to serve the Crown. Thus religious persecution at first took only a negative aspect and it was long before positive and active persecution began.

The precise nature of this breach with the old order was at first hard to realize. In the eyes of Rome, Elizabeth's new prayer book made the Church of England and of Ireland both schismatic and heretical. It was some time, however, before the Pope abandoned the dream of winning this woman back, and it was not till 1570 that Pius V excommunicated her and released her subjects from their obedience. Up to that time, therefore, though the situation became more tense in Ireland, we must regard Religion as not playing the chief part. Nevertheless, for the first time in history a common resentment against the new Establishment and the official policy on religion began to unite the two races, Gaelic and Old English, who were to become the Irish nation.

SHANE O'NEILL, 1558–1567

Sussex remained Lieutenant of Ireland till 1566. He was the last of those viceroys of the old aristocratic St. Leger type who, whatever their particular orders were, in general respected the rights of the Irish nobility and people, and wished for reforms to go slowly and to secure national acceptance. In a dispatch to Elizabeth in 1560 he pointed out how Ireland was still divided into the two factions of the Geraldines and the Butlers, and that, while the latter favoured the Earl of Thomond and the Baron of Dungannon, the Geraldines favoured Shane O'Neill and Donal O'Brien, champions of Tanistry. He advised that the Irish captains should be summoned so that their consent should be obtained to accepting the government as coming from the Prince and paying a certain rent to the Crown, while they should rule their country in a manner according to the old order. Two years later he repeated this advice and advised that the Brehon law should be tolerated in Irish countries and even between the Irish and the March English. He was finally withdrawn in February 1566, and succeeded by Sir Henry Sidney.

Sidney ruled till 1571. He also was a manly, tolerant, and indeed a lofty-minded statesman and one of the greatest men that England has sent to Ireland; but by this time the two countries were growing more and more apart and the problem of ruling Ireland in the face of the 'strong policy' which was now in favour became more and more difficult. Of the many problems which Sidney had to face that of dealing with Shane O'Neill was the greatest.

Shane was the most uncompromising opponent of English

rule in Ireland that had yet appeared. A most skilful politician and a man of humorous and attractive address, a handsome and proud personage also, he proved more than a match for that official class which now had the State behind them, or if he came to an interview proved disarmingly attractive. After all, he commanded three whole counties in Ulster as well as the vassalage of Maguire, MacMahon, O'Reilly and other chiefs. In 1560 Elizabeth ordered his subjugation, with the unfortunate result that the young Brian, Baron of Dungannon, was slain in 1562. His younger brother, Hugh, was rescued by the Government and brought over to London, where he was taken into the Earl of Leicester's household. But Shane could not be ignored or crushed, and so at the end of 1561 he was summoned over to London to see the Queen herself and stayed there from January to May 1562. Considering the fate of Silken Thomas before him and many a chief after him, it was a bold step to march into the lion's den even with a royal safe-conduct. On January 6th he made his submission to the Queen, who admired him as she did all handsome men, while London partly jested and partly was impressed with the 'Great O'Neill' and his tall galloglasses. Shane returned to Ireland high in favour, with the unofficial title of Lord of Tyrone, and with encouragement for his offer to expel the Antrim Scots whom at the present the Dublin Government disliked. For several years Shane was the greatest figure in Ireland. According to a report of Sidney, 'Lucifer was never puffed up with more pride or ambition than O'Neill is. He continually keepeth six hundred armed men about him and is able to bring into the field one thousand horsemen and four thousand foot. He is the only strong man of Ireland, his country was never so rich or inhabited, and he armeth and weaponeth all the peasants of his country, the first that ever did so of an Irishman.'

Expeditions, partly military, partly diplomatic, were made against Shane at various times by Sussex and Sidney, but both in arms and in diplomacy O'Neill fenced skilfully, for he was not a great soldier. He was ready to acknowledge the Queen as sovereign but was resolute against the introduction of English law into Ulster. He was proud of his descent from an Earl of Kildare, which thus gave him friends in the Pale, for by this time, though the law made a distinction between the Irish and the Old English, in fact through intermarriage the Butlers, Burkes, Desmonds, O'Neills, and other great families were of mixed blood. On one occasion Shane declared to Government envoys: 'I care not to be an earl unless I be better and higher than an earl, for I am in blood and power better than the best of them (the new Irish earls), and will give place to none but my cousin of Kildare for that he is of mine house. My ancestors were kings of Ulster and Ulster is mine and shall be mine.' Such was the main aim of Shane, in whose programme Religion or the union of Ireland counted less than the maintenance of the O'Neill kingship. In this aim his two opponents were the O'Donnells and the Antrim Scots, and he won his greatest victory against the latter at Glenshesk near Ballycastle on May 2nd 1565, where James, the head of the MacDonnells was slain. His death was not forgiven by the Scots, who found a new leader in James's brother, Sorley Boy ('Buidhe').

The victorious Shane then turned against the O'Donnells whose chief Calvach he defeated and captured. Calvach died in 1566 and was succeeded by his brother Hugh Duv ('the Black'), whom the Government determined to support. For the first time the idea occurred of seizing Derry in order to attack Ulster from the sea, and this port was occupied by Colonel Randolph, but a gunpowder explosion led to the evacuation of the garrison. Encouraged by this, in 1567 Shane marched into Tyrconnell, but at Farsetmore on the Swilly was completely routed by O'Donnell. Having lost his army, Shane took the wild idea of throwing himself on the protection of the Scots of Antrim, but when he fled to them they murdered him in a drunken quarrel at Cushendun when they brought to mind their defeat at Glenshesk. Thus perished the greatest O'Neill that the old Gaelic order had produced.

On the news, both Sidney and Cecil urged the confiscation and then the shiring of Ulster, which lay vacant, but the Queen was content to have Shane attainted, the name of O'Neill legally extinguished, three counties confiscated by

legal process, and then to allow Turloch Luineach O'Neill to
succeed as practical lord of Tyrone. Turloch was second
cousin of Shane and had been his Tanist. It is illustrative
of the Irish law of kingly succession that Turloch's claim to
succeed went back to Conn More, who died in 1493, his great-
grandfather, and grandfather to Shane, and that since this
Conn there had been at least fifteen 'royal heirs'. Turloch was
a cautious and on the whole a loyal man and for some twenty
years under him it appeared as if native Ulster might safely
be allowed to continue. Meanwhile the young Hugh, now
Baron of Dungannon, with the Queen's favour, 'trooped the
streets of London with sufficient equipage and orderly respect'.

The interest again shifts to Dublin and the Pale. With Sir
Henry Sidney a 'forward policy' was ordered from Whitehall
which was the first step towards the general reduction of
Ireland on Tudor lines. Whether this could be done by peaceful means and general content was doubtful; in any case the
growing religious tension complicated the question, for we
cannot doubt that had there been no Reformation the loyal
element in Ireland would have been very large and would have
included a great majority of the Old English.

Sidney's instructions, as given to him in October 1565,
outlined much of this new policy. He was to inquire into the
best means available of establishing 'Christ's religion' among
the people. The whole of the existing counties of Munster and
Leinster, save Clare, were to be considered as under the law.
English manners were to be substituted for Irish customs,
money rents for arbitrary exactions of the lords, and the chiefs
were to be induced to accept 'estates of inheritance'. It was a
large programme and Sidney was given great powers, such as
the appointment of all Church officers except archbishops and
bishops and of all civil offices except the Chancellor, Treasurer,
and chief justices. He rightly could complain, however, that
the revenue on which to do all this was inadequate, for Tudor
parsimony continued almost to the end, and that he had only
twelve hundred soldiers in a land where lords and chiefs had
on foot some twenty or thirty thousand men.

Sidney continued the Surrender and re-grant policy which

during the reign made apparently loyal a considerable number of Gaelic chiefs. The granting of titles continued, and another great dynast, Donal MacCarthy More, was in 1565 made Earl of Clancarthy. In the next year Calvach O'Donnell again acknowledged the Queen, and in 1567 Donal O'Connor Sligo surrendered his captaincy and received a grant for life of his whole country. Now, this O'Connor was an 'urragh' or chief vassal of O'Donnell, and though the latter was for the present loyal the Government's evident scheme for withdrawing the 'urraghs' from under the paramount chiefs and bringing them directly under the Crown was to cause further trouble.

Sidney's parliament of 1569–1570 enacted the new policy. It was again more representative of Ireland than the parliament of 1560, but Ulster, Connacht, and the Desmond country were still unrepresented. There appeared in it for the first time what was to be of permanent consequence, namely, a constitutional, Catholic, and loyalist opposition led by Sir Edmund Butler, eldest brother of the Earl of Ormond, which was supported by the Lords of the Pale and the lawyers and deputies who appeared for the towns. Among his other measures for making Ireland a monarchy Henry VIII had established the King's Inns in Dublin as the centre of the Irish legal profession, for without it the much-desired English law could not spread. This weapon was now turned against the Government, for the lawyers of the Old English stock who were trained there henceforth opposed the Reformation and set themselves to defeat whatever penal laws might be passed. It was not yet possible generally to exact the oath of Supremacy and many of the chief government officials remained Catholic. Especially did the old self-governing towns remain strongholds of the old Faith and until 1624 even their mayors were generally Catholic. The lawyers were the obvious people to elect for the towns and along with the Lords and gentry of the Pale they formed what was called a 'country' party as against the 'Court' or 'English party'. For the first time a Deputy had to use skill and persuasion amounting to force to carry through measures against a stout and conscious Opposition. Sidney wanted Poynings' law suspended so that measures proposed by him could be put at once before this parliament. But the Irish party now saw in Poynings' law a weapon to their hand, and a check upon arbitrary measures, religious or otherwise, on the part of viceroys, for the procedure it entailed it gave them time 'to appeal to Caesar'. Finally, however, a Suspension bill was accepted, but with the provision that in future such a bill must secure a majority of both Houses.

The effective result was that any penal measures against Catholics or even active measures to endow the State Church had to be dropped and the parliament ended in a triumph for the Opposition. It was, however, a loyal opposition and Sidney found no difficulty in getting an act to attaint Shane O'Neill, to abolish the O'Neill title, and declare three counties forfeited. Henceforth the Old English Catholics in parliament were always ready to attaint 'traitors and rebels' at the Government's wish, in order to have a greater claim for indulgence on the religious question. The result of such tactics was that by 1603 the Irish Statute book contained much less penal legislation against the Roman faith than did the English.

Sidney's other measures were also passed; such as a parliamentary subsidy for ten years in lieu of the 'coign and livery' which had formerly maintained the army; an act to shire all the countries that were not yet shire-ground; and another to abolish Irish captaincies except where established by law. Under the shiring act, Connacht was in 1570 divided into counties. The intention of this act was indicative of the Government's policy to anglicize all Ireland, namely 'that her Majesty's laws may have full course through the whole realm'. The act 'for taking away captainships and all exactions belonging thereunto from all lords and great men of this realm exercising absolute and regal authority within large circuits', though it could not be at once enforced, was sufficient to alarm not only Gaelic 'lords of countries' but also great feudal princes such as the Earl of Desmond and the Burkes, whose powers went back to the original conquest.

Another act of this parliament set up presidencies for Connacht and Munster and for a hundred years these two provinces were subjected to what was in effect a local form of the all-powerful Council at Dublin, with the object of suppressing feudal and chiefly privileges and bringing the whole country under the law. Sir Edward Fitton was the first President of Connacht and Sir John Perrot, reputed an illegitimate son of Henry VIII, the first President of Munster.

Before this parliament ended Sir Edmund Butler, who had begun as the leader of the loyal Catholics, was in rebellion, and by an act of this very parliament an attainted traitor. How this came about is instructive of the situation that was developing in Ireland.

The chief motives of rebellion under Elizabeth were destined to be: the insecurity of land-titles among the Old English of Leinster and Munster, threatened by English-born adventurers and planters, the attack upon feudal and chiefly lordships, and the religious grievance. At first it was the two former which agitated men, and it was not till Hugh O'Neill attempted to make a national combination that the three were united. The temporal sovereignty of Elizabeth was not repudiated in any thorough fashion, but the attacks on what the Irish considered their rights of land and liberties and to hold office gradually brought more and more of them into the field against the official government.

A curious bit of antiquarian buccaneering drove Sir Edmund Butler with others into revolt. When the Presidency of Munster was set up a band of young gentlemen from Devon, Somerset, and other south-western counties began to arrive in Ireland, such as Sir Walter Raleigh, Sir Humfrey Gilbert, and others. Among these Sir Peter Carew of Mohun Ottery in Devon was certainly the most aspiring. On the strength of a pedigree whose value is very uncertain he claimed to be the heir of Fitzstephen and the original Carews of Ireland, and so to be the inheritor of most of Carlow and the moiety of the old 'Kingdom of Cork'. The Carews of Ireland had in fact expired about 1370 and their chief barony in Carlow, Idrone, was now in the possession of the Kavanaghs. The northern part of Idrone, called the Dullough, had come into Butler hands and belonged to Sir Edmund. Peter Carew's claims were seriously put before the Council, which declared them valid, and as the Council was all-dominant in the area which it could control, nothing but strong protest, armed or otherwise, was of any use. Sir Edmund with his brothers went into rebellion, and though after three years he was pardoned he was never restored in blood and so did not inherit the Earldom in due time. The Kavanaghs, who by this time were much weakened by division into several septs, made their protest to the Lord Deputy Sidney and the Council in 1568, and three of their chiefs declared that their ancestors before the Conquest and ever since had been lawfully seized of Idrone. The answer of the Council was, however, that Dermot 'Ny Gall', king of Leinster, had but one daughter and heir 'who was married to the Earl Strongbow, from whom descended divers noblemen of England, of which stock the defendants were not come, but a wild Irish race and kindred sprung up since within the realm'. The right and legitimate descent of the Kavanaghs was thus denied, and the title of the Carews, whose heir Sir Peter was, was affirmed. The Carews had been barons there, 'until the MacMurroughs, a rebellious nation of Irish people, in time of common rebellion, wrongfully and by force seized the said barony and lands and with strong hands and without right or title maintained it; from which MacMurroughs the present defendants are descended, but not born in lawful marriage or legitimate by the laws of Holy Church'. The defendants not being able to prove the contrary, the Lord Chancellor and court decreed that Sir Peter and his heirs should have the possession of the barony. There was nothing left for the Kavanaghs to do but to accept Sir Peter as their lord (for in default of a native lord the Irish generally wished to have a strong and just master, even of English blood), and, as it happened, Sir Peter proved a kindly and easy lord. But the case was most illustrative of what was to happen when Irish chiefs, no longer able to make a fight, found their claims to their lands challenged either by the Crown as representing the Mortimers and other families or by Anglo-Irish claimants going back to the original conquest.

Meath and Leinster having by this time been more or less brought under the law, the rich and accessible province of Munster was the next experiment. Perrot, President of Munster, declared the Earl of Desmond's palatine liberty of Kerry null and void, while that of the Earl of Ormond in Tipperary was not to be infringed. Sir Humfrey Gilbert did not hesitate 'to infringe the pretended liberties of any city or town corporate, not knowing their charters to further the Queen's service, answering them that the Prince hath an absolute power and that what might not be done by the one (prerogative) I would do by the other (force) in case of need'. Thus was the doctrine of the State proclaimed, and as a result Munster was soon in commotion. It was a part of the trouble that in the rich lands around Cork harbour, when Sir Peter Carew got his claims allowed, the Gilberts and Raleighs managed to feather their nests also.

Religion entered into the general grievances, and the Old English of Munster, a rich and prosperous country, full of towns and abbeys and inhabited by a strong feudal caste and their tenants, felt the religious appeal more strongly than did the native Irish. Already abroad the dispossessed Church had its bishops, papally appointed, and soon had its colleges in the Low countries, Spain, Portugal, and Italy. A strong and enthusiastic Irish world was being built up abroad, and as the idea of the counter-Reformation grew the Irish abroad, acting with the leaders at home, determined on a Crusade to recover Ireland for the Faith. The easy-going religion of the old sort was replaced after the Council of Trent by zeal, determination, and the conscious knowledge of the grounds for one's religion. The Jesuits and the bishops were the guiding spirits of this movement, while on the other hand the Crown for the success of the State Church relied upon Englishmen such as Adam Loftus and others, who 'by her royal pleasure' were installed in Armagh, Dublin, and the nearer sees. Loftus was a complete example of the new type of State bishop, unable to understand the language of the country, putting the English interest first, and yet as Chancellor and member of the Dublin government able to thwart the more generous viceroys such as Perrot. Successively during his long life, which ended in 1605, Loftus was dean of St. Patrick's, archbishop of Armagh, then finally of Dublin (1567–1605), and Provost of the new college founded by Elizabeth. To the common man of the time no doubt the Pope and theories of religion were far-off things, but the old familiar Mass and Sacraments were what touched him close, and when the service in St. Patrick's was in English, and Loftus removed the altar from the east end and put a communion table in the centre, the majority of Irishmen felt that this was not the old religion which they believed Christ founded and committed to Peter.

There was of course plenty of honest attachment, zeal, and intellect on the other side, and the Puritan spirit, now growing in England, was to be a militant antithesis of the Jesuit spirit on the Catholic side. When in February 1570 Pius V declared Elizabeth excommunicated as a heretic and her subjects released from obedience, the position of the peaceful Roman Catholic between the two kinds of zealot became more and more difficult. How was he to obey the Pope in spiritual things and be a loyal man to the Queen in temporal things? How was he to deny the right of the Pope to excommunicate, depose, and even sanction the murder of heretic sovereigns when Rome itself made no official statement as to this doctrine? Luckily for the ordinary man the Prerogative was high and was able by the Dispensing power and in other ways to shield him from the penalties of religious laws. The great failure of the State Church was that it was not made national or attractive enough and that its bishops were not of saintly and patriotic character fitted to win over the old population to itself.

THE FIRST DESMOND REVOLT, 1569–1573

Gerald, fourteenth Earl of Desmond, who succeeded in 1558, was a weak and incapable man, and his character was particularly unfortunate because for long his family had been out of royal favour and a palatinate so huge and independent as that which he inherited was almost certain to be attacked. Thomas, Earl of Ormond, had powers almost as great, but then he was the 'white-headed', as Desmond was the 'bad', boy of the piece in southern Ireland in Government eyes, and in any case Thomas was an exceedingly wise and acute man. The winning over of Desmond was attempted, and in London in 1562 he promised to pay the Queen her feudal dues, and to suppress

Brehon law and the poets 'who by their ditties and rhymes in commendation of extortions, rebellion, rape, and ravin do encourage lords and gentlemen'.   But he showed no inclination to carry out his promises, which were indeed difficult considering how great a power and revenue the Earl derived from the masses of his Gaelic tenants.   He had a standing feud with Ormond over boundaries such as Clonmel where their territories touched and over the prise of wines from the ports of Munster, and indeed the Ormond-Geraldine quarrel was a century old. Finally it came to a pitched battle in 1565 at Affane on the Suir, in which Earl Gerald was defeated and taken prisoner. Both earls were then summoned to London where Desmond along with his brother John was kept in honourable confinement till 1573.   Their detention was condemned by the Deputy as not only unjust but dangerous, because no Irish lord could afford to be absent from his country for long.   That Sidney was right was shown when Sir James Fitzmaurice, the Earl's cousin, summoned the chief Geraldines, declared that their lord's rights were in danger, and got himself elected their Captain.

Fitzmaurice was a Catholic enthusiast and made the Irish cause predominantly a religious one.   When the Pope declared Elizabeth deposed, his Bull was taken seriously by many of the Irish leaders, both the Church and the nobles, for the idea still survived that the Pope was the final suzerain of Ireland.   In common with the Catholic party in England, they looked to Mary, Queen of Scots, now in captivity, as the rightful sovereign of both realms.

This first revolt of the Old English of Munster was led by Fitzmaurice and Sir Edmund Butler who, for his part, declared, 'I do not make war against the Queen but against those who banish Ireland and mean conquest'.   In short, the reduction of the Desmond palatinate threatened that proud race which had made the former conquest with a new conquest directed against themselves.   Carew's claim to half of the old kingdom of Cork brought into the field even MacCarthy More, the new Earl of Clancarthy.   Carew, however, like Raleigh, Grenville, and the other Devon men now in Ireland, was of the fighting gentry type, who, as the Normans had done before them, backed up their charters with their swords.   He took Butler's castle of Cloghgrenan, and Perrot and Gilbert suppressed Munster with the merciless slaughter of garrisons. In the midlands and Wicklow the discontented septs rose under Rory Oge and the famous Fiach MacHugh O'Byrne, but no great battle is recorded or victory for the Irish side. When the allies besieged Kilkenny in 1569 it was a failure, but the composition of the rebel army is interesting, namely 4,500 men, of whom 1,400 were galloglass, 400 musketeers, 400 pikemen in mail, and the rest horsemen and kerns. Formidable in numbers, such Irish armies, however, were seldom a match for the small but disciplined armies of the government backed by artillery. The rebellion ended without any sweeping vengeance on the government's side and Fitzmaurice departed to the continent in 1573, while Sir Edmund, though he remained attainted, henceforth ceased to be a rebel.

In the lull that followed, the Lord Deputy Sidney, who had been recalled in 1571 but held office again from 1575 to 1578, was able in peace and in state to travel through Ulster and Connacht. For the present Ulster was left to its native chiefs, the loyal Hugh Duv O'Donnell, the semi-loyal Turloch O'Neill, and the apparently loyal Hugh, baron of Dungannon, who was sent back in 1568.

In his journey Sidney made shires of Connacht and of Clare, and when the 'degenerate English' of the west trooped in he found with surprise that few of them could speak English and that, though they knew their origin and surnames, Prendergast had become MacMorris, De Angulo Costello, and so on. In Connacht Richard, Earl of Clanrickard, was the great man and Conor, Earl of Thomond, the same in Clare, but the old Irish order died hard.

Connacht had its own wars, or rather constant disturbance, quite different from the other provinces. Though Clanrickard was a loyal man, his two sons, Ulick and John, called the 'Mac-an-Iarlas' or 'Earl's sons', led the resistance to the President of Connacht, whose orders were to introduce English law and abolish Irish 'cuttings and spendings'. The native nobility looked on this as a way of depriving them both of power and revenue, and making the 'churl as good as a gentleman'. Irish feudalism, whether Norman or Gaelic, was undoubtedly most oppressive to the poor man upon whom the quartering of mercenaries was a constant curse, and the haughty pride of the gentry in their ancestry and blood was extreme. It now took the form of hating the English language and the middle-class English who came as commanders and officials, rather than the Queen, to whom in general they did not refuse allegiance. The 'rising out' of the Burkes was supported by a remarkable female, Grace or Grania O'Malley, queen of Clare Island and Clew Bay, a famous commander of war galleys, who was said to be 'for forty years the stay of all rebellions in the west'.

The furious pride of the Burkes is shown in one or two incidents. In 1572 President Fitton sent the Earl of Clanrickard over to London to be detained and examined by the Privy council, whereupon his two sons and the Mayo Burkes flew into rebellion, and hired a whole army of 1,400 Scots and 2,000 galloglass. The sporadic fighting simmered on till 1582. In 1576 the Earl's sons submitted and went to Dublin with Sidney, but on their return, contrary to their agreement and in the sight of the castle of Athlone, 'they shook off their English clothes in the Shannon and resumed Irish dress'. In June of that year they attacked Athenry, which the English forces had occupied. Sidney reported: 'In this town was the sepulture of their fathers and their mother was also buried there; the chief church of which town they most violently burned, and Ulick, being besought to spare the burning where his mother's bones lay, blasphemously swore that if she were alive and in it he would burn the church and her too rather than any English churl should inhabit or fortify there.'

There was indeed as yet no Irish nation and the aims and local pride of the Connacht lords were a whole world removed from those of burgesses and landlords in the Pale, though a general attachment to Ireland united them, and even the Irish language was by now common with all Irishmen. Opportunism was indeed the general policy of lords and chiefs, for loyalty itself was hard to maintain. When Clanrickard died in 1582 he adjured his sons to serve the Queen of England and left his curse on any who would do the contrary. Ulick, the elder son, obeyed his father's words and as earl of Clanrickard became a loyal man; at the battle of Kinsale his son Richard was foremost on the English side. Even the famous Grace O'Malley, who married Richard 'the Iron' Burke, became mother of Theobald Burke 'of the Ships', first Viscount Mayo.

Meanwhile the Pale had its grievances too, for it had to support the main charges of the Government, and the Deputy's army was quartered upon it by 'cess', the coinage was a debased one, and the Lords and gentry of the Pale felt more than others the exclusion from office and fines which they suffered as 'Recusants'.

No wonder that able and honest men like Sidney groaned over their charge, for which they were provided with neither sufficient troops or men or even allowed a generous policy, for Elizabeth 'would never consent to let a great nobleman serve in his own country'. Indeed the government became more centralized still when in 1580 a Court of Castle Chamber was set up in Dublin, a parallel to the Star Chamber court in England, through which the English-born junta in Dublin controlled the whole government, and the lords of the Pale found themselves more and more excluded from that share in the Council of Ireland, which they believed they had under Poynings' law. These general grievances, however, such men as Fitzmaurice believed they could cut like the Gordian knot by a general Catholic confederacy backed by Spain and the Pope.

Philip II, indeed, though he continued to be the Catholic hope, proved a very disappointing patron, who actually during his long reign never sent over more than a few hundreds of men directly to the Irish cause. His hands were full with the revolt of the Netherlands which began in 1572, and with maintaining the greatness of Spain in Europe and the New World. When England helped the Dutch and the Huguenots he thought himself entitled to help Irish rebels in return, but mainly as a way of hitting back at his enemy, England, and without any enthusiasm for the Irish cause, which like a politician he waited to see become really formidable before he would help it. The Papacy was more whole-hearted but had not the money or the armies to back an Irish Catholic rising. Hence when Fitzmaurice returned, the show of support behind him was not impressive.

Fitzmaurice arrived at Dingle in Kerry on July 18th 1579, bringing with him a few soldiers, some money, and promises of further aid from Philip, and the Bull of Gregory XIII which declared Elizabeth deprived of her kingdoms. There accompanied him the Legate Saunders and the Jesuit Allen, both Englishmen, and a Spanish friar, Oviedo, papal commissary to the troops, who was to devote twenty years or more to bringing the Irish cause to success by Spanish aid. The leaders of this revolt had a moral justification for rebellion, which they declared to be sacred and lawful, 'a war for the Catholic religion and against a tyrant who refuses to hear Christ speaking by his Vicar', hence they called upon the people of Ireland without distinction to join them. John and James, the Earl's brothers, did so with numbers of the Munster gentry, but Desmond himself for the time stood aloof. Many native lords actively opposed the rising, especially Barrymore and Sir Cormac McCarthy of Muskerry, both good 'Queen's men'. Unfortunately for the cause, Fitzmaurice was killed on August 18th in a petty affray with the Burkes of Castleconnell, and the one real leader and man of pure principle in the rising disappeared. Nevertheless a widespread rising showed what discontented elements there were. The O'Mores and O'Connors took arms again, though Rory Oge was soon slain, and in Leinster FitzEustace, viscount Baltinglass, a typical lord of the Pale, revolted on the religious question and allied himself with the Wicklow rebels. In 1580 in the lonely pass of Glenmalure Fiach McHugh O'Byrne gave a complete overthrow to the forces of the Deputy, Lord Grey de Wilton.

The Munster rising was suppressed by Perrot, Ormond, 'General of the army of Munster', Carew, and other English commanders. Again pitched battles were rare and the war took the form of the siege and the massacre of garrisons and the destruction of the country which brought on all the horrors of famine. The promises of Philip and the Pope materialized

In a force of seven hundred Spaniards and Italians who landed at Smerwick west of Dingle in October 1580 and fortified themselves there. But rapidity of decision and combination was all on the English side, and the fort at Smerwick (remembered in Irish tradition as 'Dún-an-óir' or 'fort of gold') was besieged by the Lord Deputy and Sir Walter Raleigh, compelled to surrender, and its garrison pitilessly massacred.

Saunders and Allen both died during the rising and the Earl's brothers were the one slain and the other executed. Desmond himself was finally driven into rebellion, proclaimed a traitor, his castles stormed one by one, and at last when the rebel forces had been reduced to a handful was tracked down and killed at Glenageenty in Kerry on November 11th 1583. Thomas of Ormond might perhaps have procured the unfortunate Earl his life or pardon, but on the one hand Irish chiefs had now a natural dread of ending their days in the Tower and on the other Ormond was not averse to seeing the Geraldines overthrown. A large part of the shame must also rest on Philip, who left the unfortunate Irish to their fate.

By 1583 the rebellion was over and Munster was a devastated land. The introduction of colonists to support the English Church and government in Ireland had often been urged, and it was now resolved to try it on a large scale in this fertile but depopulated province. Henceforth for over a century rebellion, or whatever was styled so, was to be followed by confiscation and Plantation. The modern idea of redress to cure grievances was not thought of. Desmond had chosen to 'rebel', and it had cost Elizabeth half a million pounds to suppress him and his supporters, so he and they must pay for it. It was a simple and sufficient piece of logic for English rule in Ireland.

THE PLANTATION OF MUNSTER, 1586

In June 1586 Elizabeth approved the final 'Articles' for the plantation of the Desmond lands. The Earl and his chief supporters were attainted, and their attainder and the Plantation approved by the Parliament of this year. At first, out of the 5,000,000 acres of Munster 500,000 were intended for confiscation, but in the end only 210,000 were granted to the

new settlers. These were required to be English, but it was
not precisely demanded that they should be Protestant, and
indeed at the time there were too many gentlemen of the old
Catholic upbringing to insist on this point; in fact, some of the
planters, such as Sir Nicholas Browne, ancestor of the Earls
of Kenmare, were soon found on the Catholic side. The lands
confiscated were the richest in the south-west, and with the
imperfect measurements of the time (for the extent of an
estate depended on the evidence of sworn juries of the neighbourhood) it was always possible by pressure or persuasion to
add a great deal of supposed 'unprofitable' to the 'profitable'
lands. By this scheme 'Seignories' or chief grants of 12,000,
8,000, 6,000, and 4,000 acres were created. Those who were
granted them, called 'Undertakers', were to plant English
tenants under them. The grants were made in socage, not
tenure-in-chief, but a head or 'quit-rent' was to be paid to the
Crown. In Kerry, for example, the quit-rent was a mere
hundred pounds for the seignory of 12,000 acres. Along with
the planters, many of whom were at least brave soldiers, came
the lawyers, and in this and later plantations chicanery and
the cruel ingenuity of the law was used to extend the grants
and to swindle the natives. Thus, though no grantee was to
have more than one seignory, Sir Walter Raleigh was ultimately in possession of 40,000 acres.

The Plantation of Munster had for the time but a limited
success. It certainly led to a number of landlords of English
stock being added to the Old English and Irish of Munster,
who naturally hated them, but the grantees did little to fulfil
the planting conditions, and as Elizabeth received but little
revenue from the whole transaction she was soon disappointed,
and never again in her lifetime was such a plantation attempted.

SIR JOHN PERROT, LORD DEPUTY, 1584–1588

Perrot was a gallant and handsome man who, as President
of Munster, had acted with severity to the rebels, but now in
times of peace was for moderation and fair treatment both on
religion and land. He was indeed of the St. Leger type but
his pride and choleric temper were to ruin him. On being

appointed, he found himself thwarted by the English junta in the Council, led by the Chancellor Loftus, who wanted stronger measures against the Catholics. Perrot refused to have a Court of High Commission in Ireland and was against persecution for religion's sake. By now the government in Ireland was a despotism controlled from Westminster and checked by few of the institutions which checked it in England, and the Court of Castle Chamber, which lasted till 1672, was Ireland's Star Chamber and less controlled.

Among other checks, a frequent meeting of Parliament should have been the principal, but Perrot's was the first held since 1569. It met in April 1585 and lasted till May 1586. Again a wider area of Ireland than ever before was represented, and thirty-one towns and twenty-seven shires sent in all 118 deputies. But the more numerous the Commons were, the more they could organize resistance.

For the twenty-six peers who attended, Perrot prescribed parliament robes, and his Assembly had more pomp than had yet been seen. The Deputy began with a bill to suspend Poynings' law, in order that legislation could be carried through without consulting England, but by this time the Opposition well realized the advantages to them of this law, and the bill was rejected. Perrot, whose intended measures were thus thwarted, had to be content with a subsidy bill, and with acts for the attainder of Desmond, Baltinglas, and other rebels, and for the plantation of Munster and the Composition of Connacht. The Catholic party again pursued the skilful game of 'holding up' legislation which might be of a religious character. But to prove how loyal they were, though Catholics, they assented to the attainder of 'the great rebels'.

Perrot found himself thwarted on another side when, according to instructions, he proposed to convert St. Patrick's into a university but was defeated by Archbishop Loftus. His quarrel with the Loftus party finally led to his being withdrawn in June 1588 and charged with various offences. He finally died in the Tower in 1592. Loftus made it a great point against him that before his parliament there had been but twelve Recusants of any standing in the Pale, 'but since then they have grown to great obstinacy and boldness', for the Lord Deputy had said, 'This people are not to be dealt with hardly in matters of religion'.

THE COMPOSITION OF CONNACHT

Perrot's most effective achievement was the settling of the land-tenure question in Connacht and Clare. It had been a standing problem under the Tudors how to bring the Irish chiefs and old Norman lords under the Crown, to have their estates legalized in English law, and to decide on what terms their tenants were to hold of them. It was a problem answered in several ways, and not always with wisdom, while the violent way of ousting chiefs like the O'Connors and O'Mores led to nothing but long guerrilla resistance. In the Surrender and Re-grant treaties sometimes a whole vast country would be handed over to a Clanrickard or an O'Brien; at another time provision would be made for the vassals and freeholders of Irish law to retain their rights. The Composition of Connacht was at least an equitable and peaceful solution, though it was in favour of the great men.

In 1585 a Commission was appointed for the counties of Connacht and Clare, local juries were summoned and their inquisitions were made the basis of a great number of individual agreements with the lords and chiefs of the West. By these the Old English lords and 'chieftains of countries' were to hold their lands by secure tenure under the Crown in return for ten shillings on every quarter of arable land and a fixed amount of 'rising out' or military service to the Lord President of the province or the Deputy of Ireland when summoned. By the inquisitions the lords and chiefs were found to have enormous countries, thus O'Kelly of Hy Many was lord over 80,000 acres. In addition to the castles and demesnes which they held in virtue of their office, the chiefs derived from their tenants tributes in kind, military service, and what the English called 'cuttings and spendings'. The Normans had followed this system, but maintained primogeniture as against the Irish system of elective chieftainship and Tanistry. By the Composition the demesnes were to become the private and family property of the chiefs with succession to the eldest son.

though provision was made for the Tanists and 'royal heirs'. The office and title of chieftain, such as O'Connor Don and O'Kelly, with all that pertained to it, was abolished. Instead of the old 'cuttings and spendings', the chief's tenants were on the death of the present lords and chiefs to pay money rent, and the under-lords of the paramount chiefs were to grant the same terms to their tenants. This great Composition was to be ratified by Parliament, but unfortunately this was never done. Nevertheless it was a wise measure which quieted most of the turbulent aristocracy and allowed for the continuation of Gaelic law and tradition. As a result, and because Connacht and Clare were by Cromwell left to the Irish, the western province has remained until the present a predominant Norman and Gaelic land.

Another act of Perrot, though it seemed of little importance at the time, was to have great and lasting results. This was the kidnapping at Rathmullen in September 1587 of the young Red Hugh O'Donnell, who spent four years as a prisoner in Dublin Castle. But he was to be heard of again.

THE ARMADA AND IRELAND

As the reign of Elizabeth proceeded the religious atmosphere heightened and Ireland reflected the growing war of Reformation and counter-Reformation on the Continent. The Government was bent on enforcing the State religion, but for the present proceeded slowly, so that many found it possible to be complete Queen's men. Nevertheless the preaching of Jesuits and the papal bishops had its effect, and combined with religion was the resentment over the savage treatment of Desmond and far more loyal men such as Baltinglas. Religion, Land, and local Lordship were to be the great trio of Irish wrongs. Many who remained attached to the Queen as sovereign resented English methods and hated the new English settlers and officials; this was the spirit of the Lords of the Pale. It is one which has been common even with the most loyal of the Anglo-Irish in later times, and is one of the hardest things for Englishmen to understand.

Spain had long been the favourite among foreign countries to the Irish, and while the Gaels believed they came thence, and the bishops looked to Philip to restore the Church, the old Irish towns, especially Galway, Limerick, and Cork, had their chief trade and intercourse with Spain. 'Spanish hearts' were common in Ireland, and what between religious, racial, and commercial feeling, we can hardly doubt that a Spanish monarchy would have been acceptable to Ireland and that the success of the Armada would have led to a general and most dangerous rising in the country.

But when 'that great fleet invincible' in 1588 suffered complete defeat on the English coast and only a remnant of its ships managed to get round to the rocky coasts and wild seas of western Ireland the result was indeed disastrous and pitiful. The galleons that reached Ireland were many enough and contained so many soldiers, arms, and money that even then if they could have landed safely they could have provided the chiefs with a first-rate army. But the storms which were their fate drove them headlong from Malin in Inishowen down to the Blasket Island, and everywhere save for some lucky exceptions they were driven on the rocks or sunk off lonely islands. Instead of a united Catholic people ready to welcome them, they found a people terrorized by the Government, officials active against them, and the septs divided, some like the Mayo Burkes sheltering them, others like the O'Malleys slaughtering them as they came ashore. The Government was pitiless, the Deputy Fitzwilliam ordered all provincial governors to execute any Spaniards taken, and Bingham, President of Connacht, by proclamation declared that any one harbouring them for more than twenty-four hours would be proclaimed a traitor Acting on such orders, several over-loyal chiefs murdered the unfortunate foreigners, and Boethius Clancy, the Irish sheriff of Clare, had 300 despatched at Malbay. Probably in all some 10,000 Spaniards were lost or murdered on the west coast. The Ulster chiefs were an honourable exception to this cruel treatment. Hugh O'Donnell harboured 3,000 refugees for some time and he and Hugh O'Neill finally got them safe away to Scotland. Sir Brian O'Rourke (called 'na Múrtha', 'of the Ramparts'), lord of Leitrim, sheltered

1,000 Spaniards and as a result was driven out of his country by Bingham, fled to Scotland, was basely handed over by James VI to Elizabeth, and tried and executed as a common criminal in London in November 1591.

Meanwhile the eyes of the English Government were perforce turning more and more to Ulster, the last unconquered province.

THE POSITION IN ULSTER, 1568–1592

After the death of Shane, Turloch O'Neill ruled Tyrone in general with satisfaction to the Government. But as dowry with his wife Agnes Campbell, daughter of the fourth Earl of Argyle, he got 2,000 Hebridean Scots, and the enlistment of these professional fighters aroused suspicion. 'One Scot', it was said, 'was worth two of the Irish.' The maintenance of the new Scots became now the thing with the O'Neills and O'Donnells as that of the older galloglasses had been. It was they who kept the Connacht rebellion simmering and gave a stiffening to the later Ulster rising. In 1586 two MacDonnells with 2,000 Scots invaded Connacht to aid the rebel Burkes, but Bingham surprised them on the river Moy, and most of them were drowned in the complete rout that followed. This ended their career in Connacht, and Sorley Boy MacDonnell in the same year submitted and was granted most of Mac-Quillan's country of the Route, so that the Scots now had all north Antrim. Nevertheless Scots mercenaries continued to serve in the rebel armies and at Kinsale some 800 of them fell on the Irish side.

Hugh O'Neill was the figure on which because of his innate greatness and secretiveness the eyes of Dublin Castle turned more and more inquiringly. In 1585 he sat in Parliament as Baron of Dungannon and Perrot divided the rule of Ulster between him, Sir Turloch, and Sir Henry, son of Nicholas Bagenal. In March 1587 he went to London, where he was well known, and was recognized as Earl of Tyrone like his grandfather Conn, but not with the same authority over his 'urraghs' and reserving to the Government ground for a royal garrison at Portmore on the river Blackwater between Armagh and Tyrone.

For more than a century now adventurous or greedy Englishmen saw in Ireland a country full of fertile land and rich estates, easily acquired either after rebellion or by the favour of the Court. Ulster thus in its turn became a field for colonization as Leinster and Munster had been. The Queen was by descent from the Mortimers 'Countess of Ulster', and this title was considered enough to entitle her to the whole of the province, regardless of native rights. In particular De Courcy's old lands of Ulidia in Antrim and Down were considered by law hers, and the recent O'Neills of Clandeboy had no right there. In 1572 Sir Thomas Smith, with her consent, planned without success to colonize the peninsula of the Ards. In 1573 one of her favourite courtiers, Sir Walter Devereux, Earl of Essex, proposed to plant the North-east and the Queen made him a grant of all the country between Coleraine and Belfast, she to bear half the expenses and get half the dividends. This mean and shameful bargain Sidney criticized sharply, saying that the conquest of Ireland should not be 'a private subject's enterprise but at the Queen's purse'. The opposition of the MacDonnells and the Clandeboy O'Neills was too great for Essex and his few hundred of Elizabethan gentlemen, and he had to abandon the enterprise and received in compensation the barony of Farney in Monaghan. But before he withdrew two atrocities stained the English name, one the massacre of the Scots on Rathlin Island by a force which he landed there, and the other the seizure of Brian MacPhelim O'Neill of Clandeboy and his wife and others, who were executed to the number of some forty in Dublin in October 1574. We can well imagine with what secret indignation men like Hugh O'Neill saw events like this take place, which made clear to them that in English law they had no title to their lands or captainships.

Hugh O'Neill's plan was to succeed Sir Turloch as 'The O'Neill', the most famous of all Irish names, entailing not only personal loyalty but all kinds of military service and tributes without which, though Earl of Tyrone in English law, he could not count on the obedience and devotion of the ancient kingdom of Tyrone. It was not, however, till May 1593 that Turloch retired (dying in 1595) and that Hugh was able to

unite in a powerful combination the titles of Earl and The
O'Neill (a title actually forbidden by law). He was already,
by six years spent in London in the household of Leicester and
at Court, acquainted with the arts of war and diplomacy and
English politics and statecraft. He was an excellent soldier
and for the time was a loyal man, even serving with an English
troop against Desmond. Being allowed to keep six hundred
men in the Queen's pay, he cunningly changed them from
year to year, and on the pretence of roofing his new castle at
Dungannon he procured a great quantity of lead which might
be used for bullets. He was to be the first Irish leader to bring
into the field an army trained and equipped after the best
fashion of the time and wearing red coats.

By 1587 it was noted that 'all men of rank within the province
are become his men'. Fitzwilliam said of him: 'As long as Sir
Turloch lives he is not dangerous, but when he is absolute and
hath no competitor he may show himself to be the man which
in his reason he has wisdom to dissemble.' Later it was
written of him: 'His rebellion will be more dangerous and cost
the Queen more crowns than any that have foregone him since
her reign began, for, educated in our discipline and naturally
valiant, he is worthily reputed the best man of war of his
nation. Most of his followers are well-trained soldiers and he
is the greatest man of territory in the Kingdom and absolute
commander of the north of Ireland.'

In Hugh O'Neill the Irish cause was to find at last a man of
real greatness, a statesman as well as a soldier, a born leader
who combined thought with action and caution with energy,
no out-of-date Gaelic chief intent on his own rights and wrongs,
but a man of intellect who understood his times and who called
on Ireland to combine all her wrongs and seek redress as a
united nation. The great rising began in the North with an
alliance of Tyrconnell and Tyrone, formerly hostile, and while
the elder Hugh proved to be a cautious leader, in Red Hugh
O'Donnell was found a lieutenant, a young hero, and the
forward fighter of the cause.

To explain Red Hugh we must go back. Hugh 'the Black'
had succeeded his brother Calvach as chief of Tyrconnell and

married a woman who became famous in Irish history. This was Finola, daughter of James MacDonnell killed at Glenshesk, and therefore niece of Sorley Boy. Finola, who was thus a Highland woman, was known to the Irish as 'Ineen Duv' ('the dark lady'). Her mother Lady Agnes Campbell, wife of Sir Turloch O'Neill, had brought to her husband some thousands of Scots and Finola did the same for her husband, the O'Donnell. 'Dealing with the Scots' was now common with the Ulster chiefs and much feared by the government, for they were the backbone of any Irish army. By Hugh, Finola had three sons, Aodh Ruadh, best known in history as 'Red Hugh', Rory, and Caffar. She is described in the *Annals of the Four Masters* as being 'like the mother of the Macchabees, who joined a man's heart to a woman's thought', and indeed it was her ambition for her sons and then her determination in their cause that inspired much of the later rising. Hugh was born in 1572 and grew up as the hero of the clan for his beauty and gallant character.

In 1587 the Deputy Perrot, who feared that the O'Donnells were going over to the Irish side, by a mean stratagem had the young Hugh captured, and brought to Dublin, where he remained in wretched captivity till he finally escaped by his flight along with Art O'Neill to Glenmalure at Christmas 1591. Although he was got safe away to Tyrconnell, the memory of his cruel captivity and his sufferings in the snow, which left him permanently crippled, rankled and made him a bitter enemy of the English. His mother ardently embraced his cause, his father resigned in his favour, and in 1592 Red Hugh was inaugurated as 'The O'Donnell'. It was the last true Gaelic 'enkinging', and Hugh was to be the last of the old Gaelic kings. Except for the submission of Manus in 1542, Tyrconnell had never submitted to an English monarch, and as it commanded Fermanagh and Sligo also, it was able to make a last great fight for freedom.

Red Hugh was not in fact the senior of his race, for Calvach had left a grandson, Niall 'Garbh' ('the turbulent'), who might have been The O'Donnell. For the present and until 1600, however, Niall remained faithful to his cousin.

THE SETTLEMENT OF MONAGHAN, 1591

By a surrender and re-grant treaty the reigning chief, Ross MacMahon, had received all Monaghan, with succession to his brother Hugh. The latter succeeded, but when he proceeded to distrain for rent upon his tenants he was seized and finally executed by the Government in 1589. His fate was regarded as most unjust by the Irish, for, as O'Neill said, 'cattle driving is merely distraining for his right according to Irish custom'. Hugh MacMahon was attainted and all Monaghan save Farney came by the usual easy attainder method into the hands of the Crown. But Elizabeth was disappointed over the Munster plantation, and this time a new and equitable plan was adopted. The country was divided between seven chief MacMahons and a MacKenna, who received from 2,000 to 5,000 acres each in demesne with chief rents from the freeholders of ten pounds for every 960 acres. The chiefs themselves were to pay a quit-rent to the Crown, which was to be represented by a Seneschal. Thus the rights of chiefs and native freeholders were recognized, and Monaghan, though there was no chief 'MacMahon' left, remained loyal. As a result it was not included in the final Plantation of Ulster.

THE TYRONE WAR, 1594–1603

The great confederacy of the Northern chiefs was the last stand of the old Gaelic world in the province which, west of Lough Neagh, the English had never settled, and where the warlike Northerners were in full possession. By geography Ulster was well fitted to make a desperate resistance, for on the south its border was one long chain of lakes, forests, and mountains, where the only passes were the Gap of the North beyond Dundalk on the one hand and the fords of the Erne at Enniskillen and Ballyshannon on the other. There was no English garrison on the north coast, and this left open the communications with the Hebrides and with the citizens of Glasgow, who had no scruple in supplying Irish rebels with munitions of war. In Ulster also the old Gaelic order of poets, brehons, and chroniclers was intact, and this had always been the greatest enemy of English civilization, which had no regard for the vested rights of the literary class. It was a land also of Gaelic lordships, of which that of O'Neill was the greatest, and Tyrone was a great Gaelic state just as Desmond had been a great feudal state. Nowhere were the chiefs more proud or warlike. The 'shiring' policy of the Crown, by which English law was continually spreading, had not yet reached Ulster along with the rule of sheriffs, etc., but already such State officials were being appointed and naturally they were bound to clash with the Gaelic kingships. And again, while in the other provinces the Crown had asserted itself in some fashion or other, in Ulster the Catholic party saw the last hope and prop of the Roman Church. As long as even one province could hold its own the Reformation could not be made final for all Ireland, and hence many dreaded the coming of peace because it would be followed by religious persecution.

The first chief to appear in arms was Hugh Maguire, lord of Fermanagh, who stood at bay on the Erne, which the English wished to seize as the western gateway into Ulster. The expulsion and fate of his neighbour O'Rourke naturally alarmed him, and though he paid not to have a sheriff one Willis was appointed in his country, who had behind him the cruel but vigorous Bingham, President of Connacht. There was much fighting about Enniskillen in 1592, and soon Hugh O'Donnell as Maguire's suzerain came to his aid, so did Tyrone's brother, Cormac MacBaron, and between them in August 1594 they defeated a small English force at the 'Ford of the Biscuits' near Enniskillen. Thus began the great rising of the Northern chiefs.

Elizabeth had little money or men which she cared to spare for Ireland and the Deputy Fitzwilliam had at this period of comparative peace an army of less than a thousand men. The Ulster chiefs alone could command thousands of Irish and Scottish mercenaries and at need could call up their free-holders in arms, so that at first the advantage seemed all with them. O'Neill himself did not take the field till 1595, but O'Donnell already struck for his hereditary claims over North

Connacht, where he set up a MacWilliam of Mayo, a Mac-Dermot, and an O'Connor Sligo of his own. Meanwhile the Gaelic cause became a Catholic cause, and Magauran, archbishop of Armagh, in 1592 was sent by O'Donnell and Maguire to solicit help from Philip and the Pope.

O'Neill had always resented the existence of an English force at Portmore, and in 1595 he attacked and took it. His coming into the open field alarmed the Government more than anything, especially after he defeated at Clontibret an English force under his brother-in-law, Sir Henry Bagenal. In May of that year Norris, President of Munster, arrived in Ireland with two thousand veterans from the Netherlands, and on June 28th 1595, O'Neill was proclaimed traitor as being 'the principal and chief author of this rebellion and a known practiser with Spain and her Majesty's other enemies'. Hugh had also taken the title of O'Neill. Without this he could not command the sacred authority of the name, but it was illegal in English eyes and made his offence the greater. Nevertheless a truce was made which lasted from October till the next February 1596.

THE WAR IN 1596

In January of this year the two leaders met Government envoys near Dundalk. They both stood out for liberty of conscience and O'Donnell asked to have no sheriff or garrison in his country. The Queen's answer refused to guarantee liberty of conscience, though yielding on other points, and finally the truce was prolonged, peace was declared later in April, and in August O'Neill and the chiefs were pardoned. They were in fact playing a waiting game, for which O'Neill had particular skill, and were in communication with Philip II. In a letter of May 16th they asked Spain for six thousand soldiers with arms and munitions and swore they would continue the war though the English terms were favourable. They suggested that Philip should send the Archduke of Austria to be king of Ireland. Maguire and the other chiefs also sent letters, and Philip was appealed to that 'with your aid we may restore the Faith and secure you a kingdom'. Tyrone also was working up a general confederacy of the Irish, and on July 6th wrote to a number of southern chieftains, urging them to rise and assist 'Christ's Catholic religion', in which he pledged himself never to make peace with the English except along with them. In the local areas of Wicklow and Leix he could count on certain gallant figures such as Owny O'More and Fiach MacHugh O'Byrne, but the latter was in this year finally hunted down and slain, and by now England had in Ireland a large and trained army of seven thousand men.

THE WAR IN 1597–1598

Fitzwilliam had been succeeded as viceroy by Russell and he again by Lord Brough on May 22nd 1597. Under him the war was renewed in May and a threefold attack on Ulster was planned. O'Neill had two good commanders in the midlands, Piers Lacy and Captain Tyrrell. In July it was decided that (1) Brough should march from Dublin to Portmore; (2) Clifford, now President of Connacht after Bingham, should march from Boyle against O'Donnell, having with him Donough O'Brien, Earl of Thomond, the Baron of Inchiquin, and Ulick, Earl of Clanrickard; and (3) Barnewall, son of Lord Trimleston, with a force from the Pale, should march from Mullingar, all three to meet at Ballyshannon. The result was a disaster on the three fronts for the English, for O'Donnell repulsed Clifford, Brough was defeated near Benburb by O'Neill, and Barnewall with a thousand men was ambushed at Tyrrell's Pass in Westmeath by Lacy and his army cut to pieces. After such a threefold failure, the Government in December made a further truce with the northern chiefs, which was finally prolonged till June the next year, and a fresh pardon made out for Tyrone. At last the war in its final stages was renewed over Portmore. It was again in English hands, and in July the Lord Deputy sent Sir Henry Bagenal to relieve it from a threatened attack. He had with him 4,000 foot and 300 horse, all trained soldiers. The allies decided to put the matter to the test of battle and O'Neill and O'Donnell collected 5,000 men from Tyrone, 2,000 men from Tyrconnell and 1,000 from Connacht, to oppose Bagenal on his march from Newry. On August 15, 1598, at the Yellow Ford on the

Blackwater, the Irish won a complete victory, Bagenal was killed, a third of the English army destroyed, and the rest driven back upon Armagh. According to Camden: 'Since the time the English first set foot in Ireland they never received a greater overthrow, thirteen stout captains being slain and over fifteen hundred common soldiers.'

This complete victory for the time seemed to lay Ireland at Tyrone's feet. The discontented and patriotic everywhere took up arms, and by the end of the year the rebel forces in Ireland had swelled to some 30,000 horse and foot. In Munster O'Neill was already in communication with the Geraldines who had suffered in the plantation, of whom the chief was James FitzThomas, who claimed to be Earl of Desmond, and among the Irish Fineen (or Florence) MacCarthy Reagh, claiming to be MacCarthy More. Into this promising field for rebellion Tyrone's commanders Tyrrel and Lacy descended in October 1598, and within a fortnight the whole Munster plantation was swept away and a rebel army took the field, though at least half of the Old English remained loyal. The reputation of O'Neill 'now stood as high among his country-men as that of Hannibal after Cannae'. In Spain and Italy he was regarded as a great commander and a Catholic hero, and when an envoy of his went to the court of Scotland it appears that James VI received him kindly and promised he would remember Tyrone 'when it shall please God to call our sister the Queen of England to death'. In fact, however, O'Neill knew the weakness of his own position. Without artillery and siege weapons he could not hope to take walled towns like Dublin. Connacht had been quieted by the Com-position and Leinster was for the most part in English hands. In Munster great lords like Barrymore were Queen's men, so were the Earls of Thomond and Clanrickard in Clare and Connacht, and the skilful policy of the government in religion had kept the Catholic majority quiet. O'Neill's hopes had in the first place to be in Spanish aid, which so far had been disappointing, and secondly in prolonging the fight, by the cautious tactics that he was a master of, until Elizabeth should die, when a possible succession war in England would give him the victory, or the accession of James of Scotland, a

H

supposed Catholic, would enable him to lay down his arms on terms acceptable to his allies and himself. In this waiting game, however, which one great and many small victories illuminated, O'Neill was to be beaten by new English tactics and the rashness of Red Hugh.

In September 1598 Philip of Spain died, but his son, the third Philip, to whom the Irish again appealed, promised them help. And so the winter and spring passed with the Council of Ireland only daring to peer out of the Pale, while Elizabeth in her feminine fury against 'the Arch-traitor' prepared to launch 'the royallest army that ever went out of England'.

ESSEX AND MOUNTJOY, 1599–1603

Sir Robert Devereux, second Earl of Essex, was given the chance by his adoring Queen to distinguish himself as Lord Lieutenant in Ireland and with an army of 16,000 foot and 1,300 horse arrived in Dublin on April 15th 1599. The Queen ordered him to march straight against O'Neill, whom she was determined not to pardon. The Council in Ireland, however, induced him not to attack Ulster till the grass had grown and cattle were fat, and therefore, early in May, he marched with a fourth of his army in a vain expedition into the South, during which a detachment was cut off by the O'Mores in the 'Pass of Plumes' near Maryborough. In Wicklow Fiach O'Byrne's son, Phelim, again defeated an English force in Glenmalure. So the Lord Lieutenant's army began to dwindle and by July, through sickness, dissipation of his forces, and other losses he had but 4,000 men under his direct command.

Meanwhile in Connacht O'Donnell won the last of his victories. The Government had set up a loyal O'Connor Sligo and the President Clifford marched to his help from Boyle with 2,000 men. He was held up on the high road that crosses the Curlew mountains by O'Donnell and O'Rourke, and there the English were routed and lost among others Norris, President of Munster. It was the last victory of those tall gallo-glasses that had served the O'Donnells for over three centuries.

Essex now marched northwards, but not to gain the final triumph which Elizabeth demanded. He met O'Neill at the

Ford of Annaclint on the borders of Monaghan and Louth, and there, after some parleys between them which were never revealed, a truce was declared which lasted till the end of the year. Recalled in anger by the Queen, Essex left Ireland on September 24th 1599 to meet his death by the headsman's axe on February 25th 1600.

The Essex episode prolonged O'Neill's cause and was a triumph for those waiting tactics and small engagements by which he hoped to wear the English out and snatch a final victory. But with the appointment as Deputy of Sir Charles Blount, Lord Mountjoy, a new kind of war began which was to beat O'Neill at his own game. Mountjoy, who arrived in February 1600, had a splendid army of 20,000, but rather than trusting to battles he decided that the war could only be ended by a general famine. His plan was not to give Tyrone battle but to hem him into Ulster by forts such as Derry, to cut him off from his southern allies, and, after reducing them, to make the final attack upon him. Elizabeth had entrusted Mountjoy with great powers, but one thing she would not grant him, 'the pardon of the arch-traitor, a monster of ingratitude to her and the root of misery to her people'. At the same time Sir George Carew, cousin of the original Peter, was made President of Munster, and he and Ormond set to work to crush the southern rebellion.

In January 1600 O'Neill himself entered Munster with an army and held a camp of the Catholic confederates at Holy Cross in Tipperary. The main rebels collected around him and there they made Fineen MacCarthy, 'MacCarthy More', James FitzThomas earl of Desmond, and Oviedo archbishop of Dublin. In March, however, he retired north and the war continued with no more truces to its end. Hugh Maguire was slain in an encounter near Cork. The Munster rising was so rapidly and savagely suppressed that a general pardon was proclaimed in the province at the end of the year. During the fighting both the unfortunate FitzThomas (called by the Irish the 'Súgán Earl' or 'Earl of straw') and Fineen were seized and sent over to London, where they ended their days in the Tower. In October of that year Earl Gerald's son, a delicate and ailing man, was sent over from his captivity in London and set up as

Earl to content Munster, but as he was a Protestant the people rejected him and he returned to London to die. Such was the end of the Munster Geraldines.

The massacre of garrisons and the systematic destruction of crops by the troops finished off most of the rebellion in the South. In Leix, for example, Owny O'More bitterly protested at the burning of crops, £10,000 worth of which was destroyed in his country alone. By this time most of the heads of the O'Mores and O'Connors had perished, and in 1600 the gallant Owny himself was killed: 'a bloody and bold young man, chief of the O'More sept in Leix, after whose death they never again held up their heads'.

The war was now confined to the North, where O'Neill still commanded a proper army of 4,000 men and where a long line of ditches called 'Tyrone's trenches' mark the elaborate defences that barred the Gap of the North. A price was put on his head of £2,000 alive or £1,000 dead, but 'the name of O'Neill was so reverenced in the north as none could be induced to betray him for so large a sum'. What could be done was to sap the strength of the confederates by detaching their vassals and commanders from them. This was achieved by Sir John Docwra, who occupied Derry in May 1600 in order to attack the chiefs from the north. Sir Arthur O'Neill, a son of Turloch Luineach, Niall Garbh O'Donnell, and Donal O'Cahan, lord of north County Derry, were successively bought over, and Niall in particular was promised the earldom of Tyrconnell. O'Neill's hopes had to centre more and more upon Spain, where a fleet was being prepared to assist him. The danger was well realized in England, and Mountjoy said: 'The coming of the Spaniards will be the War of England made in Ireland.'

But when the fleet of Philip III came, it was disappointing both for where it landed, the size of its army, and the nature of its commander, Don Juan D'Aguila.

Some western or northern port should have been the Spanish objective; instead they occupied Kinsale on the Cork coast on September 23rd 1601, in a province already subdued and all the length of Ireland from the Northern chiefs. Philip's aid consisted of only some 4,000 men and a few ships, while

D'Aguila was a commander of no eminence or resolution and was soon out of sympathy with those he had come to help. His proclamation calling on the Irish to rise against a heretic Queen ('Elizabeth is deposed of her kingdom and all her subjects absolved from fealty by Popes Pius V, Gregory XIII and Clement VIII, to whom the King of kings has committed all power, even to deposing of temporal monarchs') was most injudicious, for even Philip II would not have consented to the deposing doctrine, and O'Neill and O'Donnell could have had no wish to see the national cause made a mere outflash of the counter-Reformation. But disappointed though they were, they marched to join the Spaniards, while O'Sullivan Beare and O'Driscoll put into Spanish hands their castles of Dunboy, Castlehaven, and Baltimore.

Rapid action was necessary for all parties and Mountjoy at once besieged Kinsale from land and sea, while Carew was sent off to intercept the Northerners. But O'Neill and O'Donnell outmarched the forces which would have stopped them and by the end of November 1601, with an army of some 12,000, were encamped around the Deputy's forces, thus besieging the besiegers.

The whole fate of Ireland hung upon a single battle. A victory for O'Neill would have led to further aid from Spain and a great flocking to his standard, for Mountjoy himself records how much of the population, even the Old English, had 'Spanish and Papist hearts' and that 'in the cities of Munster the citizens were so degenerated from their first English progenitors as that the very speaking of English was forbidden by them to their wives and children'. So much had the Irish language and sympathy prevailed. But those who were actively on the Irish side were a minority, and it is notable that among the Deputy's commanders around Kinsale were Richard, the new Earl of Clanrickard, O'Brien, Earl of Thomond, Cormac MacCarthy of Muskerry, and St. Lawrence from the Pale.

Everything favoured O'Neill's Fabian tactics, for by wastage on December 2nd the Deputy had only some 6,500 men fit for arms, while Tyrone had 6,000 foot and 500 horse, with 3,000 Spaniards inside Kinsale. But the Spaniards pressed for a decisive battle, which took place on December 24th 1601, in which through mismanagement the combination of Spaniards and Irish failed, and O'Neill, who favoured waiting for another day, was forced into action by O'Donnell, which ended in a rout for the Irish. In this the losses of the Irish were reckoned from 1,000 to 2,000, among whom a Spanish regiment on the Irish side, and 840 out of 900 Scots under MacDonnell captains, were slain outright.

Such was the sudden and astonishing termination of a long war in which the Irish had gained victory after victory. O'Donnell in terrible agitation took ship for Spain, where next year he died in Salamanca, with the suspicion that an English agent poisoned him. O'Neill marched back to the north, while D'Aguila shamefully surrendered without making any terms for his Irish confederates. Of the castles which had been surrendered to him, that of Dunboy made a heroic resistance worthy of the last stand.

There was nothing left for the stubborn O'Neill but to stand on his defence among the woods and wilds of Tyrone, leaving Dungannon to be taken and the famous inauguration stone of the O'Neills at Tullahoge to be destroyed by Mountjoy as a symbol of the ending of Gaelic independence. In Tyrconnell, Red Hugh's brother Rory with difficulty maintained the cause, but famine and the desertion of allies finished off the faithful. Mountjoy recalls that in Tyrone alone he saw 3,000 bodies dead of famine and Ulster was becoming, like Munster before it, depopulated. Though O'Neill urged them to hold together for terms, successively Rory O'Donnell and other chiefs submitted to the Government. Elizabeth was now dying, the war in five years from October 1598 to March 1603 cost some £1,200,000, and Mountjoy was a man who, when his cruel measures had succeeded, had considerable feeling for a beaten enemy. Finally O'Neill, who stood almost alone, offered to submit and was received by the Lord Deputy at Mellifont. There on March 30th 1603 the ageing but indomitable patriot laid down his arms and made humble submission to the offended Elizabeth. But in fact she was dead on March 24th and Mountjoy, as Lord Lieutenant for the new king, extracted from O'Neill a fresh submission to King James.

It is a pitiable thought that had O'Neill known in time he would certainly have held out to extract honourable terms for himself and his confederates from the new sovereign who had formerly professed friendship for him.

By the terms of his submission Tyrone renounced the title of O'Neill (the real source of his power); abjured dependence on any foreign power, especially Spain (to whose King he wrote a manly letter of farewell which must have stung the proud Philip); renounced his authority over former 'urraghs', and resigned all lands and lordships save such as the Crown might grant him.

The beginning of the new dynasty promised brighter things for those who had been in arms and for Ireland as a whole. O'Neill and Rory O'Donnell went to London with Mountjoy, who was now made Lord Lieutenant and later Earl of Devonshire for his services. James received them kindly and O'Neill was restored to his earldom with all the lands of Conn Bacach, while O'Donnell was made Earl of Tyrconnell. In both cases, however, the lordship was greatly limited. Some of O'Neill's former 'urraghs' were set free of him, such as Sir Henry Oge O'Neill and the O'Neill of the Fews in south Armagh. The rich fisheries of the Bann and Lough Neagh were also taken away. O'Donnell was limited to his county and had to leave Inishowen to O'Doherty and surrender the fort of Ballyshannon and the rich fisheries of the Erne to the Crown. Niall Garbh, who had been promised the earldom, might well consider himself shamefully treated, but at least he received a large estate at Lifford. Thus to outward seeming Gaelic Ulster was restored, but in fact the old order had gone, and after four years attempting to reconcile themselves to the new, the Earls had to quit their ancient province.

The submission of O'Neill, following on the extinction of Desmond twenty years before, did in fact bring to an end Gaelic and feudal Ireland. The last unconquered province was thrown open to English law and Government. There were to be no more 'lords of countries' and 'captains of their nations' and no wide territory in which the poets, Brehons, and chroniclers could practise freely their art. In the struggle the hereditary poets had thrown real inspiration and passion into their verse, giving a Biblical fervour to their exhortations to the chiefs to save their mother Erin. Now came the violent and sudden ending of the whole Gaelic world. But though the ancient learned and literary caste came to an end (for the law took little heed of their rights) and were ruined along with their noble patrons, the Irish language was to find more genuine expression in poets and writers who lived, and felt, with the common people.

Ireland, Gaelic and Norman, had been for centuries a 'land of war'. In 1530 the chiefs alone could have collected twenty thousand armed men. Now the country from end to end was disarmed and save for foreign aid could not be armed again. No longer could some petty chief lead out with impunity the small army of his state against the now victorious State. Irish 'cuttings and spendings' were replaced by the lord's money rents. English landlordism took the place of the older tenures of Brehon and semi-feudal law. The change was a disastrous one for the numerous free tenants of Irish society but of advantage to the Irish aristocracy, had not the political disasters of the new century destroyed most of their class.

The fight of the Northern chiefs was an apparent failure. Nations, however, are made in many ways, and among these is the heroic example of great men even when they seem to fail. Few of the great names of Irish history come better out of the tangled treachery, cruelty, self-seeking, and indifference of their times than the wise and long-lived Hugh O'Neill and Red Hugh O'Donnell, that fiery spirit soon quenched.

CHAPTER XIII

THE EARLY STUART MONARCHY AND CROMWELLIAN PERIOD, 1603–1660

THE new reign began with an Act of Oblivion in February 1604, by which all offences against the law done up to the present time were forgiven, and all the Irish without distinction were received into his Majesty's immediate protection. It was obvious that the old order was to be done away with and a proclamation of Lord Deputy Chichester in 1605 declared ended the 'servitude and dependence of the common subjects upon their great lords and chiefs'. Yet instantly an incident showed that at least in Religion there was a definite breach between the Government and the people, and that in this question at least the recent rebellion had had a far-spread sympathy. The liberties of Ireland, constitutional, feudal, chiefly, and religious, had been swept away but those of the old towns remained. They had been seemingly loyal during the rebellion and hence were regarded as 'the sheet-anchor of the State'. James the First was believed to be an open or secret Catholic. Acting on the belief that religion was now to be free, the southern towns such as Cork, Kilkenny, and Waterford in 1603 reoccupied their old churches and celebrated the Mass openly. But this Mountjoy would not tolerate and his victorious army of 14,000 men, after a short resistance, brought the towns to due submission. It was seen that Toleration would not be guaranteed by law but must depend upon the favour of the Prince.

Mountjoy, however, once the fighting was over, proved himself a man of noble thinking, and though he left Ireland in 1604, he continued to urge the better way upon the Court, but unfortunately his early death in 1606 removed a wise statesman and a friend of Tyrone.

In a letter of February 25th 1603 Mountjoy had dwelt upon the curable evils of Ireland. The nobility, towns, and the English-Irish, he said, though weary of the war, feared that a reformation in religion would follow upon a peace. The Church as established was full of abuses. There should be no persecution for religion's sake, save the oath of Supremacy for office, and there should be no plantations save on the sea-coast or the great rivers. And actually that a general 'Reformation' would follow upon peace was shown in the fact that after the defeat of Kinsale the Recusancy fines were generally inflicted and a High Commission Court, set up in 1593, began to act with vigour. But according to the charges of Councillors such as Loftus, the liberal-minded Mountjoy put an end to it and stopped rigorous measures in the matter of religion.

From the battle of Kinsale onwards Ireland entered upon a new phase in her history. A new Irish nationality emerged, Catholic by conviction, a mixture of English and Gael by race, becoming in the upper classes ever more and more English-speaking. But in the common people we see a blended race who in the long run have proved to be the characteristic Irish people, feeling a sense of common history and a common Faith, with an intense passion for the land which nothing has been able to shake, and speaking that Gaelic language which was the speech of the majority up to 1800. Milesian or Old English, Danish or Norman, whatever their origin they have all accepted the Irish legend as against the English legend. How to reconcile this Catholic nation, fast forming because of a general ill-treatment, with an Anglican government was a problem, but how to make it fit in with a greedy, intolerant, and pampered Protestant ascendancy, which increased with every plantation, was a harder problem still.

There was no doubt that a new order had begun and that all Ireland was to be united as a kingdom under an English monarchy. The whole country was for the first time shired, and English sheriffs, justices on assize, juries, and all the other forms of English law, land-tenure, and local administration appeared everywhere. Sir John Davies, an exceedingly able Englishman, was made Attorney-general for Ireland, and in his circuits through the country enforced for the first time the Common law and inquired into the principles of the Brehon code and the Irish system of land-tenure, which was now swept away and replaced by the ordinary rules of English land-lordism. At first, in the cases of Cavan and Fermanagh, he gave decisions recognizing great numbers of the Irish as freeholders, but when later ways had to be found of ousting them he was not above making judgments unworthy of law and his former impartiality. Decisions by him and other judges abolished the Irish law of chieftainship, Tanistry, equal par-tition among the heirs, Irish serfdom, and so on, and thus the whole Irish Brehon system became of mere antiquarian interest, A royal commission for Defective titles was insti-tuted, by which all who owned or claimed estates under the old system were encouraged to bring them in and to receive confirmation of them by royal patents.

How to deal with the majority in Religion was a standing problem, especially as the towns and the nobility and gentry of the Pale and of Munster were increasingly proud and stubborn in the matter. To enumerate the faults and explain the failure of the State Church to capture the great majority of the people one need only read the dispatches of Mountjoy, the writings of Spenser, or the confessions of honest bishops. Thus Edmund Spenser, in his *View of the State of Ireland*, speaking of the planting of Religion, says: 'wherein it is great wonder to see the odds between the zeal of Popish priests and the ministers of the Gospel. For they spare not to come out of Spain and from Rome by long toil and dangerous travelling, where they know peril of death awaiteth them and no reward or riches are to be found, only to draw the people unto the Church of Rome: whereas some of our idle ministers, having the livings of the country offered unto them without pains and without peril, will neither for the same nor any love of God nor zeal of religion be drawn forth from their warm nests to look out into God's harvest, which is even ready for the sickle and the fields yellow long ago.'

Of positive persecution and still more of actual martyrdom for Religion's sake the government cannot fairly be accused. It was clear that, unless some great genius rose to draw the people over to the Established faith, the Jesuits and papal bishops had already won the day in Ireland, and that, quite apart from the towns, the mass of the country gentry were now Romanist, as firmly as Scottish gentlemen were Presbyterian and English gentlemen were Puritan or High Church Anglicans The amount of persecuting statutes in Ireland was actually small compared with England, and the chief grievances centred round the oath of Supremacy which excluded the Old English from lucrative offices and the Recusancy fines which fell most on the middle classes. Only one striking case of martyrdom positively for religion is recorded in the reign, that of O'Devany, bishop of Down and Connor, in 1612. It was over the proscription of the Catholic upper classes from what they considered their full rights as loyal citizens that trouble arose.

In 1604 Sir Arthur Chichester was made Lord Deputy and ruled till 1616. It was now that the constant bickering over the religious question arose when the viceroy, the judges, and the new bishops strove to put the laws into effect. The mayors of the old towns, the officials of the State, and others had the Oath presented to them, fines or exclusion from office and place followed, nevertheless it was only as the reign proceeded that it became possible to limit the jobs entirely to Protestants. A petition against interference with the private use of their religion was in 1606 presented to the Deputy by five peers and some two hundred gentlemen of the Pale, all Old English, headed by Sir Patrick Barnewall, brother-in-law of Tyrone, 'the first gentleman's son that was ever put out of Ireland to be brought up in learning beyond the seas'. The Government prosecuted him and sent him to England, but he returned in March 1607, for the authorities could not find a legal case against the petitioners. All Roman Catholic Ireland contributed to the fund of his defence and it ended in a triumph for the Recusants.

James himself was an amiable man, well disposed to Toleration, but the unfortunate Gunpowder Plot in England made it harder for him to oppose that anti-Popish feeling which was becoming a rooted and bitter tradition with the English. In 1606, when his English parliament passed severe laws against Roman Catholics, which were the model of the later Penal code in Ireland, the King got inserted a new oath of

Allegiance by which Roman Catholics could qualify as loyal men if they accepted him as lawful and rightful King and repudiated the right of the Pope to depose him, as well as the doctrine that Princes excommunicated by the Pope might be lawfully deposed or murdered. The oath, however, was condemned by the Papacy, and again it was shown how difficult it was for a peace-loving Catholic subject of the King to keep safe between militant Puritanism on one side and a Roman Curia on the other which would not encourage compromise. Nevertheless the compromise expressed in this oath, which said nothing as to repudiating the spiritual supremacy of the Pope, remained a device attempted several times later in Stuart Ireland. The fact was that James himself could not grant open and legal toleration, and that even at their most willing the Stuart kings could only secure to the Catholics by the exercise of their prerogative an 'indulged' or 'connived' toleration.

The Deputy Chichester now reversed Mountjoy's liberal policy, and a royal proclamation in July 1605 was the first of those 'strong measures' which continued for eighty years to be launched with little success against the majority and their priests. All were ordered to conform 'to that religion which is agreeable to God's word and is established by the laws of the realm', and within six months Jesuits, seminary priests, and others ordained by the authority of Rome were to abjure the realm. One can be sure that few had obeyed the order when the date came, especially as officials knew that the King was merely conciliating English opinions. The walls of all the old towns, the castles of many peers, the houses of the country gentry, and the unbribable devotion of the common people continued to shelter the wandering bishop and the harmless priest.

Persuasion and the cultural appeal were not wanting on the loyal side. The long-needed University of Dublin was at last founded in 1592 by charter of Elizabeth with endowment of lands and money from the city of Dublin and many of the gentry, and a gift of over £600 from the English forces serving in Ireland. From the first, Trinity College was on the Anglican and indeed the Puritan side in religion and it was unfortunate that it was founded at a time of religious cleavage. But as far as learning went, under its first Provost, Loftus, it began to produce very able men such as James Ussher, sprung from an old Anglo-Irish family, bishop of Meath in 1620 and archbishop of Dublin in 1625. Until the time of Wentworth indeed the college at Dublin continued to be frequented by the 'natives' and all the liberal-minded, to whom it opened its gates.

THE PLANTATION OF ULSTER

In the final reduction of Ireland 'the Flight of the Earls' was an event second only to the submission of 1603, but its causes are obscure. Most of Ulster had been restored to a few great chiefs, but O'Neill and O'Donnell had a new situation to deal with and a difficult game to play, harassed as they were by the new officers and bishops of the Crown and with the steady pressure against them of their former enemies. A long dispute between the Earl of Tyrone and Donal O'Cahan, his former 'urragh', who on his submission in 1602 had been promised his country under the Crown, made O'Neill realize that he was now only a great English landlord instead of a Gaelic king. Rory O'Donnell was in the same position, and both at last began to fear that they would be called up before the Irish Council on charges of conspiracy and put in danger of their life and liberty. Wearying of what they believed to be an untenable position, they decided to abandon Ireland. An exiled Maguire and Tyrone's son Henry, an officer in Spanish service, sent a ship into Rathmullen on Lough Swilly in which on September 14th 1607 Tyrone, Tyrconnell, and his brother Caffar, Maguire and others, ninety-nine in all of the leading men of the North, departed to find at last an asylum and their graves in the Holy City. With their departure, we may truly say, came to an end that Milesian aristocracy which had lorded over Ireland from the dawn of history. Spain welcomed and honoured hundreds of such exiles, who became more and more numerous as Plantation went on. For long it was hoped by great numbers, not only of the native race but of the Anglo-Irish who now regretted the exiled hero, that he would return to set Ireland free, but when the news of his blindness and then of his death in 1616 came they abandoned hope 'and trooped in in hundreds to get their patents from the Crown'.

Several advisers such as Bacon had urged generous treatment of the Irish, but the opportunity to plant a whole province seemed too good to miss and the Government determined to carry it into effect. At the close of 1607 a jury was summoned at Lifford and another at Strabane of Irish and English freeholders, of whom the Irish were in a majority, and in the first case Sir Cahir O'Doherty was foreman and in the second Sir Henry Oge O'Neill, now the leading man of his name. Their Bills of indictment against O'Neill, O'Donnell, and others for supposed treason and conspiracy were duly returned to the King's Bench, upon which, according to English law, they stood attainted and all their lands escheated to the Crown, an act of Parliament only being necessary to complete the attainder.

Those Irish gentlemen who thus outlawed their chiefs supposed that, save for them and their particular demesnes, other freeholders would be left in undisturbed possession. Davies had encouraged this idea by former judgments, and the natives had every reason to believe that only the Earls were to suffer, but now the Attorney-General turned round and in a letter to the Earl of Salisbury wrote: 'both by Irish custom and the law of England his Majesty may now seize these lands and dispose of them at his good pleasure.' Of this we may remark that, whatever the power of native chiefs was, they certainly did not under the accepted principles of Brehon law actually *own* the whole land of their 'country', nor can we imagine that in England the rebellion of a few great men would have led to the dispossession of the whole body of their tenants in several counties.

Having thus got Tyrone and Tyrconnell, the Government went boldly forward until Confiscation, on the plea of a rebellion which had been pardoned in 1603, embraced six whole counties —Donegal, Tyrone, Derry, Armagh, Cavan, and Fermanagh. In Fermanagh the last admitted chief, the famous Hugh, had fallen in rebellion; a kinsman, Conor Roe, was now granted a considerable estate and the rest of the county was confiscated to the Crown. In Cavan also Sir John O'Reilly had been killed in rebellion, and though one or two of his name received grants, Cavan had the fate of Fermanagh. In Armagh, O'Hanlon, the ruling chief of a large part of the county, was attainted with O'Neill. And before another year was ended a foolish and belated rising brought in further lands. The young Sir Cahir O'Doherty by the more generous policy of 1603 had been granted his father's whole country of Inishowen and had every reason to be a loyal man. But in April 1608, on words arising between him and the governor of Derry, Sir Cahir was struck in the face. This was an affront that it was scarcely possible for a proud Irish chief either to endure or to get peaceable satisfaction for; O'Doherty therefore flew into rebellion, but was very soon hunted down and slain. The whole of that great peninsula was then added to confiscated Tyrconnell. Charges were then brought against Niall Garbh O'Donnell, a discontented and much-deceived man, and Sir Donal O'Cahan of favouring this rising, and Niall was sent up to Dublin, where, however, a jury would not and could not find him guilty. Davies pointed out the moral, which was not forgotten: 'We must have an English colony, for the Irish will never condemn a principal traitor.' Finally both Niall and O'Cahan were sent over to the Tower of London, in which, some twenty years later, they died. The treatment of these chiefs is too shameful for comment, but only Docwra, who had won them over by what he believed to be genuine offers from Government, had the decency to protest.

The final plan was issued in May 1609 under the name of 'the articles of Plantation'. In all some 500,000 acres of 'profitable' land were thrown open to settlers. Land measurements were then of an uncertain character, and to the 'profitable land' conveyed in the grants might be added 'unprofitable land as the county could afford'. English and Scottish 'Undertakers' were invited to take estates of 1,000, 1,500, or 2,000 acres, to hold of the Crown in socage. They were to be 'English or inland (i.e. Lowland) Scots' and 'civil men well affected in religion'. A second rank of grantees were called 'Servitors', on less favourable terms, who were generally Scots. All were compelled to take the oath of Supremacy admitting the King to be head over the Church. A third rank consisted of 'Natives', who received grants from the Crown, but were not required to take the Supremacy oath. Undertakers and Servitors were after a period to pay head-rent to the Crown of £5 6s. 8d. for every 1,000 acres. Neither of them might alienate the fee to the Irish, but the Servitors might take Irish tenants at £8 for every 1,000 acres, i.e. they must pay a heavier rent if they took Irish tenants. The natives were to pay a heavier head-rent, viz. £10 13s. 4d., for every 1,000 acres or in proportion, and might take Irish tenants. It is estimated that of the total some 58,000 acres were thus granted out to 280 native free-holders, but it is to be remembered that already in 1603 the Crown had confirmed some of the Irish landowners in their estates, which still remained theirs. Even so the native gentry became a minority in their own province and in general the best lands passed to the settlers. Chichester himself protested that half the land should have been left to them and Sir George Carew, formerly President of Munster, in 1614 addressed to James a paper in which he pointed out the wrongs of the Irish and said that there had always been a Royalist population among them but that now religious feeling had brought to-gether the Old English and the native Irish, and he prophesied that they would rebel under 'the veil of Religion and Liberty than which nothing is esteemed so precious in the hearts of men'. As generally happens, the soldiers were more generous than the officials, and whereas the Elizabethan English had shown a certain generosity and admiration for the Irish, the new Puritan race of English and Scots was to be very lacking in both.

In dividing the spoils, provision was made for the Estab-lished Church, which had formerly little footing in Ulster, but was now well endowed. So was Dublin University, and land was also set apart for a Royal school in each county. James also revived some of the decayed towns such as Carrickfergus and Coleraine and created nineteen new boroughs in Ulster, the corporations of which were strictly Protestant. The grantees were bound by strict 'Plantation terms' to build castles and 'bawns' and plant in 'British' tenants, for this word was now applied to the English and Scottish planters, the latter of whom were generally Presbyterian. But the most striking transaction was that the City of London was granted for money all the north part of county Derry, i.e. the land between Coleraine and Derry, wherein they were to build towns. The vast woods and rich fisheries of this area went to them, with freedom of export and import for all commodities. For all this the twelve London Companies were to pay a head-rent to the Crown, to lay out a sum of £20,000, and to take only Scots and English as tenants. To manage these estates they set up the present Irish Society. It was later on the theme of much comment from Wentworth that the Crown had granted out this great province with all its natural riches to the planters on very poor terms for itself.

The Plantation of Ulster has naturally been the subject of much passion and much misconception. In the first place, we must note that it did not include the three counties of Monaghan, Antrim, and Down. The first of these was, under the settlement of 1590, left to the Irish. The second was for the most part in 1603 granted to Sir Randal MacDonnell, son of Sorley Boy, who as a Scot (though a Highlander and a Catholic) was favoured by James. Later he was made Earl of Antrim and his vast estates covered the whole of the Glens and the Route, from which the unfortunate MacQuillans were ousted. One branch of the Clandeboy O'Neills retained a portion of Antrim and are represented to-day by the O'Neills of Shane's Castle. In Down there existed such native chiefs as O'Neill of South Clandeboy and Magennis of Iveagh, while in Lecale and around Downpatrick there survived some of De Courcy's English, such as the Whites, Russells, Savages, etc., who for their origin were now left generally in possession. But already in 1603 the foundation of a flourishing Scottish colony had been laid in the Ards of Down and in the neighbourhood of Belfast by two Scottish adventurers, Sir James Hamilton and Sir Hugh Montgomery. These wily, active, and tenacious Scotsmen, by various clever devices or for small sums, got possession of White's country of Dufferin and two-thirds of South Clandeboy, leaving to Sir Conn O'Neill of Castlereagh, a drunken and sluggish man, only a portion of his lordship, which his descendants failed to keep. It was in actual fact north Down and south Antrim which were the real home of the new Scottish colony which later reinforced those in the Escheated counties and formed the Presbyterian race of to-day in the North.

Secondly, it is a rhetorical exaggeration that the Irish *en masse* were driven to the hills and bogs. In fact, as we have seen, several hundreds of native freeholders received grants; not only they but the bishops and servitors were allowed to take Irish tenants (leaseholders), and other native grantees already existed. The distinction must be kept between those Irish gentry who had grants from the Crown, those who were tenants and leaseholders under the planters or Irish landlords, and the mere tenants-at-will or labourers which the mass of the population became.

Actually a considerable Gaelic aristocracy was left in Ulster, though little of it was to survive the Cromwellian period. The O'Donnells indeed disappeared from Tyrconnell, but two sons of Niall Garbh got land in Westport, Mayo. Several of the O'Neills were left, either with small grants now or by former grants. Thus Sir Henry Oge O'Neill retained a great estate; his grandson, Felim of Kinard or Caledon in county Armagh, was to be the leader of the 1641 rising. Sir Turloch MacHenry O'Neill retained the Fews in county Armagh, some 10,000 acres. Sir Art, son of Turloch Luineach, kept a large estate in the barony of Dungannon, and Shane MacBrien O'Neill retained much of North Clandeboy. In Cavan some small grants were made to the O'Reillys, and in Fermanagh Connor Roe Maguire, having surrendered his claims in 1607, was granted a large estate and his son Brian in 1628 was created Baron of Enniskillen. In county Down (not a planted county), Magennis of Iveagh had his whole country re-granted to him, 22,000 acres in all, and in 1623 was created Viscount of Iveagh. In Monaghan (also not planted) the MacMahons were left in possession. There were thus many chiefs left, but the fate of many of them was to see their estates dwindle, often by their own recklessness, to feel the smart of being reduced to small landlords, and to disappear as a result of 1641. In the desperate rising of that year the leaders were an O'Neill, a Maguire, a Magennis, and a MacMahon.

Thirdly, the colony was not an immediate success. The

displacement of the population was difficult, and finally by 1612 the orders for the expulsion of Irish from the Plantations were a dead letter. The London companies in particular, being absentees, retained thousands of Irish as small tenants or cultivators on their lands. The new landlords found that the spare-living and industrious Celt would generally outbid the Scot or the Englishman when it came to paying rent. 'Plantation terms' were far from observed and were hard to enforce. The colony grew slowly, and it was not till after 1660 that the Scottish element in Ulster became a pronounced success and the only case of a real democratic, industrial, and labouring colony established in Ireland. Ulster finally became a province almost entirely Protestant as regards the land-owners and mainly so as regards the population, and it is reckoned that in 1641 of the 3,500,000 acres in the six counties the Protestants owned 3,000,000 and the Catholics the rest. But even this proportion was to be reduced after 1660, and after 1690 scarcely anything of the Gaelic and Catholic aristocracy remained.

It should be remembered that this Confiscation and Plantation, like others which followed it in the next twenty years, was done at a time of peace, after a solemn and general Act of Oblivion and Pardon, and when all the Irish were disarmed and a large army of occupation could silence all resistance.

Though Ulster was to be the one success in making Ireland Protestant, a large Irish and Catholic minority in the whole province has tenaciously persisted to this day, and up to 1840 or so the two races lived curiously side by side, the Irish in general living in the mountainous and poorer lands, retaining their religion and language, and even producing a number of poets in Irish who have written some of the most inspired verse which remains to us.

The apparent success of the Ulster Plantation inspired others, and the view prevailed in the Government that colonies everywhere were necessary to secure a loyal population which would provide juries and other officers, elect the right sort of members of parliament, support the State Church and intro-duce the English language, methods of land-tenure, agriculture and so on, and through whom trade and industry, the towns, and consequently the King's revenues, would steadily increase. From 1610 to the beginning of Charles I's reign various Plantations were carried out. The areas selected were those which were regarded as particularly Irish and where a title for the Crown as representing extinct owners could be found. They were: a large area in north Wexford, south Carlow, and the adjoining part of Wicklow, where the MacMurroughs were dominant, and which represented the old Hy Kinsella; Annaly, or Longford; Leitrim or O'Rourke's country; and Ely O'Carroll in the present south Offaly. MacMurrough's country contained the large amount of 67,000 acres, and the other portions were similarly extensive. The general scheme was to get the natives to surrender a third or a quarter of the land, in order to be given secure possession of the rest. The chiefly names and all survivals of Irish law and custom were to be abolished. The numerous freeholders under the Irish system were to be reduced, for the Government did not favour small freeholders and the intention was to establish English landlordism and its dependent tenures. The grantees were, as in Ulster, to be Britons and Protestants. The natives fought their case stubbornly through those Catholic lawyers who could now be trained in Dublin, but finally they retained possession only of the major parts of the land, not always the best parts, and the number of freeholders was, for example, in MacMurrough's country reduced from 667 to 150, the others being made leaseholders instead. Among these the largest grantee was the ancestor of the present MacMurrough Kavanagh.

These plantations caused general exasperation, and even men like Walter, Earl of Ormond, wondered who would be the next even of the most loyal to have his property attacked. This exasperation was to have its effect in 1641 and 1689. The plantations had the still further result of bringing the old Gaelic order to an end, with its hereditary bards and Brehons whose occupation was gone. But socially its worst result was to establish English landlordism without its best features in Ireland and to reduce the masses of the people at best to mere leaseholders or even cottagers and tenants-at-will. Up to 1640, however, Roman Catholic landowners, great or small, the Old English being the more important, held two-thirds of the land,

and this made their part in political and religious life very strong.

CHICHESTER'S PARLIAMENT, 1613–1615

The Lord Deputy finally summoned a parliament to Dublin in order to confirm the Ulster and other Plantations, to vote money, and to legalize the introduction of English law in the country. It was feared by the Catholics that he also contemplated the enforcement of penal measures or even the introduction of new ones. This led to a trial of strength, therefore, between the two religions and to the appearance of a Catholic Opposition strong in numbers and skilfully led. The numbers of the Commons had, by the representation of all Ireland and many new towns, been increased up to 232, the peers, though not a large body, were mainly of the Old English loyal and Catholic type of the Pale and nearer counties, and the Irish Parliament thus presented an imposing front. Roman Catholics were not barred from the Commons as in England, and therefore, a Protestant majority, necessary from the Government point of view, had to be secured by 'management', the influence of sheriffs, and, above all, the creation of thirty-nine new boroughs returning Protestant deputies. There was an initial struggle over the election of the Speaker, the Catholics putting forward Sir John Everard and the English Sir John Davies, but finally the latter was elected by a small majority, which proved the strength of the parties. The Catholics again played the loyal note and without much hesitation confirmed the attainder of the Earl of Tyrone, etc., and the Plantations. They acknowledged the King's title gladly, granted a generous subsidy, pronounced the Statutes of Kilkenny obsolete, and declared all subjects and natives of Ireland without distinction to be under one common law.

It was on the religious question that this anti-rebel party showed determined resistance. They believed that the majority which had been procured was for the purpose of passing penal measures against their faith. The Lords of the Pale claimed under Poynings' law to be part of that Council which should be consulted as to new laws, and on the eve of the Parliament eleven of them petitioned the Deputy in person protesting against 'miserable villages by whose votes extreme penal laws shall be imposed on the King's subjects'. As these Recusants had all the proud names of Talbot, Roche, Barry, Butler, Nugent, and so on, all the Old English of the Conquest, they had to be listened to. The Commons themselves sent a deputation to the King, led by Sir William Talbot, and claiming to represent twenty-one counties and twenty-one ancient towns. On April 12th 1614 James gave them one of his usual pawky lectures, saying, 'What if I created forty noblemen and four hundred boroughs?, the more the merrier.' As regards religion, they were but half subjects and therefore deserved only half privileges. He charged them with believing in the doctrine that heretic sovereigns, deposed by the Pope, might be lawfully murdered, a charge which Talbot and others said should be submitted to the Catholic Church. Finally James conceded that eleven boroughs should be abolished. In fact, this parliament, dissolved in October 1615, ended in a triumph for the Recusants, for, though no open toleration was promised, no new measures were added and forced attendance at church was dropped.

The Stuarts were not fond of parliaments, and as in Ireland it was possible to do for long periods without them, there was not another till 1633. It had been shown, indeed, how strong the Irish side was, but the Protestant element was growing, and during the rest of the reign the peerage was added to so as to increase it in the House of Lords. Among the new creations, however, several were of the Old English and Catholic stock, such as Dillon, earl of Roscommon, Plunkett, earl of Fingall, Brabazon, earl of Meath, and Barry, earl of Barrymore, while a few such as MacDonnell, earl of Antrim, Murrough O'Brien, earl of Inchiquin, Maguire, Baron of Enniskillen, and Viscount Magennis of Iveagh, represented the old Gaelic race.

For the rest of James's reign Ireland was ruled by Oliver St. John till 1622, and then by Lord Falkland till 1629. Prosperity slowly increased and there was apparent peace and growing order. On the religious side in general the viceroys maintained 'connived indulgence', but with difficulty owing to the bitter Puritan and intolerant spirit then on the increase in both countries. In Ireland the only acts of importance on the Statute Book were that of Supremacy and the Recusancy fines, the latter were not or could not be enforced, but were hung as a threat over the heads of the Roman Catholic upper and middle classes and indeed were reckoned to amount to £20,000 per annum, if they could be duly enforced. The oath of Supremacy kept all the Old English out of office, but even then it was not always demanded of office-holders. It was, however, a standing grievance that loyal subjects, however eminent, could not serve their sovereign, and this led to that state of mind which officials call the 'Old English Irelandized'. The law, too, if enforced, debarred Catholics from the practice of the law, from keeping a school, and from university degrees.

What the more recent Protestant element in Ireland thought was shown in people like Archbishop Ussher who in 1627, along with twelve other bishops, declared that 'the religion of the Papists is superstitious and heretical and Toleration is a grievous sin'. In 1615 the first Convocation of the whole Irish church met and issued 104 articles of Religion as against the thirty-nine of the Church of England and much more Calvinistic; these lasted till Strafford came.

In 1617 King James established a Court of Wards to educate and administer the estates of minors who were tenants-in-chief of the Crown, the Deputy and Chancellor being permanent members. The opportunity could be taken to ensure that these minors must be educated in the new College at Dublin or in England, and as a result the heirs of some of the old families were soon found to be of the State Church. According to the law, tenants-in-chief on 'sueing out livery' were obliged to take the oath of Supremacy, and though this was not generally exacted, it could be used against Roman Catholics. Such was the pressure which the Crown and other centres of power could use against the majority religion. The young James, later Earl and then Duke of Ormond, was thus educated at Lambeth as the first convinced Protestant among the Butlers, and by 1640 four other peers of native stock, the earls of Kildare, Barrymore, Thomond, and Inchiquin, were Protestant. Clanrickard and Antrim were the two greatest Catholic peers, and yet such was the complexity of things that Richard, fourth Earl of Clanrickard, married Frances, daughter of Elizabeth's Secretary of State, Walsingham.

Indeed, to keep the more aristocratic settlers Protestant was a constant problem. Already several of the Elizabethan settlers were found on the other side, such as Sir Nicholas Browne, who got great estates in Kerry, and was the ancestor of the Earls of Kenmare. Another striking case was that of the family of Bagenal, whose main estates came to be in Carlow, and who under Charles I were Roman Catholic and officers in the Confederate army.

Munster was now by way of becoming a Protestant province, at the time even more so than Ulster. This was largely due to the ability, energy, and fortune-seeking of a remarkable man, Richard Boyle, Earl of Cork, the outstanding example of the new magnate type that had supplanted the lords and chiefs of Ireland. In the distribution of lands and offices and the general scramble for confiscated property many 'new men' arose, some of whom were of, indeed, the lesser Irishry, such as Crosby and Shaen. The undeveloped economic wealth of Ireland brought the business-man into prominence, and out of the woods, fisheries, linen, and cloth-weaving of Ireland huge fortunes were made. Richard Boyle came to Ireland penniless in 1588. Before his death he had become a magnate on an enormous scale, was created Earl of Cork in 1620, and had four sons who were peers, the most famous being Roger, Lord Broghill, later Earl of Orrery. The first Earl of Cork bought up Raleigh's vast estates for a sum of £1,000, for a mere song got hold of abbey-lands and the Earl of Desmond's old college of Youghal, built several towns such as Bandon, founded industries such as iron-smelting and linen-weaving, and everywhere brought in English settlers. He also commanded eight votes in the Irish House of Commons, and in short was a magnate of a modern type which made the old landed peers insignificant, and whose rise, riches, and political importance naturally filled them with fury.

CHARLES I AND IRELAND

The new reign promised a new régime in Ireland. Charles had a Roman Catholic wife and his High Church sentiment made him even more desirous to continue religious indulgence. Ireland also had an army to support, and though the revenue was increasing it was necessary to get it increased still further by national consent. The obvious way was to promise concessions on Land and Religion, the two great questions for the Irish people. Lord Falkland therefore was instructed to offer what were called 'Graces', and finally in 1627 the Romanist peers and bishops sent agents to the King and made a bargain to this effect. Land titles for sixty years back were to be valid against all claims of the Crown, Catholics might practise at the Bar on a simple oath of allegiance based on that of 1606, and other minor concessions were included. On the question of land titles, those of Connacht were particularly in question. The Composition of 1585 had never been confirmed by parliament, although in 1615 Chichester had been instructed to grant patents confirming the various agreements. In return for the Graces the Recusants were to pay £120,000 spread over three years, and a parliament was promised which should confirm the whole bargain. The money was paid, but the most important of the Graces were never legalized. The Irish naturally considered themselves badly tricked, and it is difficult to find any justification for Charles and Falkland. The Puritan pressure, represented now in the English parliament, was indeed great and what the Irish Catholics might expect from it was shown in the protest of Ussher and his fellow-bishops that 'the religion of the Papists is superstitious and toleration a grievous sin'. Charles did indeed continue toleration by Prerogative, and the strength of the Catholics even in the capital is shown by the existence of thirty 'mass-houses' in Dublin at the time.

After the rule of Lords Justices for three years, Ireland found one of its greatest viceroys in Sir Thomas Wentworth, created Lord Deputy in 1632, and in 1639 Lord Lieutenant and Earl of Strafford.

Wentworth came to apply to Ireland the régime of 'Thorough' which King Charles and Archbishop Laud were now enforcing in Church and State. The idea recurred as at several times in history, that Ireland should be made the second jewel in the Crown and after paying for its own Government should provide a surplus for the Crown. In the struggle between King and Parliament this island might also be put on the royal side, for however Irish Catholics might be ill-treated it was well understood that their religion and their nature was for Monarchy. Wentworth intended first of all to staff the Irish government with Englishmen of his own choosing in place of the inefficient, corrupt, and persecuting Anglo-Irish junta. Then he intended to increase the royal revenue, which was pitifully small, for Ireland was lightly taxed and its land and wealth had been shamefully disposed of to planters and officials for a mere song. Wentworth knew that to attack the new vested interests of men like Boyle or of the London Companies meant determined and malignant resistance, but he was a man of unfaltering courage and determination.

Wentworth indeed considered the new Protestant moneyed class a far greater danger to the Crown than the submissive native race. On his appointment he found that there was an annual deficit in the revenue of £20,000, for the Government as it stood preferred to have it so so that England would have to make up the balance.

The first step was soon achieved, to set the Court of Castle Chamber in working order as the Star Chamber of Ireland and to see that no appeals from Ireland could go to England. He told the Council, in which men like Loftus had long resisted such viceroys as Falkland, that it became them better to consider what might please the King than what might please the people. Ireland, he declared, with its great men and its weak Crown, was like England in the Wars of the Roses. There were to be no intermediaries between the King and his subjects, and he would make an act of State equal to an act of Parliament.

To balance the Protestant and the Catholic elements for the advantage of the Crown was an obvious policy. The penal statutes could be kept suspended over the heads of the Catholics and used or not, as policy dictated. The Recusancy fines were not dead, and at the beginning of his rule he extracted £20,000 from the Catholic party on condition of escaping these fines for another year. Nevertheless the régime of Toleration was maintained. To enforce decency and order of a Catholic character in the Church of Ireland and to get her properly endowed was another great aim. In 1634 he imposed the Thirty-nine articles of the English Church upon the Convocation of the Church of Ireland. New statutes drawn up by Laud were imposed on Trinity College, and for the first time Roman Catholic scholars were asked to take the oath of Supremacy, with the result that though they continued to attend for educational purposes they were unable to attain degrees, fellowships, and scholarships. In his Church policy Wentworth's great agent was Bramhall, bishop of Derry. The act of Uniformity was enforced, laymen in possession of church lands were induced or compelled to return them, and in the confirmation of titles provision was made for the rights of the Church as well as the Crown. Wentworth realized well that the real enemies of both were the stubborn Protestants of the North.

In 1634 Wentworth summoned a Parliament which lasted till 1635. The House of peers contained twenty-four Anglican bishops and the Catholic nobles were now outvoted by the many Protestant creations of recent years. Again it was necessary to balance the two religions in the House of Commons; in the case of the Catholics they were won over by a promise of Graces, and Wentworth scored at the beginning by procuring handsome subsidies. Trouble then arose over the viceroy's evident intention to water down the Graces and not to grant that confirmation of land titles which both parties demanded. Catholics were merely permitted to practise at the minor side of the law, with some such small concessions. As regards land titles, both parties had demanded an Act of Limitations, but Wentworth said that to legalize all grants for sixty years back was to bar out those who had held land before that and would cover all sorts of abuses and grants on terms detrimental to Church and Crown. Instead he got an act passed establishing a Commission for Defective Titles, under which each grant was to be examined in turn by the Commission, which he controlled. Having got his way he dissolved Parliament in 1635.

Armed with such powers, he compelled landowners and planters to have their grants reviewed, and if they were confirmed, he generally managed to increase the King's rent and to recover tithes and advowsons. In doing so he naturally clashed with those who had benefited, but he was fearless in exercising the strong hand against the great. Thus he made the Earl of Cork surrender the college of Youghal and further fined him £15,000 for the flaws and evasions of this grant. His boldest measure, however, was to get the charter of the London companies in the North forfeited, with a fine of £70,000 for non-fulfilment of conditions, and the customs of Coleraine and Derry were annexed to the Crown. As the companies had the City of London behind them, this made a dangerous and in the end a fatal enemy for Wentworth.

The next great plan was for a plantation in Connacht and Clare. The West was still Gaelic and Norman in its landed classes, and the Composition of Connacht, never fully confirmed, had established them on easy terms. The revenues of the Earl of Clanrickard in this province were greater than the King's. Wentworth therefore in July 1635 set up a commission at Boyle, and grand juries were summoned for the various counties. Wentworth made light of the promise of Chichester in 1615, and declared that the King's title went back to the De Burgos. Resistance was only too likely, so he said that if the juries would find for the King they should keep three-quarters of their property, otherwise he would take all by process of the Exchequer. The juries of the counties save Galway yielded and found a title for the King, but there they stood out and were finally brought before the Castle Chamber and heavily fined. Wentworth's time, however, was to be too short for planting a Protestant colony in the West.

More admirable was Wentworth's energetic policy of reducing the selfish liberties of the old towns, whose corporations were very corrupt, and throwing them open to new industry; of clearing the seas of pirates, of building up a mercantile shipping, and of fostering Irish industries. He encouraged the linen industry and invested £30,000 of his own in it. The woollen industry he discouraged because Irish woven cloth might compete with the finer drapery of England, but the trade in the rougher manufacture was permitted. In this he expressed his policy openly to the King: 'We must not only endeavour to enrich them (the Irish) but make sure still to hold them dependent upon the Crown and not able to subsist without us.' His economic policy, however interested, undoubtedly made Ireland highly prosperous, but this was all swept away by the disasters of the next twenty years. In an account of his office to the King in 1636 he could rightly boast that he had endowed the Church, wiped out the Irish debt, given the Crown a surplus of £50,000, and raised an army to keep the peace between parties.

Strafford's work and schemes were alike to be ruined by what the Irish called 'The War of the Three Kingdoms'. When the Scots revolted against Charles and took the Covenant in February 1638 Strafford imposed upon their kinsmen in Ulster a Non-resistance oath. When the war against the Scots began in 1639 he assembled an Irish army of 9,000 men at Carrick-fergus and was ready to take against the rebels measures which Charles would not accept. He then summoned a Parliament in Dublin which met in the most loyal mood and voted sub-sidies of £200,000 to be spread over three years. This assembly, which combined Protestants and Catholics, lasted till 1641. In November 1639 Strafford was summoned to England, leaving James, Earl of Ormond, as general of the army. On his departure all the discontented elements combined and his fine army was disbanded under pressure of the English Parlia-ment. In November 1640 the famous Long Parliament began in England, and the complaints of Ireland, sent in by all the aggrieved sections, did much to bring the great viceroy to the scaffold in May 1641. By this time the subsidies were yielding only half the original grant, and in order to win Irish support Charles abandoned the proposed plantations, reduced the powers of the Castle Chamber, and withdrew the commission of Defective Titles, confirming the Graces and proposing a bill to confirm sixty-year titles in Connacht, Clare, Limerick, and Tipperary.

In this crisis Charles should have certainly given the command of Dublin to the loyalist Earl of Ormond, a great man of the old Norman-Irish stock, though a Protestant. Instead, he appointed the Earl of Leicester, an absentee, and the real power was exercised by two Lords Justices, Borlase and Parsons, who were Puritans and Parliament men. Their rule was destined to be most disastrous and to drive Irish Roman Catholics, even of the most loyal type, into rebellion. In August 1641 they prorogued Parliament, thus stopping a bill for the grant of the Graces, which Charles had ordered them to prepare; and when Parliament met again in March 1642 all unity was gone, the Catholic members were absent, and rebellion had spread all over the land. The mishandling of a delicate situation was perhaps intentional on the part of these two, who unjustly regarded all 'Papists' as rebels, had no objection to rebellion spreading because it meant more confiscations, and were glad to embarrass the unfortunate King.

The general revolt against Monarchy in Britain naturally inspired Irishmen with the thought of getting their grievances redressed by force, which otherwise were not listened to. These were: the confiscations, the unjust treatment of the natives, the favour shown to the colonists, and exclusion from office and civil rights as Roman Catholics. On the religious question, as one Irishman was heard to say, 'If the Scots may fight for their religion, why not we?' But it is to be noted that the leaders of the subsequent rising never formally repudiated the English monarchy; at the utmost they demanded the rights of Ireland as a Catholic kingdom with a viceroy acceptable to native feeling, Parliament set free from the shackles of Poynings' law, and full civil and religious rights for the Catholic population.

The elements of this rising existed both at home and abroad. At home it found a leader in Rory O'More (a nephew of the famous Rory Oge), Sir Felim O'Neill, and other gentlemen whose estates had all but vanished in these later times. Abroad there was a whole world of Irish soldiers in the service of Spain and Austria, and of priests and friars in the Irish colleges of the Low Countries, Spain, and Italy. A union was now formed between them, and while Rory O'More led the cause at home Father Luke Wadding, head of the Irish Franciscans at Rome, organized the cause abroad and sought the aid of the Pope and of Cardinal Richelieu.

The rising at home began with a plot formed by O'More and Conor Maguire, Baron of Enniskillen, to seize Dublin castle on October 23rd 1641. The plot failed through treachery, but many of the Leinster Irish appeared in arms, and there was a general rising in Ulster under Sir Felim, in which the long-suppressed fury of the native race found vent in cruel massacres of the planters, whose losses amounted to perhaps some 10,000, but were greatly exaggerated in horrified England. The Ulster colony for the time was swept away, and Sir Felim held most of the province. On hearing the news, the Long Parliament voted money for the suppression of this Rebellion, but how to raise it was the problem. This was finally done by declaring forfeit the estates of the leading rebels and offering them for sale to subscribers called 'Adventurers'. In February 1642 Charles had to accept the so-called 'Adventurers Act', by which he was further forbidden to pardon rebels. Until the settlement under Charles II this sweeping act of the Long Parliament bound the hands of every English government, and was the basis of the later Cromwellian settlement. For the present, however, only a limited sum was raised, which actually Parliament soon employed against their own King, and it was not till 1649 that the English Parliament could effectively deal with Ireland.

A small victory at Julianstown near Drogheda in November 1641 by Rory O'More over Government forces was the first encouragement to the Irish, and the English troops sought refuge in garrisons such as Derry, Drogheda, Bandon, and Cork. But O'More found the Lords of the Pale reluctant to join in active rebellion, and it was only after two meetings with them at Crofty Hill and Tara that in December he induced these loyal Old English to join the cause by dwelling on their disabilities and declaring 'we are the only subjects in Europe not allowed to serve their Prince'. The insurrection then steadily spread and embraced Munster, in which the Irish were commanded by Lord Mountgarret, a Butler, and

Connacht, where Clanrickard was a Royalist but for the present stood aloof.

The King and his parliament now bargained with the Scots for an army to suppress Ireland, and in April 1642 General Munroe landed at Carrickfergus with a large force. The Ulster Scots joined him, and the Parliament side found able leaders in Sir Charles Coote, Roger Boyle (Lord Broghill), and Murrough O'Brien (Earl of Inchiquin), one of the old Gaelic aristocracy but a determined Protestant. So the war became general, and when in August 1642 Charles set up his standard at Nottingham against Parliament the Monarchy for all effective purposes ceased to control its three kingdoms.

Ireland had technically been in a state of war for a year before the Great Rebellion began in England, hence it was possible for the victorious Parliament later to accuse the Irish of having begun the struggle. The official opening of war in England now caused a definite alignment of forces in Ireland. In August 1642 the Irish parliament met again, but it was now a Protestant body, which excluded Catholics. Charles made Ormond Lord Lieutenant and there rallied to him considerable English royalist forces. But so far in Ireland it had been a fight between Catholic and Protestant, or rather of the Old Irish against the New English. For this reason many of the Protestants preferred to obey Parliament's orders as issued by the Lords Justices in Dublin. In Munster this side was commanded by Inchiquin, President of Munster for the Parliament, and Lord Broghill, whose family had built up a great land-power stretching from Bandon to Youghal. In the north-east Munroe's army held the field under joint orders of the Parliaments of England and Scotland. In the north-west the settlers united as 'The Laggan army' under the two brothers Stewart, and Derry and Enniskillen became Protestant 'cities of refuge', as Cork and Bandon were in the south.

The Roman Catholic party, expelled under the Lords Justices from the Dublin parliament, now set up an executive council to represent and give legal force to their side. This council again formed in October 1642 the Catholic Confederacy of Kilkenny, with a supreme Council and an assembly of two Houses. They represented the four provinces, each of which was to have an army with a general-in-chief. Rory O'More was the presiding spirit of the Confederation, and it was a Royalist though Catholic body, whose motto was: '*Pro Deo, pro Rege, pro Patria Hibernia unanimis.*'

Thus did the Irish nation, which was now a blend of Gaels and Old English, who stood firm by the Roman faith, appear in arms in what they declared to be a just and lawful cause. The oath which they took was modified for any Protestant royalist who might join them, but their general aim was Catholic and they were pledged to establish if possible the Catholic Church. It was found, however, impossible to get those of them who owned abbey lands to restore them. Their general aim, expressed in many declarations, notably that of Brussels in 1642, was to procure: liberty of conscience, government by officials who should be Catholics, restitution of lands confiscated 'for religion', liberty of trade in the Empire, and the independence of the Irish Parliament by the repeal of Poynings' law. They expressed a preference for the 'moderate Protestants' of the King's religion, and their constant fear was what they might suffer from the Roundheads in England, whom they accused of disloyalty to their sovereign and an intention to extirpate the Catholic religion. Nevertheless they had assembled and taken arms without royal permission and so it was possible for later English governments technically to declare they were not a legitimate body.

It was not easy to procure one mind among the Confederates. The majority were Anglo-Irish Catholics, while the Old Irish, who had suffered most by confiscation and plantation, were more bent upon the recovery of their estates and the maintenance of the old Gaelic language and tradition. Among the Old English many thought that the best game to play was to support the Monarchy, with whose fall their own would come, while others, among whom the clergy were the most determined, thought that 'England's difficulty was Ireland's opportunity', and that a full Catholic government and nation might emerge out of the general upset. Ormond himself, whose own brothers and cousins were Catholics, strove hard to convince them that their best hope was to support the Crown and be content with whatever terms Charles could grant. MacCarthy,

Viscount Muskerry, threw in his lot with the Confederates and so did Clanrickard; Antrim also gave help, but all three were distinctly on the moderate and cautious side.

At this time the best Irish soldiers were to be found in Spanish service, in which even the Protestant Inchiquin had been trained, and so in August 1642 two famous commanders were summoned from the Continent, who arrived with arms and money supplied by Richelieu and other sympathizers, viz. Owen Roe O'Neill, a nephew of the famous Earl of Tyrone, and General Preston. O'Neill was the natural leader of the Old Irish, while Preston represented the Old English Catholic side.

O'Neill took command in Ulster and soon controlled most of this province. A man of cautious, silent, and patient genius, he formed the Ulster rebels into a disciplined army, by far the best that appeared on the native side. But in Inchiquin he found a man of Gaelic descent and military genius equal to his own. Ormond, created Marquis in 1642, was a statesman of humane and liberal mind, though not a great commander, who was determined that the cause of the King must come first. In March 1643 he defeated Preston at New Ross, and in general, in the several battles that followed, the Old English leaders showed little ability or determination.

In England the Parliament cause now began to triumph, united as it was till 1648 with the Scots, and all who feared that the Monarchy would be destroyed began to veer to Charles's side. The help of Ireland became more and more necessary as the King's cause declined, and when the battle of Marston Moor in July 1644 marked the arrival of a new military genius in Oliver Cromwell and of a Roundhead army of Independents and Sectaries, who were the enemies both of Anglicans and Presbyterians and were ready to go as far as a Republic.

In August 1645 Charles sent an English Catholic, Lord Glamorgan, to treat with the Catholic confederates for help. They were to send over 10,000 men and in return were to have legal toleration and possession of the churches then in their control. But this was a secret treaty and when it leaked out Charles repudiated it.

The whole situation was altered in Ireland by the arrival in October 1645 of the Papal Nuncio Rinuccini, who landed in Kerry and arrived in Kilkenny with money from Rome and from Mazarin. He had been invited by the majority of the Confederation and by the labours of Wadding, to restore public Catholicism and bring Ireland again under the spiritual authority of the Pope. The Nuncio at once took the lead of the more extreme clerical party and saw in O'Neill the one general who could win the Catholic cause. He did not, however, repudiate the Monarchy, for his was not a political mission, and probably his supporters would have been content with Ireland under a Catholic viceroy of the Crown, which Ormond was not. But the arrival of a papal envoy and foreign intervention only made the victorious Puritans of England the more determined to reconquer Ireland.

On June 5th 1646 Owen Roe won a brilliant victory at Benburb in Tyrone. Munroe had formed a combination with the Stewarts to march from opposite directions and to crush O'Neill, but by superior tactics he prevented their junction, and completely routed the English-Scottish army, of whom over 3,000 fell. Like the battle of the Yellow Ford won by his great uncle on the same river, O'Neill's victory should have led to final results. Unfortunately, when Preston united with him, their differences prevented such final fruits and Dublin remained in the hands of the Lords Justices.

Charles's final defeat at Naseby in July 1645 made him still more dependent on Irish aid, and so he instructed his viceroy in August 1646 to offer what is called the 'Ormond Peace'. By this the oath of Supremacy was not to be required of office-holders, religious penalties were repealed, and all land-titles from 1628 were confirmed. A large party of the confederates welcomed the terms, but the Nuncio's party were strongly opposed, and Ormond found that even many of the Old English were not, as he said, 'excommunication proof'. The spirit of the moderates was expressed by Colonel Walter Bagenal, who declared, 'We shall certainly be overwhelmed if we do not support the King.' But the clergy excommunicated those who favoured the peace, O'Neill was on their side, and under the pressure of his victorious army the Assembly rejected it in February 1647.

By this time the army of Cromwell and the Independents

dominated the Long Parliament itself and the royal cause was almost lost. Ormond therefore decided to surrender Dublin to the Parliament forces that were on their way, preferring, as he said, 'English rebels to Irish rebels'. Colonel Michael Jones arrived with 8,000 Roundheads, and on July 28th Ormond surrendered the sword of State to the Commissioners of Parliament and quitted Ireland. It was fatal for the Irish cause that the capital should thus be handed over to the English enemy, but we must equally blame the Irish commanders for not seizing it in time. Preston indeed attempted to do so, but was routed by Jones at Dangan Hill with the bloody slaughter of over 5,000 of his men. From this moment Cromwell had a safe point of entry into Ireland. Meanwhile Inchiquin was sweeping all Munster, and on November 13th 1647 he finished off Lord Taafe's Catholic army at Knocknanoss near Kanturk. In the battle a force of Antrim Highlanders on one wing of the Irish army swept all before it at its first charge, but in the general rout was surrounded and cut to pieces, and their commander, the famous Alastar 'Colkitto' MacDonnell, perished on the field.

The triumph of the Independents in England created a new alignment everywhere, in which the Scots, the Presbyterians in the Long Parliament, the Ulster settlers, and many of the English of Ireland united to save the cause of monarchy. Even Inchiquin turned over and was voted a traitor at Westminster in April 1648, but Broghill and Coote stood true for Parliament. A majority of the Catholic party also united with Ormond when he returned in September 1648 to lead the royal cause. O'Neill and the Ulster army stood true to the Nuncio, but Rinuccini finally left Ireland in February 1649 at the request of the Confederacy itself. The execution of Charles in January 1649 still further united those who favoured his son. Ormond was continued by the new King as Lord Lieutenant, but in an attempt to recover Dublin was defeated by Michael Jones in August at the battle of Baggot-rath. The way was thus cleared for Oliver Cromwell, who arrived in Dublin on August 15 1649 as 'Lord Lieutenant and General for the Parliament of England'. He commanded an army of 20,000 men, all determined and enthusiastic members of various sects, highly disciplined, perfectly equipped, and inspired by Old Testament christianity. Their commander, however, as well as being a Protestant zealot, was a sturdy English nationalist, a great soldier, and a cool-headed politician. Here was a combination which only a union of all Ireland could have beaten and the spirit of which promised little quarter to 'papists' and their religion.

Cromwell's objects were: to recover Ireland for the rule of the Commonwealth or Republic of England, which had abolished alike Monarchy, the Church, and the Peerage, to enforce the Adventurers Act of 1642, and to punish the Ulster massacres, for which he quite mistakenly held all Irish papists responsible. Turning northwards, early in September he attacked and stormed Drogheda, where in a general massacre some 3,500 people, both soldiers and townsfolk of both sexes, were put to the sword, in what Cromwell declared to be a just vengeance for 'innocent blood'.

Turning south, he attacked and treated Wexford in the same way, and the subsequent surrender of other towns such as New Ross showed what terror the first two examples had created. In a public proclamation he charged the Roman clergy with being responsible for the war, and declared, 'I meddle not with any man's conscience, but as for liberty to exercise the mass, I must tell you that where the Parliament of England has power, that will not be allowed'—a bad outlook for Ireland under his rule.

Before Cromwell's landing, Ormond had striven to unite the Irish armies under himself, Inchiquin, and O'Neill, and it was a Royalist garrison which was massacred at Drogheda and Wexford. But the death of Owen Roe O'Neill in Cavan on November 6th 1649 removed the only commander who could have faced Oliver with success and the last great man of a race that had played so large a part in Irish history.

While Cromwell continued his campaign in the South, Broghill reduced Munster, Inchiquin's men joined him, and Coote gained the upper hand in Ulster. In March of the next year (1650) Kilkenny surrendered, and the Confederacy dissolved except for the more extreme section, which sought refuge beyond the Shannon. The Ulster Irish army was brought down to serve in the south, and when Cromwell attacked Clonmel on May 9th 1650 he suffered his one repulse at the hands of Hugh O'Neill, a nephew of Owen Roe, who then slipped away with his whole army while the mayor was treating for surrender.

Oliver himself left Ireland on May 26th 1650, leaving as commander and Lord Lieutenant his son-in-law Ireton. His campaign had not ended the war, for the Roman Catholics dreaded the fate that would follow their defeat, and Ormond spun out the fight as long as possible in the interests of his master, Charles. He himself, Preston, and Inchiquin all forsook their unfortunate country in 1650, but Clanrickard remained as viceroy, several armies still held out, and in fact Irish resistance did not end till 1652. In June 1651 Coote gave a final overthrow to the Ulster army at Scarrifhollis near Letterkenny, and the savagery of these wars is shown in Coote's ordering Owen Roe's only son Henry to be murdered after the battle. Limerick yielded to Ireton under the gallant Hugh O'Neill in October 1651, and the war may be regarded as over with the surrender of Galway in May 1652. But still various Irish armies of over 30,000 men in all were holding the field, and how to induce them to surrender was a problem for the Government. The Cromwellian army itself was some 34,000 strong. Finally, however, in the course of 1652 the Irish forces submitted, separately and without making terms for their side as a whole. The Republican 'army officers' even now complained of leniency to the Irish, and a report drawn up by Dr. Henry Jones, bishop of Clogher, by exaggerating the massacres of 1641, worked up English feeling to a pitch at which Catholic and rebel Ireland could expect little mercy.

It was first necessary to get the soldiers out of the way, and over 30,000 of them were given leave to transport themselves to France or Spain, while thousands of common Irish were dispatched to the West Indies as practical slaves. The population in the last ten years of war and ravage had fallen to some half million, and Ireland was almost a blank sheet on which the English Commonwealth could write what it wished.

To avenge the Ulster massacres and other crimes a high

Court was set up in Dublin in August 1652, but the usual English instinct of fair play asserted itself even with the Cromwellians, and in fact only fifty-two victims were executed by its orders. Among these was the unfortunate Sir Felim O'Neill and (a curious instance of the English turned Irish) Sir Walter Bagenal, an officer of the Confederates, executed for having put an English soldier to death 'out of the course of lawful warfare'. Luckily for himself, Rory O'More had died in the remote island of Inishboffin before the final collapse.

Policy and vengeance inspired a far more cruel treatment of the whole race than a few hundred executions could be. It must be remembered that the Sectarian republicans were in command of the whole British isles and that their hero Cromwell had successfully laid low the Anglicans of England, the Presbyterians of Scotland, and the Catholics of Ireland. His military rule, lasting till 1658, which his opponents call 'the Usurpation' or 'Interregnum', was in fact exercised over the whole of the three kingdoms through an invincible army. Ireland, as possible Stuart ground, had to be held down, but the Irish were also to be punished as rebels and as 'papists', and the fate dealt out to them was only possible to minds steeped in the story of the Jews and the Amalekites.

THE CROMWELLIAN SETTLEMENT

In August 1652 the Parliament of England, which was a mere remnant representing the army, passed an act for Ireland, generally called the Cromwellian 'Act of Settlement'. By this, 'Irish papists' (a term which embraced many English settlers of the old faith) were divided into several classes according to their guilt.[1] The mass of the poor with not more than £10 in goods were given a general pardon. The arrears of pay of the Cromwellian army and the claims of the adventurers under the Act of 1642 were met by the confiscation of nine counties. Ireland had to pay for its own conquest and, says Clarendon, 'was the great capital out of which the Cromwellian government paid all debts, rewarded all services, and

[1] A good many Protestant Royalists suffered forfeiture also, beginning with Ormond and Inchiquin.

performed all acts of bounty'. Under the Act of Settlement certain classes of the Irish were excluded from pardon, the rest were allowed to keep all or some of their lands and property and were ordered to remain where they were for the present. But the claims of the Army officers for more land for themselves and their men led to the idea of Transplantation, and Cromwell finally accepted the great scheme which bears his name. By ordinances in June and July of 1653, and then in a final Act of Satisfaction in September 1653, Ireland was divided into two parts, viz. Clare and Connacht which alone were to be left to Irish gentry and landowners, and the rest, which was confiscated in order to meet the claims of the Adventurers and of the soldiers and officers, with their arrears of pay. The common people were too valuable as labourers and cultivators to be expelled, and the fate of Transplantation beyond the Shannon was reserved for the upper classes, who were given estates in the West to compensate them for their estates in other provinces.

To move the whole aristocracy with all their retainers was a problem, but the Cromwellians did not lack energy or ruthless determination, and by the end of 1655 the transplanted classes were all west of the Shannon and twenty-six counties were left in English hands. The work of apportionment was speeded up by the genius of Sir William Petty, who produced what is called 'the Down Survey' of Ireland, the first scientific mapping out of Ireland, so-called because the topographical details were laid *down* by measurement on maps.

In this elaborate confiscation the government took over also the towns, and the property of the Church, which it disestablished, leaving full toleration at least to all Protestant sects. The towns were also planted with new English, and the former burgesses of Galway, Waterford, etc., were ordered to move two miles out of all such corporate and garrisoned towns.

In December 1653 Cromwell was made Lord Protector of England and, as a result, of Ireland also, and continued so till his death. Ireland was ruled in his name by Fleetwood, and then from 1655 by the Protector's son Henry, who showed some humanity towards the Irish. The great business was the carrying out of the Act of Settlement, the general intention of which was, in addition to installing the Adventurers, to colonize Ireland permanently with a Cromwellian army. This army, originally 34,000, was in 1655 reduced to 19,000, but it was sufficient to hold Ireland down. The amount of land confiscated and planted is reckoned by Petty as 11,000,000 (English) acres out of the whole 20,000,000 acres of Ireland, nearly 8,000,000 of these being 'profitable'. Actually as a scheme of colonization the Settlement was a failure, for the soldiers in large numbers sold their debentures in Irish lands to officers and speculators for whatever they could get and returned to England. Nevertheless many thousands of the common soldiery were planted on the land and with their families formed a new and considerable element in the Protestant and English population of Ireland. The real result was to create a new landlord class in Ireland; for the Adventurers, and also great numbers of army officers, were installed in Irish estates. The Catholic landowners were reduced to a minority, and the new English element in the towns never again lost their dominance in the civic and industrial life of the country. Thus Galway, which up to this had been a strong Catholic centre in which Gaelic culture could survive, henceforth ceased to be that old prosperous 'City of the Tribes' which it had been since the De Burgos first came to Connacht.

The brevity of the Cromwellian régime, however, prevented the full success of the great scheme for turning Ireland into a second England. In 1653 Ireland was declared part of the Protectorate and there was a union of the three kingdoms, in which Ireland (viz. the Cromwellian element) was represented in the English Parliament by thirty members and was granted free trade with Great Britain and the colonies.

The death of Oliver Cromwell on September 3rd 1658 removed the strong hand that kept the military usurpation together. In Ireland as in England, the majority of the Roundhead soldiery would willingly have fought if they could have found a successor to their dead hero. But in both countries the Army leaders determined to restore the Monarchy on conditions of constitutional and religious liberty. And so when General Monck marched from Scotland and declared for a free Parliament in London, Broghill and Coote did the same in Ireland, and Charles II was proclaimed king in Dublin on May 14th 1660. The restored monarch put the Cromwellian leaders into power as Lords Justices and created Coote Earl of Mountrath and Broghill of Orrery, with other titles and rewards for the Cromwellian renegades. It is to be particularly remembered that the restoration of the Stuart monarchy in Ireland was the work of the Cromwellian leaders and their army, and not in any way that of the Royalist Irish, whether they were Protestant or Catholic. All that the disarmed and leaderless people could do was to cheer when they heard their tyrants proclaim the son of the king that they had murdered. This consideration ruled the mind of Charles II when he had to meet the claims of Ireland for redress.

CHAPTER XIV

THE LATER STUART MONARCHY, 1660–1691

IT was an obvious piece of justice that Charles II should attempt to redress what Ireland had suffered from the Cromwellian 'usurpation'. In its later years the Kilkenny Confederation had thrown itself on the Stuart side, and after the final defeat hundreds of Irish gentry had served Charles abroad in various ways as 'ensign-men'. Ireland was now Royalist ground, for the Irish Catholic leaders saw that only in the Monarchy lay their hopes for toleration and their recovery of their property. The English parliament now shared the power with the Crown and had no friendly feelings for the Irish. The Dublin parliament itself became a Protestant assembly, even if no actual law was yet passed to exclude Roman Catholics; the Irish Protestants were in possession of all the main seats of power; and it was only as a landed class and a majority of the people that the Catholics were formidable. The real division was Protestant *versus* Catholic, and public opinion in England was opposed to weakening the 'Protestant and English interest' in Ireland. Charles himself, though he wished well to the Irish, had to tell them: 'My justice I must afford to you all, but my favour must be given to my Protestant subjects.'

To satisfy the two interests, the whole land of Ireland was put at the Crown's disposal. The Catholic Irish in arms since 1641 and even up to the Ormond peace of 1646 were treated as technical rebels against the King, and it was not enough to argue that they had stood on their defence as Catholic Irishmen and not repudiated the King.

A royal Declaration of November 1660 laid down the details of the second Act of Settlement. The Crown was pledged to the Adventurers act of 1642, but the Cromwellian settlement, as done under the 'Usurper', might be revised to the advantage of the Roman Catholics. The lands of the Adventurers were confirmed to them, and 'innocent Protestants' were restored at once. 'Irish Papists' were divided into classes according to their 'guilt or innocence', and those transplanted merely as such were given back their former estates. 'Ensign-men' were restored if they had accepted nothing as transplanters, but where adventurers and soldiers were in possession of their estates they were to be 'reprised' out of the forfeited lands yet undisposed of, the amount of which was much exaggerated by the Cromwellian leaders Orrery and Mountrath. Papists 'not innocent' included, for example, those who had joined the Nuncio or been in the Confederacy before the Peace of 1646, for, very unjustly, the Irish cause of 1642–1646 was considered a 'rebellion'. The royal favour still meant much, and by the Declaration and in the Act eighteen peers and many other proprietors were restored at once, such as Antrim and Inchiquin. But in general, while considerable numbers of Catholic landlords returned from beyond the Shannon, many had to be content with their transplanter portions there, and many more were excluded from grace under the sweeping definition of 'rebellion'. Charles would have liked to do more for them but was not the man to insist, English public opinion was unfriendly, and the Cromwellian party in Ireland was too strong and militant to be dislodged.

In May 1661 an elected Irish parliament met, which by the imposition of the oath of Supremacy proved to be a Protestant one, and the Act of Settlement as completed in England was laid before it. It met with stubborn resistance from the Cromwellian wing, which meant to keep all it could, but Poynings' law operated to their disadvantage, for a Bill once returned from England could only be accepted or rejected in full. It was finally pushed through, and Ormond, now a Duke, who had been appointed Lord Lieutenant in 1661, in July 1662 gave it the royal assent.

Charles now set up a Court of Claims, consisting of seven honest Englishmen, which restored great numbers of Catholic gentry, much to the indignation of the Cromwellians. In 1663 an Act of Explanation was passed by the Irish Parliament by which the Cromwellians had to surrender to 'unreprised' Catholics one-third of the estates which they held in May 1659. This Act was due to Ormond, who had the backing of the King and Cavalier party in England and of a Protestant but loyalist element in the Irish parliament, led by the Earl of Kildare. The Court of Claims lasted till August 1667, but it was too favourable to the Catholics to please Protestant opinion in England and Ireland, and after this date no more claims were heard. Some three thousand of the old proprietors remained excluded, among whom even a number of 'Ensign-men' got none of the 'undisposed forfeited land', because there was not enough of this to go round. The Catholics had no voice either in Parliament or Council, they were now mere suppliants for justice, and Charles preferred to sacrifice his friends to his enemies. Otherwise he and the Duke of York and Ormond did what they considered all that was possible under the circumstances. But the Act of Settlement remained a standing grievance with the Catholic aristocracy, which only closed with the battle of the Boyne. A particularly shocking case of the legal injustice of the act was that of Lewis O'Dempsey, Viscount Clanmalier, who had been a Confederate Catholic. His claim to be restored was not even heard and the great estate of this head of an ancient sept of Leix was granted to an English official. At least the conquerors of Ireland up to this had been aristocratic fighting men, and it is no wonder that now the blood of the 'ancient families' grew hot within them to see their land ruled by 'a generation of mechanic bagmen, strangers to all principles of religion and loyalty'.[1] Gaelic Ulster suffered most, for its surviving chiefs had led the Rising of 1641 and got no mercy. The great names of MacMahon of Monaghan, Maguire of Fermanagh, O'Neill of the Fews, and O'Neill of Tyrone, now vanished for good from the landed aristocracy of the North.

The final result was a Protestant Anglican ascendancy owning most of the land and dominant in parliament, the government, the towns, and trade. According to Petty, in 1672 the new Cromwellian settlers owned 4,500,000 out of the 12 million profitable acres which Ireland then had, the Catholic 3,500,000 and the older Protestant settlers the rest. The Catholics were 800,000 of the total population, and the

---

[1] So Richard Bellings wrote to Ormond. Secretary to the Catholic Confederacy, he had been lucky enough to be restored to his estates.

Protestants 300,000, but the majority of these were Ulster Presbyterians and English sectaries.

The restoration of the Monarchy was accompanied by that of the State Church, of which in a single day in January 1661 two archbishops and ten bishops were consecrated in St. Patrick's. This was the only religion now recognized officially, and what amount of toleration Catholic and Protestant dissenters would get was the question. Ormond's policy aimed at balancing them against one another so as to keep the Episcopalian ascendancy safe. In Ireland, as in England, the Puritan gentry who had fought against the Crown and Church or their sons now accepted both, and Protestant Dissent was confined to the middle and lower classes.

Along with the Church and the Crown the Parliament of Ireland was restored, supreme in internal affairs but controlled from England under Poynings' law, and for the most part a Protestant Anglican assembly, though the Catholics were not legally excluded and still had the vote. By the theory of the Constitution it was an admitted principle that 'the Crown of Ireland was appendant and inseparably annexed to the Imperial Crown of England, and that whoever was King *de facto* in England was King *de jure* in Ireland'. But, while the Crown had formerly been the supreme power for Ireland, the Parliament of England now shared the sovereignty with it and, though for some fifty years the claim to legislate for Ireland was not laid down, it was already working in practice. The later 'restrictive Trade acts' passed in England to the disadvantage of Ireland rested, however, on the ground that after 1660 Free Trade between the three Kingdoms had been done away with and that the trade of the Empire was an English preserve in which Scotland and Ireland as long as they had their own parliaments had no right to share.

The next question affecting the Irish, next to the Land, was that of Religion. The Roman Catholics were divided into a moderate party and an extreme or Ultramontane party, but the moderates were in the minority and found it hard to create a pro-English sentiment, especially as the State would make no provision for the Catholic clergy, who had to depend on their flocks or on support from abroad. Ormond attempted to encourage and increase the moderate section. In 1661 Father Peter Walsh and Richard Bellings drew up a Remonstrance on the questions over which Roman Catholics were in disrepute, such as the 'deposing' theory. The Remonstrance admitted that all princes and governors, irrespective of their religion, are God's lieutenants, that the King's power is supreme in civil and temporal affairs, that it binds all subjects, and that no foreign power may pretend to release them from their allegiance. Twenty-one peers and 164 prominent laymen accepted the Remonstrance but out of 2,000 priests only seventy would sign it. It was finally submitted to a congregation of bishops and laymen at the end of 1665. To repudiate the 'deposing power' of the Pope was further than the bishops in the congregation, led by O'Reilly of Armagh, would go, though they accepted monarchy as of God, and the Inter-Nuncio, who from Brussels now ruled the Roman Church in Ireland, formally condemned the Remonstrance. It thus failed to bring about legal toleration for the Catholics, but at least those who swore temporal loyalty were not molested, and the royal power saw to it that as far as possible the penal measures were not enforced. This continued for the rest of Charles's reign, interrupted only by the Popish plot, and during it the Catholic element increased greatly in power and public importance. By the treaty of Limerick later the defeated Irish Catholics asked for nothing better than to return to the 'connived toleration' which in spite of the statutes they enjoyed at this period.

Ormond ruled Ireland from 1661 to 1668 and rightly complained later that he would have made a success of his office had he not then been removed from it. Under him a considerable reversal of the Cromwellian settlement took place, and it was he who encouraged Charles to use the prerogative in favour of Ireland and used his own authority for the same purpose. This was especially necessary when in 1666 the English parliament passed one of those commercial measures against Ireland which were to continue for some thirty years.

This was the 'Irish Cattle Bill'. The landlord and farming interest in England resented the competition of cheap cattle from Ireland, and as a result the import of Irish cattle into

England was forbidden. They were termed a 'public nuisance', in the act, which prevented the King from using his power to issue licences for individual Irishmen to import cattle contrary to the Act. The great source of wealth in Ireland, whose other industries had perished in the last twenty years, was in the provision trade and the export of beef, mutton, butter, etc. These being debarred from England, the trade with the Continent, however, was left to her, and Ormond freely encouraged this.

Another commercial restriction was expressed in the Navigation Acts. In 1651 the first of these famous acts, on which England built up her maritime and trading supremacy, included Ireland in its benefits and allowed Irish ships to carry goods freely abroad and to all parts of the Empire. The Act was passed again in 1663 and again in 1670, and in these re-enactments Irish ships were not put on the same footing as English ships, and direct export from Ireland to the colonies and direct import from the latter to Ireland was forbidden. Thus Ireland could only get colonial goods through England or send her goods out through England, the building of a mercantile fleet for overseas trade was made impossible, and Ireland remained for over a century excluded from the trade of the Empire. Nothing did more to create the bitterness felt by the Protestant 'patriots' of Ireland in the next century, when Swift wrote sardonically of men who 'with the spirit of shopkeepers framed laws for the administration of kingdoms'. And, a result scarcely foreseen, the main damage fell upon England's own Protestant colony in Ireland which formed the main strength of the commercial and manufacturing class.

The Irish Parliament lasted from 1661 to 1666, but there was none again till 1690. As in England, this assembly of landed gentry abolished all tenancy-in-chief of the Crown, all military tenures, the Court of Wards, and the rest of the feudal side of the monarchy. Large subsidies after the English fashion were voted, mainly derived from the Customs, the Excise, and the new Hearth-tax. The latter had also been introduced in England in 1660, but was abolished there in 1689 as oppressive to the poor; it continued, however, in Ireland till nearly the end

of the eighteenth century, a shameful infliction upon the poor
peasant, to whom even two or three shillings in the year for
such a tax was a burden and a wrong. The abolition of the
Court of Wards and of tenure-in-chief of the Crown favoured
the Catholics as well as the Protestants, for heirs of estates-in-
chief on succession had formerly been subject to the oath of
Supremacy. Minors who were orphans now fell under the care
of the Chancellor, and even still he could use his authority to
have them educated in the Anglican faith.

Ormond was succeeded as Viceroy between 1670 and 1677 by
Lord Berkeley and Lord Essex. This was a favourable time
for the Catholic Church, which was led by Oliver Plunkett and
Peter Talbot, one the archbishop of Armagh, the other of
Dublin, and both of the Old English and loyal element. Under
Essex, Dublin, formerly a small medieval town, began to be
extended and greatly beautified and four fine stone bridges
now spanned the Liffey, over which since Norse times there
had only been the old Ostmen's bridge.

This hopeful time was an opportunity for the Roman Catholic
party again to attack the Cromwellian settlement and for the
English Government to favour the Roman Catholics, as far as
constant criticism and anti-Popish feeling in England permitted.
Colonel Richard Talbot was sent to London in 1670 and secured
a Commission which, under Prince Rupert, examined the
claims of the dispossessed gentry. Roman Catholics had also
been excluded from the towns under the Cromwellian régime,
and in all the old corporations the merchants' houses and the
businesses were in the hands of Protestants, nor could Catholics
purchase houses in them without taking the oaths of Allegiance
and Supremacy. The Lord Lieutenant was now authorized to
permit any one to purchase such houses on a simple oath of
allegiance. The 'Re-modelling' of corporations was now being
pursued in England as a way of strengthening the Anglican and
Tory element, and the same policy was extended to Ireland,
where the Catholics were regarded as true royalists. Hence
under Essex 'New rules' for Irish towns were issued, to apply
to the capital and all the other chief corporations. By these
rules, the election of the mayor, sheriff, and other officers was

to be confirmed by the Lord Lieutenant, the elective power was confined to the aldermen, and the oath of Supremacy was to be taken by all mayors, officers, councillors, and members of guilds and companies, but it might be dispensed with in the case of Catholics at the discretion of the Lord Lieutenant, on condition of taking an oath of temporal allegiance and repudiating the supposed papal 'deposing power'. Thus the Government was able to restore Catholics to a large extent to the towns, but it all rested upon mere favour and on how strong the Monarchy remained. In fact, the Protestant control of the corporations and of the rich and powerful trading guilds remained for the future practically unbroken, since their favour was necessary for the admission of non-Anglicans.

The English Parliament, especially the Whigs, watched all this with growing hostility, and in 1673 compelled Prince Rupert's Commission, under which some of the claimants had been restored, to be withdrawn, as well as the Declaration of Indulgence which Charles had issued in the previous year for both countries, suspending the penal laws.

Ormond returned as Lord Lieutenant in 1677 and lasted out the reign of Charles II. He aimed at summoning another Irish parliament to get subsidies in return for a fresh revision of the Act of Settlement, but the Popish plot of 1678 ruined his plans. The Protestant mania in England spread to Ireland, and one victim of it was Archbishop Plunkett, who was sent to England and tried and executed there. Ormond was instructed to carry out strong measures, to disarm the Roman Catholics, and to banish their clergy, but when the plot subsided and a Tory triumph ended the reign, the policy of connived toleration was restored.

On February 6th 1685 Charles II died and Ormond ceased to be Lord Lieutenant in March. Ireland was now in somewhat of the flourishing condition which she had been in in 1640, and in the last twenty years the revenue had doubled itself. During the reign the balance of the Catholic and Protestant elements had been reversed and the former had lost both political and religious rights. But they still had a large part, possibly a third, of the freehold land, and the royal Prerogative protected them from the worst forms of religious persecution. Unfortunately the Prerogative had not the whole-hearted support of any English party, not even the Tories, nor did any strong English party favour Irish claims or the repeal of disabling religious statutes. The hope of Catholic Ireland was absolutely in the Stuart monarchy, which with the new King became a Catholic one, and had James showed the right skill and caution his dynasty might have continued and Ireland remained a loyal and contented dominion.

The economic condition of Ireland in actual truth was neither sound nor progressive. English landlordism had been introduced without its better features and the majority of Irish peasants had been reduced to mere cottiers and tenants-at-will. Economically their standard was low and their general diet was the potato, a root introduced within the last generation. Petty records that of the 184,000 houses then in Ireland only 24,000 had one chimney or above and the rest had no chimney. What with the penal laws and the exasperation they caused, the claims of the dispossessed gentry, and the poverty of the Gaelic-speaking peasantry, all the materials existed for a fresh Rising, if such were possible.

THE LAST STAND OF CATHOLIC IRELAND, 1685–1691

The reign of James II offered the hope that two of these grievances, Land and Religion, might be mitigated by constitutional measures. James had at first the full support of the Church and Tory party in England and with their aid might well have kept the throne. Colonel Richard Talbot had long represented the Irish Catholics in England and was thought of as the man for Ireland. He was created Earl of Tyrconnell and as Lieutenant-general was given the command of the army in Ireland. Up to this only a Protestant militia was on foot, now a Roman Catholic standing army was designed. In December 1685 James appointed his brother-in-law, Lord Clarendon, as Lord Lieutenant, and he arrived in Dublin in January 1686, but only the civil government was committed to him.

Tyrconnell stood for the old Anglo-Irish Catholic party,

which had little sympathy with the native race and the Gaelic tradition. Ireland was to him a Catholic kingdom, as to the earlier Confederates, and now the hope seemed realized under a Catholic king and possibly a viceroy of this faith. 'Ireland', he said, 'is in a better way of thriving under the influence of a native governor than under any stranger to us and our country.' Roman Catholics should be secured in full civil and religious rights and the upper classes admitted to office, political and military, by the suspension or repeal of the Oath of Supremacy. The Irish aristocracy should be restored to their rightful place under the Crown, and this entailed revising or repealing the acts of Settlement and Explanation. Talbot was more of a soldier than a statesman and believed in having a Catholic army to secure these ends. This army, he represented to James, would be a support to him against the Whigs or other opponents in his three kingdoms. A clash with Clarendon, who as an Anglican, though a Tory, did not share these views or aims, was inevitable, and the revocation of the Edict of Nantes at this time (1685) still further increased English prejudice against Popery and France.

Clarendon was instructed to admit Roman Catholics to office in the Council, the law, the corporations, and the sheriffdoms. The charters of the corporations were remodelled under writs of *Quo Warranto*, and under the new charters Roman Catholic members secured their places in the town councils. Before long two-thirds of the judges were Roman Catholics and every county save Donegal had a sheriff of this persuasion. Meanwhile Tyrconnell staffed the army with Catholic officers and secured the chief garrisons. To him everything was a preliminary to a parliament, representative of the old race, which would repeal the Act of Settlement and the penal statutes. To such an active policy Clarendon could not give his assent, and was recalled on January 8th 1687. He was succeeded as Lord Deputy by Tyrconnell, and the way seemed open for that religious and national ideal which was expressed in the phrase: 'Reducing everything to that state that Ireland was in before Poynings' law and the Reformation of Henry VIII.'

James now, disastrously for himself and his dynasty, broke with the Church and Tory party in England and proceeded to secure general toleration by the royal Prerogative alone and the possible support of the Protestant Dissenters. In Ireland the Anglican minority similarly began to waver in their loyalty, and the Dissenters, especially the northern Presbyterians, preferred to wait on what the English parliament would do. The first Declaration of Indulgence in April 1687 was extended to Ireland; so was the second in April 1688. It was the second which led to the trial of the Bishops and the invitation of the leaders of both parties which brought William, Prince of Orange, to England on November 5th 1688. He was 'the Whig deliverer' whom even the Tories reluctantly accepted, but to the majority of Irishmen James was lawful King and the true heir after him the newly born prince, his son James Edward.

Again, as in 1642, the three kingdoms were to be divided over the Stuart cause, but this time the Stuart king found no one to fight for him in England and only a few thousand Highlanders in Scotland, so that after Killiecrankie ruined the hopes of the Scottish Jacobites in June 1689 Roman Catholic Ireland became his one hope. Thousands of Irish Protestants now poured over into England, the rest were disarmed, but numbers were ready to fight for William if the chance came. Seeing how dangerous the situation was, some of the Irish leaders, such as Chief Justice Keating, favoured coming to terms with William, but with the army in the hands of Tyrconnell and Ireland full of discontent the die was cast otherwise. Tyrconnell had now a Catholic army and had secured most of the garrisons, but it was fatal for the Stuart cause in Ireland that he did not secure Derry and Enniskillen. In the former, on September 16th 1688, the apprentices closed the gate against the Earl of Antrim and his Catholic regiment, and both towns became Protestant cities of refuge. James was still the only king, but when on February 13th 1689 William and Mary accepted the Crown of England by vote of parliament, Irish Protestants in general transferred their allegiance. Scotland also accepted William, and Ireland alone offered James a refuge. He had fled to France, and on March 12th 1689 landed at Kinsale, escorted by a French fleet bringing money, ammunition, and some French officers but no troops. These Tyrconnell could provide and he offered James the support of a kingdom. As for Louis, he wished to see James restored to his British throne, but for the time was not prepared to send an army to support him; he did, however, send arms for 10,000 men.

Thus the cause of Ireland was once more transferred from statesmen to soldiers and put to the ordeal of battle. Tyrconnell was in control of most of the country, and for the first time for a century practically the whole Irish nation was in arms, this time under the command of the lawful King. According to the allegiance which they owed him the aristocracy found little hesitation in flocking to the royal standard, and the most loyal of the Old English and the surviving Lords of the Pale were found side by side with the Old Irish gentry among his commissioned officers. The subsequent war of 1689–1691 can certainly not be called a technical rebellion on the Irish side. The novel situation was seen of a King *de jure* who till lately had been King *de facto* in all three kingdoms appearing in arms against a King whom the English and Scottish parliaments had made monarch *de facto*. According to the accepted constitutional position, however, which had prevailed ever since Henry VIII took the title of monarch of Ireland, the latter kingdom had been inseparably annexed to whoever was King *de facto* of England. On this theory, which naturally was resented on the Irish side, was based the claim in turn of the English Commonwealth, of Cromwell, and then of William III and the Parliament of England to rule Ireland. William himself, however, a tolerant and reasonable man, realized the Irish position and was undoubtedly willing to secure Ireland after submission in her former rights.

The objects of what is called 'the Williamite War in Ireland' differed in the eyes of the various actors. Tyrconnell was concerned with Ireland first and her rights, and if these could not be secured under a Stuart king he was ready to put her under the wing of France. James II looked on Ireland as a stepping-stone to the recovery of England. He was at heart a good Englishman and realized that yielding to extreme Irish claims would do him harm in his native country. Louis's main purpose was to use the Irish war to embarrass William and prevent or delay his return to the Continental war. He was sincerely wishful to see James restored to England and impressed on him not to alienate his Protestant subjects by relying too much on his Catholic subjects. French aid proved to be not quite as feeble as Spain's had been in 1573–1603, but it was half-hearted in spite of the fact that the French fleet had full command of the sea. The Irish war was but a sector of the great war waging between Louis and his enemies in the League of Augsburg, an alliance which included the Catholic Emperor Leopold and the Pope, Innocent XI, who objected to French domination in Europe and to Louis's treatment of the Church in France. Of the League the guiding spirit and the most determined member was William of Orange, who, if he could quickly reduce Ireland, could then throw the weight of Great Britain into the European contest. William was sincerely free from bigotry and a statesman of enlightened and liberal mind. We cannot doubt that had the Prerogative remained as high in his hands as it was even in those of Charles II he would have secured, as well as offered, honourable terms to the Irish on their defeat. Unfortunately for them, Parliament in England had now reduced the monarchy to a constitutional limit, it was both Protestant and anti-Irish, and could insist that the royal word needed its confirmation. Out of these conflicting hopes James was personally to come out worst, while the Irish nation was to lose even what liberties and favourable prospects it had had under his brother.

The war commenced with the siege of Derry, which lasted from April 17th to July 30th 1689. Meanwhile James summoned to Dublin an assembly of the Irish Estates which met on May 7th 1689; it is generally called 'the Patriot Parliament'. This was the last legislative assembly of the older Irish race up to 1922 and the last in which the Roman Catholic faith was represented. Only a handful of Protestant bishops and loyalists attended. Among the fifty peers, the Earls of Clanrickard, Antrim, and Clancarthy (formerly Viscount MacCarthy of Muskerry); among the viscounts, Magennis of Iveagh, Roche of Fermoy, O'Dempsey of Clanmalier, Justin MacCarthy, Lord Mountcashel, and Donal O'Brien, Lord Clare; and among the barons, Fleming, Bermingham, FitzMaurice, Plunkett, Purcell, Burke, Butler—were famous names of the Gaelic and Norman past. Many of them were destined to be outlawed and attainted and to disappear from Irish history, or survive only among the peasantry. Of the 230 members in the Commons many also were to meet the death of exiles; the great majority were Anglo-Irish Catholics who would doubtless have understood the Gaelic speech, but the language of the Parliament and of the army was now English, and for the most part this was an 'Old English' assembly. The great names of Kildare, Ormond, and Inchiquin were not there, and even Antrim and Clanrickard were to be found early in the next century on the Protestant side.

The proceedings of this Parliament were natural enough in men who had suffered so much over religion and confiscation, but they were scarcely wise or creditable. James favoured liberty of conscience and admission to office for his Catholic subjects and was willing to revise the act of Settlement, but had no desire to estrange his Protestant Irish subjects. Parliament, however, proceeded to repeal the acts of Settlement and Explanation outright, without regard to the claims of subsequent purchasers. An act of Attainder was passed against some 2,400 landowners and others who had left Ireland in the Protestant exodus or were absent elsewhere. Their property was vested in the Crown and they were ordered to return to prove their innocence and loyalty or to stand their trial by fixed dates, according to distance. These dates gave little or no time for refugees and absentees, however innocent, to return. To this act James was strongly opposed but had to give way. It naturally infuriated the Williamite party in both countries and brought about in its turn severe treatment for the Jacobites. England could, and often did, pass most unjust measures of confiscation, but Ireland had not the power to do so, and her leaders should have learned better from their own wrongs.

Another act ordered Protestants and Catholics to pay tithes to their own clergy respectively. Another declared the independence of the Irish courts and it was proposed to repeal Poynings' law, but against this James stood firm. He had little reason to be pleased with his Parliament, especially as no subsidies worth speaking of came in, but the affection of Ireland for the Stuarts was not so much personal as national, and James was reminded: 'If your Majesty will not fight for our rights, we will not fight for yours.'

Derry was relieved on August 1st 1689. The Protestant irregulars of Fermanagh under Colonel Wolseley next defeated Mountcashel at Newtown Butler and the Jacobite siege of Enniskillen was abandoned. The loss of Ulster followed, and on August 13th William's commander, Marshal Schomberg, landed at Bangor with an army of 20,000 men. During the winter he faced James's army along the river Fane near Dundalk without coming to a battle. In numbers James's forces were superior, but in equipment the thousands of hardy peasants who were ready to serve 'Rí Shamus' and were natural soldiers were far inferior.

A stiffening of Continental soldiers was necessary, and so in March 1690 Louis sent 7,000 French regulars under Marshal Lauzun to Ireland, to compensate for whom Lord Mountcashel sailed to France with 5,000 men, the best of the Irish army, who were destined never to return.

On June 14th William himself landed at Carrickfergus, and his united forces amounted to 36,000 men, who were mainly foreign mercenaries, Danes, Germans, and Huguenots. Meanwhile the English fleet was able to land troops in Munster or wherever opportunity offered. On July 1st 1690 the battle of the Boyne decided the contest of the two kings and lost the greater part of Ireland for the Jacobites. It was not a stubbornly fought battle, for though the Irish horse fought well, the Irish foot did not, and gallant officers such as Patrick Sarsfield could only regret that they were not able 'to change Kings and fight it over again'. When James fled to Dublin and then returned to France for good it was left for the Irish under Tyrconnell to continue the fight with French aid, not so much now for James as for the preservation of their barest rights as a nation and as men.

The importance in history of the battle of the Boyne is

beyond all comparison with its interest as a clash of two armies. As a European event it was part of the coming and the final triumph of Louis's European enemies. The strange event befell that what was the final defeat of the Catholic and national cause of Ireland was greeted with a *Te Deum* in Catholic Vienna, though with mixed feelings by the Pope. In the history of Ireland it is one of the half-dozen events that have completely changed her destiny. Kinsale in 1603 had spelled the downfall of the Gaelic order. The Boyne marked the doom of the Old English loyalist aristocracy. Mainly Norman with some Gaelic survivors and later Elizabethan additions, it had in the last thirty years still retained the greater part of the soil of Ireland. But now it fought its last fight and by subsequent attainder, outlawry, and pressure of the Penal laws was to become an inconspicuous and timid minority in its own country. Gaelic peers such as Iveagh, Mountcashel, Clare, and Clancarthy vanished for good, the Old English lords fared better, but in general the history of the old Norman and Celtic aristocracy and its leadership of the race may be said to end at this fatal date. The Protestant and Anglican ascendancy, social, religious, and political, became securely established for another century and a half. The blow to the still surviving Gaelic tradition, culture, and speech was fatal. Though badly broken under James I, these had still found patrons among the surviving nobles and gentry. Henceforth such patrons were to be few and the Irish language descended into the ranks of the peasantry, who themselves, as a result of frequent confiscations, were soon a blend of the noblest names of the old order and the blood of the common people.

From the Boyne it was an easy march for William into Dublin, and Ulster and Leinster fell into his hands, while John Churchill, the famous Marlborough, in Munster captured Cork and Kinsale. The Irish army fell back across the Shannon, where they held the bridge-head of Athlone, and the main army took up its stand at Limerick under Tyrconnell as Lord Lieutenant representing the government and Lauzun and Brigadier Sarsfield (whom James had created Earl of Lucan) in military command.

William's first attempt to take Limerick ended in a repulse and he soon left Ireland. Athlone held out, and the decisive struggle was deferred till the next year with Ginkle acting for William and Sarsfield for Ireland. Louis withdrew Lauzun's army, but in May 1691 Marshal St. Ruth, an enthusiastic soldier, arrived from France with arms and stores and a commission to unite all the Irish forces. He soon raised 15,000 men and for the first time put purpose and honesty into the French alliance with Ireland. On June 30th Ginkle forced the passage at Athlone in face of a gallant resistance and St. Ruth fell back to the hill of Aughrim, beyond Ballinasloe, where on July 12th 1691 Ireland was once again lost and won. The stand made by the Irish army was worthy of the last field, where all that was dear to them as a nation and as men was at stake; the priests urged them to die or conquer for the Faith; and, inspired by the leadership of St. Ruth, they had almost won the day when a cannon-ball ended his career. In the rout that followed, thousands of them strewed the fields of Connacht, and Sarsfield could only collect the remnant and fall back on Limerick. Waterford and Galway surrendered on terms, and the old city on the Shannon became the Irish 'City of refuge'.

The second siege lasted from September 4th to October 3rd 1691. Tyrconnell had died in August and supreme command devolved on Sarsfield, whose Irish spirit, military skill, tall stature, and manly beauty made him the hero of this fight as Owen Roe had been of the former one. Old English on one side, on the other he was an O'More and grandson of the leader of 1641; and so typifies well the final union of the two races. It was his fate to die two years later at Landen, fighting for France and sighing 'Oh, that this were for Ireland', ending thus the soldier story of that wronged sept which began with Rory Oge in 1560.

At last he decided to treat with the enemy since France had failed him. On October 3rd the Treaty of Limerick was signed by William's commander Ginkle and the Chief Justices on one side and Sarsfield with his lieutenants on the other. Scarcely was the ink dry when a great French fleet came up the Shannon with a real army on board, but it was too late for

Sarsfield to go back on his word, and in any case he was a man both of valour and honour. The fleet's main use was to transport immediately some 5,000 Irish soldiers to France, while 2,000 more departed on English ships. This was arranged under the military articles of the treaty, which permitted Irish officers and men the choice of taking an oath of allegiance to William and returning to their estates or homes, enlisting in the English forces, or departing to France in French or English ships. Of the whole of Ireland's last army 11,000 finally sailed for France with most of the officers, of the rest 2,000 went home, and 1,000 enlisted with Ginkle. Seldom in history have a few thousand men, departing into exile, represented as these did almost the whole aristocracy, the fighting force, and the hope of a nation. Had men like Sarsfield, who had after all only loyally served their lawful King, returned now to their estates they would have had every right to be restored, and to dispossess them again would have been difficult. But they thought themselves still bound in honour to James and hoped to return one day along with him. Such devotion to a King who was hardly worth it does honour to them, but one may regret that they did not put Ireland and the national cause first. Their great estates, left ownerless, were destined to enrich still further the English ascendancy and reduce Catholic Ireland to the shades. Already the Dublin government had set up a Court of Claims, under which 4,000 Jacobites finally forfeited their estates.

The Civil articles of Limerick were thirteen in number. By the first the Catholics of Ireland in general were to enjoy such privileges 'as they enjoyed under Charles II and as were consistent with the laws of Ireland'. Ginkle pledged his word that their Majesties would endeavour to reduce the number of attainders and procure further securities for the Irish Catholics from Parliament. By the second article 'all the inhabitants of Limerick or any other garrison now in the possession of the Irish', 'all the officers and men now in arms under commission of King James either in the English quarters or the counties of Limerick, Clare, Kerry, Cork, Mayo (and Galway by separate capitulation)', and '*all such as are under their protection in these counties'*, should keep their former estates, properties, and privileges and enjoy their professions and callings, on condition of taking the simple oath of Allegiance enacted in the English Parliament in the first year of William and Mary, *and no other.*

'All such as are', etc., was to be famous as 'the omitted clause'; when the fair copy reached William it was found to have been omitted, but he reinserted it with his own hand when he signed the Treaty on February 4th 1692.

Article 7 recognized the rights of those protected by the treaty to keep horse and arms sufficient for their defence. The 9th article laid down that the oath to be taken should be that mentioned in the 2nd article, and no other. This, we may note, did not include the oath of Supremacy or any abjuration of the papal spiritual power. Finally article 12 pledged their Majesties to ratify the Treaty within twelve months and to have it fully ratified by the Parliament of England. Such were the terms that Sarsfield and his Irish army were able to exact after two years of a losing war. If carried out both in the spirit and the letter by William and his English Parliament they might have restored the Catholic religion in Ireland at least to the tolerable position of Charles II's time, limited the amount of confiscation, and left the former landowners a still considerable aristocracy. But, while Ginkle could speak for William, both were foreigners who could not understand the place of the King in the new constitution of England, and it was soon shown that the English Parliament meant to interpret the Treaty both in letter and spirit in the most narrow and ungenerous way.

CHAPTER XV

THE MONARCHY OF WILLIAM AND ANNE,
1691–1714

THE period 1691–1714 was for Ireland an interim period, in which in a sense the Stuart monarchy survived and the Prerogative remained considerable; so between the liberality of William and the Toryism that triumphed under Anne the final subjection of Catholic Ireland was deferred. Nevertheless the Anglican ascendancy was secured after the fall of Limerick, and it remained for the new King and the Protestant parliaments of both countries to decide how the terms should be carried out. There was no hurry for the victors, and it was not till 1697 that the Irish parliament ratified the Treaty of Limerick and 1700 that the confiscations were completed. This may be called the Williamite settlement of Ireland. In 1692 Lord Sidney was sent over as Lord Lieutenant to represent the new régime. He summoned at Chichester House the Irish parliament, a body of three hundred in the Commons and twelve bishops and sixteen peers in the Lords, which henceforth became as long as it lasted a Protestant body, for an act of the English parliament passed in 1691 was now extended to Ireland by which members of both Houses were required to take an oath of allegiance, a declaration against the Mass, Transubstantiation, and other Roman doctrines, and an oath abjuring the spiritual supremacy of the Pope. This effectually debarred conscientious men and the few Catholic members and peers who presented themselves, and it was not till its repeal in 1829 that Roman Catholics were enabled to sit in parliament. For a century or more they could only humbly petition the King or plead as suppliants at the Bar of the House.

The double question of the carrying out of the Treaty of Limerick and of the attainders now for years occupied the government. A Court of claims was set up at Chichester House in Dublin, under which some 4,000 landowners were attainted, and there were forfeited to the Crown lands amounting to 1,100,000 plantation acres (1,700,000 English acres). William used his royal influence, as he had promised, in favour of the attainted, and got restored sixty-five great landowners who were not protected by the Treaty. As a result the amount of confiscated land was reduced by one-fourth. This angered both parliaments, especially as William made vast grants to his Dutch favourites, the Earls of Portland and Albemarle, and his former mistress the Countess of Orkney. The Irish House was well bridled under Poynings' law and in 1697 had finally to pass a Government bill which ratified the main force of the Limerick terms, though it whittled them down considerably. The conclusion of the matter in England was a Resumption bill passed in April 1700, which set up a Board in which were vested all the confiscated Irish estates, and, with the exception of seven of the favoured landowners, all the King's grants were resumed. But some 400,000 acres were restored to 'innocent papists', and finally about a million English acres were sold in the open market, representing the final amount of confiscated land in the last confiscation in Irish history. When the lands were publicly offered, Irish Roman Catholics were debarred by act of the English Parliament from purchasing or leasing more than two acres, for the Protestant ascendancy was determined to limit the Catholic landowning class to the narrowest limits possible.

It is reckoned that by 1700 the Roman Catholics had the freehold of about one-eighth of the land, but even this was to be greatly reduced in the next thirty or forty years by the proprietors conforming to the Established Church either willingly or under pressure of the Penal laws. Many great names had vanished by the attainders of over fifty years; others now ceased to be leaders of the majority. The second Duke of Ormond was a Williamite; so was the Earl of Kildare; the Earl of Antrim in the next generation was a Protestant, and so it befell with other names such as MacMurrough Kavanagh. The 'Lords of the Pale' now only survived in a few timid Catholic peers such as the Earl of Fingall, while in Munster of the old nobility Browne, Earl of Kenmare, became the leading name. Of all the great Gaelic patronymics of 1500, only O'Brien, Earl of Inchiquin, finally remained in the peerage, but as a supporter of Church and State.

The other great question was the Treaty of Limerick. The terms covered not the whole Irish Roman Catholic population but merely the officers, soldiers, and garrisons of the Irish army in the cities of Limerick, Galway, and Waterford, and the counties of Limerick, Clare, Kerry, Cork, Mayo, and Galway, and all such as were *under their protection in the said counties*. This famous 'omitted clause' had been restored by William, but when the whole Treaty was brought before it to be ratified with this clause restored the Irish Parliament, less liberal than the King, in 1692 showed its resentment by throwing out a Mutiny bill which had been drafted by the Councils of both kingdoms, as well as a Money bill prepared in England. Hence Sidney dissolved parliament; he himself was soon withdrawn, and finally Sir Henry Capel was sent as Deputy from 1695 to 1700. Under him the Irish Parliament in 1695 began that iniquitous Penal code which was not completed till 1727. The treatment of the defeated nation was a violation both in the spirit and in the letter of the Treaty of Limerick. But the army and the nobility to whom it had been promised were mainly in France; as to those who remained at home disarmed and harmless, when they died out it was considered the Treaty was sufficiently honoured. William endeavoured, as he had promised, to reduce the number of attainders, but on this point was finally defeated by the intractable English Parliament, which now shared the sovereignty with the Crown. His promises and his wish to mitigate the Penal laws were also overridden and his own parliament did not hesitate to dishonour 'the word of a King'. The Prerogative, which the Stuarts had used to protect Ireland, had been cut short, and the royal power to dispense with or suspend the religious statutes had been abolished at the 'glorious Revolution'.

As regards the Penal laws, the 'violation' consisted of the limiting of the terms to as small a population as possible, reviving into full operation religious statutes which under Charles II had been left dormant, and, worse still, enacting for the future far more crushing ones.

K

The Irish Parliament now became a permanent element in the Constitution. It was, and remained till the Union, a Protestant body of Cromwellians and Williamites of almost pure English blood who had all the arrogance of conquerors. But its independence was shackled by Poynings' law, and it was in virtue of this imperial control that Sidney could override it when in 1692 it protested about the 'omitted clause'. It did not control the army, it had not the real power of the purse, and the Viceroy, his secretary and the ministers of State, were appointed from, and were responsible to, Westminster alone. The 'Glorious Revolution' of which the Whigs boasted in England, which ended the personal monarchy of the Stuarts, did not even give the Protestant oligarchy of Ireland a responsible system of government. Only a small advance was made when, after 1692, by a procedure called 'Heads of Bills', either Irish House could propose a bill which, if accepted by the Irish Council, was then passed by the Irish parliament and transmitted to England, where the King's Privy Council could accept, alter, or reject it. On its return, the Irish parliament must accept or reject it in full; if passed it received the royal assent from the Lord Lieutenant. Above all, the imperial power of King and Parliament in England claimed the final directing and restraining power in all matters touching the Empire, its defence, its trade, and its navigation. For internal purposes, the Irish parliament remained supreme, but where English interests were touched or when it came to the 'reduction' of Ireland by an army the English parliament legislated without regarding the Irish assembly.

Ireland was so completely under irresponsible government controlled from England that a meeting of her parliament every second year was considered sufficient for carrying on; there was no fixed limit to its duration and the Viceroy could dissolve or prolong it at discretion; hence he needed only visit Ireland once in two years, leaving Lords Justices in his place. There was an hereditary revenue uncontrolled by parliament; fresh servi̅s became necessary, and so the practice was established, after the protest of 1692, by which Bills of Supply (money bills) were prepared by the Councils of the two realms in unison, which were limited in duration to two years; another reason for a mere biennial session. According to the witty Earl of Shrewsbury in 1713, the office of Lord Lieutenant was 'a place where a man had business enough to prevent him falling asleep but not enough to keep him awake'. So effectually had the sister kingdom been silenced.

The constitutional dependence of Ireland on the *de facto* government of England was frankly admitted by the new ascendancy. The Act of recognition of William and Mary as joint sovereigns was passed by the Irish Parliament 'forasmuch as this kingdom of Ireland is annexed and united to the Imperial Crown of England, and by the laws and statutes of this kingdom (Ireland) is declared to be justly and rightfully belonging and ever united to the same'. When this principle was affirmed in the act that made Henry VIII king of Ireland it did not entail the subordination of the Irish parliament to the English one; what it asserted was the imperial sovereignty of the single Crown supreme over its two realms.

But the course of English history determined that with the accession of the Georges England became an aristocratic 'crowned Republic', and Ireland was to find out, as Machiavelli said of the rule of Venice, 'of all forms of servitude, servitude under a republic is the worst'. English domination suited the upstart ascendancy for the present, but it was not long before it began to chafe.

On the Catholic question it has to be remembered that until the peace of 1697 England was engaged in a European coalition against France and that some of her allies were Catholic; again, James might possibly be restored, in which case native Ireland might rise once more. The one consideration urged some decency towards the defeated Irish—this was William's; the other—that of Parliament—urged the disarming of them and excluding them from all places of power and trust so that they should never again seize the reins. This panic and cruel spirit animated Capel's Dublin parliament of 1695.

Exclusion from parliament by the act of 1692 was the first violation of the Treaty, for under Charles II the Catholics had sat in the Lords and formally at least might sit in the Commons. What followed was in the same spirit. An act was passed for disarming 'papists' (henceforth for nearly a century the official and legal designation of his Majesty's Roman Catholic subjects), by which only those protected by the Treaty were allowed to carry the arms of a gentleman for self-defence and fowling. No 'papist' might own a horse worth above five pounds, and no gunsmith might take a Catholic apprentice. Thus was the Irish majority, which since 1590 had thrice taken the field, disarmed for a century, and only foreign aid could, as later in 1798, have properly re-armed it. Another act made it illegal for Catholics to go for education abroad and forbade them to keep a public school at home. The University of Dublin was already closed to them as regards degrees, fellowships, and scholarships. This and other 'no education' acts were particularly shameful, as well fitted to brutalize a race of aristocratic and learned tradition and reduce it to peasant status and ignorance.

The Irish parliaments of the rest of William's reign followed suit. William indeed and the nobler spirits of England should have vetoed their enactments, but it was much easier to yield to the 'No Popery' spirit in both countries. The majestic and world-wide system of the Church of Rome could not be treated like some Protestant sect at home seeking a modest toleration; the very greatness of her empire and the completeness of her claims over the souls and minds of believers marked her out for special persecution from the narrow Protestant and English nationalism of the age.

The Dublin parliament of 1697 dealt with the ratification of the Treaty of Limerick. William consented to leave out the 'omitted clause' if parliament would accept the remainder, and abandoned his promise to reverse outlawries. The Roman Catholics petitioned in vain to be heard by counsel at the Bar of the House against this open violation of the King's word. It is to the honour of some of the peers and bishops of the Church of Ireland that when the Bill of ratification left the Commons it was only carried in the House of Lords by one vote, and seven bishops and seven peers entered their protest against it. The Lords also passed the Outlawries Bill, by which all outlawries (save those already reversed or protected by the

Treaty) were to stand, but the Lords secured that certain peers and gentry were also exempted from the Bill.

This was the end of the Treaty of Limerick as far as the Irish parliament went. The anti-Popery spirit was shown by an act for the banishment of all Roman Catholic bishops and dignitaries, leaving untouched the parish clergy, who, it was hoped, would die out in time for want of due consecration. As an established Church, the Roman Catholic religion now reached its nadir point in Irish history, and those bishops who stood their ground were reduced to less than half a dozen, living the most obscure, and at any moment possibly dangerous, existence. In the next year (1698) another act excluded members of this Church from the practice of the law except by taking an oath of allegiance and abjuration of the papal authority. Exemption was, however, provided for those who were covered by the Treaty or who had practised under Charles II. Thus the trained lawyers who could defend Roman Catholic claims were reduced to a handful.

England was meanwhile passing its own equally severe penal code for Romanists, but in comparing the injustice of such laws we must remember that in the one country they affected only a small element; in Ireland they were directed against the majority of the nation by a minority which owed its victory to the armies of England and whose ascendancy depended on English support.

But the Catholic 'dissenters' from the Church of the minority were not the only dissenters. In Ulster was strongly entrenched a Presbyterian population of Scots origin, amounting to some hundreds of thousands; in the rest of Ireland Cromwellian times had left behind great numbers of English sectaries. They had all sided with William and expected toleration from him; he, on his part, though he could do nothing for Catholic nonconformists, strove hard to do something for Protestant ones. He granted to Presbyterian ministers, who had preached in his cause, a yearly sum called the *Regium donum* at £1,200 a year, and in 1695 sent over from England a Toleration bill on the basis of the English one of 1689. But in Ireland, where one would expect the whole Protestant minority to unite, the Anglican Church and aristocracy were almost more hostile to the Protestant democracy than to the dispossessed Catholics. The Cromwellians had been branded 'republicans and regicides', the Ulster Scots were denounced as stubborn enemies of Tory monarchy and episcopacy; both were, in short, obstacles to the complete success of an upper-class Anglican régime. The Tory and High Church spirit was now strong among the bishops of the Church of Ireland; that minority which owned most of the land and controlled politics supported them, and between them the Toleration bill was rejected. In spite of this, Ireland was a much better land for the Dissenters than England. There was no Clarendon Code on our statute book, and William prevented the Test act from being extended here. In the North the Presbyterians controlled many of the corporations; everywhere they had the vote and even returned some members of Parliament. Until the reign of Anne they were secure, and it is no wonder that William of Orange is still the hero of the North.

Though apparently triumphant over the Catholic majority and the Dissenting democracy, the Anglican minority had its own quarrels with the mother-country. The trade and industry of Ireland was mainly in Protestant hands, but would English commercial jealousy allow it to prosper? William here again had to yield and to promise his Parliament of England that he would promote English trade and discourage Irish trade. According to the system and theory of the times, England regarded what was imported from the other two kingdoms as its own concern; as for the trade of the Empire and the commerce of the seas, that was an English preserve, for Scotland and Ireland had done nothing to found or conquer the American and West Indian 'plantations'. An act of the English parliament in 1696 forbade goods to be exported direct from the colonies to Ireland. Another of 1699 allowed the export of Irish manufactured woollen goods only to England where heavy duties prevented their competing with this great English industry. Thus was the woollen industry of Ireland crushed. But William was allowed to encourage the linen-weaving trade, and this, of which the English had no jealousy, became a great industry in Ireland, not confined as now to the North, but spread over the whole island, whose soil and climate are favourable to flax-growing. Nevertheless the industry found its chief hold among the Presbyterian weavers of the North, and in towns like Belfast and Lurgan, where the Huguenots, such as Crommelin, introduced the latest machinery.

The Restrictive acts were a blow rather to the Protestants of Ireland than to the Catholics, who were mainly confined to the land, and such an attack by England upon its own colony roused an indignation which found vent in a famous book by Molyneux in 1698 called *The Case of Ireland's being bound by acts of Parliament in England, stated.* Its author declared that subjection of the Irish parliament to the selfish enactments of England were the main cause of trouble, and after some sixty years a large party of the ascendancy took this up as their slogan.

William III died on March 8th 1702. The reign of his sister-in-law Anne, was a return to 'High Church and State' principles and a triumph for the Tory party, which rejoiced to see a pure-bred Englishwoman and a grand-daughter of Charles I on the throne. The Tory spirit was strong in the upper-class Protestants of Ireland and favoured to a certain extent the Roman Catholics, whose religion seemed to put them on the royalist side. Unfortunately Anne and the Tories also had the 'No Popery' obsession, though the Whigs were stronger still in this. France too was the enemy of England, and when, on the death of James II in September 1701, Louis XIV recognized his son Prince James Edward as King, a fresh motive against France and against Irish Roman Catholics was found. Before long the great war of the Spanish Succession (1702–1713) began, and Ireland became once again a danger-point, for it was pretty certain that if a French army had landed the 'Pretender' (as the English affected to call James's son) on the soil of Ireland there would have been a fresh up-rising. Thus the Irish majority could still be branded as dangerous and pro-French.

So the Penal code continued, though Anne was a Stuart and though the majority of the Irish bishops and officials were Tories. The second Duke of Ormond was appointed Lord

Lieutenant in 1703 and continued in office for nearly the whole reign; at heart a Jacobite, he did what he could to mitigate the persecuting spirit, but the 'ferocious Acts of Anne', as Burke called them, were a curious comment on the last Stuart reign. In 1703 another act was passed to banish Roman bishops, regulars, and vicars-general, but a Registration act which accompanied it showed the disposition to allow at least the simple toleration of the Mass. By this any secular priest taking a simple oath of allegiance could be registered and then perform his priestly functions undisturbed. It was accepted by over 1,000 priests, whose numbers showed that it was impossible to suppress the religion of two millions of Irishmen. Unregistered priests remained liable to the penalties of treason under existing statutes. This act remained in force till 1780; henceforth the numbers of priests and their people steadily grew, and by 1750, under the authority of the Papal inter-nuncio at Brussels, twenty-four bishops ruled the Roman Catholic Church in Ireland, for the most part quietly tolerated, though never out of danger.

The extinguishing of the Roman faith as a religion was now obviously impossible, and the Church of Ireland, with its great revenues and highly endowed bishops, accepted the fact that as regards the mass of the people itself was a minority religion. But when it came to political power, to ordinary civil rights, and the pursuit of natural liberty, happiness, and prosperity, that was another question. A whole code was passed to bar the Roman Catholics from the land, the army, the electorate, commerce, and the law. In 1704 a typical act 'against the growth of Popery' enacted that estates which had belonged or might belong to Protestants should not come into Catholic hands. Roman Catholics were only to inherit from one another, they might not purchase land or lend on mortgages, or take a lease over thirty-one years. Even for such a lease they must pay a rent of two-thirds of the annual value. Further, by what was known as the 'Gavelkind act' the estates of a Catholic landowner was to be divided at his death among all his sons, unless the eldest should conform within a year or on coming of age, in which case he should inherit the whole estate accord-ing to the usual English law of 'primogeniture'. The act was

intended either to increase the Protestant landlordry or by
equal division to turn Catholic proprietors before long into an
impoverished though freeholding class. It had actually great
effect in reducing the number of the Romanist aristocracy,
some of whom 'conformed' to keep estates intact and prevent
the family being degraded into holders of a few acres. Others,
against their conscience, on succeeding to the estate attended
the Protestant service once in order to satisfy the law. For
those who stuck it out in the eighteenth century, the 'Gavelling
act' was the cruellest of the Penal laws.

Other parts of this sweeping 'anti-Popery' act excluded
Catholics from offices in the State, corporations, or army, and
also from voting at elections, except on taking a declaration
against Roman doctrines. By a later law of 1708 they were
forbidden to act as grand jurors, though allowed to sit on
petty juries, and severe penalties were imposed on such of
them as continued to practise law. By another of 1710 fifty
pounds reward was promised to any one securing a 'popish
bishop', and Roman Catholic employers were forbidden to
take more than two apprentices to their trade, save in the
linen-weaving industry. The Penal code was finally completed by an act of 1727 by which Catholics were finally
debarred from voting for members of Parliament both in
counties and boroughs.

The penal laws were to last in their entirety for some seventy
years and not to be repealed till 1829. They can be divided
into the actual *penal* measures, which positively punished
people for their religion, and the *disabling* statutes, which
excluded Catholics from office, the army, and civil employment.
Naturally, as the liberal spirit grew it would desire to abolish
the former, which were repugnant to ordinary human feeling,
but as regards the disabling statutes, these were preserved as
long as possible and were justified by many good men as
necessary to maintain the Protestant ascendancy, the aristocratic constitution, and the connexion with England. We
may divide them again into those which affected the older
population as a nation and as its various classes. Some of
the laws limited the landowners to such estates as they held

or inherited by law, but prevented their buying fresh land or acquiring favourable leases. Their heirs were encouraged to conform, and 'informers', who were favoured by deliberate statutes, were a constant terror to those who sought to evade the law or whose titles might be brought under some Attainder act. It was especially exasperating to such of a proud aristocracy as survived that they were disarmed and forbidden to carry arms or ride like their Protestant neighbours.

Then there were the laws which affected the middle classes and excluded them from the learned and lucrative professions of the law and education, or debarred them from trade and industry or the free purchase of land and property. What the law did not do the selfishness of an ascendancy could do, and Roman Catholics henceforth had little share in the trading guilds and companies of the boroughs. The only fields left open to their industry were the linen trade, grazing, agriculture, the practice of a few professions such as medicine, brewing, and so on. Both they and the upper classes were excluded from offices, from commissions in the army and navy, from the electorate and parliament. The nation as a whole suffered from all this body of law, which debarred it from all the essential civil rights which even in a despotic State they would have enjoyed, and which allowed a newly arrived minority to hamper them in every natural ambition and self-development.

The mass of the Irish people, however, were neither gentry nor freeholders nor middle-class people looking for jobs and careers for their sons. Their grievances were economic and positive, the payment of hearth tax to the State, of tithes to the Established Church, of heavy rents for their small potato plots to landlords mostly of alien stock and language, not to speak of forced labour on the roads, and the rest. English land-laws had been introduced into Ireland at successive Plantations with all the features in them which were most oppressive to the poor man. Favourable leases, the letting of properly furnished farms at reasonable rent, copyholds, and such things were not to be the lot of Ireland. 'In England the landlords let farms, in Ireland land', such was the judgment of an English peer in the nineteenth century. Reduced to an almost general status of mere tenants-at-will, their main food the potato, their wages as labourers less than a shilling a day, the lot of the Catholic peasantry was one of the worst in Europe. And how could they procure redress? Not from the gentlemanly Parliament up at Dublin, which scarcely passed a single act in favour of the poor husbandman all through the eighteenth century. Not from the parson to whom they paid tithes of corn and cattle, sometimes even of potatoes, nor the Church courts of the Establishment. Not from the grand jurors and justices of the peace, all Protestants, who now ran the county government. The Catholic aristocracy and middle class were to have all their wrongs redressed from 1778 to 1829; a far more determined and disastrous struggle had to be waged by the Irish peasant for sixty years after that before he shook off the chains of his serfdom.

As farmers, weavers and industrialists, the Protestant Dissenters, especially in the North, who were little represented in the landlord and ruling classes, had their own religious and economic grievances, far fewer and lighter than those of their Catholic neighbours, but galling enough. Their creed had received no legal recognition. The State regarded the Popish priest indeed as an enemy, but did not deny that he *was* a priest and that his functions of marriage, etc., were valid. The Presbyterian or Dissenting minister was not an ordained clergyman according to law, unless he had been ordained by a bishop, and the marriages he performed were not marriages by law. As regards the free purchase, inheritance, and enjoyment of land the Dissenters were not subject to any disability, nor were they excluded from the trades and professions, for they had no objection to the anti-Popish Declaration required. They had the vote in towns and shires and could sit in parliament with a clear conscience; if their political influence was small it was because the Church of Ireland ascendancy could be used against them. They were strong in the industries of the North and they or their fathers had received farms at low rents in order to colonize Ulster. A favourable practice called 'the Ulster custom', prevalent in the North, gave the tenant a certain right in his farm and allowed him to sell this right when vacating it. But the payment of tithes to the State clergy galled them and united them with the Catholic peasants in hatred of the Establishment. The Church of Ireland, as represented in Dean Swift later, did not hide its dislike or open hatred of the Presbyterians, whose well-organized faith, uncompromising spirit, and widespread influence in the North especially made them so formidable.

In England the Whigs were the friends of the Dissenters. But under a Tory government, the democratic sectarians of Ireland had to endure a long-sustained attack as enemies of the established Church and no true friends of Royalty, especially of that Stuart prerogative to which the Tories and High Church still clung. In 1704 when the 'act against Popery' was returned from England it was found to include a new clause added by the English ministry, requiring office-holders under the Crown to qualify by taking the Sacrament according to the Anglican Church. The clause was passed and it excluded Protestant dissenters from all offices in State and corporations. Their members at the same time disappeared from Parliament, and they lost their former control of the northern boroughs such as Belfast. Thus did the disqualifying acts exclude the Protestant as well as the Catholic dissenter from political power, local and central. Later, in 1710, the *Regium donum* was withdrawn from their ministers, in accordance with the general attack on Dissenters in both realms.

Ireland under Anne seemed like a Tory stronghold from which Bolingbroke in England might hope for support in his secret plan of restoring Prince James Edward. Many of the State bishops were well inclined, the Duke of Ormond, Lord Lieutenant, was actively on his side, and the Chancellor, Sir Constantine Phipps, was almost impeached for favouring Catholics and admitting them to the army. The hopes of the Catholics ran high and it seemed not improbable that a second Stuart restoration would restore their old lords and bring back the exiled ones. But the sudden and fatal illness of Anne in 1714 ruined these hopes. This childless woman, whose only objection to her half-brother was his religion, would express no open wish or take any open action about the succession.

The Whig Privy Council boldly took the initiative, got her to install the Earl of Shrewsbury as chief minister, by a *coup d'état* overthrew Bolingbroke's cabinet, and on the death of Anne in August 1714 brought in as king George the Electoral Duke of Hanover, great-grandson of James I. The Jacobite leader was impeached and fled to France; so was Ormond, who died in exile in 1745, though his line was restored to his titles and estates later. With his attainder the only remaining Palatinate in Ireland, that of Tipperary, was abolished. The Whigs came triumphantly into power in Cabinet and Parliament and retained their supremacy unshaken for fifty years.

CHAPTER XVI

HANOVERIAN RULE, 1714–1782

A MORE unattractive figure than George the First could hardly have been found for the Throne of these kingdoms. The triumphant Presbyterians of Scotland and Anglican Whigs of England stomached him for their own reasons and left it to Tories and Highlanders to sentimentalize about 'the Divine Right' and 'the King over the water'. To the Irish nation, now subjected for good to a colonial ascendancy, the accession of a dull German princeling was more than an offence to all the traditions of Monarchy—it was the positive death-knell of the hopes that had survived the Boyne. The religion of the majority, their political and civil liberty, and all their racial self-expression were proscribed for almost a century, or, worse still, driven underground with disastrous results. A dynasty had arrived which not only was not interested in the fate of Ireland and the treatment of its Catholic subjects but was positively by the new constitution of a limited monarchy forbidden to interfere. To the mass of the Irish people George must have seemed neither a King nor a man. As for the Stuarts who had at least attempted justice to Ireland, a Scottish Jacobite rising in 1715 and another in 1745 scarcely made a ripple in Ireland. After Philip of Spain had failed them and then Louis, after their devotion to the Stuarts had only brought on disaster after disaster, it is no wonder if the majority of those who survived began to think on the old maxim: 'Put not your trust in princes, for there is no help in them'.

The aristocratic and militant part of the old Irish nation, whose exodus had begun in the Elizabethan age to Spain, was now abroad in the armies of France, Spain, and Austria, whose Irish Brigades were for nearly a century constantly recruited by the 'Wild Geese' of Ireland. They were destined never to return as armed men to their mother-country and the hope of a foreign or native deliverer died into a pathetic legend.

The restoration of the old aristocracy was the constant

theme of the Gaelic poets of Hanoverian Ireland. The hereditary bards had inspired the resistance under Elizabeth, and O'Bruadair and others had lived to see the Jacobite armies in the field, but now all that was left for their patronless and impoverished successors such as Egan O'Rahilly and Owen Roe O'Sullivan of Kerry and Art MacCooey of Armagh, was to lament the old Gaelic and Norman aristocracy, and under many lovely and secret names for Ireland, 'the Dark Rosaleen', 'Kathleen Ní Houlahan', or 'Drumin Doun Deelish,' to imagine the return of the old order. The theme of many a melodious 'Aisling' or 'Vision' was that of a symbolic Ireland, a beautiful sorrowful maiden and her rightful spouse, a mythical Stuart. But the Ireland of a native aristocracy, generous patrons of the Gaelic literati and poets, was a dream rapidly dissolving. As for any practical hope of a Stuart restoration, it ended with 1745. The world of the 'File', the Brehon, the man of learning, art, and poetry, whose history as an established and cultured class went back to pagan Ireland, had lingered on till the Boyne, but it was now over. The Irish language which had been cultivated for a thousand years now, save for an odd printed work, remained all through the eighteenth century in the manuscript stage. In the current idiom which replaced the learned, it became confined to the peasantry and to a few wandering scholars, musicians, and poets, who in each province kept alive a poetic rivalry and a sort of Gaelic academy. In prose the language produced little of merit, but its swansong in poetry was rich and of great beauty. Though the upper and middle classes gradually forsook it, the people clung to the Gaelic speech with an affectionate attachment which only gave way in the nineteenth century.

It was the peculiar tragedy of the Irish nation that it was now left leaderless in the aristocratic sense. The pressure of the Penal laws, the frequent education of minors in the State religion, the natural disposition to go with the tide, the growing indifference of the eighteenth century to dogmatic religion, all conspired to make great numbers of the surviving gentry conform within the next fifty years and to reduce the Catholic landowning class to a mere fraction. But thus through intermarriage of the new landlord class with the old the blood of the ruling element in Ireland was in a generation or two an admixture of Celt and Norman, of Elizabethan and later planters. A similar story can be told of the peasantry, among whom were absorbed great numbers of Cromwellian troopers and other settlers. Though the religious division has persisted, no one can doubt that the greater part of the modern Irish nation is well mixed, and that there are few people in our country whose ancestors on one side or another have not been Gaelic speakers. But, blending or no blending, the tradition of Irish nationality was already founded too strong to be ever lost.

In the period 1714 to 1760 Ireland had little or no political history. The Protestant ascendancy in Church, government, law, parliament, local government, industry, was complete. It was a replica on a small scale of that of England, but at least in England the Anglican aristocracy for all its faults ruled in the Church of a majority and had the support of a nation. It was otherwise in Ireland, where both the ruling aristocracy and Church represented an alien minority. But the ascendancy here seemed just as secure. Swift, who hated the stubborn Presbyterians, describes the 'papists' as a people entirely crushed, 'harmless as women and children', and though tolerant in a lofty way he thought their religion a superstition which would naturally die out. George I or George II could do nothing, even had he wished, for his Irish subjects, and on the other hand they were unable by the laws to serve him. Whatever fighting spirit was in them was drained off by the departure of the 'Wild Geese' to enlist in foreign armies. From 1690 to 1730 it is said that some 120,000 of such departed, never to return. To keep down those who remained was for the time an easy task, but nothing can excuse the enacted injustice by which they were kept down rather than governed.

Peaceful, as opposed to military, emigration curiously enough began not with the Roman Catholic but with the Presbyterian population. In 1718 great numbers of leases, formerly granted on easy terms, fell in in the North-eastern counties. On renewal the great landlords doubled or trebled the rents

The Ulster Scot was only too ready to chafe at tithes, Church courts, and other burdens; to be also rack-rented was intolerable. Emigration to New England set in, and every year thousands of Presbyterians sailed for America, to settle in Pennsylvania and the frontier States. Here they found a land of religious and political equality, and it was not long before such ideas floated back to their cousins at home. There, in Antrim, Derry, Down, and Armagh, the native Irish, able to live more sparingly and more patient under social wrongs, could outbid them in the bidding for farms, and thus did considerable parts of the North go back to the Catholic and Irish-speaking peasantry.

The Church of Ireland ascendancy now filled the whole stage. They had excluded both the Romanist and Nonconformist elements from power and place and even deprived them of the rights of subjects. But, at least for the Protestant Dissenters, Whig rule now procured a partial freedom. The *Regium donum* was restored in 1718 at two thousand pounds yearly and, though the test clause for office had to stand, the British government at least in 1719 forced on the Irish parliament a Toleration act for the Dissenters. By this, on condition of an oath of civil allegiance and the usual declaration against 'popish' doctrines, they were exempted from attendance at church, allowed to worship freely and to serve at least in parish offices. So they remained till Emancipation began.

At least in 1714 our country, after the unrest of a hundred and fifty years, reached an equilibrium which lasted for some fifty years. Unjust as was the established order, it gave peace and security for such gains as men could make or such education as their minds could take advantage of.

Ireland had now no constitutional or responsible government. It was in effect a despotism worked from Dublin but controlled from Westminster in a double interest, that of the Protestant ascendancy at home and that of England in its relations to a subject kingdom. There was a parliament meeting every second year dealing with internal affairs and voting necessary supplies. A Lord Lieutenant, who maintained the state of a king, came over for the session. His chief occupation was to maintain the 'Protestant Constitution', to get the necessary supplies and votes when measures came before the House, and to keep Ireland 'safe' for England. But the war with France, which ended in 1713, did not begin again till 1740, and both in England and Ireland the Walpole policy of peace and 'letting sleeping dogs lie' ruled politics. It was a thoroughly inglorious age in both countries, that of a selfish and corrupt political oligarchy which got between the King and his people.

Generally Ireland was ruled by two or three Lords Justices, one of them representing the British interest, who brought irresponsible government to a fine art by 'management', namely, securing for favours in return the votes controlled by the 'Undertakers', that is, the great borough-owners such as the Duke of Leinster. The Irish House of Commons was even more packed with members from pocket boroughs and from 'decayed and rotten' boroughs than the English was, and quite as many were ready to sell their votes for bribes, pensions, sinecure offices. As in England, 'Patronage' and the nomination to offices and use of the revenue for the purchase of support had passed into the hands of the King's ministers. But in Ireland there were no political parties; the groups who owed allegiance to one magnate or another and the borough or county members who alone represented free election had no principles to bind them into opposing parties. Hugh Boulter, archbishop of Armagh from 1724 to 1742, a pure-bred Englishman, who was no less than thirteen times a Lord Justice, was for nearly twenty years 'our Walpole'. Even the recent Anglo-Irish were now suspected of not being truly loyal to the 'English interest', and Boulter filled the great offices in Church and State with Englishmen and got his majorities in Parliament by the distribution of offices, pensions, and bribes.

But all this state of things soon found critics from among the Anglo-Irish themselves. The 'rights of the subject' came to mean for them 'the rights of Ireland'. By the 'Glorious Revolution' of 1689 England had secured a Constitution in which a Prime minister took the King's place in the Cabinet, the ministry was responsible to a majority in Parliament, the army, the revenue, and the judges were under parliamentary control, and the 'Habeas Corpus' act secured the subject from arbitrary imprisonment. But all these triumphs, the Bill of Rights, the Act of Settlement, the Triennial and then the Septennial bill fixing the duration of Parliament, had not been extended to Ireland. Whatever the blessings of the 'Glorious Revolution' may have been for England they were ingloriously denied to Ireland.

While the old nation lay totally disarmed, an English army of 12,000 men occupied Ireland, paid out of Irish revenue, but legalized by a Mutiny bill of the English Parliament passed under William III and now become perpetual. England, with her much larger population, maintained only an army of 7,000 men. In Finance the power of the Irish Parliament was limited. In 1660 the hereditary revenue of Crown lands, etc., had been settled permanently on the King, and so the government disposed of it. But new supplies became necessary, and to vote these after 1692 the Irish parliament had to be summoned every second year. Parliament itself was of unlimited duration, and that of George II (1727–1760) lasted thirty-three years.

Under Poynings' law as explained by an Act of Philip and Mary, it was impossible for the Irish Parliament to pass a measure unacceptable to the Government. Any Bill it might pass must in the first place be approved and accepted by the Irish Privy Council and then by the Privy Council of England; as it left the hands of the latter it must be accepted or rejected in full with whatever modifications it had received in its passage to and fro. Suppose a great question arose like that of the Excise Bill in England in which the great Walpole was defeated, the Irish government might feel obliged to withdraw a hated measure but it itself need not retire to make place for a new set of ministers. No, for the government consisted of the Lord Lieutenant and his Secretary, both Englishmen, and the chief ministers and officials whom the Lord Lieutenant appointed or summoned to the Privy Council of Ireland, so that in fact the whole government depended on England and had as their prime duty to protect England's interests here. The Lord Lieutenant, though nominally answerable to the King, was in fact under the orders of the Secretary of State for Home Affairs.

But on this point we must remember that in England itself for the removal of a chief minister at the time it needed the withdrawal of the King's favour or his own failure to keep a majority of supporters together in the Commons. Only, in Ireland the English capacity for party action and the pressure of public opinion which occasionally compelled both King and Cabinet to give way on some great question did not exist.

This irresponsible government ruling in English interests, and this shackled and spiritless legislature, were to last almost unquestioned till 1760. In 1719 the coping-stone was put to it by the Declaratory Act (called that of 6 George I), which abolished the appellate jurisdiction of the Irish House of Lords and affirmed the right of the Parliament of England to bind Ireland by its acts. The power had been exercised in fact since 1640, it was only now, after a celebrated lawsuit called the Sherlock-Annesley case, made into a statute.

If a man filled with a burning sense of injustice turned his eyes away from this unedifying picture, he could behold far worse things in Ireland, the shocking poverty and ill-treatment of the lower classes, the callousness of the rich, the unemployment and decay due to the Restrictive acts of England, the lack of a currency to stimulate trade and the vast sums which went every year over to England as rents to great Absentees who under the recent confiscations had received large grants of Irish land. Such a man was found in Jonathan Swift, dean of St. Patrick's from 1713 to 1745. One of the Anglo-Irish colony and born in Dublin, he had employed his brilliant and sardonic genius in the cause of Harley and the Tories under Queen Anne, and since their defeat was a disappointed man. He now devoted this genius to the cause of his native country. No Irishman of the age was more talked of and quoted in his own country than he, or has been more remembered and written about since. In 1720, when he wrote his anonymous *Proposal* for the universal use of Irish manufactures the government tried to prosecute the printer for publishing a 'seditious, factious, and virulent pamphlet', but a grand jury could not be found to convict him. Swift's fame was assured by the *Drapier's Letters* of 1724, in which he denounced Wood's halfpence. Ireland was in need of copper money and the Duchess of Kendal, an ex-mistress of George I, who was already pensioned from the Irish revenues, procured a patent for an English ironmaster called William Wood to coin £100,800 worth of halfpence and farthings. It was reckoned that the profit to him would be £40,000, of which a large part would have gone to this disgusting harpy. The transaction, especially as made under such auspices, met with the opposition of the Irish Parliament which for the first time dared to stand out against both governments. But it was the intervention and the scathing wit of Swift that defeated it and caused the withdrawal of the patent. The storm made the English government send over for the first time since 1714 an able man as viceroy, namely, Lord Carteret, and Ireland for once had to be taken seriously. He used every pressure to get Harding, the printer of the anonymous *Letters*, prosecuted, but when it went to a second grand jury they retorted by presenting all persons who had attempted or should endeavour to impose Wood's halfpence upon Ireland as 'enemies of his Majesty and the welfare of this kingdom'. We must remember that grand juries, like all the authorities in Ireland, were Protestant.

This may have seemed a small triumph for justice compared with the greater wrongs of the time, but it was important as the first note of Anglo-Irish opposition to the selfish domination of Ireland by England, which led in time to the great achievements of Grattan and the 'Protestant Irish nation'. Henceforth viceroys had to be men of some ability and at least had to come in person to manage the Irish parliament by influence, bribery, and good dinners.

Swift, however, was never silenced till his death. In subsequent writings he poured forth his immortal scorn upon the vested injustice of the times. He attacked the policy by which the high offices in Church and State were filled with pure-born Englishmen, frequently of no merit, who had no scruples in serving the interests of 'the Castle'. He attacked the corrupt parliamentary system and in savage but obvious satire depicted the wrongs and starvation of the Irish poor. 'Burn everything from England but her coal,' is one of his best-remembered maxims, and he may be called the founder of the economic policy of Sinn Féin. Other famous phrases of his are often quoted. He spoke of the legislators of the inglorious times since the Whigs began as 'coming with the spirit of shop-keepers to frame laws for nations'. He compared Ireland with its splendid harbours empty of shipping to the noble prospect which a prisoner may catch from out of his window-bars. 'Ireland', he wrote, 'is the only kingdom I have ever heard or read of, either in ancient or modern history, which was denied the liberty of exporting their native commodities wherever they pleased. Yet this privilege, by the superiority of mere power, is refused to us in the most momentous parts of commerce.'

Swift ignored a good deal that we would call unjust, such as the Penal laws. His indignation was in fact more easily aroused by human than by legal injustices, and his genius with its *Saeva indignatio* directed itself chiefly against the shocking wrongs of the social order and the unreason, cruelty, and follies of mankind. Humanity as well as Ireland has much to learn from the Latin epitaph that he made for himself in St Patrick's:

> Here rests Jonathan Swift,
> Where bitter indignation can no longer rend the heart.
> Depart, traveller, and imitate, if thou canst,
> So strenuous a champion of Liberty.

Primate Boulter was, after the withdrawal of Carteret, practical ruler for nearly twenty years. This very unclerical prelate made it his business to rule Ireland in Church and State through Whigs and Englishmen, which he thought the only way of keeping Ireland safe for the Protestant and English interest. On one occasion he complained that if an Englishman were not appointed to the vacant see of Cashel there would be thirteen 'Irish' to nine 'English' bishops, 'which we think will be a dangerous situation'. As a result of this policy, continued after him, every Chancellor of Ireland was an Englishman till 1785.

Ireland was indeed ruled by three English-born prelates up
to 1764, Boulter himself, Hoadley, archbishop of Dublin
(1730–1742), and Stone, archbishop of Armagh from 1747 to
his death in 1764. Under Boulter the penal laws were completed by the disenfranchisement of the Catholic voters in
1727. In 1733 this Primate began a scheme of popular education and founded the 'Charter schools'. These were so well
endowed by private donors and grants of the Irish parliament
that by 1763 the yearly income spent on the schools was
£15,000. Unfortunately, as the scholars could only be educated
on a Protestant basis, the Charter schools never found any
favour with the Catholic bishops or the mass of the people.
Boulter was an excellent administrator, but an absolute
Protestant ascendancy man, and typical like Hoadley of the
unimaginative 'Latitudinarian' bishops who ruled the Church
in England and Ireland.

The age of positive persecution, however, was now over. In
1745 Lord Chesterfield was viceroy, and in order to prevent
any movement in favour of Prince Charles Edward in Ireland
he treated the Roman Catholics with respect and the Penal
laws were suspended. The final defeat of 'Bonny Prince
Charlie' in 1746 was in fact the death-knell of the hopes of
Jacobite Ireland. After this, the hopes of whatever survived of
the nobility and of the growing middle class among the Catholics were practical and limited to asking for modest favours
from the government. Among the peasantry who spoke Irish
and supported as best they could the wandering poets, the hope
of a Stuart restoration became a poetic fancy in which they
transferred the Golden Age of the past into an impossible
dream of the future. The upper and middle classes showed
every sign of unconditional loyalty and submission, but we
cannot doubt from the songs and poems that were in favour
among the oppressed peasantry and their old martial spirit
that had a French army landed and armed them there would
have been a popular rising once again, but mainly against
cruel landlords, tithe-proctors, and the other 'petty tyrants
of their fields'.

The spirit of the times favoured toleration. Religious zeal
died out among the Protestant upper class, and the prevalent

Deism could see no reason for persecuting people even for what it thought absurd beliefs. The liberal spirit affected the Papacy itself and made upper-class Catholics take their religion less seriously than in the former century. Protestant clerics, justices of the peace, and landowners became kindly disposed and protected their Catholic neighbours from the operation of the laws. Foreign powers such as the Empire, and France during her period of peace with England from 1714 to 1740, protested against the Code as unjust and absurd. At first it cannot be doubted that the Protestant conquerors genuinely wished the wholesale conversion of the Romanists, but this spirit soon died or was confined to more serious bishops and zealous people. To all reasonable, humane, or even indifferent men the actual *Penal* laws became indefensible, but this did not weaken the determination of the ascendancy to maintain the *disabling* statutes and prevent Jacobite land titles being revived, for on those two points the ascendancy rested. According to Edmund Burke, a man of old Norman stock and the son of a Catholic mother, 'the Protestant ascendancy is nothing more or less than the resolution of one set of people to consider themselves as the sole citizens of the Commonwealth and to keep a dominion over the rest by reducing them to slavery under a military power'.

The last years of George II saw the rapid growth of a Protestant nationalism directed against the English control of Ireland, and kept alive by the Restrictive acts in trade and by the 'management' of Parliament in the English interest by the Court party. There was a considerable lower-class Protestant population, especially in the towns, and these, who were almost entirely without voice in the corrupt and unrepresentative parliament, it was not difficult for writers and authors to stir into occasional mutiny. The tradition begun by Swift that Ireland was a sister kingdom of England's, entitled to the same rights from Magna Carta down, was carried on by George Berkeley, bishop of Cloyne in his *Querist*, and by Lucas in the *Citizens' Journal* (1747–1749). The mass of the Catholic people, who had no representation at all, could only look on indifferently or applaud what seemed to be a revival of

Irish nationalism. The Protestant ascendancy, formerly Tory,
under the general spirit of the age became Whig, and saw the
general panacea for things that were wrong in making Parliament more powerful and representative of public opinion,
while we cannot doubt that the depressed Catholics would,
on the other hand, have welcomed the revival of the Royal
power which alone had helped them in former days, for the
'King's grace' was in their tradition.

In 1751–1753 a constitutional event marked a step forward
in the claim of the Irish parliament to control government and
finance. It had become more or less continuous since 1692,
and however much Burke might blame it for its penal laws,
like a true Whig he thought that a continuous and sovereign
legislature was a supreme benefit and that the Irish parliament
by its measures improving trade and commerce had by his time
'made Ireland the great and flourishing kingdom that it is'.
A vital element in parliamentary government is the control
of the finances. In England this was secured by the Revolution of 1689. In Ireland the parliament of 1692 had protested
that Money bills were the sole gift of the Commons, a protest
for the time without effect. The national revenue was now
increasing in spite of the injustice of the laws, for Boulter and
Stone managed Ireland well, peace prevailed, and industry
prospered. In 1751 the Duke of Dorset as Lord Lieutenant
was actually confronted with the question of what to do with
a surplus in the revenue. He and Primate Stone declared that
the King would give his consent to the application of part of
the balance in the Treasury to the reduction of the public debt.
The House of Commons passed a Bill to this purpose, and so
admitted that they could not spend their own money without
the consent of the English Privy Council. The question
emerged again under Dorset in 1753. Indignant over the former
surrender, a party of opposition had formed itself in the
House of Commons under Boyle, the Speaker, and Anthony
Malone, Prime Sergeant, which was joined by no less a person
than the Earl of Kildare. Again the viceroy announced the
royal consent to appropriate part of the balance to the reduction of the National Debt, but the Irish parliament would

not admit that the surplus was the King's by prerogative and finally threw out a Money bill sent from England which embodied this principle. The Lord Lieutenant then took the whole of the surplus revenue out of the Treasury by means of a royal letter, and bribed over the opposition by creating Boyle Earl of Shannon and Malone Chancellor of the Exchequer, with large pensions, while Kildare became Duke of Leinster. So little nobility or popular spirit was in this aristocratic 'Patriot party': nevertheless it was the foundation of a nobler movement led by Grattan, Flood, and Charlemont. And further, the Irish parliament secured its claim over finance to the extent that any future surplus was appropriated to Irish needs, and spent in liberal bounties to agriculture, industries, Trinity College, and so on.

Thus did the Protestant ascendancy of Ireland become politically conscious. Meanwhile, apart from the few peers and gentry who survived of the Catholic aristocracy and the mass of the peasantry, a Catholic middle class began to grow up whose wealth was derived from occupations which were still permitted to them, from the grazier system and from the lucrative provision trade. As these formed a 'money interest' and yet by law could not lend money on mortgages, etc., or acquire land on paying terms, they presented a fresh argument for the relaxation of the Penal code both from their own point of view and that of Protestants who wished to borrow their money. The Catholics were without cohesion, for the gentry were if anything even more caste-proud than their Protestant neighbours and were also disposed to lie low and not bring the law down on them: they had a snobbish distaste for the merchant class, who again displayed little or no interest in the wrongs of the peasantry and the poor. As regards leadership, the natural leaders of the nation had been greatly diminished by conformity. Between the years 1703–1788 it is reckoned that from five thousand gentry and middle-class people of importance conformed to the Established Church, partly through growing indifference to religion and partly through the pressure of the Penal code. The Catholic bishops and clergy, though devoted to the religious side of their duty, had no desire to join in political agitation which had so often ruined

them in the past.   Nevertheless the first gleam of a more manly
spirit was shown in the 'Catholic Committee' founded in 1756
by the efforts of Dr. Curry, Charles O'Connor, and Thomas
Wyse. It was a weak beginning, which for a long time had little
democratic sympathy and only sought relief by humble addresses to the Throne.   We may say that the upper and middle
classes of the Roman Catholics had become Whigs and asked
for nothing better than to recover a portion of their civil rights
under a Protestant constitution which they constantly avowed
they had no wish to subvert.

THE 'PATRIOT PARTY' FROM 1760 TO 1782

The accession of the young George III helped to lift this age
still further out of the dead-weight of the Whig and Hanoverian rule which had prevailed for fifty years. George openly
displayed himself as a Tory, and the traditions of this party
included a certain tenderness for Roman Catholics who had
suffered at Whig hands for their Stuart and Tory attachment.
The new King was determined to end if he could the corrupt,
shameful, and unrepresentative rule of the Whigs, based as it
was on the great 'family connexions', who had reduced the
power of the Crown to a shadow. Bad as this system was in
England, it was still worse in Ireland. George, however, was
no democrat, nor had he any intellectual views as to the real
changes and reforms which the age needed. He was, moreover,
a pronounced and serious believer in the Church of England
and took his title of Supreme Governor and Defender of that
faith very seriously. His Coronation oath bound him to
maintain the Protestant succession as by law established and
to a declaration against Roman Catholic doctrines, which was
indeed offensive to great numbers of his subjects, but which
as a conscientious man he believed it his duty to maintain.
Otherwise, both in England and Ireland, he was ready to co-
operate with Parliament in abolishing the worst features of the
penal laws. Altogether the accession of a young Prince, a
born Englishman, moral and serious, devoid of the gross
manners and vices of the first two Georges, who wished to be
the 'Father of all his people', could not fail to encourage Irish

hopes of redress and to revive once more the loyal sentiments of the Catholic gentry and bishops towards the English Crown.

The Irish Parliament still presented the picture of an opposition party opposed to the Court party and led by a few magnates such as Leinster and Shannon. The former system of 'management' was maintained in full until the death of Primate Stone in 1764, but with the arrival of Lord Townshend as viceroy in 1767 a new epoch opened in Irish history. One of George's initial acts was to command that the Lord Lieutenant of Ireland should reside continuously, and under Townshend the viceregal court became a centre of splendour, wit, and hospitality such as made the Dublin season highly attractive. Ireland had now to be taken seriously, for it had a growing population, and considerable wealth, and the spirit of constitutional opposition from the Anglo-Irish had to be either opposed or satisfied. Townshend was commissioned by George to end the corrupt rule of the 'Undertakers' and the corruption and jobbery of the Irish Government, but it was too much for him entirely to defeat in his period of rule (1767–1772). In 1768 the Irish parliament, which formerly had lasted for a whole reign, was at least made more expressive of public opinion by the passing of an Octennial bill, providing for a general election every eight years. This was the first triumph for the Reform movement directed from outside parliament, which owed so much to Lucas and to public opinion. But when in 1769 the House of Commons rejected a Money bill sent over by the English Privy Council 'because it had not its origin in that house' Townshend lectured the Commons at the Bar of the House of Lords and dissolved parliament for two years. England, however, had little reason for discontent with the Anglo-Irish, for they had in their parliament loyally and generously assisted her in her continental wars, especially in the Seven Years War of 1756–1763 against France and Spain. The mother-country was now approaching the tragic conflict with her own colonies in America (1775–1783), and, as on former occasions, England needed Irish help in her difficulties, and again a large body of

Irishmen, this time her own progeny, determined to use her difficulties so as to procure concessions for their country.

From 1760 the Government had to face at once the question of Catholic relief and the Protestant demand for a constitutional parliament. All the arguments existed for at least releasing the Catholics from the more obvious injustices of the Penal code. Their upper and middle classes and their bishops took every opportunity to protest their loyalty. In 1762 Lord Trimleston, one of the surviving Lords of the Pale, presented an address to the viceroy, Lord Halifax, signed by leading Roman Catholics and asking permission to enrol their people in the service of the Crown. Trimleston dwelt on their loyal conduct during the last war and declared that 'all impressions in favour of the Stuart family were worn out with the gentlemen of consequence and fortune in this country'. The Government did not change the law which prevented Catholics from serving as officers of the army, but as a measure of condescension several Irish Catholic regiments were allowed to enlist themselves in the army of England's ally, Portugal.

A few concessions were all that the upper classes sought for, but the whole social system which few criticized at the time was against the peasantry. In the early years of George III there was a widespread agrarian movement in Ireland, especially among the high-spirited people of Munster. The pressure of tithes, highest of all in the south, rack-rents, the hearth-tax and the expulsion of the people from their ancient rights by Enclosure acts led to a general discontent which expressed itself in movements called after 'the White-boys', 'Shanavests', and other local names, and which, as the people spoke Irish, associated itself with the old hatred of the 'Saxon foreigner' and 'the breed of Calvin and Luther' and hoped for aid from France or Spain. But even the better off and more law-abiding Presbyterians of the north had exasperating grievances also, the tithes, persecution by Church courts, forced labour in road-making, the raising of rents when leases fell in, and the clearance of great areas when fines could not be paid by such landlords as the Marquis of Donegall. Wherever Protestant and Catholic tenants were mingled together, the latter generally outbid the others for farms, and

this in the border counties such as Armagh led to bitterness
and even bloody encounters between the two persuasions.
The Presbyterian emigration to America was swelled, and those
who stayed at home heard with sympathy or enthusiasm of
the later revolt of the Colonies and the establishment of a free
nation.

In these troubles both sides formed themselves into what
were in fact 'peasant trade unions', the 'White-boys' being the
Catholic, and the Ulster Presbyterians calling themselves 'Steel-
boys' and 'Oak-boys'. A more just Road Act did something to
appease the movement in the North; and severe repressive
acts and military operations suppressed the White-boy movement for the time, but to the end of the century it constantly
broke out again. Not all landlords were bad, of course, and
from the people's point of view many were of the old stock,
either still of the old religion or conforming to the new, and
even among the more recent landlords there were many good
and just men who resided on their lands and with the growing
interest in agriculture of the time brought great tracts of land
into cultivation and were proud of their model estates. But
while tithes to Protestant clergy and hearth-taxes to the State
were unjust enough, the real root of discontent was the system
itself by which the mass of the people were rightless cottiers
and small tenants holding entirely at the will of the lord, over-
rented and having no security in their holdings or compensation for whatever improvements they made. Few at the time,
whether Protestant 'patriots' or Catholic loyal-addressers,
expressed indignation at this state of things, and it was
reserved for other men in the nineteenth century to rouse a
flame over the real wrongs of the people.

There was now in Ireland among all classes a higher spirit
and indeed a general ferment, which expressed itself in literature, politics, and other forms of self-expression. This was
pronounced in the Parliament which Townshend summoned
in which the Opposition, beside the former leaders such as
Shannon and the Duke of Leinster, contained a great number
of trained lawyers skilful in debate and several new names such
as Henry Flood and Hely Hutchinson. The latter was an

advocate and a writer on Free Trade, while Flood was destined to lead a far more genuine 'Patriot party' than had yet taken that name.

Townshend was the first viceroy who was instructed to offer concessions to Anglo-Irish feeling and to satisfy it by breaking up the indefensible system of aristocratic group-corruption which had prevailed. But this was with an interested object, for England had just emerged out of a great and expensive war and trouble might be foreseen with her American colonies. Money support from Ireland had been amply given; her military support was now sought. The Octennial Bill of 1768 was a concession to the reformers; in return Townshend proposed an Augmentation of the Army Bill, by which the Irish forces were to be raised to 15,000 men, of which 12,000 were to remain in Ireland (unless by permission of the Irish parliament they could be transferred), the remainder were to be at the disposal of the Imperial government. After much resistance, for many of the patriots thought these forces might be used to coerce the Americans with whom they had much sympathy, the Augmentation Bill was passed.

When Townshend resigned in 1772 it seemed like a personal defeat for him at the hands of the Opposition. But at least he had wrought one great change, namely that he had transferred the patronage from the hands of the aristocratic groups and the Undertakers into the hands of the viceroy. This did not end corruption, but it meant that the buying and bribing of votes in parliament was now in the hands of the English governor of Ireland, who had to obey policy as dictated from London and preserve Ireland for the English interest.

Townshend was succeeded from 1772 to 1776 by Lord Harcourt. Parliament now contained a high-spirited Opposition led by Flood and joined in 1775 by Henry Grattan, a more generous and emotional spirit than Flood, but with less realism and political acumen. The new 'Patriot party', whom we may regard as a body of Irish Whigs in touch with Whig reformers in England, had now a whole programme which they were united to achieve. It was a parliamentary one, rather than a social or truly reforming one, and aimed at winning for Ireland a real Parliament and a 'free Constitution', such as

England had won for herself by the Revolution of 1689, by bringing the army under Irish control by a renewable Mutiny bill, procuring a permanent Habeas Corpus act, establishing the position of the judges, and purifying parliament from the corruption and bribery that disgraced it. From the purely Irish point of view, they proposed to end the commercial subjection of Ireland, and the monopoly of Englishmen in Church and State offices which had been the tradition since 1714. This intrusion and pampering of the 'English by birth' had, as in the fourteenth century, done much to persuade the 'English by blood' that they were a nation and inclined them towards the old native race. Flood and his supporters spoke of the 'Protestant nation', and Flood himself, like many others, not only believed that Ireland had its rights as a colony to all the liberties of English freemen, from 1172 onwards, but showed interest and sympathy with the Irish language and the Gaelic past. Behind them, though the Catholics seemed as yet negligible, existed the makings of a great Anglo-Irish movement and a spirit of at least colonial nationalism. The Protestant clergy as a whole were poorly endowed and had little love for the rich and luxurious English-born bishops who ruled them. If we can judge by men like Goldsmith, there was considerable Tory and even Jacobite sentiment among them. Above all, the middle classes were greatly irritated by the continued pressure of the Acts in Restraint of Trade, which England had imposed since 1660, and which resulted in unemployment and discontent among the town populations, which to a large extent were Protestant. Thus the commercial interest reinforced the political and legal classes in a demand for Irish rights.

Liberalism was now in the general air, and the elegant gentleman who sat for pocket or rotten boroughs were very different in Protestant zeal from the morose Puritans of a century before. Whatever the demerits of aristocratic rule may be, the ruling classes of Ireland showed in a high degree all an aristocracy's instinct for beauty and dignity in art and architecture. Dublin had now become a splendid capital, the second in the Empire, and its noble buildings are to this day a testimony to the good taste of the Anglo-Irish ascendancy of the eighteenth century.

Lord Chesterfield in 1745 gave us the Phoenix Park, one of the most beautiful and widest public spaces in Europe. In 1729 the building of the Parliament House in Dublin was begun. Ample grants by the Irish parliament made Trinity College a noble and ample specimen of eighteenth-century architecture, and the gentry themselves filled the lovely corners of all our provinces with fine houses and handsome demesnes. It was at this time that the writings of Edmund Burke and the speeches of Grattan, De Burgh, and others in the Irish parliament gave Irishmen a reputation for sustained eloquence and verbal felicity which they have never lost. But behind all this Anglo-Irish civilization and nationalism survived the old Irish nation with its Gaelic tradition, suppressed but not dead, and destined to revive when this brilliant Whig episode was over.

Concessions to the Roman Catholics began in 1750 when they were admitted to the lesser grades of the army. Twenty year later, in 1771, was passed the 'Bogland act', which enabled them to take leases for sixty-one years of not more than fifty acres of unprofitable land, to be free of taxes for seven years. It was a miserable concession, but at least it broke up the long ostracism of the native people from the free enjoyment of their own soil.

Flood was the Irish leader on Trade concessions and on the Absentee question, but his bill to tax absentee landlords, of whom there were one hundred in England, was defeated. In 1775 he accepted the post of Vice-Treasurer under the government, which he kept till 1782, and thus gave place as leader to Grattan. He was regarded as bought by the government and never fully recovered his popular influence, though, as he said, 'a patriot may do as much in office as out of it'. The year 1775 saw England at war with her American colonies and the results for Ireland were momentous. The government laid an embargo on all Irish goods going to the colonies and this caused general distress. Parliament, however, continued its loyal record, voted supplies for the war, and allowed 4,000 troops and later still more to be withdrawn from the Irish army. Lord Buckinghamshire replaced Harcourt from 1776 to 1780, and the ill-success of English arms in America pointed out the necessity for the conciliation of Ireland. Even if Ireland had not helped to conquer or colonize the original Plantations, she had at least contributed large supplies of money to hold them against the French, and the injustice of excluding her from imperial trade became more and more obvious. In 1778, therefore, the English Prime Minister, Lord North, carried concessions through the British parliament in favour of Irish trade. By these the Navigation acts were amended to include Irish-built vessels, bounties were granted to Irish fisheries, and some other slight concessions were made. The question of Catholic relief was taken up by the British Government which saw now the necessity of winning over the Irish Catholics unless it was prepared to see them won over by the Patriot party and so reinforce an already embarrassing movement. Contact between the Imperial government and the Catholic Committee was established through Edmund Burke, its London correspondent. The Munster bishops drew up a declaration repudiating the papal deposing power and denying that the Pope had any civil or temporal authority in Ireland. This was accepted by most of the Catholic clergy and was made into an Act in 1774. It is significant that the bishops did not consult the Pope and that the oath was generally accepted, in strong contrast to the opposition against the Remonstrance in the former century. Four years later this was followed by Gardiner's Relief act of 1778. By this Catholics might take leases of land of indefinite tenure, though not freeholds, on condition of an oath of allegiance. They might inherit land on the same terms as Protestants, and the Gavelkind act was repealed. Two years later a great concession was made to the Dissenters when in 1780 the Test clause imposed on them in 1704 was also abolished by law. The Dissenters were thus made eligible for office, though as things stood the Protestant ascendancy prevented the concession having much effect on Government and Parliament.

The undefended condition of Ireland, which had no militia and whose army was now mainly being used by the Imperial government in America and elsewhere, now led to the formation of the memorable Irish Volunteers. With France, Spain, and

Holland joining in against England, there was a considerable prospect of invasion, and it was realized that among the subject Catholic and Dissenting peasantry a foreign invader might find considerable support. When it was therefore proposed by the Patriot party to raise volunteers, the Government accepted the proposal and provided the new corps with arms. Martial enthusiasm became universal among the Protestant ascendancy, and eventually some 80,000 men were seen in arms and brilliant uniforms in every part of the country, raised by local subscriptions, and well provided with muskets and a certain amount of cannon. What their actual object was was not clear in view of the general enthusiasm. Grattan declared them to represent 'the armed property of the nation', and though Catholics subscribed to the funds few of them were enlisted in the ranks. It was in fact a Protestant body. The Duke of Leinster commanded the Volunteers in Leinster, and in Ulster the Earl of Charlemont. Flood's attitude was a definite one, the Volunteers were there to exact Ireland's rights from England and to remain on foot till these were secured. And indeed concessions soon followed on one another, for England was threatened not only with the loss of America but defeat at the hands of her European foes. The history of Ireland has few pages to excel the romantic events that stirred Dublin and the Irish parliament in October 1779. Everybody, on the teaching of Swift, was pledged to wear Irish manufacture only. There were now 40,000 volunteers on foot, they were all the fashion and their leaders were the idols of the nation. When they appeared to line the streets for the members who presented to the Lord Lieutenant a motion that 'only by a free trade could this nation be saved from impending ruin', there could be no doubt what forces were behind them. On November 25th the Commons, by an unprecedented act of rebellion, voted supplies for only six months, and De Burgh made the famous outburst, 'England has sown her laws like dragons' teeth and they have sprung up armed men'. Concession was imperative, wrote the Lord Lieutenant, and so in December Lord North carried through the British parliament measures permitting the free export of Irish wool, woollen cloth, and manufactured glass and freedom of trade with the colonies.

Thus did the Patriots with the Volunteers behind them win Free, or almost Free, Trade. They went on then to secure what they believed to be a Free Constitution, and as the Volunteers grew in numbers and daring it seemed certain that England would have to yield this also.

In February 1782 a Volunteer convention took place at Dungannon attended by the delegates of 143 corps and presided over by Charlemont, the commander-in-chief, Grattan, and Flood. The delegates from Antrim and Down, representing the democratic Presbyterian spirit, played a very honourable and sincere part in the proceedings. Resolutions were passed that 'the claim of any other than the King, Lords, and Commons of Ireland to make laws to bind this kingdom is unconstitutional, illegal, and a grievance'. So were 'the powers exercised by the Privy councils of both kingdoms under Poynings' law'. Also 'the ports of Ireland are open to all ships of countries not at war with his Majesty'. Grattan in his Volunteer uniform also got accepted a motion that 'as Irishmen, Christians, and Protestants, we rejoice at the relaxation of the penal laws against our Roman Catholic fellow-subjects'.

The Volunteer leaders were all ready to abolish the purely penal measures against Catholics, but on their admission to Parliament and the vote they were divided. Grattan wished to enfranchise the freeholders and admit the upper classes to office and the legislature. Charlemont and Flood did not agree with him. Flood thought the Catholic question too dangerous to touch for the present and aimed at a reform of parliament and the creation of a Protestant democracy by the extension of the franchise to Protestants at large.

The modern and democratic touch of this Convention was provided by the picturesque figure of Frederick Augustus Hervey, earl of Bristol, and since 1768 bishop of Derry, a rich and extravagant Englishman who had been promoted to the Irish episcopate. This unbalanced but generous-hearted man advocated the complete abolition of both the Penal and the disabling statutes, and was the first to propose a union of the unprivileged Catholics and Dissenters in the struggle for a free and representative constitution.

The Imperial government for over ten years remained in favour of the Catholics, whose tradition was one of loyalty and submission. Therefore in 1782 the Irish parliament, in which the liberal spirit also prevailed, passed Gardiner's second Relief act. By this Roman Catholics who had taken the oath of 1778 might purchase, hold, and bequeath freehold land and leases on the same terms as Protestants. A number of other laws were swept away, such as those against the residence of the regular clergy and against the bearing of arms, the law of registration of priests, and the acts against education. But no establishment of a Roman Catholic college was permitted, and when Grattan urged that the Roman Catholics should be secured in full civil liberties he was opposed by Charlemont and Flood. But at least 1782 marks the end of the purely *penal* part of the religious code which had lasted for over a century.

It now occurred to some that the religious emancipation of the majority might lead to the revival of land-claims going back to the great forfeitures of only a century before. Indeed, the admission of Catholics to parliament, some thought, might threaten the whole Protestant ascendancy, based as it was on English acts of Parliament since 1642. The Roman Catholic leaders disclaimed any wish to reopen this question, and in 1782 'Yelverton's Bill' gave effect and fresh confirmation to such English acts as in the past affected the land-settlement of Ireland. Yet up to recent times, among the Irish-speaking people, poor or wandering heirs of the dispossessed gentry of old, respected and sometimes supported by the people, went on hoping that some day they would get their estates back again.

Had Great Britain triumphed over her American colonies it is probable that she would have made a firm stand against the somewhat similar demands from Ireland. But the military ardour and Irish patriotism of the Volunteers were never put to the test as they might have been then, nor were the eloquent denunciations of English rule which were often heard in the Irish parliament. In 1782 Lord North resigned owing to the defeats in America and the Tory experiment of George's reign came to an end. When the independence of the American colonies was recognized next year and England ended the war against France and Spain, she was in little mood to face further armed resistance in Ireland. Moreover, the reforming Whigs under Rockingham, Fox, and Burke came for a time into power in England, and their programme included friendship with the Irish reformers. Grattan's party could now for some twenty years count on the friendship of the English Whigs as such, but unfortunately for them these went out of power for some fifty years when the younger Pitt came into office in 1783 as the head of a new Tory party.

In April 1782 the Duke of Portland arrived in Dublin as the Whig viceroy, instructed to make further concessions and to take Grattan and Charlemont into office. They, however, declined, believing their hands would be left freer and their criticism more genuine in Opposition. Judged by the light of later events it was a mistake, for it left the Irish Government in the hands of Fitzgibbon, Beresford, and the rest of the junta who ruled Ireland and were far less liberal than even the British government which was supposed to control them. The recognition of Irish parliamentary independence was made both in the British and the Irish parliaments in May 1782. At Westminster Lord Shelbourne in the Lords and Fox in the House of Commons proposed to meet the full Irish claim, and the Declaratory act of 1719 was repealed. On May 27th this was communicated by Portland to the Irish parliament, and as a result the claim of the Privy Councils of England and Ireland to alter Irish bills was abolished. The Mutiny bill was limited to two years, and the independence and salaries of the judges were established as in England. The triumph of the Patriot party was received both in the House on College Green and in the Irish nation with universal and generous enthusiasm. The Irish parliament voted £100,000 towards the British navy and allowed the Imperial government if it wished to withdraw 5,000 men from the Irish army of 12,000, for England was still at war with three maritime powers. The sum of £50,000 was voted as a mark of gratitude to Grattan, who had by now become the admitted leader of the Protestant nation. This token of national gratitude he felt himself able to accept; otherwise this great man through all his life fought an entirely disinterested fight for liberty as he conceived it. In his great speech on this day he traced the progress of Ireland from the spirit of Swift onwards, from injuries to arms, from arms to liberty. 'Ireland is now a nation. In that character I hail her, and bowing in her august presence I say *Esto perpetua*.' Unfortunately this liberty was only to last eighteen years. It can, however, be mainly attributed to this great man and 'Grattan's Parliament' has been the popular designation ever since of the new Constitution.

Henry Flood, a much colder and more realist type of man, has had his fame as a leader of the Patriot party obscured in popular memory and gratitude, though he deserved well of it. At this point Grattan was content to stop and trust England's word. Flood, however, insisted on a positive renunciation on the part of Great Britain to bind Ireland by British acts of Parliament. This also the British government decided to accept, though the generous-minded Fox himself, who was a statesman, admitted that it was an unwise surrender and that it would have been better to have instead an honourable and perpetual treaty drawn up between the two countries, providing for Great Britain's imperial rights.

On January 22nd 1783, the promised bill was brought in and passed the British parliament. Irish legislative independence was accepted in the following words:

> 'Be it enacted that the right claimed by the people of Ireland to be bound only by laws enacted by his Majesty and the Parliament of that kingdom, in all cases whatever shall be, and is hereby, declared to be established and ascertained for ever, and shall at no time hereafter be questioned or questionable.'

England was indeed 'the weary Titan'. She had lost most of her American empire and reached a low ebb in European eyes as a naval and military power. Nevertheless peace was in the air, and a political genius, the young Pitt, came in with general consent as a great peace minister. In this masterful and thin-blooded man who founded a new Tory party, George, though defeated in his attempt to restore the direct influence of the Crown, found a minister whom he leant upon for the next twenty years as one who respected his royal master's prejudices and pride. A new page began in the history of the British empire, for, having lost most of the old one by bad statesmanship, her rulers had to realize that what remained or what might be added could only be retained by wise and generous policy. French Canada, though conquered, was in 1774 confirmed in its laws, language, and religion, and the same moral could be applied to Ireland. Pitt accepted for the present the new status of Ireland honourably, and for some ten years the rights of Ireland as a sister kingdom went without challenge from the King's first realm.

CHAPTER XVII

THE RISE AND FALL OF THE PROTESTANT
NATION, 1782–1800

IN 1782 Ireland entered upon a period of great apparent prosperity which can be not unjustly attributed to her Parliament's having attained full legislative power to establish the economic prosperity of the country. The tense events of the recent struggle had ended in triumph and left a far more generous spirit and patriotic feeling than had as yet animated the ruling class. Ireland was in fashion, and the expression of this in poetry, literature, and scholarship was pronounced by comparison with the dreary silence of the first half of the century. By the abolition of the greater part of the Penal code, the upper and middle classes of the Roman Catholics were at least enabled to acquire property and to have the status of citizens again. What the old race had suffered by the pressure of this Code, prolonged over a hundred years, cannot be estimated. Its positive results were unfortunately to create in the mass of the people a total lack of confidence in or even a detestation of the law, so that to be against the law was almost the mark of a hero and a friend of the people. Had the Hanoverian dynasty but understood, another fatal result was the estrangement of the popular imagination from the Crown, for which in earlier days, little as it might do for them, both the Irish aristocracy and the peasantry had felt a pronounced loyalty. 'This race', it had been said by Sir John Davies, 'did ever love great personages.' The greatest Person in the three kingdoms now never came to visit his second realm and for all this person-loving race could know might almost not have existed. The natural alliance should have been the Altar and the Throne; unfortunately this had been rendered impossible for most Irishmen, and their sole devotion was given to the Altar of that Church to which in spite of all the laws they had clung. What Ireland has lost by the suppression of the native intellect and the possibility of genius because of the laws which for a century condemned the mass of the population to ignorance can also never be reckoned.

Half of the Penal laws had been abolished, for none could defend them, but when it came to the laws which excluded the Catholics 'from the State' there was a sharp and continued clash of opinion among those in power and those in opposition. Grattan wished to go on to full Emancipation and admit them to the franchise, parliament, and all offices except the very highest. Thus he thought their leaders and merchants would be enlisted on the side of the new Constitution, the essentially Protestant basis of which as established by law they would be bound to accept and observe. Few of the Patriot leaders went so far, although outside parliament, especially in the two democratic centres, Dublin and Belfast, and among the Presbyterians of Antrim and Down, the full claim of the Catholics was favoured. They themselves had a great genius on their side, Edmund Burke, but for the present did not show much political spirit or initiative. The Catholic Committee was an aristocratic and snobbish body, dominated by Lords Trimleston, Fingall, Gormanstown, and Kenmare, who did not relish being associated with men of trade, and had little or no sympathy with White-boys and oppressed peasants. The ruling junta in Dublin was for the most part strongly opposed to Catholic emancipation, and this spirit was embodied in a very able man, John Fitzgibbon, afterwards Earl of Clare. Although he was the son of a Catholic convert of old Norman stock, Fitzgibbon shared none of the 'Old English' or Gaelic tradition which might be expected from his ancestors and had little sympathy with their religion.[1] He was a realist in politics who despised the eloquent platitudes about Natural and National rights which were then so frequently delivered, and thought that the real grievances of Ireland were those of the oppressed lower classes. To him the British connexion and control of Ireland came first; the Protestant constitution next must be maintained at all costs, for the Anglo-Irish were 'England's garrison'; if they could not maintain themselves,

[1] Both the son and father made a fortune at the Bar. In 1778 the son entered Parliament as one of the two members for Dublin University, Hussey de Burgh being the other; after 1783 he represented Kilmallock.

the only alternative would be to throw them into the arms of Great Britain by a Union. The romantic events of 1782–1783 were to him a 'fatal infatuation', endangering Imperial control. Nevertheless, though determined not to yield up the citadel of Anglo-Irish Protestant ascendancy to disloyal elements, he was sincerely in favour of the economic measures that made for Ireland's prosperity and believed in the Kingdom of Ireland, provided it could be safely maintained.

For many years, in peace-time and growing prosperity, all seemed well and the political temperature diminished. Under the Duke of Rutland, Lord Lieutenant from 1784 to 1787, several remarkable men were placed in the Irish government, and at least it displayed vigour and efficiency. Fitzgibbon was made Attorney-General, John Foster Chancellor of the Exchequer and soon after Speaker, and Sir John Parnell Chancellor of the Exchequer in his place. Much has been written and much passionate feeling expressed over the fate and fall of 'Grattan's Parliament' and in praise or dispraise of what it was and did, but there can be no doubt that it gave Ireland a period of remarkable prosperity. The revenues were increasing and were practically in the control of Parliament, which appropriated the surplus to the encouragement of trade and manufactures, the endowment of agricultural and other societies, and such public utilities as a great canal system, or again to the beautification of Dublin. By a whole system of bounties and preferential duties Irish industries were encouraged and built up against the natural competition of the more highly developed and favoured industries of Great Britain. Free Trade and *laissez faire* were economic principles not to be adopted for over sixty years yet, and the accepted duty of a government was to protect and encourage industry by protectionist measures. Agriculture, too, was the basis of the State and the rents of landlords were the first consideration of the legislature.

Foster's Corn law of 1784 began an epoch in Irish history of lasting consequences. Under the operation of the bounties and encouragement it provided for tillage our country became a great corn-growing country, amply satisfying the home market and selling its surplus to Great Britain. There the Industrial revolution was changing the whole face of England, and the growing towns and manufacturing population in addition to what their own country produced needed the cattle and corn of Ireland. The Irish Corn laws, like those of England, designed to exclude foreign grain except on dire necessity, lasted till 1846. In that period Ireland became, what it had never been before, a great tillage country; the rents of the landlords went up, and there was abundant employment for labourers. It became a common spectacle in Ireland for harvesters from the West, who carried their own scythes and were hence called 'spalpeens', to be seen tramping in bands in every county of the fertile areas, seeking work at a shilling a day. Such was the support of one of the last and most mellifluous of our Gaelic poets, Owen Ruadh O'Sullivan, himself a man of aristocratic descent. What these men thought of their lot is to be read in Gaelic songs and poems of the time directed against landlords or still more the rich farmers ('bodachs') who underpaid them. The more spirited of the peasantry were not reconciled to the social order, whatever the middle-class Catholic might be, and their secret combinations were to be openly displayed in the Rebellion of 1798. But for those who profited, the time of Grattan's Parliament was a great one. It led to the building of noble country mansions and to the great corn mills, and the carrying trade, and the inns and beautiful houses of our numerous towns; such farmers as had favourable leases prospered; and the Catholic trading classes, now partly emancipated, became a widespread prosperous community.

Writers such as Burke and politicians such as Foster and Parnell, in their fight against the Union, were able to drive home what an advantage Ireland had in her resident free Parliament and how this had made Ireland prosperous beyond all comparison with other countries of the time. The population in the century from 1706 onwards, declared Foster in an anti-Union speech in 1799, had increased from 1½ millions to 4½ millions. Ireland's export of linen in the first of these years had been only some ½ million yards; in 1783 this had risen to 16 millions; in 1796 it reached nearly 47 millions. The total exports of Ireland in 1706 in value reached only £550,000; in 1783 nearly £3,000,000; and in 1796 over £5,000,000. Her trading and industrial classes were thus won over to the side of the Constitution and their opposition to the Union had later to be overcome. It must be admitted that in the giving of bounties and the grant of contracts much corruption and 'graft' prevailed and selfish and vested interests were created. Amid the many acts by which the legislature benefited the country we unfortunately discern little that the ruling classes would have considered a give-away of their landed and privileged rights. The noble Grattan fought hard to get Tithes set on some just basis, and Fitzgibbon attacked the high rents and exploitation of the peasantry and the poor, but, as in England, unfortunately the oligarchic age had to last for two or three generations yet, and the tradition of Irish patriots remained in the romantic and political sphere rather than in the social reforming. At least in 1793 Parliament abolished the oppressive Hearth-tax and thus encouraged the peasant to build a comfortable cottage in place of his hovel.

Although Ireland had apparently secured a 'Free Constitution' and seemed to be a sister kingdom of England's, in fact the new order presented not only many faults and defects but positive dangers for its own continuance. Parliament had no rival parties as in England, its corruption was far greater, and above all it had no regular and ordinary control over the Ministry. Although Bills now began and went through the two Houses as in England and were then sent direct to the King, the English Cabinet could still advise him to veto them. The Lord Lieutenant, with his secretary, usually an Englishman, stood to Ireland what the King had formerly been to England, but he again obeyed the instructions of the Home Secretary in England and he again was controlled by the Prime Minister. From the Irish Privy Council, the Lord Lieutenant selected the Ministers of State who formed the actual government. They could not be removed by a vote of the House of Commons, they did not think it necessary to resign either as a group or an individual on the defeat of a measure, and if having opposed, let us say, a Catholic Relief

Bill (as in 1792–1793) next year they supported it under orders from the British government or because popular feeling demanded it, they saw no inconsistency in this. In Fitzgibbon's eyes their duty was to stop all dangerous measures and to maintain the 'English connexion'. He himself more than once expressed his irritation at 'experiments' in Ireland directed by English politicians. The only way that Parliament had of bringing this irresponsible government to heel would be to refuse to pass supplies or the annual Mutiny bill. But in fact the prevalent temper of the Irish parliament was loyal and even in the days of the Union only a few daring spirits proposed such an expression of 'no confidence'.

The junta which ruled Ireland has often been blamed for bringing about the Union, by resisting Catholic emancipation, the purification of Parliament, and the extension of the franchise. But it contained several remarkable and efficient men. Among these was Fitzgibbon who in 1789 was created Lord Chancellor (the first Irishman to hold that office for a century) and a peer; in 1795 he became the Earl of Clare. Another leading figure was John Beresford (1738–1805), a son of the Earl of Tyrone. He was member for Waterford for forty-five years, was appointed to the Privy Council in 1768, was soon after made Chief commissioner for Revenue, and was practically the head of Irish affairs after 1784 and Pitt's right-hand man. Allied by marriage to Lord Clare and having many sons by two marriages, he put these into such lucrative offices in Church and State that it was said that the Beresfords finally controlled one-quarter of the jobs of Ireland. He and others of the junta were mockingly called 'the King-fishers' for their assiduous devotion to self-interest. There were men of higher moral standing among them, such as Foster and Parnell, and the Patriots were not without influence in the Government, but it must be admitted that the stand made by the junta was more effective than the attack of the Ponsonbys, Parsons, and other liberal Irishmen who battered for seventeen years at the gates of 'the Castle'.[1]

---

[1] 'Dublin Castle' was henceforth in Ireland the synonym for the narrow-minded and unrepresentative system of government which, with some generous intervals, ruled the country till 1921.

The 'management of Ireland' had now passed into the hands of the Viceroy and was to become a serious matter when after ten years Britain found herself at war with France. The viceroy had to maintain his government by the constant distribution of the patronage in the old corrupt or dubious fashion, in which, however, the eighteenth-century government of England itself was not much superior. Hence the opposition to parliamentary reform, for if members could not be bought how could the majority be kept together? The upper classes had a naïve passion for titles, Parliament was already top-heavy with Irish peerages, and these were made more ridiculous still when the Union came to be carried. But sinecures, pensions, and highly paid jobs were the usual means of bribery, and often a mere deputy of an important post would see nothing wrong in living in England and drawing his salary running into four figures from his empty office.

The Reform of Parliament was the general object of both Grattan and Flood, but while Grattan like a true Whig would be content with inside purification, the more original Flood wanted the reform of the franchise from without. Moreover, while Grattan thought the Volunteers had done their work, Flood, who felt little gratitude to England, wanted to maintain them to secure final reform.

The more important and wealthy that Ireland became and the more equality with England she attained, the more necessary it seemed in British eyes to 'manage' her, a point that was emphasized when the next great war began. She had a sovereign parliament, and parliaments which have asserted a large measure of right generally go on to claim more. Pitt and most English statesmen felt the limit had been reached. The Viceroy therefore had all the more to exercise that patronage and distribution of places and pensions, with an occasional gush of peerages, that had been in his hands since Townshend. This policy was not difficult in a parliament where out of 300 members the only unbought men were those from the thirty-two counties, elected by the forty-shilling freeholders, and a few of the great towns. In the boroughs the vote varied from place to place; in some the corporation alone elected the member, in others the local magnate, in others all the residents.

Most of them were insignificant places, owned by the patron and called 'pocket-boroughs', others, the 'decayed' or 'rotten' boroughs, had few or in several cases no inhabitants. The patrons had the nomination of 176 members, and 86 sat for 'rotten boroughs'. Above two-thirds of the seats in the House, Grattan declared in 1790, were private property. The un-bought element was steadily outvoted by the corrupt or nominated, unless public opinion were so strong at times as to compel the latter to swing over to the patriot side. Hence the failure in the end of Grattan and Flood to make the new Constitution a lasting success, in face of the bribery of the court and the negative spirit of the ruling junta. They had refused to take office, only a Whig triumph in England could now put them in power, and with their minority of votes they could not hope to capture 'the Castle'. The pension list in the six years from 1783 rose to £100,000 per annum, and the number of place-men and pensioners was nearly one-half of the whole Commons.

Even the best of the Anglo-Irish ascendancy looked on Government, as the nobles had done in the fifteenth century, as an inexhaustible treasury of salaries and perquisites. The Speaker had a salary of £4,500 per annum and £500 for each session. Aristocracy, with its splendour, art, and corruption, bore all the sway in the Europe of the time, but the Revolution in France was soon to launch the great attack on all privileged systems and spread its ferment to all lands, not least of all to Ireland.

For some years there was a lull in political agitation, a great increase of wealth, and a spirit of liberalism in politics. Several great questions were, however, merely in suspense: Catholic emancipation, the purification of Parliament, and the relations between the Imperial government and the new Constitution.

For some years Grattan and Flood worked together as leaders of a forward movement. Both thought it essential to maintain the Protestant ascendancy, but while Flood wished to increase the electorate by adding more Protestant voters and making Parliament more representative, Grattan would have been content to purify the sovereign parliament from within by reducing the pensions list and the number of the bought place-men. Both realized that the new Constitution was not safe as long as a stubborn and narrow junta ruled Ireland and as long as a majority in Parliament could be bought to support British policy. But Flood thought the only lasting foundation was that of a reformed electoral system and the support of a democratic population which could make its influence felt in the House. Flood expressed little gratitude to England, for, as he said, the advantages it already derived from Ireland were such as any country would have been glad to have. Grattan was a convinced loyalist and imperialist, generously ready to give England the full and unhesitating support of Ireland at any crisis. To show his confidence and because Parliament was to him the supreme authority he was ready to disband the Volunteers, whom, on the other hand, Flood wished to maintain as the wedge for a further advance.

The Catholic question Flood was content to leave at the point it had already reached. Grattan, who was an aristocrat, advocated throwing open the vote, parliament and all offices to the more respectable and aristocratic element among them while maintaining 'the happy Constitution in Church and State' which the Whigs believed perfect. Thus would the upper classes, the natural leaders of the people, unite loyally under the Crown to promote the temperate liberties of Ireland and the civilizing of the country.

On November 10th 1783 there was a Convention of the Volunteers in Dublin. Of its leaders the Bishop of Derry wanted to give the vote to the Roman Catholics, but his motion was defeated by Flood and Charlemont. A Reform bill, mainly the work of Flood, was next on November 29th introduced by him in the House of Commons, but as he came dressed straight from the Convention in Volunteer uniform the House which disliked the suspicion of intimidation refused leave to introduce it. In the next year, March 1784, he was given leave to introduce the Bill, which had secured great support in the country. It proposed to abolish the right of corporate bodies to return members, to extinguish decayed boroughs, to limit Parliament to three years, and to extend the vote to Protestant leaseholders. The Bill, however, was rejected, and this idea of a Protestant democracy vanished.

It marked the end of the Volunteers in their original form, for conservatives like Grattan thought they had outplayed their part. Several of their corps persisted and admitted Catholic members, their arms often got into hands which used them in the Rebellion, but, as the 'armed property of the Protestant nation' whose brilliant uniforms Grattan and most of the leaders had worn, the Volunteers now subsided. In the next year the Government introduced the proposal for a new militia which it could control, and Grattan supported this. After 1785 Flood rarely appeared in Parliament and died in 1791, while Fitzgibbon, who had formerly shown some liberalism, now became the most determined opponent of Reform.

The great interest in 1784–1785 centred round Pitt's commercial proposals. The new Prime Minister of England, like the Whig Fox, considered that the settlement of 1782–1783 had not been final because it did not provide for full imperial control or even settle the question of Ireland's trading rights in the Empire. He sent over as viceroy the Duke of Rutland in February 1784, with Thomas Orde as his Secretary, with instructions to bring forward measures which have received the name of 'Orde's Commercial Resolutions'. The general intention of these was a commercial treaty between the two countries by which Ireland was to have practically equal trading rights with England. Lord North's concessions had done much for Irish trade but excluded her from the full trade of the Empire, while between the two kingdoms themselves commerce was subject to various import duties and restrictions. In February 1785 Orde brought forward his proposals in the Irish Parliament by which there was to be free trade between the two countries, Ireland was to be admitted to the full imperial trade, and in return was to contribute out of her surplus revenue to the support of the Imperial navy when the revenue exceeded £665,000. The Irish parliament accepted the proposals, but in England commercial jealousy was so roused that Pitt had to reduce the extent of the concessions to Ireland. In their new form the propositions debarred Ireland from trading in that part of the world between South Africa and South America and from importing Indian goods except through Great Britain. Her parliament must re-enact all British laws on the navigation and trade of the colonies. The regulating power of the British parliament was to cover all goods imported from Ireland into the American or West Indian colonies, and even part of the trade with the United States. Resolutions to this effect passed the British parliament, but had such a small majority in the Irish that Orde finally withdrew them. They had become unacceptable to Irish feeling, because under them the British parliament would have the final control over the trade of the Empire, Great Britain would keep the trade monopoly of India and to some extent of the Plantations, and Ireland would be bound to trade within the British Empire. Also free trade with England might lead to the ruin of Irish industries, carefully protected by bounties and the protective measures of the Irish parliament.

From another aspect Ireland would be bound to a perpetual tribute to Great Britain which would increase with her prosperity. Grattan declared that the amended proposals involved for Ireland 'a surrender of trade in the east and of freedom in the west'. Their defeat was hailed with delight in Ireland, with mortification by Pitt. He had shown signs of favouring Reform, but now he made no further effort to displace the unrepresentative junta that ruled 'the Castle'.

Great Britain thus retained the monopoly of the imperial trade and protection against Irish trade with England, admission to which was to be one of the baits offered at the Union.

A further division took place between the two Parliaments when at the end of 1788 King George's intellect gave way. A Regency had to be provided, and the obvious person was George, Prince of Wales, then a handsome and attractive young man who had allied himself with the Whigs against his father and Pitt. The latter resolved that the Prince should only succeed as Regent under an act of Parliament which should impose limitations upon him. The Whigs declared that he ought to succeed automatically with full royal powers, one of which was that of turning out one ministry and installing another. Armed with such a prerogative, the

Prince Regent might dismiss Pitt and bring in Fox. In Ireland among the Irish Whigs hopes ran high that as Regent he would turn out the Fitzgibbon-Beresford clique and bring into power the party which had won the Constitution. On February 5th 1789 Pitt introduced into the British parliament a limiting Bill to the above effect. In Ireland the Patriot party led by the Duke of Leinster in February of the same year got carried by nearly two votes to one an address to the Prince urging him 'to assume the government of this nation during his Majesty's indisposition, under the style of Prince Regent of Ireland and to exercise the prerogative of the Crown'. The Viceroy, Buckingham, refused to transmit it to one who was still legally a subject. A deputation, however, carried it to London and was graciously received by the Prince. Before the British bill could be passed the King recovered at the end of February, and as a practical matter the Regency question dropped. Again the Government had to recover a majority and to punish the Opposition. No less than sixteen peerages were created; among others a Mr. Stewart became Marquis of Londonderry, and Fitzgibbon, who had vehemently opposed the action of the Opposition, was appointed Lord Chancellor. The incident had its effect in turning the mind of Pitt, who was greatly influenced by the ruling junta, in the direction of a Union. He had seen the Irish Parliament take its own way over his commercial propositions; he now saw the possibility, if the Regency question came up again, of Ireland's appointing a Regent who would be full sovereign while in England he would be limited by act of parliament. The moral became clear to him that the Irish Parliament might in trade, politics, and even war and peace take an independent line which would endanger England's imperial supremacy.

From 1790 to 1793 Lord Westmorland was Viceroy and his Chief Secretary was Hobart. In the parliament under him appeared another memorable figure, Robert Stewart, famous in history as Viscount Castlereagh. He was elected for Co. Down in 1789, and the curious electoral system of the time is shown in the fact that the open poll lasted forty-two days and cost his father, Lord Londonderry, no less than £60,000. Grattan remained leader of the Opposition and sought by a place and pensions bill to reduce the corrupt element in Parliament. In June 1789 he, Charlemont, and Ponsonby formed the Whig Club to promote administrative reform and maintain the Constitution of '82. But already political ferment outside Parliament was on the increase and many realized that the aristocratic monopoly of government and property was not to remain unchallenged.

Agrarian discontent was marked in the continued Whiteboy movement which stringent Crimes acts were unable to eradicate. A large cause of it was the iniquity of the tithe system. Grattan made several attempts to bring it to an end but he was defeated by the vested interests, and the evils of this system lasted till 1838, the bishops of the State Church being stubborn against any change. All he could do in 1789 was to procure that land reclaimed from the wilds should be exempt from tithes for seven years. Later, in 1793, he procured the abolition of the hated Hearth-tax. But while such agrarian movements disturbed the South, in the northern counties competition for farms and the religious difference led to standing feuds between Catholic and Protestant peasantry. In Ulster and elsewhere the Catholic tenants banded themselves into a society called the 'Defenders', who owed their origin in 1784 to an encounter between the two religions. The Defenders spread to the South and became well organized in Wexford for example. They did much to bring about the rising of 1798 when they were blended with the political movement of the United Irishmen, but their name disappeared after that. This unhappy agrarian religious feud was kept up not less on the other side in the Ulster 'Peep-of-Day Boys'.

In addition to this ferment, principles of political freedom and reform were spreading rapidly among the Presbyterians of the North and found an echo also in other parts among the unprivileged classes. Dublin had a strong democratic element, the hero of which was Napper Tandy. The movement in France that soon became a Revolution added its ideas to the ones that the northern democracy had already imbibed from the emigrants who had gone off to America and from whom news came back of a free country. 'American' and 'French' democratic and republican sentiments soon became general among masses of the Irish population.

It is significant of the altered times that the people began to find their leaders in men who were not in Parliament or even members of the ascendancy. The most remarkable of these new leaders was Theobald Wolfe Tone, a young lawyer from county Kildare and of no great social standing. Born in the Established Church, he adopted the prevalent Deism and regarded the Church as part and parcel of the privileged injustice of the time. His active and enthusiastic genius, that of a soldier rather than a politician, was deeply stirred by the news from France in the years following the meeting of the National Assembly in 1789, which led to a Constitution, the abolition of all privileges, and the Declaration of the Rights of Man, all in a few months. To thousands of earnest or enthusiastic spirits in Europe the French Revolution seemed the dawn of a new and perfect age; it was so to Tone, and he, unlike others, was never disillusioned. To him Ireland was a supreme example of all that privileged injustice which France had renounced, and he devoted his great talents as an organizer, writer, and natural soldier to attack a corrupt ascendancy and the English connexion that maintained it. But at first like most of his fellow-reformers he strove to achieve his aims within the law, and it was only the march of events that drove him and them into armed extremism.

In 1791 Tone attracted public attention by his pamphlet signed 'A Northern Whig', in which he attacked the Constitution of '82 and advocated the union of Catholic and Dissenter to secure the reform of a corrupt unrepresentative Parliament. Next, along with Rowan Hamilton, Napper Tandy, and other Protestants of education and standing, he formed the 'Society of United Irishmen' in October 1791, with its first headquarters at Belfast. Its objects were to abolish all unnatural religious distinctions, to unite all Irishmen against the unjust influence of Great Britain, and secure their true representation in a national Parliament. The union of Catholic and Dissenter had been advocated by the bishop of Derry; it now became Tone's lifework. Thus to the grievances of the common people were added the doctrinaire principles of Episcopal

Protestants in Dublin and Belfast, Thomas Addis Emmet, the brothers Sheares, Oliver Bond, Henry Joy McCracken, and others. The real danger to the established order came from the democratic Presbyterians of the north, where in January 1792 the journal, the *Northern Star* of Belfast was begun, for the sturdy, educated, and logical Scoto-Irish race now enjoyed just sufficient rights as Protestants to make them feel aggrieved that the rest were denied them.

This union of the discontented advanced a great step when in 1790 John Keogh, a Dublin tradesman, became dominant in the Catholic committee and Wolfe Tone became its secretary. This timid body now had the courage to send a deputation to Pitt himself who gave a gracious promise that the British ministry would offer no objection if the Irish Parliament proceeded further in emancipation. Next, in January 1792, they drove out of their body Lords Kenmare, Fingall and others of the aristocratic section which had long dominated it. There was general enthusiasm over this, and the Government, which had long regarded the Catholics as tame loyal-addressers, saw with consternation that they had now entered boldly into the political field. It was realized that further concessions must be made if they were not to be thrown into the arms of the Protestant reformers. Wolfe Tone regarded the aristocratic patriots of Grattan's party with much the same contempt that the French revolutionaries had for Lafayette and the Girondins, but Grattan's support of complete Catholic emancipation was sincere and continued to the end of his life. The Irish executive, which cared nothing for feeling in the Dublin parliament, now frustrated the generous intentions both of Pitt and of Grattan, and the Catholic Relief Bill of 1792 granted only minor concessions which were contemptible in view of the public demand. Grattan laboured for the cause in London and a National convention met in Dublin to demand the full franchise. The King received the deputation, including Tone, graciously, the Viceroy in January 1793 announced the King's wish that Parliament should consider the situation of his Catholic subjects, and the executive had to yield before such a positive command.

Hobart's Catholic Relief Act of 1793 in its main provisions was carried with the votes of two-thirds of the House of Commons. It enabled the Catholics to bear arms, to become members of corporations, to vote as forty-shilling freeholders in the counties and in the open boroughs, to act as grand jurors, to take degrees in Dublin University, to hold minor offices, and to take commissions in the army below the rank of General. But they were debarred from seats in Parliament and from offices in the government and State, for, while most of the humiliating oaths of former times were abolished, to be a member of Parliament or enjoy a government post still required the Sacrament and the anti-Roman declaration of 1692. The other measures had been carried by two to one, but a motion admitting them to Parliament, moved by George Knox, was vetoed by 163 to 69. 'So near was this poor kingdom to its deliverance.' Grattan especially regretted that the upper class of the Catholics had not been admitted to a full voice in the State. Nevertheless the Catholic Committee expressed their enthusiastic gratitude, voted £1,500 and a gold medal to Wolfe Tone and similarly rewarded others of the deputation, and dissolved themselves.

On January 21st 1793 Louis XVI was sent to the guillotine, and in February the French Republic, already at war with Austria and Prussia, declared war on England. For twenty-one years Great Britain was to be France's chief enemy by land and sea. The horrors and revolutionary principles of France were answered by a Conservative panic among all the ruling classes in Great Britain and Ireland, and those reforms which were so pressingly needed in politics, law, religion, and the condition of the poor were shelved for forty years. Pitt thought it no time for reforms and most of the Whigs agreed with him, inspired by the eloquent treatises of the Irishman Edmund Burke.

Of the 'New Whigs' in opposition Charles Fox led only a remnant, too small to be of much help to Ireland. The ruling junta in Dublin was firmly entrenched, for Pitt regarded it as the chief security for imperial control, and Fitzgibbon was often denounced by the Opposition as 'Mr. Pitt's delegate.'

Since corruption in the Viceroy's hands was the existing weapon, it must not be taken from him; an alliance of the discontented elements against things as they were must be resisted at all costs. The war indeed changed the whole face of Ireland's prospects and once more, as in the sixteenth and seventeenth centuries, in England's wars against Spain and France, her hopes of a lasting conciliation and contented loyalty were sacrificed to the supposed military necessities of Britain.

But the Imperial government still looked with a kindly eye on the Catholic claims. The Roman Church was the friend of Monarchy and Religion and a great bulwark against revolution and atheism. Its bishops, priests, and respectable classes in Ireland expressed unfeigned horror of the French Republic, and the famous Irish Brigade, which had so long served the French monarchy, now for the most part transferred itself to King George's forces rather than serve a godless Republic. Once again the Catholic nation of Ireland seemed on the conservative side and further concessions might safely be made to their upper classes. But among the Romanist peasantry, who had no share or interest in Parliament and government jobs, 'Jacobin' ideas began to spread, directed mainly, however, against practical wrongs and inspired by the radical teachings of the United Irishmen. 'Hereditary hatred,' wrote Thomas Emmet of them, 'and a sense of injury has always conspired with national pride and patriotism to make them adverse to England and enemies of the British connexion.' The Church of Ireland ascendancy, which possessed all the jobs and owned five-sixths of the land, but formed only one-tenth of the population, had indeed done much for Ireland in civilization, wealth, architecture, a free parliament and even religious toleration. But gratitude for all this could hardly be expected from an Irish-speaking peasantry, steeped in the past and subjected to a harsh landlord system. All the dramatic events and 'nation-making' of the last thirty years had scarcely touched them, and almost nothing had been done to win their loyalty or even manly consent to the established order.

Some small measures of reform were accepted in 1793, though a general Reform act was out of the question. The revenues

were brought under the annual control of parliament. By a
Pension Bill all future pensioners were excluded from parliament and the total amount available for this form of bribery
was reduced from £120,000 to £80,000. A Place Bill was
passed compelling members who should accept government
posts to vacate their seats and seek re-election. In spite of
this Place Bill the number of those who held posts or pensions
under the Crown was seventy-two at the time of the Union,
and it was their votes which carried this detested measure.
On the other hand, the government of Ireland sought to bring
to an end the period of popular outside organizations which
had begun in 1775. An Arms act abolished the Volunteers by
forbidding the carrying of arms except by the government
forces, and a militia was enlisted. It met with great opposition
in various parts from the common people, and the remarkable
sight was seen more than once of Catholic militiamen and
Presbyterian 'United men' firing upon one another. Further,
a Convention act forbade subjects to assemble in bodies calling
themselves representatives of the nation. This act made
illegal the National conventions which had been so much in
fashion and was for long years afterwards to hamper movements such as O'Connell's.

As in its previous wars, Great Britain had no reason to
complain of support in money and men from the Irish Parliament, and Grattan was among the first to pledge Ireland's
cordial support in the war against France. Nevertheless,
outside parliament French sympathies were pronounced and
gave point to a fresh attempt finally to win over the Roman
Catholic population. This led to what is called the 'Fitzwilliam episode'.

The war against France had led to a coalition in England
between Pitt and his Tories and the aristocratic or 'Old
Whigs'. Pitt intended to keep the upper hand, but it was
agreed that Ireland should be a Whig province and Lord
Portland was made Secretary for Home affairs, which included
this country. Lord Fitzwilliam, an Irish landowner and a
friend to Grattan and the Roman Catholic cause, was in
January 1795 appointed Lord Lieutenant in place of Westmorland. Fitzwilliam planned to take Grattan into office in

the Irish government and to carry full Catholic emancipation. For this he thought it essential to remove the junta, who obstinately stood in the way of all liberal measures. Fitzgibbon and Beresford got to know of this and used their influence with Pitt to defeat Fitzwilliam's plan. The latter was instructed not to *introduce* the proposal to admit Catholics to parliament and government offices, but to *support* it if it were brought forward. Without securing the backing of Pitt, he dismissed Beresford and proposed to do the same with Fitzgibbon and others of his band. This roused Pitt's jealousy of his Whig allies taking too much on themselves and his determination not to let down the junta which ruled Ireland. Fitzgibbon persuaded the King, in a communication through one of his ministers, that the admittance of the Catholics to parliament and offices of State would be a violation of his Coronation oath to maintain the Protestant constitution as by law established. George was a dull and obstinate man, but his conscience was a rooted one, and it might well be argued that until parliament relieved him from his solemn oath he could not be expected to change it. Portland himself became alarmed and instructed Fitzwilliam to offer only minor concessions. Finally he was recalled in February. Undoubtedly much of the failure of 1795 was due to the imperfect understanding between Fitzwilliam and Pitt, but it is tragic that a generous and final settlement of Catholic emancipation was not made now instead of in 1829.

When Fitzwilliam left Dublin on March 25th 1795 his carriage was drawn by the people to the shore through streets draped in mourning. It cannot be doubted that the majority in the Protestant ascendancy itself had been in favour of emancipation, and many noble men in the Commons had fought hard for it, such as Sir Lawrence Parsons, who reminded the government how they had voted £1,700,000 in support of Britain. But these were only individuals and their minority could not shake the Fitzgibbon clique. So ended all hope of Reform. The moral for those who had hoped to alter parliament from without unhappily was that the Constitution of '82 was a thing to be despaired of and the minds of such reformers as Tone and the United Irishmen were driven to the thought of a Revolution. The generous Fitzwilliam was succeeded by Lord Camden, who secretly was instructed to oppose both Emancipation and the reform of parliament. The one concession that did take effect was the endowment from State funds of Maynooth College as a seminary for the Roman Catholic clergy, who could no longer be educated in France and whose loyalty it was thus hoped to secure. But from this moment Ireland entered upon that period which only ended with 1803 and which saw the Republican organization of Ireland, attempted French aid, the Rebellion of 1798, the Union and the last pathetic outbreak of Robert Emmet. Wolfe Tone, whose name was to be prominent in the armed movement, now left Ireland and spent some time in Philadelphia. The United Irishmen replaced their former oath, which was legal and public, by a secret and revolutionary one, while their Directory from Dublin began to organize Ireland on a military basis and through their emissaries to enter into correspondence with the French government.

After the Fitzwilliam episode the crisis began to approach fast. Grattan and the moderates strove to exact the reasonable reforms which might have averted it, and in May 1795 he proposed a Catholic Relief bill, but in vain. In May 1797 a further attempt by Ponsonby and him at a moderate Reform bill was also in vain and was the last. The majority in parliament thought it sufficient answer that Great Britain was engaged in the great struggle against victorious France. Fitzgibbon, now Earl of Clare, was determined to save the British connexion and the Protestant ascendancy at all costs, by a Union if all else failed. He could rely on most of the Protestant population, which, though it was a minority, could be armed at any moment against Catholics and Dissenters and he was ready to oppose force to force.

The long-standing local feuds between Protestants and Catholics in the Ulster counties came to a head on September 21st 1795 in an affair called 'the Battle of the Diamond' in Armagh, when in an armed encounter between the two sides some twenty or thirty Defenders were left dead. The day closed with the institution of the Orange order 'to maintain the laws and peace of the country and the Protestant Constitution, and to defend the King and his heirs as long as they shall maintain the Protestant ascendancy'. This was followed by a continued religious war in which great numbers of harmless Catholics were driven into Connacht while the more spirited enrolled in the United Irishmen. The Orange order soon numbered many thousands of militant Protestants, for the most part Episcopalians, but it is to the credit of Lord Camden that he refused to employ them in the later Rebellion.

Early in 1796 the Irish parliament passed an Insurrection act of a severity which would have been impossible in Britain. It allowed the Lord Lieutenant to proclaim any district or districts and place them under martial law. It compelled arms to be produced, imposed the death penalty for administering an unlawful oath, and transportation for life for taking such an oath, and empowered magistrates to seize suspects and send them to serve in the fleet. In November the Habeas Corpus Act was suspended for all Ireland. Ulster was now regarded as the dangerous province, the discontented had great numbers of arms, and the Presbyterians were to a large extent sworn United Irishmen. The disarming of Ulster was next ordered by Lord Camden and carried out by General Lake from March to October 1797, and during it one of the most noble-minded of the popular leaders in the north, the Presbyterian William Orr, was hanged for administering the United Irish oath. The excesses of the ill-disciplined troops and militia, who exceeded even their brutal orders, were bitterly denounced by Grattan's minority in parliament and even in the English House of Commons, but, as we have seen in our own times, a Great War is a bad time to complain of military methods until they become too cryingly scandalous. The number of arms taken from the people, which it is reckoned included 50,000 muskets and 70,000 pikes, at least justified the Government in believing that if Ulster had not been disarmed in time the Protestant province would have been by far the most dangerous area in the Rebellion.

The government now went on to provide a further armed force, that of the Yeomanry, which consisted of Protestant tenants and townsmen commanded by gentry under commission from the Crown. These were actively used and imparted to the later operations the savage spirit of religious partisans. At the outbreak of the Rebellion the government could count upon not less that 15,000 regulars, 18,000 militia, and 50,000 yeoman, badly disciplined and shockingly out of hand. But it is to be noted that of the two latter forces the yeomanry were Irishmen and many of the militia were Catholics.

The cruelties of the troops and the firm determination of the government to flog rebellion out of the people naturally cowed great numbers, but on the other hand drove into rebellion a host of desperate or injured men who would have remained peaceful under better treatment. Many now preferred a 'union with France' to a 'union with Britain', if such had to be. According to the current patriotic song, 'the Shan Van Vocht', the French were already 'on the sea' and during two years several expeditions menaced English rule in Ireland. Fitzgibbon believed that a rebellion was imminent and that the back of it must be broken rapidly if the aristocratic government of Ireland was not to be overthrown or Ireland separated from England. She had now a population of 4½ millions, three-quarters of whom were the old native peasantry, men generally of sound physique and military disposition, of whom 150,000 were reckoned to be United Irishmen; they had able and educated leaders, local and central, and only needed to be properly armed from France.

Early in 1796 Tone, who had left America, arrived in Paris, where Carnot was so impressed with him that he gave him the rank of adjutant-general in the French Army. At Hamburg the Directory of the United Irishmen had two other envoys, Arthur O'Connor, a gentlemen of Milesian descent, and Lord Edward Fitzgerald, a younger son of the Duke of Leinster. Tone was now determined to overthrow if he could both English rule in Ireland and her aristocratic and corrupt government as the first necessity of liberty. He wrote in his diary at this time, 'The truth is, I hate the very name of England. I hated her before my exile and I will hate her always.' This product of the English race in Ireland was indeed a son of the Revolution as much as any Danton, and his optimistic, gay, and gallant character had all the makings of a great soldier.

The young Napoleon would have called him 'one of Plutarch's men'. He was not a communist any more than the French revolutionaries, who had no objection to the rights of Property as long as it was not feudal, but he relied upon the poor, who were to him the Irish nation, to save Ireland. As he rightly said, 'They were ready for any change, for no change could make their situation worse.' What Tone would have done with Ireland had he succeeded cannot be known, for he failed, but the memory of the man who founded the Republican tradition in Ireland has been the most inspiring in later history of all the names which the period 1770–1800 produced. For though unrelenting against what he considered the ruling tyranny and the classes that supported it, personally Tone was a man of sincere, generous and likeable character, a moral man, and a good husband and father.

While enthusiasts such as Fitzgerald over-exaggerated the forces of insurrection and thought they merely needed arms from France, Tone, who was more of a realist, declared that only a French army of 20,000 men could guarantee success. Finally Carnot determined upon a French expedition to Ireland and gave the command to the young Hoche, one of the most brilliant of the Republic's generals. On December 15th 1796 a fleet of forty-three ships, carrying 15,000 soldiers and ample arms, one of which carried Tone, sailed from Brest. After much bad seamanship part of it arrived in Bantry Bay on the 22nd, but again, as often before, the weather was for England, and a strong easterly gale which blew for a week made landing impossible. Grouchy, second-in-command, mismanaged everything, ship after ship made back for France, and Hoche himself, who never even reached the Irish coast, was the last to return on January 14th. The government was naturally delighted at the passing of such a peril, and most of all with the report that the Munster peasantry, led by the bishop of Cork and Lord Kenmare, had shown every sign of supporting the royal forces. It is a strange fact to look back upon that the Catholic towns of Cork, Galway, and Limerick were then the loyalist centres while Presbyterian Belfast was the rebel town.

The patriot phalanx in the Irish parliament made a last appeal to the government in March 1797 to calm and conciliate the country by repealing the Insurrection act and accepting a Reform of parliament and a final removal of religious disabilities. In the British parliament Fox also pleaded against a great majority for conciliation measures in Ireland. But from the King downwards it was clear that such measures were not to be hoped for. So between the government and the army the rising in Ireland became inevitable. When their proposals were defeated on May 15th by 170 votes to 30, Grattan, Ponsonby, and their minority left the House in despair, and constitutional reform was totally abandoned. The executive now had in its ranks Viscount Castlereagh, as Secretary for Ireland, who was as firm as Fitzgibbon on repression and later the necessity of a Union, but unlike him favoured Catholic emancipation. One cannot doubt that as things stood a French invasion on a large scale, especially if the French could have kept the sea, would have led to the greatest rising in Irish history and might have secured the independence of Ireland. But it seems equally certain that had the King's government in Ireland at this time conceded full emancipation to the Catholics, reformed to some extent the corrupt state of parliament, widened the vote, and granted the oppressed peasantry some lightening of their miserable condition under landlords and tithe-proctors, a rebellion would either not have taken place or would have been of a limited character.

The second great attempt on the part of France was when a Franco-Dutch fleet of the Batavian Republic collected at the Texel in June 1797 to convey 14,000 men to Ireland. On October 11th 1797 it was met and defeated by Admiral Duncan at Camperdown, and henceforth French aid to Ireland was insignificant. With the death of Hoche, Bonaparte was left supreme among the generals of France and he thought little of the chances of success in Ireland or the ability of the Irish leaders.

The last parliament of the old Kingdom of Ireland began its first session on January 9th 1798. It was, as before, a body little representative of the country and full of members from unimportant towns and of placemen who made up some one-third of the House. It is true that some 30,000 Catholics had been added to the voters, but their votes were too few and recent to produce much effect. This parliament was destined to pass, or rather to have forced upon it, the legislative Union with Great Britain and to watch the course and suppression of the Insurrection of '98.

The military command of Ireland had been in the hands of Lord Carhampton. He was superseded in December 1797 by Sir Ralph Abercrombie, who found the army so disgracefully undisciplined that in a general order of February 26th 1798 he declared it to be 'in such a state of licentiousness as must render it formidable to every one but the enemy'. This honourable Englishman was not to the taste of the ruling junta; he was compelled to resign and his place was taken by General Lake, who applied to the country at large the methods he had used in Ulster. Floggings, burnings, tortures, the shooting and hanging of men, were now a fate that even the most innocent might fear from hordes of soldiery living at 'free quarters' and without control. No wonder that retaliation followed and that savagery and outrage on the military side was answered on that of the rebels.

The Directory of the United Irishmen could not count upon French aid and therefore determined on a rising without it. A general insurrection was planned for May 23rd, but the government struck at once, for its spies were many, and arrested the leaders, so that the Rebellion was deprived at one blow of its organizers. The Sheares brothers suffered on the gallows-tree. Lord Edward Fitzgerald died of wounds inflicted on him when he was arrested. Wolfe Tone was in France. But a rising broke out on May 24th. Munster and Connaught remained for the most part quiet, but at various points of Meath, Leinster, and Ulster poorly armed bodies took the field, who were soon suppressed and on several occasions simply massacred by the mounted troops. In Antrim and Down several thousand Presbyterian farmers, mixed with some Catholics, turned out. But the most determined, indeed

M

the only formidable, rising took place in the quarter where no one would have expected it. County Wexford had been in the days of Strongbow planted with Normans, Flemings, and Saxons, and though the northern parts were Irish, the southern baronies were still occupied by an Old English population speaking an old-fashioned Saxon dialect. The Defenders had been strong among these sturdy peasants, and as often happened they blended themselves with the United Irishmen. The government troops practised in this county the same methods which disgraced them in other parts, and their conduct was especially aggravated by the fact that they were largely Orange yeomen who treated it as a religious war. The Catholic leaders in Dublin had assured the government of their loyalty, but in Wexford several priests were found who either sympathized with the people or at least urged them to go out and die like men. On May 26th a rebellion began in Wexford led by Father John Murphy of Boolavogue, who proved himself a very able leader, which was not suppressed till June 30th. In various engagements the Wexford men, who were generally armed only with pikes but had a few hundreds of expert musketeers, defeated small bodies of the troops, acquired confidence, and increased in numbers, until they occupied the town of Wexford and held most of the county. To maintain their cause, however, it was necessary to cut their way out to the surrounding counties, but several determined battles failed to give them the opening that they needed. On June 1st they were defeated at Newtownbarry in an attempt to force their way into Wicklow. Two days later another large body attacked Gorey so as to find a way along the coast to Dublin, won the day, but did not make use of their triumph. The most determined battle was at New Ross, where the rebels were commanded by a Protestant leader, Bagenal Harvey, on June 4th. Here some 1,400 soldiers under General Johnson held the town and defended the river Barrow, beyond which lie the counties Waterford and Kilkenny. The rebels were probably ten times as numerous but were for the most part mere pikemen. Their constant and gallant charges finally carried them into the town, but after hours of fighting the troops rallied and the rebels, many of whom had abandoned themselves to drink and plunder, were driven out and it is calculated that over 2,000 of them were left dead.

The formidable numbers of the rebels, 'led on by desperation and enthusiasm', as Camden described them, greatly increased the alarm of the government and showed what would have happened had the other provinces equalled the fighting spirit of Leinster. On June 9th another rebel army, led by Father Michael Murphy, made a determined attack on Arklow. This town was defended by 1,600 militia and yeoman under General Needham, who had to bear the onslaught of some 19,000 desperate but ill-armed peasants. Here again after several hours' fighting and almost carrying the British defences they recoiled, disheartened by the death of their leader. Possession of artillery, muskets, and fortified positions naturally gave the government troops an advantage which outweighed the numbers of their opponents. In Wexford it was clear that it was a religious rising and Catholic sentiment animated the rebel forces. But unhappily the Rebellion degenerated everywhere into a war of 'Orange and Green' between two kinds of Irishmen, a sad awakening from the ideals of the United Irishmen.

By this time thousands of English militia were on their way to Ireland. The Wexford rebels made Vinegar Hill at Enniscorthy their head-quarters, but this was stormed on June 21st by General Lake with an army of 13,000. Wexford town was recovered, and the rebellion in the county came to an end. Executions followed, among whom there suffered Bagenal Harvey. One remnant of the Wexford army under Father John Murphy penetrated into county Kilkenny hoping to raise the people, but after a defeat made their way home and dispersed, while Father Murphy was captured and executed without pity. A few other local engagements followed, but after July 2nd only a small remnant kept up the fight, made their way into the Wicklow hills, and for some time under Joseph Holt and Michael Dwyer kept up a guerrilla warfare.

The viceroy Camden was replaced in June 1798 by Lord Cornwallis, who combined the two offices of Lord Lieutenant and Commander-in-Chief. He was an experienced and humane soldier and issued a general pardon as soon as it was possible.

Ulster had been too disarmed and broken to be formidable, but three small battles took place in counties Antrim and Down, where the rebels were mainly Presbyterians. Those of Antrim were led by Henry Joy McCracken while those of Down selected Henry Monroe as their leader. On June 7th the town of Antrim was attacked by several thousands of insurgents who were finally repulsed, and McCracken suffered death for the cause at Belfast. In Down there was an engagement at Saintfield and a final pitched battle at Ballinahinch on June 13th. Monroe showed some military skill and the rebels the usual headlong courage of Irish pikemen against artillery, but they were finally routed with the loss of several hundreds. Monroe too paid the death penalty, and the Presbyterian rising came to an end. The Catholic nature of the peasant revolt in Wexford disenchanted most of them, who had hoped for an all-Ireland rising without regard to men's religious beliefs.

On July 17th an Act of Amnesty was carried in the Irish parliament and led to the general submission of the Leinster and other rebels. But when it was too late French aid again revived the embers. On August 22nd a force of 1,000 Republican soldiers landed in Killala Bay under General Humbert, which was joined by many unarmed peasants, marched inland, and defeated a large mixed force at Castlebar, but was soon surrounded by Cornwallis at Ballinamuck, and forced to surrender. Later, of several ships that had been dispatched, the *Hoche* arrived in Lough Swilly but had to surrender to an English squadron and Wolfe Tone was taken and conveyed to Dublin. He could hardly have expected his life, nor did he seek it; he only asked to be shot like a soldier in view of the French officer's uniform that he wore. He was, however, sentenced by a court martial to be hanged like a common criminal and therefore inflicted a wound on himself of which he perished in his pride on November 19th 1798.

The imprisoned United Irish leaders were offered their lives on condition of revealing the secrets of their movement. They refused to do so though they were ready to justify their motives, and were finally sent as State prisoners to Fort George in Scotland. Released some years afterwards, several of them, such as Thomas Addis Emmet, emigrated, and died in America. Most of them had begun as mere reformers and liberals and would have been contented had liberality and humanity existed in the Government. Their final fate of exile was far happier, however, than that of the hundreds of common Irishmen who were sent to Botany Bay or forced into the army and navy.

The Rebellion over, what remained was to settle a disordered country and consider the future government of Ireland. Grattan and his remnant still thought that conciliation might appease the country and preserve the Constitution, while prominent men in the Protestant ascendancy, such as Foster and Parnell, argued that there was no need for a change considering that the Irish Parliament and the Protestant gentry with their yeomen and militia had suppressed a most dangerous rebellion. But the ruling junta was now bent upon a Union with Great Britain as the only safe means of maintaining the Protestant constitution and England's imperial control. On this Cornwallis, Castlereagh, and Fitzgibbon were united, and Pitt strongly took the same course. The two sections of the population that Tone had striven to unite, the unprivileged Roman Catholics and Presbyterians, had now been crushed and the latter disillusioned. A huge British army held Ireland down and prevented even free political discussion and action, while large numbers of the propertied classes, both Catholic and Protestant, had been terrified into a state of mind which favoured a Union. Lord Camden had said, 'Ireland is like a ship on fire, it must be either extinguished or cut adrift'. The rebel leaders had failed to sever it from England, it now remained to grapple it to England's side. In the dead lull that followed the events of 1795–1798 the stage was occupied entirely by the two governments, bent on Union, and the Irish parliament, offering a varied resistance.

To Pitt the Union was an imperial necessity. The Rebellion was a moral pointing out how the Kingdom of Ireland could not have survived without British aid. The rebellious elements had received French aid and might do so again. How could a separate Irish parliament and the Constitution of '82 be maintained in face of this danger? Emancipation and the extension of the franchise were bound to come, but supposing pro-French Catholics and democratic Dissenters got a majority in the Irish parliament how long would the Anglican monopoly in Church and State survive? The panacea for all was a legis-lative Union. In the united Parliament of Great Britain and Ireland representatives of the Catholics might safely be admitted for they would always be a minority. The Church of Ireland, threatened by three-quarters of the people, could only be saved by a union of the two State churches. Once the Imperial government was entrusted with the complete control of the three Kingdoms and no longer menaced on the west by Irish nationalism, whether extreme or moderate, it would be able from Westminster to combine the whole force of these islands against France. A modern statesman, in return for such advantages for his side, would think it necessary to offer all-round terms in order to secure general consent. But this was not only an oligarchic age but one threatened by Revo-lution, in which the people were a danger to be suppressed, and the peasant must be content with his hard lot. The chief, indeed the main, thing to be overcome was the separate Irish Parliament, the citadel of the Protestant ascendancy, from which the King's viceroy distributed a rich and unceasing stream of jobs, pensions, offices, and titles. It had to be simply bought out. Had it been a body elected under a general fran-chise, to bribe its electors would have been almost impossible, and it is certain that their consent could have not been got otherwise. But it was not so, and the corrupt state of parlia-ment within and the limited number of voters outside enabled the Union to be successfully carried. It proved the former contention of Grattan, Flood, and Tone that only by Reform could the Constitution of '82 be made safe and permanent.

As it was, the majority of its 300 members *could* be bought out by present bribes or future prospects. Buying out the 'fee simple of Irish corruption' was a costly business, but money could be found for it. Outside forces had at least to be con-sidered or propitiated. The Irish Parliament had made the country prosperous by paternal legislation and the whole system of protective acts and bounties. Hence the merchant and manufacturer class was against the Union, unless it could be shown that they would benefit by full admission through Empire trade and free commerce with Great Britain. The Bar was also pro-Ireland, for great and many emoluments flowed from the separate judiciary which the Kingdom of Ireland maintained. All these forces could pull strings and offer great obstruction. But the Roman Catholics, though numbers of them had recently been admitted to the franchise, had almost no political power or influence; yet they were the majority and regarded themselves as the Old Irish nation. Their admission to full citizen rights had been one of the burning questions for thirty years, and it was recognized by all to be only a matter of time. Pitt, Castlereagh, and Cornwallis proposed to win them over to the Union by the undertaking that this measure would be followed by full emancipation in a united parliament. Horrified by the Rebellion and strongly anti-French, their bishops, clergy, and upper classes turned a favourable ear to what were mere promises which they might have insisted should form part of the actual Act of Union. As for the lower classes, they were beaten and cowed, nor, under the undemocratic system of the time, need such non-voters be considered. The separate Irish parliament could hardly be expected to swamp itself by the admission of Catholics and Dissenters, and only in a British Parliament would total emancipation be both possible and safe. Pitt and Cornwallis were sincere in wishing that emancipation should follow the Union, so that it might be 'a Union not with a party but with the Irish nation', which both had vision enough to see was mainly outside parliament. But Clare did not wish it so, and this adamant personality prevailed, at the cost of robbing the Union of all its national and statesmanlike appeal. Indeed one may go further and say that the Union was made from this point of view a shameful breach of faith, perhaps even worse than the Treaty of Limerick.

The Irish Parliament met for its last session on January 22nd 1799. Cornwallis brought forward the proposal for a Union, but when the debate on the Address came up the patriot remnant, Grattan, Plunket, and others, were joined by Sir John Parnell and other former Government supporters, and Sir Laurence Parsons's motion against the Union was carried by 109 votes to 104. Cornwallis, however, was determined not to spare men either on the right hand or the left. He at once dismissed Parnell, Chancellor of the Exchequer, and Fitzgerald, Prime Serjeant; on the other hand, he purged the Irish Cabinet of its reactionaries and the government became in fact himself, Castlereagh, and Clare. Pitt thus had an unyielding trio in power in Ireland, and it was announced that the proposal of a Union would be pressed on, no matter how often defeated, till it were carried. In the British House of Commons in February he carried resolutions for a Union, his arguments being the unsatisfactory settlement of 1782–1783, as illustrated by the Regency and other disputes, the necessity of a united front against France, the danger of the Protestant establishment in Ireland being overthrown, and the impossibility of full emancipation for the Roman Catholics except in a united legislature. On the British side the Union was carried by a great majority. On the Irish, however, a prolonged resistance held it up for a year, and its opponents had to be worn down or bought out. Placemen still numbered seventy-two; if loyal to Ireland they could be dismissed. The owners of eighty-four pocket or decayed boroughs might oppose the Union, but if they were offered compensation for this loss of property and influence they might prefer their pockets to their nation and their honour. The House of Lords offered no resistance to speak of, and when twenty-eight members of Parliament who were given peerages for their votes climbed up to it, they swamped it for the government.

Offices, pensions, threats of dismissal further helped to secure the majority, and the unbought members opposed in vain. The buying-out of the rest, as if the national parliament belonged to them, makes one of the most unpleasing pictures in history and disgusted even Cornwallis and those who did the buying.

Parliament was prorogued in June 1799, and in the months that followed offers to public opinion outside was one of the concerns of government. The Catholics were sounded, and their aristocratic leaders, such as Lords Kenmare and Fingall, readily said 'Yes'. To the Roman clergy the government gave what amounted to a promise that immediately upon the Union, though not forming part of the actual treaty, the Imperial government would offer a State provision for the clergy, along with the regulation of episcopal elections, and commutation of tithes. Thus Cornwallis endeavoured 'to give them the most favourable impression of the measure' without binding engagements, for the consent of the King and the British cabinet would have to be secured. At Maynooth in January 1799 a meeting of the bishops under Dr. Troy passed resolutions accepting the offer of State provision and admitting the right of the government in return to confirm the papal election of bishops and the appointment of the parish priests. To the Catholic laity was thrown out the prospect of admission to the Union parliament. They, however, were less complaisant than the bishops, for they represented an ancient nation, not only a Church, and the Dublin Catholics at a meeting in the Exchange declared as one man that the Union would mean the extinction of Ireland's liberty and denounced as a calumny the imputation that they could be induced to sacrifice the independence of their country. An impressive young barrister called Daniel O'Connell here made his maiden speech and passionately declared that he would sooner have the Penal laws back than lose the national parliament.

Apart from the Catholics and the ruling class there was a large Protestant population which was not so easily bought or intimidated and which was clearly in a majority against the Union. But 'the Will of the People' was a doctrine out of fashion and no suggestion was made that the Union should be submitted for approval to the whole nation. Indeed Pitt would not even consider having a general election and the return of a new parliament on this great issue. In the Commons Grattan's liberal remnant was reinforced by conservatives such as Parnell and Foster, proud of the Protestant constitution of '82, while outside parliament the Bar, the Dublin Catholics, and even the Orange order showed great hostility. But free expression of opinion and still more public indignation was hardly possible, for Ireland was held down by 100,000 troops. The Rebellion had failed; the United Irish Society, though thousands secretly belonged to it, was a broken force;

and the brutal victors in the late civil war did not mean to permit public meetings. Inside the House all that Grattan and his party could say or do did not avail to shake the ministerial intention. When Parliament met on January 15th 1800, the government was certain of its majority. Creations and promotions in the peerage amounted to forty-eight, the buying out of the pocket boroughs was to cost £1,260,000, and office-holders were to get compensation for their lost jobs.

On September 5th 1800 Castlereagh outlined the proposals of the Union. Ireland was to be represented in the Imperial parliament by a hundred members and in the House of Lords by thirty-two peers. The Churches of England and Ireland were to be united and the Anglican establishment in Ireland to be maintained. The viceregal office and courts of Law were to remain. As regards trade, there was to be free commerce between both countries and the full trade of the Empire was opened to Ireland, but certain bounties, as for example on linen, were to be retained in the interests of Ireland. As regards imperial contributions, Ireland was to share for twenty years in the general expenses of the Empire in the proportion of two to fifteen, after which the matter should be re-opened. During that time she was to retain her Exchequer and a separate National Debt. All members of the united parliament were to take the oath which excluded Roman Catholics. But the forty-shilling freehold in the counties and the vote in the boroughs, as restored to the Catholics in 1793, was maintained. On June 7th the Bill was carried on a third reading, this time by 153 to 88, and on August 1st it received the royal assent.

The dramatic protests of the last scenes have often been described. Grattan's lament for the Constitution that he more than other men had created was a noble piece of eloquence, mingled with hope for the nation that yet outlasted it: 'Yet I do not give up my country. I see her in a swoon but she is not dead; though in her tomb she lies helpless and motionless, still on her lips is the spirit of life and on her cheeks the glow of beauty.' It was a fine dirge for the Irish Protestant nation which he at least had striven to broaden and make real by the

admission of representatives of every creed. Yet the after-
thought remains that this nation of a minority, for all its
merits and in spite of all it did for Ireland, was from first to
last an upper-class oligarchy based on a particular creed and
not even representing the whole of it. To secure the Union,
Pitt had to buy it out, and whatever he might say in the
English parliament he knew in his heart that the Union was
not 'a treaty between the two nations'. It has certainly never
been regarded so in Ireland, and with calm judgment one
may say that had it not been a time of rebellion followed by
a military terrorism the Union, even if attempted, would
not have succeeded. Pitt and Cornwallis were English gentlemen who did not relish the way the Rebellion was crushed or
the Union carried, but Fitzgibbon unblushingly justified it all.
They intended to complete the Union by making good their
promises to the Catholics. Early in 1801, after the Union was
safe, Pitt proposed to the King on behalf of the ministry and
as part of the Union measures the admission of the Catholics
to parliament, with the removal of tests for office, and State
provision and regulation for the Roman Catholic bishops and
clergy. George's dull and obstinate mind was now constantly
on the verge of insanity and it was his fixed idea that consent
to Catholic emancipation would constitute a breach of his
coronation oath. He was now strengthened in this opinion
by the Chancellor, Lord Loughborough, a member of the
Cabinet but an enemy of Pitt, but Fitzgibbon had already
made up his mind for him in 1795. He answered Pitt at once
that his coronation oath prevented him from discussing such
a proposition, 'which tended to destroy the groundwork of our
happy constitution'. To oppose the King's will was not
merely a ticklish matter but it might throw him off his mental
balance again. So Pitt dropped the subject and sent the King
an assurance that during his Majesty's reign he would never
again raise the Catholic question. In this way Catholic emancipation, which should have been carried in 1793, was nearly
carried in 1795, and was distinctly promised in 1799, was
dropped till 1829. It added to the many great lost oppor-
tunities of Irish history, the things not done when they should
have been done and then done too late for any gratitude.

Pitt's memory must bear most of the blame. He had not pledged his whole cabinet on the question, he had not consulted or informed the King sufficiently and so had roused the dull old monarch's stubborn pride. Yet he was England's political master and could still have carried the day. When George raised the objection that his coronation oath in conscience bound him to maintain the established religion and the disabling acts, Pitt might well have answered that Parliament, which had in 1689 imposed this oath on the King, could also in 1800 relieve him from it. But the hopes of Ireland and the rights of her people had to be abandoned because of the stupid prejudice of a King, because of English party politics, and because of Protestant dominance and gentlemanly agreements 'to drop things' in Downing Street. It was a lesson that Ireland had painfully to learn over and over again in the course of the next century.

CHAPTER XVIII

FROM THE UNION TO 1848

WITH the Union the Kingdom of Ireland as vested in the Monarchy and Parliament since 1540 came to an end, the separate government by the King, Lords, and Commons of Ireland ceased, and the political connexion with England was expressed legally as the United Kingdom of Great Britain and Ireland. With the separate Crown passed away the nobility and aristocratic rule, for there was no reason for noblemen's seats in the capital once the legislature had departed. Only the office and name of Viceroy, a Privy Council, a number of necessary officials, the Established Church, and a judiciary left complete and imposing, remained to tell of the former Kingdom of Ireland. For Dublin the change meant one from a prosperous and stately capital to that of a dull provincial city with a stagnant trade. Parliament House became the new Bank of Ireland and the splendid insignia and trappings of the two Houses the perquisites of former peers and officials. Of the stirring age from 1780 onwards most of the chief actors had gone, and the death of Clare in 1802 removed the principal author of the change, but Grattan still urged the Catholic cause in the united Parliament.

The Union had not been a treaty made with the Irish people, and even had it been so the national sense would probably have resented it later. But the failure to carry out on the British side the promises that were made to the Catholic majority deprived it of its greatest argument from the first. Indeed the history of the next forty years is simply a commentary on the fact that the British Crown, the ministries, and the parties at Westminster were averse to, or by the party game chose not to satisfy, Ireland's just expectations. These promises which took so long to fulfil had embraced full Catholic emancipation, State provision for the Catholic clergy, and the settlement of the Tithe question, thus offering hopes to the Catholic upper and middle classes and even to the peasantry.

Ireland was now a nation of $4\frac{1}{2}$ millions, of whom more than half lived in poor habitations with only one hearth and existed mainly on potatoes, but it was a race which felt itself an ancient nation, and in spite of two centuries of oppression was naturally high-spirited and intelligent. The 'predominant partner', England, now had on her hands a problem greater than before. Would rule from Westminster prove better than rule from College Green? Would the Imperial government be content with merely having solved the danger of a possibly independent Ireland or would the wisdom of her rulers and the conscience of her people seek to lift Ireland out of all those injustices which could be directly traced to English mis-government? The aristocratic and unreformed government of England lasted till 1832 and at least in this period settled the Catholic question. After the Reform act of 1832 the great middle class of England got their share of political power but the common people not till 1867 and 1884. Unfortunately the strong Protestant prejudice of the middle and even of the upper class was stubbornly opposed to the Catholic spirit of Ireland, though it could be generous enough in money charity at periods of famine and distress.   The House of Lords, a far more formidable barrier, also now appeared as the great enemy of Irish demands and continued for a century to impose its veto on Bills passed by the lower House on the three great questions of the land, the Established Church, and the restoration of Irish self-government.

Out of a total membership of some 660 the Irish members in the Union House of Commons were 100 and were thus in a permanent minority. For nearly thirty years, except for such men as Grattan, they were not representative of the unprivileged classes in Ireland, and it was not till a great party leader arose in O'Connell that the tactical advantage of a pledged Irish party in Parliament was realized.

The insurrection of Robert Emmet in 1803 was a belated flash out of the failure of '98 and a protest of a young Protes-tant idealist of the same calibre as Wolfe Tone and the United Irishmen, among whom his own brother Thomas Addis had been prominent. Rebellion under the circumstances could only be a protest, for Ireland was still held down by a large army and by an Insurrection Act. The young hero's death on the scaffold, the moving verses written on him by his friend Thomas Moore, and the idealism of the whole affair places it in the realm of poetry and tragic romance rather than politics, but as a solemn sacrifice the execution of Emmet has had an effect on Irish political sentiment far beyond that of any act of Parliament or political event.

Under the dull rule of Lord Hardwicke and the Duke of Bedford, Ireland was a very dead country which it was the main aim of government to keep down by the Convention act, the suspension of Habeas Corpus, and the Coercion acts which make the melancholy story that from 1796 to 1823 only four or five years were of normal civil government. The justification was the simmering of armed revolt following on '98 and the continued agrarian disorder and crimes of the White-boys, 'Shanavests', 'Caravats', and other peasant bodies protesting against tithes, rents, and their other oppressions. Pitt died in 1806, having done nothing on the Catholic question; though admitting the justice of a Catholic petition, he could only reply, 'Time must always enter into questions of expediency.' English statesmen, whose country was in a more static condition, could not be made to understand the urgency of Irish questions, and this alone was a bad omen for the Union. It can hardly be doubted that the best government for Ireland for the time would have been a firm, autocratic, just, and reforming administration, continuous and independent of party politics, and addressing itself mainly to the needs cf the depressed population.

Of the three Churches traditional in Ireland, only the Established Protestant one was highly endowed and controlled by the State and formed what men like Castlereagh called and valued as 'an ecclesiastical aristocracy'. The Presbyterian had for a century received a modest endowment called the *Regium donum* of some £2,000 or £3,000 yearly, but this had done little to win the loyalty of their body and a number of their ministers had been implicated in 1798 and one even publicly executed. The failure of the Rebellion and the religious note that had been given to it had left the Presbyterians depressed and disillusioned over the union of all

Irishmen irrespective of religion. In 1802 the government increased the *Regium donum* very considerably and in future payments were made to Presbyterian ministers, on scales ranging from £50 to £100, paid directly from the State if the government were satisfied of the particular minister's loyalty. Thus were the clergy of the Presbyterian Church to be made a second 'ecclesiastical aristocracy' and weaned for good from all disloyalty. For all that, democratic sentiment and a desire for religious equality continued to be strong in the North, where the Dissenters also had their own disabilities. The Roman Catholic Church of the vast majority alone now depended on its flocks for maintenance, but at the time of the Union offers had been made of State provision along with Government regulation of episcopal appointments. The bishops, who were conservative and loyal, were well disposed, but the laity, as represented by Daniel O'Connell, were opposed to seeing their Church also harnessed to the State, and the new type of priesthood, educated at Maynooth instead of on the Continent, felt themselves too much at one with their people and their anti-English sentiments to wish to be made dependent on the government rather than on the people. This proved itself a stumbling-block in the way of Catholic Emancipation.

After the death of Pitt, emancipation was taken up again, and in 1807 Daniel O'Connell appeared as the dominant figure in a new Catholic Association. The great question was urged over and over again in Parliament. The Irish bishops seemed ready to accept the principle of a government Veto on episcopal appointments by the Pope, and acting upon this Grattan in 1808 presented a Catholic petition which the House rejected. But later in that year and in 1810 the Irish bishops refused the Veto proposal and this delayed emancipation, for Grattan and his supporters thought it fair that the Crown should have a control over the papal appointments. Grattan's bill of 1813, which gave all the later rights of 1829, practically passed, but when Canning got the royal Veto inserted in it, Grattan disclaimed it and the Bill dropped. In 1814 Monsignor Quarantotti, head of Propaganda and acting for the Pope in Rome, declared for the Veto, but was denounced by O'Connell.

who said, 'How dismal the prospect of liberty would be if in
every Catholic diocese there were an active partisan of the
Government and in every Catholic parish a priest as an active
informer.' The Veto question was thus defeated, at the cost
of alienating from O'Connell, Lord Fingall and the Catholic
peers in Ireland and Grattan in Parliament. The latter
continued, however, 'with a desperate fidelity' to serve the
Catholic cause till his death in 1820. O'Connell was making
an Ireland very different from the Whig, aristocratic, and
rational eighteenth century that Grattan had adorned. Nevertheless to the nationalists of his time, such as the poet Moore,
Grattan was the noblest figure in the great age that had now
ended. He had written of himself in 1810 the best tribute that
could be paid him: 'I hope I shall now as at all other times
prove myself an Irishman, that Irishman whose first and last
passion was his native country.'

In 1815 the final overthrow of Napoleon brought to an end
the great Revolutionary age that had begun in 1792. The
reactionary monarchies were restored all over Europe and a
period of unsteady peace set in, but in spite of the Grand
Alliance of emperors and kings middle-class revolutionary or
reforming temper was soon to be found everywhere. In
Ireland as in England economic distress set in, for the Corn
laws had brought agricultural prosperity with high rents and
prices for landlords and farmers, and Ireland had done well out
of the high prices prevalent in war. But the slump that follows
a war brought about a fall in the price of wheat, a return to
pasture, and unemployment for the peasant population which,
already large, was increasing fast. Agrarian discontent
expressed itself in crime and disorder and was suppressed by
Coercion acts, while at the same time an army of 25,000 men
garrisoned Ireland. A Bill of 1816 made easier still the already
great powers which landlords had in Ireland for the ejectment
of tenants in arrears of rent. In 1817 there was a partial
famine and another in 1822, due to the failure of the
potatoes, and England generously subscribed three-quarters
of a million pounds in charity. But Ireland needed more
lasting remedies.

In 1817 the two Exchequers were amalgamated, according to the terms of the Union. In 1793 the Irish National Debt was but 2¼ million pounds, but by 1817 it was 113 millions, for Ireland had to bear as a separate debt all the costs of the troubled times of rebellion and her contribution in the great war. Henceforth the National Debt was one for the whole of these islands, but it is certain that so poor a country as Ireland bore too much of the burden.

Until O'Connell became 'the Uncrowned King' of Ireland and until some nobler action from England could happen, a strong ascendancy spirit prevailed in the ruling class and magistracy of Ireland, who thought themselves the victors in the late rebellion, and the Orange order was widely spread over all the provinces. In Parliament, Plunket succeeded Grattan in the advocacy of the Catholic cause, and in February 1821 his resolutions in favour of Emancipation passed the House of Commons, but they contained the Veto clause to which O'Connell was obstinately opposed. In any case the House of Lords rejected the Bill, and this was the first case of their obstruction to a necessary Irish measure which was to continue for nearly a hundred years. Later in the year a royal visit of George IV to Ireland was the first sight of a king that Ireland had had since the Boyne. It aroused great enthusiasm, but unhappily neither George nor his successors William IV and Victoria had a genuine, as distinguished from an official, solicitude for Ireland. In the general neglect of Ireland there was nothing for it but agitation in the country itself to stir the official government into action.

The Catholic Association was suppressed in 1812 under the Convention act of 1796, and a mild 'Catholic Board' took its place which was divided on the question of the Veto, on which the Catholic gentry were on one side and O'Connell and the priesthood on the other. In 1823, however, a real forward body appeared in the 'Catholic Association of Ireland', led by O'Connell and Sheil. O'Connell, a clever lawyer, saw to it that it escaped coming under the Convention act by not claiming to be a representative body of delegates. Pledged to obtain emancipation by legal and constitutional measures, and confining itself to petitions and correspondence, the Association had members paying a modest annual subscription and a body of supporters throughout Ireland, where collectors in every parish collected what was called the 'Catholic Rent' of poor supporters at a penny per month. The movement spread like the heather alight, and with the funds thus raised the Catholic cause could be advanced in the newspapers in both countries, popular opinion formed, and the unjust proceedings of landlords and Orangemen contested in the courts.

O'Connell, the son of a small Catholic landlord in Kerry, a native speaker of Irish, a man of tall and commanding presence with a magnificent voice which tens of thousands could hear, a born organizer of open-air mass meetings and party conventions, and a sincere though not bigoted son of the people's religion, was destined to bring a totally new spirit into Irish affairs. Emancipation to the upper and middle classes meant admission to the army, parliament, government, and professions, but to the masses it meant the liberation of the peasant from local tyranny. For the ignorant, ill-used, and Gaelic-speaking masses of the Irish people, a new Moses arose who was neither of the Court, the government, the parliament, nor the Protestant ascendancy. The law had for ages done nothing for the poor earth-tiller, in fact it had continued to make his lot even harder, and now it was realized that deliverance could only be looked for in forming into mass to overbear the law and the government. The people found a national hero such as they had not had since Sarsfield, and him and his condemnation of disorder and vengeance they obeyed, though Insurrection acts could not make them do so. In the Catholic Association they found popular amateur tribunals whose decisions they obeyed as they would not obey the State courts. In the former century Dean Swift and the liberal Protestant Grattan had first stirred their hope or at least their interest. Wolfe Tone and his Protestant republican idealists, had the rebellion been effective, would certainly have been followed into battle by great masses of the Gaelic peasantry. But these men were not of their own religion or class, and in O'Connell they found a man who could speak to their hearts. O'Connell was indeed no friend to the Gaelic past, and though he could and often did address crowds in Irish he told them that the old language was a barrier to modern progress.

He believed in Ireland a Nation and the union of all Irishmen as much as Wolfe Tone, but he opposed rebellion and force, expressed sincere loyalty to the Crown, and stated that Irish freedom was not worth the shedding of a single drop of blood. Up to this time the masses of the Old Irish knew nothing of the English Crown, of politics or parliaments; they harboured old poetic ideas of a Stuart return and later hopes of a French invasion, and meanwhile did their best to defy the law and seek redress in secret societies. Such Gaelic songs and verses as survive of '98 have the old note of a leaderless and depressed nation which was still monarchic and aristocratic in feeling, Gaelic in speech, and ready to fight the old fight in arms again. Under O'Connell they were led into new ways of English speaking, of party politics, with the Catholic sentiment dominant, and of leadership by political organizers and parish priests. The Protestant aristocrat, the middle-class Liberal, and even the Catholic peer and bishop lost that leadership which they had in fact only half-heartedly attempted. The Union with England and the difficulty of securing redress from distant Westminster unfortunately made politics necessary in Ireland and turned the eyes of the race for a whole century towards England until politics became a passion to which true nationalism was sacrificed.

O'Connell once declared that 'nations have been driven mad by oppression', but he taught Ireland to trust to methods which no army could be called on to suppress. In 1825 Parliament passed a Suppression act which ended the Catholic Association, but by skilful reorganization it emerged as a new 'constitutional' society whose first object was to 'promote concord among all classes of Irishmen'. Its strength was soon put to the test on the emancipation question. The Catholics had got the vote in 1793 and there were now 100,000 forty-shilling freeholders in the counties, but as they were practically the slaves of their landlords they generally voted as they were told. But at the Waterford election in 1826 Lord George Beresford, whose family owned a large part of the county, was to his surprise and indignation rejected in favour of a liberal Protestant, Villiers Stuart. It was a sign that the feudal bond, which rested on fear more often than affection, was weakening.

In 1828 the Duke of Wellington became Prime Minister with Sir Robert Peel as Chief Secretary for Ireland. Emancipation seemed bound to come, though it had the Crown, the House of Lords, and great public opinion in Britain against it, but it was made inevitable here and now by the Clare election of July 1828, where O'Connell was elected on the limited franchise of the time by 2,057 votes to 982 cast for Vesey FitzGerald.

This remarkable victory had been wrested from a whole official opposition by a leader who owed almost nothing to the ascendancy, by a priesthood who wished to owe nothing to the State and who had moved through the ranks of the voters urging on them that it was a fight for the Faith, and by a disciplined and sober crowd of small farmers who had long been helots, but now under the teaching of the 'Liberator' dared to have 'a public mind and a public spirit'. The Parliamentary declaration of 1692 still barred the victor, but it was clear that Ireland's cause was won. In March 1829 Peel proposed the abolition of tests for office and parliament, and Wellington, remembering that he was an Irishman too, declared the only alternative was civil war. In April the Emancipation bill passed the House of Lords, which, like the Crown, had to yield to such a solemn warning, but, with a display of that niggling and half-measures spirit which was long to spoil such concessions, Peel saw to it that the forty-shilling freeholders were deprived of the vote, and the franchise raised to ten pounds. The Catholic Association was also dissolved. Nevertheless the Constitution was at last opened to the loyal upper-class Catholics of England and Ireland, reserving in Protestant hands the Monarchy and the offices of Regent, Lord Lieutenant, and Chancellor of England. A new oath of allegiance displaced the former declarations, and the removal of the Sacramental test for Parliament finally emancipated Protestant Dissenters. But while the law now opened public and municipal posts to Catholics and others, admission to them was controlled by a caste which was reluctant to share them, and it was long before the majority could secure their share in public jobs from the hands of the ascendancy which had been in the saddle since 1660.

On the death of George IV in 1830 the Whigs came in after an exclusion of fifty years, and Lord Grey's Reform act of 1832 began a middle-class age in England, which, however, with its strong Protestant and Anglo-saxon prejudice was scarcely a better friend to Ireland than aristocracy had been. A Reform act was passed for Ireland which gave the parliamentary vote to £10 householders in towns, and in the counties to £10 freeholders and leaseholders of £20 and upwards. Attempts to settle the Tithe question and to reform the Established Church, which, it had to be admitted, was only the Church of a minority, failed and gave more argument to O'Connell's demand for the Repeal of the Union which was his next great cause. In 1831 Chief Secretary Stanley introduced a system of National Education to meet the popular need and the Catholic demand for religious instruction. The system became a great success as an educational one, but it had fatal effects on the Irish language and the old Gaelic tradition. According to Thomas Davis, at this time the vast majority of the people living west of a line drawn from Derry to Cork spoke nothing but Irish daily and east of it a considerable minority. It seems certain that at least two millions used it as their fireside speech, and those of us who remember the old generation in the West who were born before the Famine cannot doubt that they had a great and tenacious affection for the ancient language. But the institution of universal elementary schools where English was the sole medium of instruction, combined with the influence of O'Connell, many of the priests, and other leaders who looked on Irish as a barrier to progress, soon made rapid inroads on the native speech and helped to extinguish that old 'Clanna Gael' pride and isolation which the mixed Norman-Irish race had long cherished.

The boasted 'Age of Reform' was slow to do anything really to appease Ireland. But at last some of the inevitable advance took place under the ministry of Lord Melbourne (1835-1841), during which the young and attractive Queen

Victoria succeeded her absurd old uncle William IV. A
Municipal Reform act in 1840 abolished the picturesque and
ancient but corrupt governing bodies of our greater towns and
provided a uniform constitution with a popular electorate.
The ascendancy had so far taken care to exclude Catholics
from office and freedom, but before long the latter soon began
to rule in their ancient cities and O'Connell became the first
Catholic mayor of Dublin for two centuries.

The Tithe question, which Grattan had first raised in 1787,
had been for long beyond all endurance, and a strike of peasant
Ireland, encouraged by the writings of Bishop Doyle, had now
made it impossible for these taxes to be collected. In the
course of this 'Tithe war' several armed encounters took place,
and at Carrickshock in Kilkenny in 1831 the police were routed
and eighteen of them killed. At last in 1838 a far from generous
Tithe act, which merged this exaction in the rent, removed
an old grievance out of politics. In 1838 a Poor Relief act
gave Ireland for the first time a system of poor law and
extended here the dreary and degrading workhouse system
recently set up in England. It was of course a bad time for
the poor, whether deserving or not and whether English or
Irish, a time too when if property was assailed in Ireland the
propertied classes in the sister-country would certainly rush
to its assistance.

For the first time since the Union an 'Irish party' now
appeared in parliament, due to the Reform act, led by O'Connell, and holding the balance between Whigs and Tories. In
return for O'Connell's support and promise to help in Ireland,
Melbourne for five years did his best to conciliate the country
in spite of the miserable give-and-take of the party game.
Lord Mulgrave, a noble-minded Viceroy, saw to it that Catholics and Protestants, rich and poor, were treated as equal
before the law, that the Orange spirit was discouraged, and
Catholics got a share in government and legal jobs. For this
policy, which met with the bitter opposition of landlords and
ascendancy men, a rare and upright minister was found in a
Scotsman, Thomas Drummond, under-secretary to Mulgrave,
a splendid administrator, fearless and just and inspired with
a deep sympathy for the poor. But his task was made easier

by the instructions given by the adored O'Connell to the people to keep quiet and trust to the law.

The country had in fact since 1796 been under a terrorism which survived both the Rebellion, the Union, and Emancipation, a terrorism in which the normal ascendancy was reinforced by an Orange bigotry which meant to keep the power in Protestant hands in spite of emancipation and to make rebels and 'Croppies' (for so they called the discontented) 'lie down', as their song ran. This menace did much to justify O'Connell's banding of the long-dispirited Irish majority and the fighting of the Catholic and peasant cause in every arena except the battle-field. But while he declared that federated Orangemen were regarded by the people as enemies and exterminators, he added: 'The Liberal Protestant is an object of great affection and regard from the entire Catholic population.'

For the first time now and, in a sense, for good, the terrorism was broken by Mulgrave, Drummond, the Attorney-general Perrin, and the Irish administration. The new police force, called the Royal Irish Constabulary, whose ranks were filled with native Irishmen, became a force of high efficiency for keeping order, though indeed it was more like an army, and later was used for eviction purposes and as the first line for suppressing rebellion. The Orange Order, which numbered 125,000 men, became discredited even though a royal duke commanded it, and was broken up in 1837, and not revived till 1845. The magistracy and local government were opened to Catholics and purged of party taint. On the other hand, the faction-fights, which showed what wild and lawless blood still survived in the old Milesian peasantry, were suppressed. To this appeasement contributed a noble friar, Father Mathew, whose Temperance crusade had marvellous, though unhappily temporary, results in weaning the people from the drinking habit which was common among all classes.

The highly endowed State Church remained one of those rusty chains which must be burst asunder if justice was to prevail for all Irishmen, and, while the Orange Order wanted to keep it intact, Catholics and Presbyterians were united against it. But Landlordism in the form it had assumed in Ireland was the more galling chain of everyday life. A French inquirer, Gustave de Beaumont, who visited us at this time, wrote that though he had seen the Red Indian in his forests and the negro in his chains, in Ireland he had seen 'the very extreme of human wretchedness'. Part of the genius of O'Connell lay in enlisting enlightened and liberal opinion in Europe on his side. There he was far more admired as a states-man and champion of liberty than in England, yet there were plenty of honest men in England too who admired and aided the Irish fight. Drummond was a type of this friend of Ireland, but when in 1837 he wrote to the Lord Lieutenant and grand jury of county Tipperary that peasant crime rose from peasant wrong and that 'Property had its duties as well as its rights', he roused astonished indignation from the people's masters. Unfortunately his early death in 1840, a bloodless martyr to this cause, removed a true friend of Ireland and left her to the politicians.

There was to O'Connell's mind the greatest chain of all left in the legislative union of Ireland and Great Britain, and while he was all against *national separation* he was now resolved to win back *national independence*. The Repeal of the Union filled the rest of his days, but the restoration of 'the Old House on College Green' was a greater task than two more generations of Irishmen by persuasion were able to achieve.

On the defeat of Melbourne and return to power of the Tories (1841–1846) under Peel, the 'Liberator' resumed outside action and with his Repeal Association roused the people to tremendous fervour. 'Monster meetings' were attended by thousands marching in military array though without weapons to some point where their beloved 'Dan' swayed them with an extraordinary blend of eloquence over Ireland and vitriolic or humorous, though often coarse, attacks on her enemies. On the sacred Hill of Tara it is said a quarter million of people listened to him. The greatest meeting of all was to be at Clontarf on October 8th 1843, but the government prohibited it and O'Connell ordered the people to stop their march and disperse; they obeyed though many believed he meant there 'to give them the word'. He and five others were next prose-cuted for conspiracy; they were condemned by a Protestant jury in Dublin, but the verdict was reversed in the House of Lords in September 1844. After such a failure O'Connell never recovered his unique leadership, and his magnificent health began to fail.

Concessions to Ireland, however, of the minor order continued, and in response to the demand for a popular university the 'Queen's colleges' were founded at Dublin, Cork, and Galway. But, being undenominational, they did not satisfy the Catholic prelates. And by now the great majority of the Irish people on the national question believed that the Union must go. How was this to be achieved? Ireland was destined to oscillate for a century between Repeal (in forms such as Federalism and Home Rule) to be won by consent with England, and Separation to be achieved by force. O'Connell had been the great advocate of the one method; a new generation now appeared of 'physical force men' with the aims and the principles of '98.

In 1842 the *Nation* newspaper was founded and the young men who wrote for it or surrounded it were called the 'Young Ireland Party'. Their leaders were mainly Protestants, inspired by the memory of the United Irishmen, with some Catholics such as Gavan Duffy. Among them Thomas Davis, a Trinity man, who died in early manhood in September 1845, has left the most moving memory since Robert Emmet though he was not destined to see Ireland in arms. The Young Irelanders believed that the first and last aim was 'National independence', compared to which 'Irish grievances' on the one hand and 'concessions from England' on the other were minor points. They were full of the romantic liberal nationalism of the time which animated men like Garibaldi and Kosciusko. Only one of them, Fintan Lalor, put forward as the first essential the securing of the peasant's right to his land. While they stood for the principles of Wolfe Tone and also honoured Grattan, they drew their inspiration from far back in Irish history and the Gaelic and Norman past, an inspiration expressed by the poet James Clarence Mangan and in the many stirring poems and ballads in popular metres which circulated from the *Nation* into every village of the land. To a large extent it was a revival of the Gaelic, militant, and aristocratic spirit, and the cult of 'the Dark Rosaleen', formerly expressed in the native tongue but now poured into the new mould of the English language which was steadily spreading among the common people.

At first Davis, John Mitchel, and the others of this party were willing to work with O'Connell, who naturally resented their arrival. But O'Connell had against him not only the extreme Protestant spirit, which took the form of violent hatred, but the hostility or suspicion of the liberal Protestant element which either had stood by Grattan or disliked the Catholic aspect of O'Connell's crusade and the way he had wrested the leadership out of the hands of the landlords and the patriots of the former generation.

Meanwhile Ireland was approaching the dreadful crisis of the 'Great Famine'. Her population in 1845 was about eight millions, of whom half were wretchedly poor and dependent on the potato for food, at a time when Ireland was intensely cultivated and some three-quarters of the soil was under wheat and other crops. The people depended almost entirely on the land without any outlet in industry, for the flourishing trades and industry of Ireland had since the Union suffered from the free import of English goods, manufactured under greater economic advantages, as well as from strikes and other local troubles. The day's pay of an Irish agricultural labourer ranged from a shilling in the more prosperous North to eight-pence in the South, though at harvest eighteen-pence was usual. Undoubtedly the country was over-populated, or rather its population was not based upon a proper and healthy economic system. In 1843 the Devon Commission made a report which, though it had no practical result, exposed the dangerously impoverished state of the people and the injustices of the landlord system. 'In England and Scotland', said the Duke of Newcastle, 'the landlords let farms, in Ireland they only let land', and the small farmer had been robbed of all tenant right.

In September 1845 the potato blight appeared and it was not till 1848 that the Great Famine ended in complete exhaustion. Peel was becoming a convert to Free Trade as against the Protection on which the wealth of Great Britain had been founded, and the state of Ireland was a final argument. In January 1846 he introduced a Bill for the repeal of the Corn laws for both countries; it was carried and along with the repeal of the Navigation acts opened up the British isles to the import of cheap corn from America. O'Connell was not to see the great disaster that ended his crusade for he died at Genoa in May 1847, a stricken invalid on his way to Rome.

Following on the failure of the potatoes a growing majority of the poor had to be kept alive by State aid or the private charity which came in generously from Great Britain and America. The Government retailed Indian meal from America at low prices and established relief works where starving men, if they had the strength, could earn ninepence or a shilling in the day and buy meal for their families. In the summer of 1847 it was calculated that 3 millions were being kept alive by public works or charity. The potato harvest, however, of that year was fairly good, and by March 1848 the worst was over. In the course of this dreadful visitation, by death from famine or fever or by emigration to America the population fell from over 8 millions to $6\frac{1}{2}$. The upward curve which had gone on since the Corn Laws began suddenly fell and a steady decline set in, so that by 1881 the population was only some 5 millions. Whatever the landlords may have been before, most of them had now done what they could as individuals for their people, and it is said that one-third of them emerged ruined. It was necessary for parliament in 1849 to pass an Encumbered Estates act allowing for the sale of the estates of ruined owners. Under this act great numbers of estates passed into new hands (the purchase-money by 1858 amounted to 23 million pounds) and great numbers of new landlords appeared, some of them English and Scotch, who, wishing to improve their estates, often evicted and ill-treated the tenants even more harshly than the landlords 'of the ould stock', whom the people often had cause to regret. But at least emigration relieved the pressure and diminished the number of tiny holdings. while day-wages slowly increased.

The Famine, the worst event of its kind recorded in European history at a time of peace, staggered the conscience of England

on the Irish question and caused Carlyle to write some of his
most burning pages. In Ireland it evoked sentiments ranging
from indignation down to rebellion. Many asked why was not
the abundant wheat and corn harvest used to feed the people,
instead of its being sent to England which was its chief market,
or otherwise used to pay landlords' rents? Some thought that
a continued Irish parliament, resident in Dublin, would have
seen that the people did not starve and that at least it could
not have handled the situation worse. Others replied that
after all Ireland had now the public wealth, capital, and
charity of England at its back, which as a self-managing small
country it could not have. Moderate men of the upper class
such as Smith O'Brien, a landlord in Clare, pointed out in
parliament the failure of the Union as regards Ireland, and
that while time after time measures which would have passed
an Irish parliament without difficulty were contemptuously
rejected in the British, coercive measures or Bills unacceptable
to Ireland were forced upon her by large majorities. The
extreme wing of the Young Ireland party turned to the idea
of arms. The events of the time seemed to give them hope,
for 1848 was a year in which the French monarchy fell at last
and other crowned heads had to fly from their capitals, and
even the Chartist movement in England seemed encouraging.
O'Brien, Meagher, and Dillon attempted a revolt in Munster
but it proved a lamentable failure, and the only armed encounter was at Ballingarry in Tipperary between O'Brien and
some half-armed peasants and a garrison of police on August
5th 1848, in which a handful of rebels were killed or wounded.
State trials followed, Smith O'Brien, Meagher, Duffy, and other
leaders were condemned to death, but the sentences were
commuted and they spent some years of imprisonment in
Tasmania and elsewhere. Mitchel had already under a Treason
Act been transported. This was the end of the Young Ireland
party. In the next year Queen Victoria visited Ireland and
received an enthusiastic welcome, but it was fifty years before
she came over again, and nothing effective was done to make
the monarchy popular and visible in the realm it had always
neglected.

CHAPTER XIX

FROM THE FAMINE TO PARNELL, 1848–1891

SELDOM has a nation experienced so definite an ending-point and a starting-point in its history as Ireland had in the Great Famine. The Repeal movement, the insurrectionary and even the constitutional agitation spirit all suddenly collapsed. The country lay prostrate, and in the course of a few years the population declined by some two millions. Emigration to America set in with a vast and steady flow (in 1852 there were two hundred and twenty thousand emigrants) and continuing for the next sixty years kept the population at home in a state of decline and made a greater Ireland in America of millions to whom Ireland has been either a passionate memory or an ancestral poetry. Those who emigrated did so for the most part at their own expense and in turn sent back the money for their relatives to follow them, so that the Irish in America have never felt gratitude to England even for that State-provided emigration which should have been an Imperial duty. Great numbers also crossed over into the English manufacturing towns or London. The support given by the Irish abroad in money to Irish political causes as well as to revolutionary agitation, and the way they have helped to make the Irish question a world one has been of momentous effect.

The departure of so many allowed what remained of the old Irish race more room on their own soil and there set in a rapid decrease of the poorer cabin homes and an increase in the larger holdings. But the repeal of the Corn Laws which permitted the free entry of cheap corn from abroad, though it did much good, was a blow to Irish tillage and meant that the land began to go back to pasture. There was thus less labour needed, and as there was none or little outlet of industry in the towns there was much distress on the land. The new landlords under the Encumbered Estates act were an 'improving' race and in many cases used the powers which the law gave them to clear off their tenants, so that the Famine was followed by a huge increase in evictions. This found retaliation in Ribbonism and continued agrarian combinations marked by much crime and disobedience to the law, which again brought on Coercion acts or the suspension of Habeas Corpus. It was a dead time in politics, but the Land question was one of grim reality and was destined to be dominant for fifty years.

The Great Famine also had a fatal effect upon the old Gaelic language and tradition. Those who have talked with aged survivors of the times before the famine understand what a change then took place in the numbers who spoke Irish and in the purity and richness with which it was spoken and the poetry and folklore that was embodied in it. The losses by famine, fever, and emigration were greatest among the cottar class and in the most Gaelic parts of the country. In Mayo and Kerry, for example, the population fell by over half. The small labourer type that in the eastern counties still spoke Irish was almost wiped out or ceased to find employment as tillage declined, and within fifty years county Meath, for example, ceased to be an Irish-speaking district. Though Munster and Connacht, Donegal, and other sea-board counties continued up to our times strongly native-speaking, the decline finally affected them also, and by 1900 it left only a few counties with a large Irish-speaking population. It is one of the hardest tasks of our modern Government to turn back the tide which has ebbed so strongly and suddenly in the language which dominated Ireland for two thousand years The decay in the language was also aided by the use of English by political leaders, especially by the great O'Connell and the Young Ireland party. Political agitation had to be in English, for the eyes of Ireland were turned towards Westminster. It must be admitted that the Catholic Church of the majority of the Irish people has been indifferent, if not hostile, to the old tongue. A great attempt made from 1840 to 1850 to win over the Irish peasantry to the Established Church through the medium of their own language failed in that object, but unfortunately struck a further blow at the language when the priests adjured the people to abandon it lest it should be the vehicle of their conversion. Strong as Nationalism has remained in Ireland, unfortunately the language has not been a vital part of the national cause, and the English language has become that of patriotism, politics, religion, and even of the fireside, among the great majority of the Irish race.

An Irish Franchise act of 1850, though of a limited nature, raised the total electorate to some one hundred and sixty thousand voters and enabled an Irish party to hold together in Westminster, but it was not till after 1884 that practical manhood suffrage gave popular sentiment full play in politics. Remedies for the land laws in Ireland were obviously necessary but were barred by the general spirit of the age which believed in the sanctity of Property, a spirit which often regarded 'tenant-right as landlord-wrong'. The propertied classes in both countries looked upon Irish agitation as a blow to the foundations of society, and the House of Lords could always put its veto on measures for tenant relief. Yet, as Lord Dufferin showed in the House of Lords, the new landlords were harder masters than those of the old stock who, even if the tenant had little legal right, recognized customary and unwritten right. Now the tenantry had the right to ask 'that legal right under definite law should now become the substitute for equitable right under uncertain custom'.

In 1850 the Tenant Right League was formed with the object of securing for the tenant fair rent and security from capricious eviction, but though at the General Election of 1852 the League returned a party of fifty to Parliament its three-years' agitation was a failure. Some dreary years followed in which agrarian outrage was constant and on the other hand the spirit of Orangeism which had now entrenched itself mainly in the North brought a new and invincible spirit of opposition into Irish politics. Such evictions on a large scale as those of the Adare estate of Glenveigh in Donegal in the winter of 1860–1861 added to the bitterness which was to culminate later in a Land war. In spite of many honourable exceptions and although many of them were of the old Gaelic, Norman, and Elizabethan stock the final verdict must be pronounced of the Irish landlord class that they were, as De Beaumont called them, *une mauvaise aristocratie.*

A nobler, if for the time it seemed an impossible, spirit came into Ireland with the Fenian insurrectionary movement. The Irish Republican Brotherhood was founded in Dublin in 1858, and thousands of emigrants who fought in the American civil war pledged themselves to return and fight for Ireland. The Republican ideal had begun with the Protestant Wolfe Tone; it was now taken up by Catholic Irishmen and remained the other wing to the constitutional Home Rule movement up to our own times. The Fenians (whose name was derived from the famous 'Fianna' of Irish legend with their commander Finn MacCool) despised both constitutional agitation and 'concessions from England' and set the old claim of National independence above all minor questions. Their newspaper, the *Irish People*, revived among the masses the ideal of Ireland a nation, and in Stephens, O'Leary, O'Donovan Rossa, Kickham and their band were found romantic leaders. At the close of the American war the Fenians were numerous in Ireland and England, but the Government was able to crush insurrection without much trouble. In March 1867 the armed rising was a failure and though no blood-vengeance was enacted most of the leaders were sent to prison for life or long terms. The only victims of the law were three young Irishmen hanged for attempting the rescue of two Fenian prisoners in Manchester in November 1867, in the course of which a policeman was shot dead. They are called 'The Manchester Martyrs'. Fenianism thus apparently failed but in fact it was destined to remain alive and have lasting consequence. It found its support rather among the labourers in the country and the thoughtful Irish-minded populace in the towns than among the farming class, and it was strongly opposed by the Catholic Church, but the manly ideal of a fight for Ireland and the stern, thoughtful, and disinterested character that marked their leaders entitle the Fenians to all respect.

The two aspects of the national fight, Land and Home Rule, were to be the national passion from 1870 onwards, with University education for the Catholics striking a minor note. The way was cleared by the disestablishment of the Church of Ireland in 1869. The highly-endowed State Church commanded the allegiance of only an eighth of the population, she had

N

against her both the Romanist and Presbyterian elements, and though she claimed to be the ancient Church of Ireland with uninterrupted succession it had to be admitted that she had never been nor could be the Church of anything but a minority, even though that minority was powerful in the upper classes. In spite of her fine record in scholarship and learning and for the noble men she had produced it was clear that her claim to remain the national Church could not be supported, though it was secured by the Act of Union. Further, the age was making for justice to all classes of Irishmen, and the disestablishment of the State Church was part of the undoing of the grossly unjust subjection of Ireland from Elizabeth onwards. Disestablishment had the support of England's great Liberal statesman, Mr. Gladstone, himself a sincere Anglican, and when he came into power in 1869 he carried through the Act by which the Church of Ireland was disestablished and put on a footing with other churches. Henceforth she was to be ruled by a representative Church Body and made self-governing. Of her former revenues, £7,500,000 was paid to her to maintain the existing clergy for life; from the surplus, appropriations were made to education and other public causes, £770,000 was voted to the Presbyterian Church as compensation for the *Regium donum*, and some £372,000 granted as a final lump sum to Maynooth College.

Until a great leader arose in Parnell to lift up the Repeal banner which O'Connell had let fall, the Land question occupied almost the whole field of politics. On the University question the Catholic bishops had denounced the Queen's colleges of 1845, and when they attempted in 1854 to found a 'Catholic university' with the famous Newman as president it was a failure. In 1879 the 'Royal University of Ireland' was established, an examining and degree-giving institution which made way in 1908 for the National University of Ireland. In 1878 an act was passed for Intermediate education and £1,000,000 was voted to it from the Irish Church surplus. Thus Ireland was endowed with an education system ranging from the National school to the University. Meanwhile, by an Act of 1873, fellowships and the higher degrees were opened to all creeds in Trinity College.

The landlord system in Ireland, which was far more unjust than that of England, had its roots in the unjust confiscations and plantations of earlier centuries and the importing of English land-laws without their better features. Few or none of the ties that bound the English farmer and villager to the resident squire and Anglican parson existed here, for the clergyman represented an alien Church and the landlord a potentate of recent and unwelcome arrival in Ireland differing at first in race and in language. Naturally the system was mitigated by good individuals and personal generosity, but the system itself was bad. In the great attack now to be made upon it there were few defenders save those who benefited by it, and numbers of noble-minded Englishmen and women gave their help in the Irish fight. Two centuries before, the Irish peasantry, though the law had degraded great numbers of them from freeholders to leaseholders or tenants-at-will, had at least been protected by survivals of Irish usages, such as the 'Ulster custom' which had been universal at one time but now was confined to the North. This gave the tenant an interest in his holding, secured him as long as he paid his rent, and on his quitting possession enabled him to sell his interest in the farm. But it was only a custom, and the time had come for the Irish farmer to demand a legal right in the land. From the landlords' point of view, the land was theirs to let or recover at their wish, but the people, who had never acquiesced in the plantations and confiscations of past history, continued to regard the soil of Ireland as belonging to the people of Ireland. Had wisdom prevailed in time, Tenant Right and Landlord ownership might have been reconciled together and made a permanent system; as it was, landlordism was doomed to be swept away and Ireland became a land of peasant proprietors.

Mr. Gladstone had become and remained for the rest of his life a friend of Ireland, determined to do what he could to redress the injustice of centuries, including, finally, the Union. In 1870 he introduced and carried a Land Act, the first of many such, which gave legal force to the Ulster custom in the other provinces and protected tenants from the unjust forms of ejectment. But it had little effect, for it left the landlord's rights practically intact. and this and a series of bad years

brought the question again and again to the front. Finally
the Land act of 1881 conceded to the tenants the principles
advocated at the Tenant Right convention of 1850, and
secured to them 'the three F's' (fair rents, fixity of tenure, and
free sale). Their leaders, however, went on to claim that the
peasantry should become *the owners of the soil* and this step
forward coincided with the Home Rule cause from 1879
onwards.

In 1873 a Home Rule League was founded with a Protestant lawyer, Isaac Butt, as chairman, and among its first
members were prominent men of the Protestant and educated
classes. The name 'Home Rule' was a happy invention of the
Irish genius for political phrases, it essentially implied that
Ireland was to manage her *internal* affairs, leaving to Westminster the supreme control over trade, the army and navy,
foreign policy and all imperial matters. At the General Election of 1874 Butt entered the British parliament with fifty-
nine followers, but his was a party of moderate claims, and
fire and passion had to be put into it by a younger man,
Charles Stewart Parnell.

The rival English parties were now called Conservatives and
Liberals, a modern variant for Tories and Whigs. Lord
Salisbury represented the solid English weight of one, Gladstone, eloquent and emotional, the advancing spirit of the
other. The latter was already old when he took up his mission
'to pacify Ireland', and he was the first English statesman who,
as a matter of principle and justice, sought to meet Ireland's
claims. The Irish members now held the balance in the party
game at Westminster, and every democratic advance favoured
them. The Secret Ballot Act of 1872 enabled Irish peasants
to vote without fear of their masters, and the conservative
gentlemen who represented them in Parliament were before
long swept out of politics. It was thus that in 1879 the
O'Conor Don was beaten by a Parnellite for County Roscommon, the last representative of the old Catholic gentry in
politics.

Charles Stewart Parnell was born in 1846, one of a long

family at Avondale, County Wicklow, where in due time he became the squire of a handsome estate.

He was destined to become in his time like O'Connell the 'uncrowned King of Ireland', but the place of the eloquent Hibernian and Catholic 'Liberator' was strangely filled by this reserved, handsome, proud man of the landlord class, the Protestant faith and the Anglo-Irish ascendancy, who in his taciturn, inflexible, and deep attachment to Ireland goes back to such aristocratic leaders as Red Hugh or Owen Roe O'Neill. The career of 'Charles Stewart Parnell', as he was called with a mixture of adoration and respect, was short, but no leader of the Irish nation before or since has commanded in life and death a deeper loyalty. A man of silent reflection though of little reading, he had become convinced of the long injustice of Ireland from the great broken treaties down to the atrocities of the Yeomen in '98. In his hatred of England he followed after Wolfe Tone and Swift; much of it was over the Union which his great-grandfather, Sir John Parnell, had opposed to the end, and the regeneration of our legislative independence was his first aim. His career was a revival of the old Protestant leadership, but this time the Protestant aristocrat had a Catholic nation behind him. For such a general, capable lieutenants were found in Michael Davitt, the author and inspiring genius of the Land League, Joseph Biggar, the founder of 'obstruction tactics' in the House of Commons, John Dillon, John Redmond, William O'Brien and others. A signal example of the art of obstruction was over the South African Bill (to annex the Transvaal) in 1877, when seven Irish members, including Parnell, held up the bill for twenty-six hours by continuous speeches, to the indignation of the British members and the sorrow of Mr. Butt.

Parnell used all the weapons and employed all the talents of his lieutenants, but his was the inflexible will, the power of unalterable decision, the sticking and unbeatable tenacity, and the instinct of command. His reserve and silent personality impressed even the British House of Commons, 'the finest gentleman's club in the world'. Irish leaders had often tried to flatter England before, but Parnell always spoke as an equal and never apologized either for Ireland or himself. To the mass of Irish people, still accustomed to aristocratic leadership, he became 'The Chief', a name which recalled the Gaelic past.

It was in 1875 that this shy and haughty young man decided to enter Irish politics, a course to which the influence of his American mother and of his sister Fanny, already a young poetess and patriotic enthusiast, helped to draw him. In April of that year he was elected member for Meath in Butt's party and on June 30, 1876 created a sensation in the House of Commons by interrupting the Chief Secretary for Ireland who had spoken of the 'Manchester murderers', and icily declaring that neither he nor Ireland had ever regarded or would regard the three executed men as anything but martyrs. This made him a hero with the Fenians and made the House of Commons wonder to see one who appeared to be a perfect English gentleman take up the despised Irish cause.

Michael Davitt may be regarded as the second name in the cause. Born in Mayo in 1846, evicted with his family which sought a home in Lancashire, he became a Fenian and in 1871 was sentenced to fifteen years imprisonment for his part in an attack on Chester castle, but was released in 1877. His real life-work was the cause of the oppressed tenantry whom almost all Irish leaders had ignored for centuries.

Davitt, himself of the tenant class, taught that the Land struggle must go along with the national struggle. It was he who said that the Irish at present would never find a chief from among themselves and that an aristocratic leader was already provided them in the young Parnell. The latter was elected chairman of the Home Rule Confederation of Great Britain in 1877 and in the next year Chairman of the Irish party in the House of Commons, whom he ruled, an accepted despot, for twelve years. Butt had already retired, a disappointed man, and died in 1879.

Parnell, since 1877 the real leader, and member for Cork city, now united the Land and the political issue and became convinced that a million Irish farmers should own each his own farm and that landlordism of the old type must go down before peasant ownership. To this double cause he attracted such a mixture of peasant self-interest, national enthusiasm, and personal devotion that the physical-force alternative seemed for a generation less real and even less romantic. Home Rule Ireland had the eyes of the world turned to it; there were now in America and Great Britain as many Irish as in Ireland, and their pockets were generously emptied for frequent delegations from home. It was on one of these that at Toronto the young Timothy Healy, a devoted retainer of Parnell, hailed his chief as 'The Uncrowned King of Ireland'. The Irish leader had to ride several horses—agrarian, political, revolutionary—at once and he rode them with superb skill. A large part of the Fenians under John Devoy and Patrick Ford were for him, but some of the older ones such as O'Leary were against him in his plan of uniting all Irishmen at least to try a parliamentary solution for Ireland's many questions.

HOME RULE AND THE LAND WAR 1880-1892

The General Election of 1880 saw thirty Irish members returned under Parnell, pledged to stand independent of all English office and parties and to promote the Irish cause by all possible devices within the law. In the country itself the Land League, founded by Davitt in 1879, and the weapons of the boycott and 'No-Rent' campaign united to bring land-lordism to its knees. It seemed as if Ireland was attacking England and carrying the war into English politics. In Ireland Parnell's was the final voice and the law of the Land League was stronger than British law itself. Opposition and extremism shrank before this astonishing leader who in the worst of election riots 'looked like a man of bronze'. But underneath the more or less legal agitation ran the fierce old stream of agrarian crime that had gone on for over a century, enhanced by bad harvests, falling prices and numerous evictions. The harvest of 1879 was the worst since the Great Famine, in 1880 there were 2590 agrarian outrages and between 1874 and 1881 some ten thousand evictions. The peasant's 'wild justice of revenge' displayed itself in the shooting of many landlords and their agents. 'Captain Moonlight' was the phrase for the secret terror, and in the towns secret societies were pledged to obtain Ireland's independence by methods of assassination.

Gladstone was Premier again from 1880 to 1885 and complained of receiving little help or gratitude from the Irish party for such measures as the Land Act of 1881, or help in the difficulty of ruling Ireland. Yet his portrait as 'the Friend of Ireland' adorned thousands of peasant homes. In October 1881 the viceroy, Lord Cowper, had Parnell lodged for seven months in Kilmainham gaol, and the Irish leaders retaliated with a 'No Rent' manifesto. England realized that anarchy was the alternative to Parnell and a 'Kilmainham Treaty' set the prisoner free and amended the Land Act of 1881.

'The Chief' had elements behind him hard to quell or unite. The wise Davitt for long advocated 'Land nationalization' instead of 'Peasant ownership'. The people's resistance to evictions and bad landlords was not always confined to standing sieges in their cabins, their anger often showed itself in murder and outrages. 'Coercion acts' and other modes of suspending Habeas Corpus were Government ways of asserting the law.' Parnell himself urged the peasants to 'keep a firm grip on their homesteads', and left it to them to interpret the words. He declared it right to 'boycott' those who took evicted farms, and the people ingeniously applied this form of popular resentment to landlords (one of whom, Captain Boycott, thus enriched the English language with a new word). Most of the Catholic bishops and priesthood were dubious as to the moral aspect of the Land Campaign, though Walsh of Dublin and Croke of Cashel were hailed as 'patriot archbishops'.

Indeed the Head of the Church himself attempted to interfere in a matter which concerned the rights of property and the sanctity of law and contract. In 1882 Gladstone tried indirectly to get the land agitation condemned at Rome but a mission to Leo XIII, managed by a Mr. Errington, proved a failure in view of Irish opinion. Again in 1882, when a 'National Tribute' was started for Parnell, the Pope sent a letter to the Irish bishops condemning it and forbidding loyal Catholics to subscribe, but the bulk of the people refused to obey and finally some £40,000 was raised. Again in 1887 a Monsignor Persico was sent from Leo XIII on a mission to Ireland, and next year a Papal rescript condemned the 'Plan of Campaign' as breaking voluntary contracts, and denounced boycotting and intimidation. But the Irish bishops declared that the facts were misrepresented and the failure of these efforts showed once again, as in the time of O'Connell and the Veto, that 'the Irish take their politics from Ireland and their religion from Rome.'

The instincts of Parnell were in fact conservative and though he was the leader, he was the controller, of a revolution. The 'No Rent' manifesto received only his reluctant approval, and when in 1886 John Dillon and William O'Brien launched 'The Plan of Campaign' (by which, if a landlord refused any offer of 'a fair rent', all the tenants on the estate should unite in a common fund to support that tenant against ejectment and forced sale, and so compel the landlord to accept a re-duced rent) Parnell did not like the scheme, though it met with much success.

On the Land question Parnell's greatest triumph was Gladstone's Act of 1881 which gave the tenant a right in the land without destroying the landlord's right, reduced the rents 20 per cent, and provided for a further reduction in fifteen years. Most of the landlords became convinced that England had abandoned them and that it was best for them to be bought out by the State under Land Purchase rather than continue a losing fight. Another enactment in 1887 enabled 150,000 farmers to take advantage of the 1881 act, and the Land Purchase Bill of 1891 set in full flow that transference of property which has made Ireland a land of peasant proprietors. The Land War was by now almost over.

But such 'concessions' did not bring the desired peace, and in May 1882 the murder of Lord Frederick Cavendish, Chief Secretary for Ireland, and Mr. Burke, Under-Secretary, in Phoenix Park by the members of a secret gang of 'Invincibles' horrified England and made Parnell's constitutional leadership difficult. At a General Election late in 1885, however, by an overwhelming vote (for a recent Franchise act had established

almost universal suffrage in both countries) he was returned
as Chairman of an Irish Party of eighty-six, out of Ireland's
total representation of 103[1].

Mr. Gladstone, now seventy-six years of age ('The Grand Old
Man', he was fondly called) became premier with a following
of 335 against 249 Conservatives, and took up the last great
fight of his life, to reverse the Union.

Home Rule for Ireland thus enlisted the genius of two of
the greatest parliamentarians of the nineteenth century, and
the alliance seemed to promise victory. Parnell made moderate demands, though in a dramatic speech at Cork in 1884
he had declared 'No man has a right to fix the boundary of the
march of a nation'. He and his party would be content with
a subordinate Parliament for Ireland which would leave the
power and supremacy of the Imperial Parliament untouched
and unimpaired. "That the Irish people should have the
legislative and executive control of all purely Irish affairs,
subject to the supreme authority of the Imperial Parliament"
remained till 1914 the compromise of the moderate nationalist
elements in Ireland. They hoped, if they could win such a
victory, that the extremist elements would be contented and
that Ireland would settle down to a middle-class constitutional
nationalist self-government which would leave the imperial
supremacy of Westminster untouched. They themselves,
however, knew better than Englishmen such as Gladstone how
determined these elements were, that the Fenian tradition
was still strong, and that the Irish Republican Brotherhood,
founded in America in 1858, was pledged to the complete
separation of Ireland from England. But a successful bargain
between the moderate elements in England and Ireland on a
parliamentary basis seemed possible and timely, and Gladstone argued that such was the way to win the eternal loyalty
of Ireland to the Imperial connection.

[1] The Irish representation in the House of Commons had been increased from 100 since the Union. The Franchise bill of 1867 had
given householders and lodgers in the towns the electoral vote, the
above one in 1884 extended this to the country. In England it added
1¾ million voters, in Ireland the electorate rose from 200,000 to 700,000.
As regards Ireland, it was contemptuously called by Conservatives
'the mud-cabin vote'.

Gladstone introduced his first Home Rule Bill in April, 1886. An Irish parliament was to be set up with an Executive responsible to it. The imperial legislature was to retain fiscal control, Ireland was to pay an imperial contribution *per annum*, Free trade was to be maintained between the two countries, and the Imperial government was to retain the control of the army, navy, ports, foreign affairs. etc.

But already the opposition was organized which was to defeat Home Rule right up to 1914. The cause of Ireland became for the first time a *party question* and remained so till the end. The Tories took up the cause of the maintenance of the Union and of the Protestant cause in Ireland. Those who stood for the Union in Ireland were a minority of about one million out of five, they were generally of the Protestant faith, and included most of the landlord class, the richer and more favoured elements of the nation throughout the island, and in the north the majority of the population. The House of Lords and the Tory party conceived it their duty to support them and to prevent that disintegration of the British isles, the very seat of Empire, which was the danger, according to Pitt, when he forced the Union of 1800. The Irish majority, that is the Catholics, were in the main nationalist: the poorer they were the more intense was the old Irish sentiment among them, nurtured on hundreds of years of Irish history, but in the higher ranks and among the priesthood there was a considerable adherence to the Union.

ULSTER AND HOME RULE

North-east Ulster was to be for thirty years the citadel of the Union cause. Lord Randolph Churchill, a Tory leader, though much of a free-lance, in February 1886 addressed enthusiastic Orange crowds in Belfast and the North, urging them to resist Home Rule. He made popular the famous phrase "Ulster will fight, and Ulster will be right'. The anti-Home-Rule cause in Ireland and England began to be associated with a strong 'No-Popery' sentiment reminiscent of the seventeenth century, and encouraged by English political allies. 'Home Rule is Rome Rule' was another famous slogan.

Religious animosity has on the other hand been inconspicuous in the South, where the intensity of Protestant feeling in the North has hardly been realized.

The excitement of Belfast was expressed, after Churchill left, in serious riots. They were not the first of their kind, for in August 1864 riots had followed the burning of an effigy of Daniel O'Connell by a Protestant crowd, as an off-set to a demonstration in Dublin in honour of 'the Liberator'. In subsequent years the Orange operatives of Belfast showed themselves determined to permit no Catholic procession or Home Rule demonstration in their city. So now in June 1886 a collision began between Protestant and Catholic workmen which led to riots which were prolonged into September, in which many lives were lost and the military had to be called in to the help of the police.

Meanwhile, in the House of Commons, Gladstone made a superbly eloquent appeal to all sides to pass the Home Rule Bill and end the feud of England and Ireland. But already some of his ablest lieutenants had forsaken him. Mr. Joseph Chamberlain, a Radical, seceded and founded a new party, the 'Liberal Unionists', and a Whig section under Lord Hartington also revolted. In spite of all the old man's eloquence and solemn warnings, the enthusiastic support of his main party, and a temperate speech from Parnell, the Bill was finally defeated by 343 to 313 votes. A General Election followed and a Conservative government came in under Lord Salisbury, strong enough with the help of the Liberal seceders to finally defeat Home Rule. Lord Salisbury's nephew, Mr. Arthur Balfour, as Chief Secretary for Ireland, was bent upon crushing Irish agrarian crime by 'twenty years of resolute government', but hoped by administrative measures 'to kill Home Rule with kindness'.

But a second attempt upon the Unionist fortress in Parliament was preparing. The Liberal centre remained true under the magic of Gladstone's name. In 1887 and 1888 came the famous Pigott case. No less an organ than *The Times* published articles entitled *Parnellism and Crime* which accused the Irish leader of encouraging the murder of landlords. Her Majesty's government were suspected of wishing the charge to be proved, so when a Special Commission cleared Parnell and the forger Pigott committed suicide, it lost much credit, while the Irish leader's popularity became all the greater. When his complete vindication was made public, he was cheered by all parties in the House of Commons, and everywhere in England there was a generous reaction towards a former enemy. 1889 was indeed his great year, but he received all tributes with his usual distant politeness.

Great Britain, however, was now split over the Home Rule question, Protestant Ulster was determined to resist even to blood, and public opinion in both countries ranged itself strongly for or against Ireland's demand.

But in 1890 the hero of Ireland fell with a Napoleonic suddenness that gave the perfect finish to the drama of his leadership. A secret love-attachment to the English wife of Captain O'Shea, one of his own party, became the subject of a divorce case in which he was found guilty. His party and Ireland at once renewed their confidence in 'the Chief', but Mr. Gladstone on the moral issue declared he could not continue in *his* leadership if Mr. Parnell retained *his*, and the Roman Catholic bishops on the same moral issue also declared against him. A majority of his party, among whom his former adorer, Tim Healy, played the leading part and which included Dillon and Davitt, deposed him from the chairmanship of the Irish party in the famous 'Committee Room No. 15,' of the House of Commons. The rough-tongued but staunch Joe Biggar, who might by his good Ulster common sense have saved the situation, was already dead, and passion prevailed. A majority of the Irish people followed the anti-Parnellites. The Dissenting bodies in England had generally supported Home Rule, more from admiration of the great Liberal hero than for love of Ireland, but now 'the Nonconformist Conscience', so powerful in Britain, joined the Catholic hierarchy in their condemnation.

Our 'Uncrowned King', whose pride never stooped to apologize for himself, after marrying Mrs. O'Shea, fought heroically to recover his leadership. Ireland was rent as by a civil war of vituperation, insult and mob-violence. The mental strain and the physical hardships of a desperate campaign, in which he characteristically refused to believe that all was lost, were too much for a nervous constitution, and Charles Stewart Parnell died at Brighton on October 7, 1891, prematurely worn out at the age of forty-five. He was buried in the national mausoleum at Glasnevin and was followed to the grave by a vast concourse of mournful followers or repentant foes, who for the last time united in honouring the fallen Chief. The dramatic exit of the heaven-born leader left the national cause for thirty years to wander in the wilderness.

What this proud and inscrutable man had planned for Ireland's future can never be revealed, but he had lifted her cause to its full height again, and the white heat of his devotion to her puts him as a national hero among the silently passionate men, such as Red Hugh O'Donnell and Owen Roe O'Neill.

A year after his death, Gladstone was again Prime Minister and the Liberals had a majority with the aid of the Irish vote. He introduced his second Home Rule Bill in July, 1892 and it was finally carried by 301 to 267 in the Commons, but the House of Lords, who had abandoned the Irish landlords but would not flinch on the question of the Union, flung it out by 419 to 41. It seemed clear that till the House of Lords was reformed no Home Rule Bill could pass. 'The Grand Old Man' himself retired in 1894 and died four years later, leaving the last chapter unwritten. His advocacy of the Irish cause proved disastrous for his party, and from 1886 to 1906, save for an interval of three years, was effective in putting all the Conservative elements into power.

CHAPTER XX

FROM PARNELL TO THE TREATY OF 1922

IN the brief years of his leadership, Parnell had taken upon him to secure for his country the Land for the People and Home Rule for Ireland. Before his death he had gained the one but failed in the other. The peasantry, though they had not yet entered into the Promised land, had been brought to the Pisgah whence they could survey it, and if Parnell was not their only leader, or the first to take up the cause, he was the unquestioned leader, such as seldom comes to an enslaved people. Nothing remained, now that the principle had been accepted, but for successive Land acts to complete the movement begun by a Liberal government in 1870. The great Conservative party, with the House of Lords behind them, themselves accepted Land Purchase, the buying out of the landlords, and smaller 'concessions' to Ireland—provided the Union was maintained. But while this aristocratic party abandoned landlordism in Ireland, it was far otherwise with Home Rule, which in their view was 'marching through rapine and ruin to the dismemberment of the Empire'. So vital did they deem the maintenance of the *status quo* that, reinforced by the Liberals who had forsaken Gladstone in 1885, they assumed the name of Unionists.[1] To all appearance they had triumphed. Gladstonian Home Rule without the 'Grand Old Man', seemed unthinkable. As for the Nationalist party, split not merely into two, but into several factions, it

[1] This was because the Hartington Whigs and the Radicals under Chamberlain after 1885 joined them or voted with them on this question. In the General Election of 1895 the Conservatives numbered 340, the Liberal Unionists (Chamberlain's wing) 71, the Liberals 177 and the Irish Nationalists 82. The proportion varied little till the Liberal triumph in 1906. It was in this year that the name **Unionists** was finally adopted for the whole alliance.

387

was like an army that has lost the leader that created it. The
driving force of the Land agitation diminished, for the 90's
were good years for the farmer compared with the disastrous
80's and the first decade of the twentieth-century better still.
It seemed that only a sudden triumph in the party game
at Westminster, or some unexpected event in world-
politics, could make Home Rule once more a burning
question.

After Parnell there could not fail to be a dull epoch for
Ireland. His party was split and John Redmond took the
place of the dead chief, but Tim Healy, William O'Brien and
John Dillon were rivals rather than lieutenants, and it was
1900 before even the seeming of unity was restored. The
Imperialist wing of the Liberal party under Lord Rosebery
dropped Home Rule as too dangerous a question and it went
out of practical politics till 1905. There set in the age which
went on to 1912, the Irish party still loyally keeping its pledge
to hold aloof from English parties and government office, still
including able and sincere men, still able to enlist popular
support and money in America and these islands, and
still promising to give us back 'the Old House on College
Green'. But hope deferred maketh the heart sick, and in
the grand disillusionment that followed Parnell the national
cause took new and deeper channels than mere politics.
Rather wearily Ireland accepted the concessions which it
was thought would satisfy her while maintaining the
Union.

Land Purchase was now completed under Tory rule. By
the Balfour Act of 1891 and another of 1896 the claims of the
selling landlords were met by the issue of Land Stock backed
by the British Treasury. Mr. George Wyndham, Secretary for
Ireland, was in 1903 responsible for an Act which offered a
bonus to landlords who would sell, so facilitating the sale of
entire estates, and enabled the tenant to purchase on easy
terms of sixty-eight years' repayment. It was a 'settlement
by consent' of all sides. The management of these great
operations, which were backed by millions of money on
British credit, was entrusted to an Irish Land Commission
Court, while the due payment of the annual interest to

the selling landlords became a charge on the Imperial Exchequer.[1]

After fifty years of agrarian struggle the Irish tenantry became, as long as they could pay the annual interest, the owners of their farms, and Ireland has become like France, a land of peasant proprietors, of whom the greater number have but a modest acreage. This triumph would have seemed amazing to their grandfathers of 1840, who lived like serfs under landlords who were by law sole owners of the land and could eject the occupiers on default of one year's rent. Successively in a long, violent and often cruel campaign the Irish peasantry had recovered that right to the land which they believed had been theirs long ago.

Many lovers of Ireland hoped that the dual interest of landlord and tenant might be maintained and the landed gentry continue to rule the country, though no longer with the autocratic powers of old. But in 1902 a landlord gentleman named Shawe Taylor brought about a conference between landowners and the leaders of the Home Rule party as representing the tenants, and following their report which was accepted at a landowners' Convention, it was decided that dual ownership m the land should be abolished. This was the principle expressed in the Act of 1903. The landlord in modern Ireland, whose ancestor was a grand *seigneur* owning thousands of acres, now seldom has more than a handsome country house and a demesne of a hundred acres. Landlordism in Ireland came to an end at that date. The history of this class has gone through curious stages since, in the seventeenth century,

---

[1] These annuities, or annual payments, which the tenants of purchased estates made in order to repay the sums lent them to buy their lands (sixty-eight years from the Act of 1903 was the final date), were the occasion of a standing dispute between the governments of Great Britain and the Irish Free State. From the Treaty onwards they were collected by the Irish Government and handed over to the British National Debt Commissioners, to be paid to the holders of Guaranteed Land Stock, who have acquired the original landlord's interest. Mr. De Valera's Government, however, retained them on the ground that they were, or should have been, surrendered by the British at the Treaty. The result was an Economic war in which Great Britain collected the equivalent of the annuities in duties on our cattle, etc., going into British ports (some £3,000,000 per annum). Agreement was reached in May 1938 by which the Irish Government paid a lump sum of £10,000,000 to Britain as a settlement of all claims.

they became absolute owners in law of the land of Ireland. Robbed of their political ascendancy in 1800, they continued still for nearly a century to retain their social, landed and local ascendancy. The events of 1870 to 1922 have deposed them from all except the social and intellectual side of their leadership in a land which their fathers, for good and evil, both owned and ruled and have done much to make into a nation.

A Congested Districts' Board, established in 1891, to enlarge and unify the small uneconomic holdings in the west, was all part of Balfour's policy of 'killing Home Rule with kindness'. So were the light railways which, by an Act of 1899, were laid to open up the remote areas of the western seaboard. An officially-founded Department of Agriculture and Sir Horace Plunkett's privately-founded Irish Agricultural Organization Society aimed at teaching the Irish farmer how to apply modern and co-operative methods to the land of which he had become the possessor. Otherwise how could a community of small individual cultivators make their land profitable in face of modern competition? It has long been said, in explanation of the survival value of the race, that 'potatoes and turf have saved the poor Irishman', Something more was needed if the rich but neglected soil of Ireland was to *prosper* under a system of small holdings. Modern science provided us for example with a system of spraying against potato blight which, had it been known and applied in 1847, could have saved the food crop, and consequently the lives of hundreds of thousands.

An Act for the establishment of County Councils in 1898 was part of the slow process by which from 1829 the government of the towns and counties has been opened up to the Catholic majority. Since the time of Charles I the counties had been governed by Grand Juries. Under this system the Justices of Peace in their Quarter Sessions, assisted by juries of a certain standing and limited in number to 23, all of them unpaid, struck the county rate or 'cess', looked after the upkeep of bridges and roads, and administered the county generally. They were landlord bodies, generally Protestant, and addicted to giving the more important jobs to their adherents. The claims of the majority and of the Catholic population were now met by the establishment of elected bodies, so that before long the popular vote controlled most of the local government. But in proportion as the dominance of the Catholic majority was established in the southern counties, so the Protestant majority came to control the northern ones.

The claims of the Roman Catholic population in Education were met in various ways and crowned in 1908 by the creation of the National University, a teaching as well as an examining and degree-giving institution, by its charter undenominational. A modicum of Irish ('Compulsory Irish'), as the result of an agitation by the Gaelic League, was made essential for entrants. This has given the keynote to the enforcement of Irish since the creation of the Free State wherever the State controls. The older University, however, Trinity College, long a Protestant preserve, has kept the character of an independent body, owing nothing, until 1947, to State subsidies. Since 1873 all its fellowships, degrees, and emoluments have been open to members of all creeds, and the study of the Gaelic language, past and present, has been encouraged within its walls in every way except that of compulsion.

Ireland, though her population still fell by emigration, was undoubtedly prosperous from 1900 onwards. The money voted, for example, by Parliament to public buildings such as University College, Dublin, or the College of Science was on a princely scale. A Commission in 1894 on the financial relations between England and Ireland found that Ireland had been greatly overtaxed since the Union; this has been often quoted, but in justice we must wonder, if the old Irish Parliament had continued, where would the hundreds of millions of pounds necessary for buying out the landlords have been got if not backed by the credit of the British Empire?

Many therefore, both in England and Ireland, began to ask, what does Ireland want more? The answer was that Ireland is an ancient nation deprived of her national legislature standing at the bar of that Parliament which had taken it away and demanding to have it restored. The Irish party only asked to have it restored as in the 18th century, broadened, made representative, and established without danger to imperial authority. But many excellent men declared that one could be a Unionist and believe the Union to be best for Ireland, and yet a patriot and 'kindly Irish of the Irish'. Such a one was seen, for example, in Sir Horace Plunkett, a man of unselfish and enlightened patriotism.

By 1900 the Fenian and 'physical force' element seemed completely out of the picture. The centenary of "98' stirred the old dream of armed rebellion among the 'hillside men', but passed over without an incident, and when the South African War broke out in 1899 the Dublin Fusiliers and other Irish regiments maintained the fame of Irishmen as 'Soldiers of the Queen', though they cheered for Kruger on embarking.

The Land question having been settled by consent, the hope was entertained of a settlement of the Home Rule question on moderate lines by consent of the great English parties, the Irish Nationalists party, and the Irish landlords. Mr. George Wyndham was Secretary for Ireland in 1903 in Mr. Balfour's ministry and his Act in effect settled the Land question. Why should not the Conservative party meet the Irish demand for self-government? They alone could answer for the House of Lords which remained closed to Liberal measures. Wyndham, a descendant of Lord Edward Fitzgerald, felt the romantic appeal of Ireland, while his Under-secretary, Sir Anthony MacDonnell, was an Irishman and a Catholic. Lord Dunraven and other Irish gentry united in an Irish Reform Association to advocate in 1904 the 'Devolution' of strictly Irish affairs to a semi-elected Council which would have the spending of £6,000,000 *per annum* on national services. William O'Brien, M.P., on the side of the Irish party favoured the scheme, so did Wyndham, so did, it is said, the new monarch, Edward VII himself. A bill was prepared to this effect, but the extremists, both Irish and Conservative, wrecked it, and Wyndham had to resign from his office in 1905. Later events have made it clear that any such mild solution of Ireland's national claim could not have contented her for long.

THE OPPOSITION TO HOME RULE

In 1906 a remarkable 'swing of the pendulum' displaced the Conservatives from office and brought the Liberals into power for eight years. The forward advance of this party was now resumed under Asquith and his Chancellor of the Exchequer, Lloyd George, whose 'democratic budgets' and 'Land taxation' schemes alarmed the land-propertied class and made it certain that only a reform of the House of Lords could secure the passing of Liberal measures. Among these was Home Rule. In 1900 Redmond had been elected Chairman of a far-from-united Nationalist party, and now at last Home Rule became again a primary objective to which the Liberals were bound and for which the Irish votes in the House of Commons were pledged to them.

Even the grand alliance of Parnell and Gladstone in 1886 had only partly obscured the difficulties in the way of an ultimate triumph. The Nationalist party in general voted with the Liberals, for their instincts were democratic and popular, and their record in supporting humanitarian legislation in Parliament is a very creditable one. But from 1895 to 1906 the Conservatives ruled England and Home Rule was an Opposition cause. Though it had behind it the majority of the Irish people at home and financial and other support from the Irish abroad, it had against it a combination of forces strongly entrenched and socially and politically very powerful.

The House of Lords under the constitutional system had a final veto on measures passed by the House of Commons, it could be relied upon to throw out any Home Rule bill. This meant that English Society was mainly against Home Rule and so was the Crown till Victoria died in 1901, though her son and successor, Edward VII, was popularly believed to be a 'friend of Ireland.'

England was still in its middle and even in its lower classes a very conservative, imperialistic and Protestant country, and the Irish cause won the allegiance only of the Liberal elements. In Ireland itself the Protestant population, though dominant only in the north, was widely and strongly spread over the rest of the country and only slowly lost its position as a ruling minority. It amounted to about a quarter of the population, but in wealth, trade, the land, and social influence was even stronger than its numbers. The landed and social ascendancy of the Anglo-Irish in Ireland long outlived the Union which destroyed their political ascendancy. A large British army, stationed at various points, especially on the Curragh of Kildare, helped to maintain the numbers, the confidence and the prestige of the minority.

THE PROTESTANT NORTH

The Orange Order was the strongest bulwark of the Protestant and anti-Home-Rule cause. Since it was founded in 1795 it had at various times suffered the disfavour of Government, especially under the Under-secretary Drummond, but by the middle of the century it had recovered in numbers and organization. The twelfth of July, commemorating the victory of the Boyne, was the great annual day of the Orangemen and was celebrated not only in Belfast, Derry, and other Ulster towns as it is to-day, but outside the province also, though it became more and more dangerous to flaunt the Orange flag there as the century advanced. The Order professed complete religious tolerance under the British Crown for all, with a preference naturally for the 'Good Old Cause', but since their Catholic fellow-Irishmen had declared for Home Rule they feared that the triumph of this would establish a Roman Catholic domination throughout the whole island.

It could be answered that Irish nationalism since Wolfe Tone had always been tolerant on religious differences and put Ireland before religion. Daniel O'Connell, though it was inevitable that his movement should have a Romanist character, had boldly opposed Rome and the bishops on the Veto question. Parnell himself, as a Protestant, had been very cautious on the religious side; though he led a Catholic laity, not more than a minority of the priesthood were for him. The bishops and clergy of this Church had always deprecated armed insurrection and advocated to their flocks 'moral force, patience and perseverance', and 'keeping within the law' for the bettering of their condition. Though they were prominent in many ways in the public questions that agitated the country, and powerful locally, it was not from them that the Moses came to lead the people out of bondage. The British government was well aware what a valuable ally it had in a church which has such well-defined doctrines as to civil obedience, the justification of rebellion and the sanctity of property. But it had failed to win the Roman Catholic Church in Ireland over to its side by self-interest. Of the three great historic denominations it alone, save for the endowment of Maynooth, received no emoluments from the State. Its clergy had accepted this position since the days of O'Connell, though the old conservative foreign-educated bishops and priests of the Union times had inclined towards government control and maintenance. But 'the less you are bought by the State, the more you are responsible to the people' was the lesson of that position, and the priesthood and the bishops of later days, drawn from the ranks of the old Irish race, have felt for, even if they did not always counsel, the popular movements of Ireland.

In spite of such evidence that 'loyalty' and Catholicism were not irreconcilable, the Orange Order continued to profess suspicion of Popery and Home Rule as an alliance that threatened them, and to maintain the sturdy and militant Puritanism of their ancestors of 'Derry, Aughrim, Enniskillen, and the Boyne'.

The city of Belfast had now become a first-rate factor in all considerations of Irish politics. In 1800 its population was only about 25,000 as against that of Cork, 70,000, and Dublin 172,000, and it was considered a rebel centre. But subsequently the North-east, already the seat of prosperous home industries in the eighteenth century, became a highly specialized modern industrial area. Linen and cotton weaving passed into the factory stage and the great ship-building industry of Harland and Wolff was founded. By 1881 Belfast had a population of 186,000 which has steadily increased since to over 400,000. Alone in Ireland it has capitalized industries worthy to rank beside those of Great Britain and a very numerous and highly-skilled artisan class, mainly of the Orange fraternity. Ulster has continued to believe that its great industries have flourished by Free Trade and through the political union which enable it to send its goods out through the whole British empire. If Ireland had remained under the old Dublin parliament and there had been no Union, probably the Ulster problem would not have arisen. But the Protestants who in 1800 had been against the Union were now for it, while the Catholic majority were against.

By 1906 it was clear that Orangeism was a marvellous combination of the ruling class in Ulster, of the working classes in Belfast, and the majority of the Protestant farmers of the North. Belfast was its stronghold, its disciplined strength was impressive, and it had the political alliance of the Unionist party and of British society.

The worst feature of Orangeism has been the periodic outbreaks and riots in Belfast, largely due to the rivalries of working-class people of different persuasions and deprecated by the upper classes. In the province itself hostility between 'Orange and Green' and Catholic and Protestant tenants had been a tradition since the eighteenth century. The plantation of Ulster indeed is a *fact* which has remained one to the present day, the planting, namely, of a new Protestant and Anglo-Scottish population in the province, who have proved to be 'England's one successful colony' in Ireland.

A striking fact to be observed in the nineteenth century was the going over of the Northern presbyterians to the Unionist side. In the latter half of the eighteenth century they had displayed, especially in Antrim, Down and Belfast, a strong spirit of democracy and tolerance, but the principles of the United Irishmen were now rare among the descendants of those who were rebels in '98. Their Church had since been won over by the *Regium Donum*, greatly increased since the Union; and the removal of religious disabilities, the extension of the franchise, the various Land Acts, and the rapid growth of industry in Belfast and other northern towns had removed their grievances and given them economic prosperity. By the end of the century the majority of them were found on the Unionist side, though they still favoured Liberalism where Home Rule was not concerned. Also their ministers and the older generation among them held aloof from the Orange Order, which was founded as and long remained an Episcopalian organization.

The history of the Ulster Presbyterians is a very definite and compact piece of Irish history. It was under James I that they were first planted in Ulster, and it was under Charles I that the Scottish Church in Ireland first assumed the organized form it still retains. In 1642, seven Lowland Scottish regiments under the command of General Munroe arrived at Carrickfergus, despatched by the Scottish Estates at the request of the Long Parliament. They had already taken the Solemn League and Covenant and now extended it to the Ulster colonists whom they came to defend. After a triumphant campaign, the chaplains of the army at Carrickfergus on June 10, 1642, organized the first Presbytery of their Church in Ireland. From that time the Presbyterian Church has maintained itself in the North, but it was destined to suffer much persecution in the next century and a half. Seeing that their ancestors were known to be of a Calvinistic turn when they were deliberately invited by favourable terms to plant Ulster for England's benefit, the Presbyterians might well complain that religious disabilities, subjection to the State Church and oppression by great landlords were a betrayal of the original Plantation. Yet under Anne and George I they could always be reckoned as a sure bulwark for the Protestant and Hanoverian cause. It is true that American and then French republican or democratic principles spread among them in the last quarter of the eighteenth century and there was a prospect of a rising in Ulster in 1798, but in the period after the Union the nationalism of the presbyterians waned fast. The United Irishmen had been even stronger in Belfast than in Dublin but Daniel O'Connell did not find the North sympathetic ground and at the time of Catholic Emancipation and Repeal their most famous leader and preacher, the Rev. Henry Cooke, Moderator of the Ulster Synod, was a vehement opponent of the Liberator. Liberalism remained characteristic of the Scoto-Irish, and indeed comes from their democratic religion, but their theoretic sympathy with Irish Nationalism waned as they became an industrial community compacted in the North-east, and as Nationalism itself became more romantic, Catholic, and Gaelic. Allied though they were for some generations with the Catholics to remove the common bonds which they suffered under Landlordism, the Anglican ascendancy and the Established Church, the first Home Rule Bill (1886) may be taken as the date when the Presbyterians forsook their old allies. Their final adhesion to the Unionist alliance was at the signing of the second Covenant in their history in 1912.

THE ANGLO-IRISH

No survey of modern Irish history can be just which disregards the division of Ireland into Protestants, Presbyterians, and Catholics, that is, namely the adherents respectively of the Church of Ireland, the Presbyterian Church in Ireland, and the Roman communion.[1] The name 'Anglo-Irish' designates the former, who in the eighteenth century had a legal ascendancy over the rest of the population. While the Catholic people have retained an instinctive nationality which goes far back, the Anglo-Irish, whose blood is through descent, marriage or conversion, largely derived from the old English and Gaels of earlier centuries, developed in the eighteenth century a pronounced nationalism of their own. This, though in men like Grattan and Flood it went far in the Irish direction, had always in mind loyalty to the Crown and allegiance to the British connection. The Union ended the conservative, loyal, and aristocratic nationalism of 'the middle nation'. But up to our own time the Anglo-Irish population, strong among the landed and the middle classes, has produced no small number of politicians, writers, and poets who have supported the Home Rule cause and the memory of 'Ireland a nation'. Parnell himself, one of them, was only aiming at the restoration of Grattan's Parliament, thrown open, however,

[1] 'Protestant' naturally in its widest sense includes all non-Roman Catholic churches but traditionally in Ireland in its most definite sense it means the Episcopal Reformed Church, the formerly established church of Ireland.

to all creeds and classes. Many Protestants supported Home Rule as a *practical*, rather than a *romantic*, solution of the Irish question, and it is certain that Parnell knew nothing of, and would have had little sympathy for, traditional Irish nationalism and the revival of Ireland as a Gaelic nation.

The balance between the three dominant creeds of Ireland is a primary factor in modern Irish history. Had the Protestant element been in a majority at any given time, history might have taken a very different turn, but the existence of a far larger Catholic and native population than themselves always inclined them against any out-and-out break with England. This is as true of the Anglo-Irish in the days of the Great Earl of Kildare as of their successors of Grattan's time. The huge exodus of the native Irish after the Famine seemed to promise an increase in the Protestant section of the population, but the former balance was before long restored, and the waning of the Protestant element has long been a feature outside Ulster since the Land war and Land acts. According to the last census of all Ireland, taken in 1911, the Church of Ireland population out of a total of 4,390,219 numbered 576,611, the Presbyterians numbered 440,525, there were some 60,000 Methodists and other sects, and the Roman Catholics constituted seventy-five per cent of the whole.

Among the three main elements of Ireland the Anglo-Irish have always considered themselves an aristocratic, enlightened, and in many ways a very Irish stock. Living for centuries, as they have done, among a race of innate Catholic and Celtic temperament, they have learned much from them, and their opposition to Home Rule has been based more on political grounds than on religious or racial prejudice. The course of politics indeed had produced a fresh division of Ireland, not as formerly into Episcopalian and Presbyterian, but into Protestant Ulster and the rest of Protestant Ireland. Though united with the North on the question of the Union, the Protestants of the rest—notably Trinity College—showed a reluctance to join in with the religious sentiment that animated the North. Their attraction was more for the old Ireland, and so a remarkable rift was supplied between the

Anglo-Irish minority in the South and the mainly Scottish-descended majority in the North.

All this organization of the Protestant North, and the going over of the Presbyterians to the Unionist side, was ill-perceived by the Home Rule leaders. But its importance was to be attested in the events of 1912 to 1922, and in the establishment of the modern Six-Counties State. The Nationalist party conceived their struggle to be for Ireland as a whole but already, apart from the resistance of the Anglo-Irish in the rest of the Island, a solid core was forming in the North which was far more serious and was under-estimated both by Redmond and the Liberal leaders. The democratic advances of the age in themselves fostered the grouping for and against; if the Franchise act of 1884 gave the electoral majority to the Catholics elsewhere, it gave it equally to the Protestants in the North. Finally all the elements of opposition to Home Rule for Ireland here and in Great Britain were united and defined in a great leader, Sir Edward Carson, one of the Anglo-Irish born in Dublin, who at the age of fifty-seven and after a long and distinguished career as a lawyer, took up the Union cause. In the very month, February 1910, in which Redmond declared that he held the casting vote in the House of Commons Carson became leader of the Irish Unionist party.

The 'Irish question,' then, had now become a party one and an Imperial one, and it was to constitutional means and the now accepted Liberal alliance in Great Britain that up to 1914 the Home Rule leaders looked for victory. But politics were not all, and both in Ireland, Britain and America wherever the Irish were, a romantic note was added which enlisted generous sympathies.

THE CULTURAL RENAISSANCE

Irish nationalism since it was first formed in the sixteenth century has seldom been purely material and has not remained contented for long without some spiritual aim high above politics and material wrongs. So it was now. Ireland had been gorged with politics and those of the not very edifying

type which circumstances had forced upon her, even if Parnell
had ennobled them. But now a growing spirit manifested
itself which went back to the Anglo-Irish nation of the seventeenth and eighteenth centuries on the one hand, and the old
Gaelic ancestry on the other. Its inspiration came from
scholars, historians, and poets and went back to such idealists
as Thomas Davis and other lovers of the old Gaelic tongue and
tradition. The younger men who believed in Ireland a nation
turned rather to Wolfe Tone and '98 than to the ballot-box,
the political platform, and Ireland's fight at Westminster.
Others thought Ireland's destiny was never to be a political
nation but that she was and might win fame as a spiritual and
cultural nation. In many the two conceptions were blended
and found their fulfilment in the leaders of 1916.

The literary renaissance of modern Ireland began about
1890 and is illuminated by the great names of Standish
O'Grady, Yeats, Æ, and other poets, dramatists, and imagina-
tive writers. But their work has been in the English language
and has not made the wide appeal that the attempt to revive
the Irish language has had. In 1893 the Gaelic League was
founded by Douglas Hyde for the revival of the native language and, soon after, the appearance of a weekly paper,
Fainne an Lae ('Dawn of Day'), and the writings of Father
Peter O'Leary (the first man to use modern Irish as spoken for
true literary purposes) enchanted old speakers who could read
the language and thousands of the new, who turned with enthusiasm to study the speech of their grandfathers.

By 1900 the Irish language, though something like half a
million people still spoke it along the western and southern
coasts and great numbers of the older people spoke nothing
else, was rapidly dying. The neglect and abandonment of the
old speech had begun with the upper classes in the seventeenth
century, continued with the middle classes in the eighteenth,
and in the nineteenth had reached the peasantry also. While
the Welsh Celt has retained his language and has made it the
badge of his nationality and the expression of his religion, the
Irish Celt has not been taught by his leaders to maintain his
distinctive language nor has it been much heard from the
altar. In the courts and in the schools English has been for

generations the sole permitted language. Yet as late as 1600
not only was Irish the sole language of the old Gaelic population but it had captured even the Norman settlers and it is
certain that the majority of the Irish people have ancestors
who at one time or another have spoken Irish. Even the
English language in Ireland is saturated with Gaelic idiom,
sounds, and words. The cultural, literary, and poetic wealth,
going back over a thousand years, of the language has been
made known by scholars, Continental and Irish. The de-
ciphering and publishing of the ancient epics such as the *Táin
Bó Cualgne* revealed the fact, long hidden by the cataclysm
of the seventeenth century, that Ireland had a vernacular
literature older than that of any other Western races. So on
many a side the appeal for Irish has been both a romantic
and a reasonable one. But in spite of thirty years of the Gaelic
movement and since 1922 its enforcement by a native government, statistics tell of the continued decline of this old speech
whose future depends less on the hundred thousand or so of
native speakers who survive in Donegal, Kerry, and Conne-
mara than on the tens of thousands in the towns and elsewhere who have learnt it and consider it essential to Ireland's
claim to be a nation.

It would be hard to enumerate all the movements for
her regeneration which from 1890 made Ireland interesting
and drew back to her thousands who cared less for her
politics than her poetry, and who, like Red Hugh O'Donnell,
wished to make 'Kathleen Ní Houlahan' a queen once
again.

THE LAST FIGHT FOR HOME RULE, 1906-1914

With the abdication of the landlords the Protestant
ascendancy passed away, but Dublin Castle had still to be
captured if Ireland were to be ruled according to Irish ideas.
Edward VII was regarded as a friend of Ireland and was the
first of his line to be so, but after his visit in 1903 he had

reluctantly to admit that he was not in the true sense King of Ireland.

How was Dublin Castle to be captured? Parnell and his party had failed in Westminster; would the Fenian solution be tried again or could Ireland by concentration at home win the victory? In 1899 Mr. Arthur Griffith, a clever journalist back from South Africa, founded his newspaper, the *United Irishman* (later called *Sinn Féin*), and soon won adherence to his gospel of passive resistance to British rule, recalling her representatives to work for her at home, and reviving Irish industry by the boycott of British goods. A continuous advocate of 'government by the King, Lords and Commons of Ireland', his ideas were eighteenth century, but the gospel of 'Sinn Féin' ('Ourselves', i.e. self-help) got its sting from the continued failure of the Irish party at Westminster. To the teachings of Swift and Flood the young generation, such as Patrick Pearse, added those of Tone, Robert Emmet, Davis, and the Fenians, but the idea of force for the present was unthinkable.

Home Rule as a constitutional movement was given its last chance when in 1906 the Liberals returned to power in the Imperial parliament with a huge majority. Their leaders, whose programme meant at battle with the House of Lords, were pledged to give some form of self-government, but realized what a dangerous combination against them existed in the Conservative and society forces of Great Britain, and the Protestant sentiment of Ulster. At the moment, by the Old Age Pensions act and other social measures, Ireland for the first time since the Union ceased to pay for herself, and in 1910 more money was spent on her than she contributed. To many this was an argument against Home Rule, but according to others 'good government is no substitute for self-government.'

In 1909, after Lloyd George's land-taxation Budget was rejected by the House of Lords, the Prime Minister, Asquith, with the support of Redmond, leader of the Irish party, carried through the Parliament Act of 1911 which practically ended the veto of the Peers by anacting that a Bill, once passed in the House of Commons, should within two years automatically become law. This great barrier once removed, in 1912

the third Home Rule Bill was introduced and up to the outbreak of the European war was a subject of furious debate in
the realms of George V.

The Bill reserved to Great Britain the strategic and external
control which even before the Union she had exercised but
added a further point, namely fiscal control. That the kingdom of Ireland should not be able to raise and spend its own
money seemed an anomaly, especially considering that the
three colonial Dominions of Australia, Canada, and South
Africa now after 1907 all enjoyed full self-government. Yet
even as it stood the great majority of the Irish people supported
Redmond in his acceptance of the Bill. But there was to
be no plain sailing for the unfortunate barque. In Ulster the
Protestant population, under the lead of Sir Edward Carson,
and while the Bill was before the Commons, expressed their
resolve to resist Home Rule at all costs. Though Orangeism
gave this movement most of its force and made the opposition
religious as well as political, the Presbyterians, who had been
with Catholic Ireland in the eighteenth century and far into
the nineteenth on the two questions of Tenant Right and
religious equality, now in the main joined the opposition and
swore to the Solemn Covenant of September 28, 1912, which
got the signatures of 200,000 Northerners.

As if to show the final unity of Protestant Ulster, gentry
and commons, Church of Ireland and Presbyterians, cleric and
lay, the Covenant was signed immediately after Carson by
Lord Londonderry, the Bishop of Down, the Moderator of
the General Assembly, and many other heads of Society and
the Churches in the North. By its solemn wording 'the men
of Ulster, loyal subjects of King George V,' swore 'to stand
by one another in defending for ourselves and our children
the cherished position of equal citizenship in the United
Kingdom, and in using all means which may be found
necessary to defeat the present conspiracy to set up a
Home Rule parliament in Ireland, and in the event of such
a parliament being forced upon us to refuse to recognize its
authority.'

Never before was such a bold defiance made of Parliament,

whose acts, when passed in due form, have, ever since Parliament began, had binding force upon all subjects of the Crown, whatever they may have thought of them before passing. But all men are entitled to their conscience, a higher law than that of the State, if they are prepared to suffer.   This principle was put forward by the Protestant North, had it not been for generations equally true for the Catholic South?

Mr. Bonar Law, leader of the Unionist opposition in Parliament, now took up the cause of Ulster, and the open enemies of Home Rule seemed less dangerous than the secret forces in high places.   Redmond was now fully pledged to the Liberal alliance.   His position was one that called for all the genius of his dead Chief.   An amendment by Carson to the Bill proposed the exclusion from its scope of the province of Ulster. The Irish leader could only reject such an amendment, as he was bound to do, because 'for us Ireland is one entity'.

In January 1913 the Bill passed the Commons but it was rejected by the House of Lords, so that under the Parliament Bill it could not pass automatically till 1914.   The Ulster Covenanters were already arming and drilling openly under a provisional government, and a British soldier, General Richardson, was found to command their army of 100,000 men. On the other side in October 1913 a National Volunteer force was organized in Dublin under Eoin MacNeill, Pearse and others.   So was a 'Citizen army' of the Irish Labour party, led by James Connolly.   The condition of the poor, and the low wages paid in the Irish capital, shocked all fair-minded men, but a General strike organized in 1912 by James Larkin had been defeated by the employers, a disastrous victory it was to prove.   Though at first dummy rifles, in North and South, made the marchings of the respective Volunteers a little ridiculous, there was no doubt of their determination. Both sides soon got real arms from abroad, and it looked as if Home Rule would bring about a civil war which would involve Great Britain, the first since 1642. In March 1914, the refusal of General Gough and other officers in command of the British forces at the Curragh to obey government orders to move against Ulster showed how high up the resistance to an

o

Act of Parliament might go. Reluctantly Redmond advised his supporters to join the National Volunteers, but it was clear that between his moderate wing and the extremist one led by Pearse and others of the Irish Republican Army co-operation would not last long.

IRELAND AND THE GREAT WAR

The outbreak of the Great War in August 1914 altered the whole face of things. The unexpected event in world politics *did* happen. The Home Rule Bill received the royal assent but it was not to be put into force till the war was over; and Ireland remained under the Union till the world conflict ended. Some 100,000 Irishmen altogether served in the British ranks, though Conscription was not, and indeed could not be, enforced. To outward seeming Ireland was for the Allies, but as often before in her history, the apparent stream of things hardly represented the secret stream beneath.

A European war in which Great Britain is engaged has always made Ireland a danger-spot, for its people, whatever they feel for the Monarchy, have little enthusiasm for Imperial expansion, and there was always a minority wishful to seize the opportunity to 'fight the old fight again'. The menace of conscription created great excitement, and Redmond's efforts to enlist Ireland's manhood as a separate unit under the Irish flag by their failure showed how little he could do with the Coalition government. A rising was planned by the Irish Republican Brotherhood, and on Easter Monday 1916 the Post Office and other buildings in Dublin were seized by about 1,000 men, and Pearse for the Volunteers and Connolly for the Citizen army proclaimed the Irish Republic. A large British force was landed and after a bombardment of four days the main body of the rebels surrendered. General Maxwell under martial law executed Pearse and fourteen others of the leaders; among the commanders who escaped the death penalty Éamon De Valera was to be the most prominent. The Rebellion, though a small affair and soon over, served its purpose as a blood sacrifice in a country which had become apathetic about Nationalism, and Pearse and the others took their place on the accepted roll of 'the dead who died for Ireland'.

While thousands of suspects were interned and popular opinion rapidly became Sinn Féin, the Coalition government could not give Redmond that firm offer of Home Rule for the whole country which he needed to maintain his hold on Ireland, and *Sinn Féin* came out as a political force by winning an election in Roscommon in February 1917. A Convention summoned by the government, intended to be of all parties and to hammer out a settlement, was ignored by them, and Redmond died a broken man in 1918. He was a noble and sincere gentleman and a splendid orator of the old Grattan type, but he had outlived the day when mere Home Rule within the Empire would content the new Ireland.

THE TRIUMPH OF SINN FÉIN

When the Great War ended in October 1918 it was certain that Sinn Féin would claim the rights of a nation for Ireland at a time when the Allies were setting so many free. The initial step was to act as one. In January 1919 the deputies elected to *Dáil Éireann* ('the Assembly of Ireland') met as a parliament and proclaimed *Saorstát Éireann* (the 'Republic' or, more correctly, the 'Free State' of Ireland). Neither Nationalists nor Unionists attended, and it was left for Sinn Féin to win and to command the victory.

A General Election in England following the close of the War returned again a Coalition government of which Mr. Lloyd George became Premier, and in so far as Home Rule for the majority was achievable all British parties were now in agreement. The English Conservatives abandoned their resistance of before the War, for too many promises had been made to go back upon, and the shock of the world-conflict had brought old-fashioned Conservatism to an end. But, while to deny Home Rule as it was on the Statute book was impossible, to force it on Ulster was no longer to be thought of.

Ireland was now after the Great War a country with over four millions of people, of great agricultural prosperity (for Ireland always profits by great wars, being a food-producing country) and a numerous manhood which during the War had not been drained off as in the last sixty years of emigration. Politically Sinn Féin commanded their allegiance, for the Home Rule party had ended with Redmond. In April 1919 a Sinn Féin Convention elected De Valera President and Griffith Vice-President of the organization, for De Valera represented the military wing which was more powerful than the civil wing as represented by Griffith. Then began a perplexing state of things in which there were two governments in Ireland and in which people often preferred the Sinn Féin courts to the established courts. But while civil Sinn Féin functioned in public, some 2,000 militants of the Irish Republican Army in small bands took to the gun, and the seizure of government buildings and sporadic deeds of bloodshed between police and insurgents heralded a growing period of war. In December 1919 Mr. Lloyd George proposed an Amending act for the Home Rule Bill by which Ireland was to be self-governing, but 'Ulster', consisting of the six counties in which the Protestants have a total majority, was not to come under the Dublin parliament. This became an Act in December 1920, but though it contented Carson and his following it did not content Sinn Féin.[1] Abroad, American sympathy for Ireland and the influence of the Irish-Americans there, as well as the feeling in the Dominions and Great Britain, made the Irish question a world one, which England in pursuance of the avowed aim of the war 'to set small nations free' had to take into account. For some time, however, the British Government was reluctant to hand Ireland over to

[1] This six-county area, which, now as 'Northern Ireland' has a government and constitution of its own, is formed of the counties Antrim, Armagh, Derry, Down, Fermanagh and Tyrone. It contains now (1949) about 1¼ million people as against rather less than 3 millions in the Free State. Of these counties the first four have a majority of Protestants (of all sorts) ranging from Antrim (70 per cent) to Derry (59 per cent), but Fermanagh has a Catholic majority of 56 per cent and Tyrone of 55 per cent. The city of Belfast of course is overwhelmingly Protestant. 'Northern Ireland' is not an exact description, since it does not include Donegal.

such an avowed enemy or to believe that Sinn Féin represented Ireland.

By 1920 sporadic fighting between the Royal Irish Constabulary and the Republicans and the assassination of prominent opponents became so frequent that the British Government decided that neither the hard-pressed police force, nor the maintenance of a more regular army was sufficient to secure order in Ireland, and determined to do so with a small but select force who would track down the leaders of the militant Republicans. Part of these, who were ex-officers, were called the Auxiliaries; the others from their emergency costumes received the famous name of Black-and-Tans. On the Irish side, De Valera, Griffith, William Cosgrave and others conducted the civil government; prominent among the leaders in the military side were Michael Collins and Richard Mulcahy who led 'flying columns'. The object was a Republic, but the old-fashioned Griffith only reluctantly abandoned his original demand for Home Rule by 'the King, Lords and Commons of Ireland'.

The result of all this was a dreary record of reprisals and counter-reprisals, burnings, murders, and outrages, not between armies, but between expert gunmen on both sides.

In 1920 under Lloyd George's Amending Act the six counties of the North began their separate existence as a self-governing area with a parliament and government of their own, located at Stormont, with limited powers and subordinate to Imperial control. Thus was the Partition of Ireland achieved, a momentous event which no Irish leader had ever contemplated. The Covenant had pledged those who signed it to resist Home Rule for *all* Ireland. Now, since post-war Britain would no longer countenance this, Carson, Craig, and their supporters fell back upon the Six-counties area in which alone they could be sure of a Protestant majority, and reluctantly abandoned their co-religionists elsewhere. Their Parliament was opened on June 22, 1921, by King George V, who expressed his hope for a final re-union of Ireland.

As for the South, in April 1921 Lord FitzAlan, the first Roman Catholic viceroy permitted by law to rule Ireland since

Tyrconnell, ordered a general election to be held to a Dublin parliament under the Amending act. But Sinn Féin returned a majority of the members and then refused to work the Act. Thus disappeared from history the Irish pledge-bound parliamentary party, founded over forty years ago by Butt and made real by the genius of Parnell.

There was a complete deadlock in which the Anglo-Irish 'war' continued. The Church of England expressed the horror of the nobler England at the state of things, and King George was sincerely anxious for reconciliation. At the end of June a truce was declared and the British government decided to negotiate with the leaders of Sinn Féin, for, like Henry VII and the Earl of Kildare, it came to the conclusion that since all Ireland could not rule these men, they should rule all Ireland. But even advanced offers of something like Dominion status did not succeed and there was an impasse between the demand for a Republic and the British claim that Ireland must at least remain within the Empire. In October 1921 Lloyd George summoned a conference to London in which he and other leading statesmen represented the British side while Griffith, Michael Collins, Éamon Duggan, Robert Barton and George Gavan Duffy were envoys for De Valera's government. Finally on December 6th a Treaty was signed for both sides, by which the Irish Free State was recognized as a Dominion with full powers of self-government and determination, but leaving Great Britain the control of certain harbours for purposes of defence. The demand for an 'out and out Republic' was dropped. The right to maintain its own exclusion from Ireland was admitted for the unit of six counties henceforth called Northern Ireland. 'Ulster' had in fact already 'voted itself out' and though provision was made for re-union under one Parliament at some future date, it was a date none could foresee.

According to the new constitution of the Empire since the war, Great Britain and her Dominions form 'the British Commonwealth of nations' and are recognised as 'autonomous communities within the British Empire, equal in status, in no way subordinate to one another in any aspect of their external or domestic affairs, though united in a common allegiance to the Crown'. This was the great circle into which the ancient nation of Ireland was now invited to enter, and the King again became as before 1800 the King of Ireland.

The powers of freedom conferred by this treaty upon the Irish majority were far beyond what any Irish national party had ever won since 1660. But when *Dáil Éireann* was summoned to consider the treaty Éamon De Valera opposed its acceptance, because it had gone too far on the question of allegiance to the Crown and inclusion in the Empire and because the Irish delegates had not sufficiently consulted him and his cabinet. The *Dáil*, however, ratified it on January 7th 1922 by 64 votes to 57, whereupon De Valera resigned and withdrew with his following, and Griffith became President of the Executive council of *Saorstát Éireann* (an office corresponding to that of Prime minister in Great Britain). England honoured her word with the greatest scrupulosity and dispatch and the Lord Lieutenant handed over to the new government Dublin castle, the Viceregal lodge, the barracks and all the other centres of British rule in Ireland. For the first time for over seven centuries an Irish national government took possession of all the seats of power and exercised the rights of a representative sovereign assembly over most of Ireland. It was significant of altered times since 1800 that, instead of sitting in 'the old House on College Green', so often sung about, they chose as their permanent meeting-place 'Leinster House', a noble group of buildings in Kildare Street which recall the days before the Union when such Irish peers as the Duke of Leinster had a 'town house' in the capital.

Irish self-government was thus restored in 1922. The history of a nation never ends, and time alone can decide its destiny; but at least the Conquest which began in the twelfth century was now reversed, and it is certain that no Irish government will ever again, as it did in 1800, surrender the rights of the Irish people as a separate nation.

RECOMMENDED FOR FURTHER READING

GENERAL:

Richey, A. G., *A Short History of the Irish People.* 1887.

Hyde, Douglas, *Literary History of Ireland* (Gaelic literature from earliest times). 1889.

Hayden, M., and Moonan, G., *Short History of the Irish People.* 1921.

Dunlop, R., *Ireland from the Earliest Times to the Present Day.* 1922.

Gwynn, Stephen, *The History of Ireland.* 1923.

Hull, Eleanor, *A History of Ireland* (two vols.). 1926, 1931.

Curtis, E., and McDowell, R. B. (ed.), *Irish Historical Documents, 1172–1922.* 1943.

Cronne, H. A., Moody, T. W., and Quinn, D. B., *Essays in British and Irish History in honour of James Eadie Todd* (includes nine studies on Irish history, 1642–1879). 1949.

Irish Historical Studies (standard periodical on Irish history; bi-annual). 1938–.

THE EARLY PERIOD:

Macalister, R. A. S., *Ancient Ireland.* Rev. ed., 1949.

MacNeill, Eoin, *Phases of Irish History.* 1919.

—— *Celtic Ireland.* 1921.

—— *Early Irish Laws and Institutions.* 1935.

Green, A. S., *History of the Irish State to 1014.* 1925.

Meyer, Kuno, *Ancient Irish Poetry.* 2nd ed., 1913.

Gougaud, Dom Louis, *Christianity in the Celtic Lands,* translated by Maud Joynt. 1932.

Kenney, J. F., *Sources for the Early History of Ireland* (ecclesiastical). 1929.

History of the Church of Ireland, ed. by W. Alison Phillips, vol. i. 1933.

THE MEDIAEVAL AND TUDOR PERIOD:

Orpen Goddard, *Ireland Under the Normans, 1169–1216* (four vols.). 1911–20.

Curtis, E., *History of Medieval Ireland.* 2nd ed., 1938.
—— *Richard II in Ireland.* 1927.
Wilson, Philip, *Beginnings of Modern Ireland* (covers the first half of the sixteenth century). 1912.
Bagwell, R., *Ireland under the Tudors* (three vols.). 1885–90.
Bryan, D., *The Great Earl of Kildare.* 1933.
Maxwell, Constantia (ed.), *Irish History from Contemporary Sources (1509–1610).* 1923.
Butler, W. F. T., *Confiscation in Irish History.* 1917.
—— *Gleanings from Irish History.* 1925.
History of the Church of Ireland (as above), vol. ii. 1934.
Knott, Eleanor, *Bardic Poems of Tadhg Dall Ó h-Uiginn* (excellent introduction on the Irish Bardic Schools). 1922.
Ronan, Rev. M. V., *Reformation in Dublin* (under Henry VIII); *Reformation in Ireland* (under Elizabeth). 1926, 1930.
Edwards, Dudley R., *Church and State in Tudor Ireland.* 1935.
Longfield, Ada K., *Anglo-Irish Trade in the 16th century.* 1929.
Moody, T. W., *The Irish Parliament under Elizabeth and James I* (in *Proceedings of the Royal Irish Academy*, vol. xlv). 1939.
Hayes-McCoy, G. A., *Scots Mercenary Forces in Ireland (1565–1603).* 1937.
O'Faolain, S., *The Great O'Neil.* 1942.

STUART PERIOD:
Bagwell, R., *Ireland under the Stuarts* (3 vols.). 1909–16.
Butler, W. F. T., *Confiscation in Irish History.* 1917.
Moody, T. W., *The Londonderry Plantation, 1609–41.* 1939.
Mahaffy, J. P., *An Epoch in Irish History.* 1903.
Prendergast, J. P., *Cromwellian Settlement of Ireland.* 3rd ed., 1922.
Dunlop, R., *Ireland under the Commonwealth* (two vols. of documents, with excellent introduction). 1926.
Seymour, Rev. St. J. D., *Puritans in Ireland, 1647–61.* 1921.
MacLysaght, E., *Irish Life in the Seventeenth Century: after Cromwell.* 1939.
O'Brien, George, *Economic History of Ireland in the 17th Century.* 1919.
Falkiner, C. L., *Illustrations of Irish History and Topography.* 1904.
—— *Essays relating to Ireland.* 1909.

IRELAND SINCE 1689:
Froude, J. A., *The English in Ireland in the Eighteenth Century* (three vols.). 1881.

Lecky, W. E. H., *A History of Ireland in the Eighteenth Century* (five vols.). 1892.

Reid, Rev. J. S., *History of the Presbyterian Church in Ireland*, ed. W. D. Killen (3 vols.). 1867.

History of the Church of Ireland (as above), vol. iii. 1933.

Murray, R. H., *Revolutionary Ireland and its Settlement* (the war of 1689–91 and William III's reign). 1911.

O'Brien, George, *Economic History of Ireland in the 18th century; Economic History of Ireland from the Union to the Famine.* 1918, 1921.

Murray, Alice, *History of the Commercial Relations between England and Ireland, from 1660.* 1903.

MacNeill, J. G. S., *Constitutional and Parliamentary History of Ireland till the Union.* 1911.

Kiernan, T. J., *History of the Financial Administration of Ireland to 1817.* 1930.

R. Barry O'Brien (ed.), *Two Centuries of Irish History, 1691–1870.* 2nd ed., 1907.

Corkery, Daniel, *Hidden Ireland* (a picturesque study of Gaelic Ireland in the eighteenth century). 1925.

Maxwell, Constantia, *Dublin under the Georges.* 1936.

—— *Country and Town in Ireland under the Georges.* 1940.

Beckett, J. C., *Protestant dissent in Ireland, 1687–1780.* 1948.

McDowell, R. B., *Irish Public Opinion, 1750–1800.* 1944.

Lecky, W. E. H., *Leaders of Public Opinion in Ireland.* 3rd ed., 1903.

Madden, R. R., *Lives and Times of the United Irishmen* (four vols.). 1857–60.

Tone, T. W., *Life of Theobald Wolfe Tone, written by himself, and continued by his son* (two vols.). 1826.

MacDermot, F., *Theobald Wolfe Tone.* 1939.

Bradley, Patrick B., *Bantry Bay.* 1931.

McAnally, Sir Henry, *The Irish militia, 1793–1816: a social and military study.* 1949.

Dunlop, R., *Daniel O'Connell.* 1900.

Gwynn, Denis, *Daniel O'Connell.* Rev. ed., 1947.

—— *Young Ireland and 1848.* 1949.

Duffy, C. Gavan, *Young Ireland; Four years of Irish history; The League of North and South.*

O'Brien, R. Barry, *Life of Parnell* (two vols.). 1898.

Hammond, J. L., *Gladstone and the Irish Nation.* 1938.

Davitt, Michael, *Fall of Feudalism in Ireland.* 1904.

O'Connor, Sir James, *Ireland 1798–1924* (two vols.). 1925.

Mansergh, N., *Ireland in the Age of Reform and Revolution.* 1940.

Pomfret, John E., *The Struggle for Land in Ireland, 1800–1923.* 1930.

Henry, R. M., *Evolution of Sinn Féin.* 1920.

Phillips, W. Alison, *Revolution in Ireland, 1906–23.* 1926.

Pakenham, F., *Peace by Ordeal* (the Treaty of 1921–2). 1935.

Marjoribanks, E., and Colvin, I. D., *Life of Sir Edward Carson.* 1932–6.

Mansergh, N., *The Irish Free State: its government and politics.* 1934.

—— *The Government of Northern Ireland.* 1936.

O'Sullivan, D., *The Irish Free State and its Senate.* 1940.

PRONUNCIATION OF IRISH NAMES AND TERMS OCCURRING IN THIS BOOK

Abú: Irish war cry ('to victory'), e.g. O'Donnell Abú, *pronounced Aboo.*

Aedh or Aed, anglicized Hugh, *pronounced Ae.*

Aileach	*pronounced*	*Al-yuch.*
Ailill	,,	*Alyill.*
Aonach	,,	*Aynuch.*
Árd Rí	,,	*Aurd Ree.*
Athenry	,,	*Ath-un-rye.*
Aughrim	,,	*Auch-rim.*
Bacach (Lame)	,,	*Bok-ach.*
Banagh	,,	*Bann-ach.*
Betagh	,,	*Betta.*
'Buidhe' (yellow)	,,	*Bwee.*

(C is always hard in the Irish language, but as Cb is guttural like Scottish 'Loch').

Cairbre 'Cinn Cait'	*pronounced*	*Carbry Kinn Kat.*
Cathal	,,	*Kathal.*
Cell (cell or church)	,,	*Kell.*
Cellach	,,	*Kell-ach.*
Cellachan	,,	*Kell-ach-an.*
Cenel Conaill	,,	*Kennel Kunnill.*
Cenel Eoghain	,,	*Kennel Owen.*
Cianacht	,,	*Kee-an-acht.*
Ciarán	,,	*Keeraun.*
Clanmalier	,,	*Clan-ma-leer.*
Clann Sinach	,,	*Clan Shinach.*
Coign	,,	*Coin.*
Colm Cille	,,	*Colum Killa.*
Conn Céd-cathach	,,	*Kayd Kathach.*
Cruithne	,,	*Krithna.*
Cú Chulainn	,,	*Koo Hullin.*
Dáil Éireann	,,	*Dau-il Ayrun.*
Dál Cais	,,	*Daul Kash.*

417

Dál Cuinn	*pronounced*	*Daul Kwinn.*
Dalriada	,,	*Dal-ree-ada.*
Decies	,,	*Deesyz.*
Derb-fine	,,	*Derrib-finna.*
Diarmaid nan Gall	,,	*Dee-armid nan Gaul.*
Diarmaid	,,	*Dee-armid* (now Dermot).
Docwra	,,	*Dock-erra.*
Donnchad	,,	*Dunn - a - chud* (Donough = Dunnach, is the modern equivalent).
'Donn' (Brown)	,,	*Dun* (or *Doun in* Munster).
Drumceat	,,	*Drum Kat.*
'Dubh' (Black)	,,	*Duv* in South, *Dhu* in North.
Dubh-gall	,,	*Du-gaul* (or *Duv-goul* in Munster).
Dullough	,,	*Dull-uch.*
Emain Macha	,,	*Emmun Macha.*
Eochy	,,	*Yochy.*
Eoghan	,,	*Owen.*
Eoghanacht	,,	*Owen-acht.*
Ériu	,,	*Ayryoo* (modern 'Erin' = *Ayr-in*).
Eoghan Mór	,,	*Owen More.*
Escir Riada	,,	*Esker Ree-ada*
Faughart	,,	*Fauch-art.*
Feis	,,	*Fesh.*
Fiachra	,,	*Fee-ach-ra.*
Fiadh-mic-Oengusa	,,	*Fee-a mick Ayngussa.*
Fianna	,,	*Fee-anna.*
File	,,	*Filla* (plural *Fili* = *Fillee*).
Fine (race)	,,	*Finna.*
Finn-ghall	,,	*Finn-gaul* (plural *Finn-ghaill* = *Finn-geel*).
Fionn MacCumhaili	,,	*Finn MacCool.*
Fir Bolg	,,	*Fir Bollug.*
Gall	,,	*Gaul.*
Garbh (Rough)	,,	*Garruv.*
Gearóid Iarla	,,	*Garrode Eearla.*
Glenmalure	,,	*Glen Malyure.*

Glúndubh	pronounced	Gloon-duv.
'Gorm' (Blue)	,,	Gorrum.
Gormflath	,,	Gormflah (anglicized Gormley or Gormlai).
Gowran	,,	Góran.
Hy Kinsella	,,	High Kinsella.
Hy Many	,,	High Maany.
Imaal	,,	Ee-maal.
Iveagh	,,	Yva (almost as in 'ivy').
Kavanagh	,,	Kav-an-a.
Kincora	,,	Kinn Kóra ('Head of the Weir').
Kinsella	,,	Kinn Sella.
Laeghaire	,,	Laeri.
Leabhar Gabála	,,	Lyow-ar Gavála.
Leix	,,	Lease.
Leixlip	,,	Lees-lip.
'Liath' (Grey)	,,	Lee-a.
MacCarthy 'Reagh'	,,	Ray.
MacMurrough	,,	Mac Murra.
Mageoghegan	,,	Magay-igan.
Manus	,,	Maanus (from Magnus).
Meiler	,,	as in 'Mile'.
Mogh Nuadat	,,	Moe Nooadat.
Móin Mór	,,	Mone More.
Murchad	,,	Murrachad.
Murchertach	,,	Mur-Kertach (a modern form is Murtough = Murt-uch).
Murrough	,,	Murr-uch (anglicized form of Murchad).
Mileadh	,,	Meela.
Naas	,,	Nays.
Niall	,,	Nee-al.
Niall Glúndubh	,,	Nee-al Gloonduv.
Norragh	,,	Norra.

Ó Cahan	*pronounced*	*Ó Kah-un.*
Oengus	,,	*Ayngus.*
Offaly	,,	*Uffaaly.*
Oisín	,,	*Usheen.*
Ó Ruairc	,,	*Ó Roo-irk.*
Rath Croghan	,,	*Rath Cró-han.*
'Reagh' (Swarthy)	,,	*Ray or Reeach*
Rhys ap Tewdwr	,,	*Rees ap Tudor.*
Rí (king)	,,	*Ree.*
Ruadh (Red)	,,	*Roo-a,* anglicized *Roe.*
Saorstát Éireann	,,	*Saerstaut Ayrun.*
Shane	,,	*Shaan* (Irish *'Seán').*
Shanid Abú	,,	*Shannid Aboo*
Sinach *or* Clan Sinach	,,	*Clann Shinnach.*
Sinn Féin	,,	*Shinn Fayn.*
Siol Muiredaig	,,	*Sheel Murredy.*
Sitric	,,	*Sitt-rick.*
Slaine	,,	*Slaun-ya.*
Suibhne	,,	*Siv-nya.*
Taig	,,	*Tyge* (as in *'tie').*
Tailten	,,	*Talten.*
Táin Bó Cualgne	,,	*Tauin Boe Coolny.*
Thomond	,,	*Thó-mund.*
Thurles	,,	*Thurl-es.*
Tiernan	,,	*Tee-arnan.*
Tireragh	,,	*Tirr-eera.*
Tír Conaill	,,	*Teer Kunill.*
Tír Eoghain	,,	*Teer Owen.*
Tuath	,,	*Tooath.*
Tuatha Dé Danann	,,	*Tooatha Day Danann.*
Tyrconnell	,,	*Tirr-connell.*
Tyrone	,,	*Tirr-one.*
Uí Faeláin	,,	*Ee Fwaelaun.*
Uí Néill	,,	*Ee Nayl.*
Uisneach	,,	*Ush-nach.*
Umhall of Ó Máille	,,	*Ooal of Ó Maulye.*
Urragh	,,	*Urr-ach.*

KEY DATES OF IRISH HISTORY

A.D. 200. Conn Céd-cathach founds the Middle Kingdom (Meath) and begins the High kingship of Tara.

377–405. Niall of the Nine Hostages, High king.

400. Niall's sons, Eoghan and Conall, found the kingdom of Aileach.

432. Patrick begins his mission in Ireland.

563. Colmcille begins his mission in Iona.

575. Convention of Drumceat.

664. Synod of Whitby.

795. First appearance of Vikings off Irish coast.

852. The Norse occupy Dublin and Waterford.

900–8. Reign of Cormac Mac Cullenan, King of Cashel.

919. Battle of Dublin and death of Niall Glundubh.

940–1014. Career of Brian Boru.

1014. Battle of Clontarf and death of Brian.

1095–1148. Career of St. Malachy.

1100–72. Reform of the Irish Church.

1119–56. Turloch More O'Connor as High king.

1134–71. Dermot MacMurrough, king of Leinster.

1152. Synod of Kells.

1155. Date of the alleged "Bull *Laudabiliter.*"

1166. August I. Expulsion of Dermot MacMurrough.

1166–75. Rory O'Connor, last native King of Ireland.

1170. August 23. Landing of Richard, Earl of Pembroke (" Strongbow").

1171. October–April 1172. Henry II in Ireland.

1172. September. The Pope grants Ireland to Henry.

1177. Henry creates his son John 'Dominus Hiberniae'.

1210. King John in Ireland, organizes the Anglo-Irish government.

1235. Conquest of Connacht by Richard de Burgo

1258. Coming of the Galloglasses to Ulster.

1260. Battle of Downpatrick and death of Brian O'Neill.

1261. Battle of Callann and triumph of the MacCarthys.

1264. Walter de Burgo made Earl of Ulster.

1270. Battle of Ath-an-Kip marks failure of Norman conquest.

1297. Beginning of the Irish Parliament.

1315–18.   The Bruce Invasion.

1333. Murder of the last De Burgo Earl of Ulster.

1366. Statutes of Kilkenny.

1376–1417.   Art MacMurrough, king of Leinster.

1394–5.   First visit of Richard II to Ireland.

1399. Second visit of Richard II.

1425. Death of last Mortimer Earl of Ulster in Ireland.

1460. Declaration of Irish parliamentary independence.

1477–1513.   Gerald, 'the Great Earl' of Kildare, rules Ireland.

1487. May 24.   Lambert Simnel crowned King in Dublin.

1494–5.   Poynings' Parliament and acts.

1504. Battle of Cnoc Tuagh (Knocktoe).

1513–34.   'Garret Oge', Earl of Kildare, rules Ireland.

1534–5.   Rebellion of 'Silken Thomas', Lord Offaly.

1536–40. The Geraldine League.

1536–7.   The first 'Reformation Parliament' in Dublin.

1540–56.   St. Leger, Lord Deputy, wins over the Irish lords and chiefs to accept Henry VIII.

1541. June.   Irish Parliament accepts Henry as King of Ireland.

1542. Conn O'Neill created Earl of Tyrone.

1556. Plantation of Leix and Offaly.

1559–67.   Shane O'Neill, lord of Tyrone.

1560. The second 'Reformation Parliament' in Dublin.

1569–70.   Parliament under the Lord Deputy Sidney passes measures for the 'reduction' of Ireland.

1569–73.   First Desmond Revolt, led by Sir James Fitzmaurice.

1579–83.   Final Desmond Revolt and suppression.

1585. The Composition of Connacht.

1585–6.   Perrot's Parliament.   Rise of 'Catholic Constitutional party.'

1586. Plantation of Munster.

1592. Foundation of Trinity College (University of Dublin).

1594–1603.   The Tyrone War or Northern Confederacy.

1598. August 15.   Battle of the Yellow Ford.

1601. December 24. Battle of Kinsale.

1603, March 30. Surrender of O'Neill.

1607, September 14. Flight of the Earls of Tyrone and Tyrconnell.

1608–10. Foundation of the British colony in Ulster.

1613–15. Chichester's Parliament.

1627. Charles I offers 'The Graces'.

1632–40. Wentworth (Lord Strafford), viceroy.

1639–41. Last Irish parliament in which Catholics sat (save 1689).

1641, October. Irish rising began.

1642, February. The 'Adventurers' Act'.

1642, June 10. The Presbyterian Church in Ireland organized.

1642–9. Catholic Confederacy.

1642. Arrival of Owen Roe O'Neill and Preston.

1645, October. Arrival of the Nuncio Rinuccini.

1646, June 5. Battle of Benburb.

1646. The 'Ormond Peace'.

1649, August; 1650, May. Cromwell in Ireland.

1652. Cromwellian Act of Settlement.

1660, May 14. Restoration of Charles II.

1662. Second Act of Settlement.

1666. English Act excluding Irish cattle.

1670. Navigation Act, excluding Ireland.

1687–91. Earl of Tyrconnell, Lord Lieutenant for James II.

1689, April–July. Siege of Derry.

1689, May. The Irish 'Patriot Parliament'.

1690, July 1. Battle of the Boyne.

1691, July 12. Battle of Aughrim.

1691, September–October. Siege of Limerick.

1691, October 3. Treaty of Limerick.

1692–1829. Catholics excluded from Parliament and office.

1695. Beginning of the Penal laws.

1697. Treaty of Limerick 'ratified' by Irish parliament.

1699. Irish woollen industry crushed by England.

1700. The Treaty 'ratified' by English parliament.

1704. The 'Gavelkind' Act.

1704. Protestant Dissenters excluded from office by Test Act.

1719. Declaratory Act.

1724. Swift's 'Drapiers Letters'.

1756. Founding of the Catholic Committee.

1767–74. Viceroyalty of Lord Townshend.

1771. Relief to Roman Catholics begins with the Bogland Act.

1772. Rise of the Patriot party in Parliament.

1778. Organization of the Irish Volunteers.

1778. Gardiner's Relief Act for Catholics.

1779. English concessions on Trade and repeal of most of the Restrictive acts.

1780. Repeal of Test Act for Dissenters.

1782. Volunteer Convention at Dungannon. Gardiner's second Relief Act. Establishment of Irish parliamentary independence.

1783, January 22. Renunciation Act by Great Britain.

1784. Foster's Corn Law (lasts till 1846).

1784–5. 'Orde's Commercial Propositions'.

1788–9. The Regency dispute.

1790. Wolfe Tone becomes Secretary to the Catholic Committee.

1791. The Society of United Irishmen founded.

1793. Hobart's Catholic Relief Bill.

1795. The Fitzwilliam episode. The United Irishmen become revolutionary.

1795, September 21. 'Battle of the Diamond'. Orange Order founded.

1796. Ireland put under martial law.

1796, December. First French fleet sails to invade Ireland.

1797. The disarming of Ulster by General Lake.

1797, June. Second French attempt against Ireland.

1798, May 24. Rebellion of '98 breaks out.

1798, November 19. Death of Wolfe Tone.

1800, August 1. The Act of Union becomes law.

1807. Daniel O'Connell becomes the leader of Catholic Ireland.

1828, July. The Clare Election.

1829, April. Catholic Emancipation Bill passed. O'Connell takes up 'Repeal'.

1831. National Education system founded.

1835–40. Administration of Mulgrave and Drummond.

1842–8. The Young Ireland movement.

1845. The Queen's Colleges founded.

1845–7. The Great Famine.

1846. Peel gets the Navigation and Corn Laws repealed.

1847, May.   Death of O'Connell.

1848, August.   Rising under Smith O'Brien, etc.

1850.   Tenant Right League formed.

1867.   The Fenian Rising. Execution of the 'Manchester Martyrs'.

1869.   Disestablishment of the Church of Ireland.

1870.   Gladstone's first Land Act. Home Government Association founded by Isaac Butt.

1877.   Parnell becomes Chairman of the Home Rule Confederation.

1879.   Land League founded by Davitt.

1881.   Gladstone's second Land Act.

1886.   Gladstone's first Home Rule Bill defeated. Riots in Belfast.

1891, October 7.   Death of Parnell.

1892.   Gladstone's second Home Rule Bill defeated.

1893.   Gaelic League founded.

1899.   Griffith begins the Sinn Féin movement.

1900.   John Redmond Chairman of the Irish Party (till 1918).

1903.   Wyndham's Land Act settles the Agrarian question.

1908.   National University founded.

1912.   The Third Home Rule Bill introduced.

1912, September 28.   Solemn League and Covenant in the North

1913, January.   The Bill defeated in the Lords. Ulster and National Volunteers organized.

1914, March.   The 'Curragh Mutiny'. Third Home Rule Bill receives royal assent.

1917, February.   Sinn Féin wins the Roscommon election.

1918–21.   'The Anglo-Irish War'.

1919, January.   The Sinn Féin deputies elected to *Dáil Éireann* meet and proclaim *Saorstát Éireann*.

1920.   Lloyd George's Amending Act allows the Six Counties in Ulster to vote themselves out.

1921, June 22.   King George opens the Northern parliament.

1921, December 6.   The Anglo-Irish Treaty signed in London.

1922, January 7.   Treaty ratified in *Dáil Éireann*.

INDEX